ETHNOGRAPHIES REVISITED

Ethnographies Revisited provides first-hand accounts of how leading qualitative researchers crafted key theoretical concepts found in their major book-length ethnographies. Great ethnographic research lies not in the rigid execution of prescribed methodological procedures, but on the unrelenting cultivation of theoretical ideas. These contributors focus squarely on this neglected topic, providing reflexive accounts of how research decisions were made in light of emerging theoretical questions.

The continuous generation of creative concepts is arguably the most important skill in developing powerful results in field research, since the originality of the ideas produced is how the study is ultimately judged. Yet, this topic is often taken for granted, treated rigidly and artificially, or is entirely absent from existing qualitative research manuals. In contrast, this volume offers candid insights into how leading ethnographers generated their initial questions, chose their research sites, made theoretical and methodological adjustments, and oriented their research to maximize the conceptual payoff, leading to such successful research contributions. This provides a fresh approach to the topic of qualitative research, by linking practical decisions in the field to the dynamic features of theory in the making, told through the first-hand experiences of some of the best ethnographers in our field.

Antony J. Puddephatt is Assistant Professor of Sociology at Lakehead University in Thunder Bay, Ontario, Canada.

William Shaffir is Professor of Sociology at McMaster University in Hamilton, Ontario, Canada.

Steven W. Kleinknecht is Assistant Professor of Sociology at Brescia University College in London, Ontario, Canada.

ETHNOGRAPHIES REVISITED

Constructing theory in the field

Edited by
Antony J. Puddephatt,
William Shaffir and
Steven W. Kleinknecht

Routledge
Taylor & Francis Group

LONDON AND NEW YORK

First published 2009
by Routledge
2 Park Square, Milton Park, Abingdon, Oxon OX14 4RN

Simultaneously published in the U.S.A. and Canada
by Routledge
711 Third Avenue, New York, NY 10017

Routledge is an imprint of the Taylor & Francis Group, an informa business

© 2009 Edited by Antony Puddephatt, William Shaffir, and Steven Kleinknecht

Typeset in Times New Roman by
Taylor & Francis Books

British Library Cataloguing in Publication Data
A catalogue record for this book is available from the British Library

Library of Congress Cataloging in Publication Data
Ethnographies revisited : constructing theory in the field / edited by Antony Puddephatt, William Shaffir and Steven Kleinknecht.
p. cm.
1. Ethnology—Research. 2. Ethnology—Methodology. I. Puddephatt, Antony.
II. Shaffir, William. III. Kleinknecht, Steven.
GN345.E74 2009
305.8'00723—dc22
2008051498

ISBN 978-0-415-45220-5 (hbk)
ISBN 978-0-415-45221-2 (pbk)
ISBN 978-0-203-87650-3 (ebk)

CONTENTS

CONTENTS

CONTENTS

CONTRIBUTORS

Peter and Patti Adler have written and worked together for over 35 years. Patti (Ph.D., University of California, San Diego) is Professor of Sociology at the University of Colorado. Peter (Ph.D., University of California, San Diego) is Professor of Sociology at the University of Denver, where he served as chair from 1987–93. Their interests include qualitative methods, deviant behavior, drugs and society, sociology of sport, sociology of children, social theory, work and occupations, and leisure. Together, they have published numerous articles and books, including *Momentum* (Sage, 1981), *Wheeling and Dealing* (Columbia University Press, 1985, Second Edition 1993), *Membership Roles in Field Research* (Sage, 1987), *Backboards and Blackboards* (Columbia University Press, 1991), and *Peer Power* (Rutgers University Press, 1998). The Adlers have served as editors of the *Journal of Contemporary Ethnography* (1986–94) and as the founding editors of *Sociological Studies of Child Development* (1985–92). Their co-edited anthologies include *Constructions of Deviance* (Wadsworth), now in its sixth edition, and *Sociological Odyssey* (Wadsworth), now in its third edition. Their book on self-injurers is forthcoming with NYU Press. In 2006–7, they served as Co-Presidents of the Midwest Sociological Society.

Partners in life as well as scholarship, **Daniel Albas** (Ph.D., Colorado) and **Cheryl Albas** (Ph.D., Colorado) have developed their academic careers at the University of Manitoba. They have directed much of their scholarly activity to the study of student worlds, and published in a wide variety of national and international journals in sociology, psychology, and education on matters pertaining to student perspectives on university life: study strategies, impression management, the use of magic as a confidence-generating mechanism in the examination context; and other aspects of student identities, relationships, and emotions. They have also published on topics such as romantic relationships, the management of space and place, and a series of conceptually focused analyses dealing with diverse matters of modesty, motives, and aligning behaviors.

A graduate of the University of Chicago, **Nachman Ben-Yehuda**'s work has focused on unconventional behavior from Durkheimian and constructionist perspectives. His work raises the age-old Hobbesian question "how is the social order possible?" by focusing on the Hegelian concept of antithesis. This general plot is occasioned by directing attention to how, why, where and when challenges to the status quo emerge and function as catalysts for processes of social change or stability. By examining that which is considered as "deviant," we gain interesting and insightful glimpses into the nature of the non-deviant social order and of cultures. His books have focused on betrayal and treason, the Masada myth, political assassinations, politics and deviance, the European witch craze, deviant sciences and scientists, and the use of archaeology for national purposes. He is currently working on a new book on moral panics (with Erich Goode) and on unconventional behavior amongst fundamentalists. Prof. Ben-Yehuda has been with the Department of Sociology and Anthropology at Hebrew University throughout his career.

Daniel Chambliss graduated from New College in Sarasota, Florida, and earned his master's and Ph.D. degrees from Yale University. Since 1981 he has taught at Hamilton College, where he is the Eugene M. Tobin Distinguished Professor of Sociology. His research is in the social psychology of organizations. In 1989, Chambliss won the American Sociological Association's Theory Prize for his article "The Mundanity of Excellence," reconsidered in this volume. He is the author of *Champions: The Making of Olympic Swimmers*, named the 1991 Book of the Year by the U.S. Olympic Committee, and of *Beyond Caring: Hospitals, Nurses and the Social Organization of Ethics*, which won the ASA's Eliot Freidson Prize in 1998 for the best medical sociology publication of the preceding two years. He is co-author, with Russell Schutt, of *Making Sense of the Social World*, a research methods textbook. His current work is on higher education.

Kathy Charmaz is Professor of Sociology and Coordinator of the Faculty Writing Program at Sonoma State University. In the latter position, she helps faculty complete their research and scholarly writing. She has written or co-edited seven books, including the forthcoming volume *Grounded Theory: The Second Generation*; *The Handbook of Grounded Theory*; and *Constructing Grounded Theory: A Practical Guide Through Qualitative Analysis*, which recently received a Critics' Choice Award from the American Educational Studies Association. Her book, *Good Days, Bad Days: The Self in Chronic Illness and Time*, won awards from the Pacific Sociological Association and the Society for the Study of Symbolic Interaction. Professor Charmaz has also published widely in medical sociology, social psychology, and qualitative research as well as held numerous offices in professional associations. She received the 2001 Feminist Mentors Award and the 2006 George Herbert Mead award for lifetime achievement from the Society for the Study of Symbolic Interaction.

Harry Collins is Distinguished Research Professor of Sociology and Director of the Centre for the Study of Knowledge, Expertise and Science (KES) at Cardiff University. In 1997 he was awarded the J. D. Bernal prize for contributions to the social studies of science. His thirteen books cover sociology of scientific knowledge (e.g. *Changing Order: Replication and Induction in Scientific Practice* (1985), *Gravity's Shadow: The Search for Gravitational Waves* (2004) both with Chicago); the relationship between humans and machines (*Artificial Experts* (1990) and *The Shape of Actions* (1998) both with MIT Press); and three *Golem* volumes (*The Golem: What you Should Know about Science* (1993), which won the American Sociological Association's Robert K. Merton book prize, followed by volumes on technology (1998) and medicine (2005)). Collins and Evans's: *Rethinking Expertise* was published in 2007 by Chicago and the same year saw the publication of an edited volume, *Case Studies of Expertise and Experience*.

Norman K. Denzin, Distinguished Professor of Communications, Research Professor of Communications, Cinema Studies, Sociology, Criticism and Interpretive Theory, received his Ph.D. from the University of Iowa in 1966. He is the author, co-author, or co-editor of over 50 books and 200 professional articles and chapters, including: *Reading Race*; *Interpretive Ethnography*; *The Cinematic Society*; *The Voyeur's Gaze*; *Performance Ethnography*; *Searching for Yellowstone*; and *The Alcoholic Self*. He is past editor of *The Sociological Quarterly*, co-editor (with Yvonna S. Lincoln) of three editions of the *Handbook of Qualitative Research*. He is the past President of The Midwest Sociological Society, and the Society for the Study of Symbolic Interaction. He is founding President of the International Association of Qualitative Inquiry (2005–), and Director of the International Center of Qualitative Inquiry (2005–). He is past editor of *The Sociological Quarterly*, founding co-editor of *Qualitative Inquiry*, and founding editor of *Cultural Studies–Critical Methodologies*, and *Studies in Symbolic Interaction: A Research Annual*.

Jennifer L. Dunn has examined the social construction of victims in multiple realms; she has published work on stalking victims' identity work as victim-witnesses in the criminal justice system; emerging vocabularies of motive in the battered women's movement; and the emotional and political resonance of social movements' framing of victims. Her work appears in the *Journal of Contemporary Ethnography*, *Social Problems*, *Symbolic Interaction*, *Sociological Inquiry*, *Sociological Focus*, and *Violence Against*

Women. Her book, *Courting Disaster: Intimate Stalking, Culture, and Criminal Justice,* won the Charles Horton Cooley Award of the Society for the Study of Symbolic Interaction, and she recently was awarded an Early Career Scholarship Award from the Midwest Sociological Society. She earned her B.A. in Sociology at Sonoma State University and her M.A. and Ph.D. in Sociology from the University of California at Davis. Her current project examines victim narratives in survivors' movements in the contemporary United States.

Robert Roy Faulkner is Professor of Sociology at the University of Massachusetts, Amherst. He is affiliated with the Social And Demographic Research Institute (SADRI), Department of Sociology. A jazz trumpet player and sociologist, he has written on Hollywood film composers and their careers, freelance musicians, and the repertoire in jazz. He is the author of *Music on Demand; Hollywood Studio Musicians; Art from Start to Finish* (with Howard S. Becker); and *The Jazz Repertoire* (forthcoming, with Howard S. Becker). Articles in the *American Journal of Sociology* and the *American Sociological Review* include "The Social Organization of Conspiracy," "Hazards of the Market," "Role as Resource," and in *Criminology* they include "Diffusion of Fraud," and "Crime by Committee." For "The Social Organization of Conspiracy," Faulkner and Wayne E. Baker won the Max Weber Award from the American Sociological Association. His research interests are in culture, social networks, socio-economic behavior, and repertoires of wrongdoing by corporations.

Jaber F. Gubrium is Professor and Chair of the Sociology Department at the University of Missouri. He has taught at Marquette University and the University of Florida, was a Fulbright scholar at Tampere University, Finland, in 1996, and has been a visiting professor at Tampere, at Lund University in Sweden, and at the Universities of Copenhagen and Odense in Denmark. His areas of specialization are aging and the life course, social interaction, identity, qualitative methods, and narrative analysis. Gubrium works empirically at the border of ethnography and narrative analysis, combining them in new ways to deal with the perennial problems of linking observational data with transcripts of stories, speech, and other narrative material.

Samuel Heilman holds the Harold Proshansky Chair in Jewish Studies at the Graduate Center and is Distinguished Professor of Sociology at Queens College of the City University of New York. He is the author of numerous articles and reviews as well as: *Synagogue Life; The People of the Book; The Gate Behind the Wall; A Walker in Jerusalem; Cosmopolitans and Parochials: Modern Orthodox Jews in America* (co-authored with Steven M. Cohen) *Defenders of the Faith: Inside Ultra-Orthodox Jewry; Portrait of American Jewry: The Last Half of the 20th Century; When a*

Jew Dies: The Ethnography of a Bereaved Son and *Sliding to the Right: The Contest for the Future of American Jewish Orthodoxy* and edited *Death, Bereavement, and Mourning* and serves as Editor-in-Chief of *Contemporary Jewry*. In 2004, he received the Marshall Sklare Memorial Award for his lifetime of scholarship from the Association for the Social Scientific Study of Jewry.

David A. Karp is a Professor of Sociology at Boston College where he has taught since 1971. He received his B.A. degree from Harvard University in 1966 and his Ph.D. in Sociology from New York University in 1971. He has written or co-authored nine books and more than 50 journal articles and book chapters. His diverse writings are animated and united by the core social psychological question, "How do people make sense of complicated life circumstances and how are their behaviors, emotions, and attitudes linked to such interpretive processes?" His work has largely clustered in three areas: urban life and culture, aging, and the study of mental health and illness. His book, *Speaking of Sadness*, won the Society for the Study of Symbolic Interaction's Charles Horton Cooley Award in 1996. In 2008 he received the Lifetime Achievement Award from the American Sociological Association's Section on Emotions.

Steven W. Kleinknecht is Assistant Professor in the Department of Sociology at Brescia University College in London, Ontario, Canada. His research interests lie in the study of subcultures, deviance, and online interaction. He has conducted ethnographic research on computer hackers and Old Order Mennonites.

Donileen Loseke received her Ph.D. from the University of California, Santa Barbara. She is Professor and Graduate Director in the Department of Sociology at the University of South Florida in Tampa. Her books include *The Battered Woman and Shelters: The Social Construction of Wife Abuse* (1992, SUNY Press), and *Thinking About Social Problems: An Introduction to Constructionist Perspectives* (2003, Aldine deGruyter). She is a past co-editor (with Spencer Cahill) of the *Journal of Contemporary Ethnography*. Currently, she is an Associate Editor of *Symbolic Interaction* and the *Journal of Contemporary Ethnography*, and an Advisory Editor for *The Sociological Quarterly*. Her recent interests center on the narrative construction of identity and relationships among narrative identity, emotions, and social problems.

Dorothy Pawluch has been a member of the Department of Sociology at McMaster University in Hamilton, Ontario for the past 20 years. She teaches courses in deviance, social problems, social constructionist theory and the sociology of health and health care. Besides her work on the social history of pediatrics, Dorothy has published (with Steve Woolgar) papers on social problems theory and as part of the McMaster HIV Research

Group, a series of papers on the social aspects of living with HIV/AIDS. She recently edited (with William Shaffir and Charlene Miall) a volume titled *Doing Ethnography: Studying Everyday Life*. The volume brings together a collection of papers presented at the Qualitative Analysis Conference, a conference with which she has been connected for many years. She is also a founding member of the McMaster Constructionist Circle.

Trevor Pinch is Professor of Science and Technology Studies and Professor of Sociology at Cornell University. He has published extensively on aspects of the sociology of science and technology. His studies have included quantum physics, solar neutrinos, parapsychology, health economics, the bicycle, the car, and the electronic music synthesizer. His most recent books are *How Users Matter* (edited with Nelly Oudshoorn, MIT Press, 2003); *Analog Days: The Invention and Impact of the Moog Synthesizer* (with Frank Trocco, Harvard University Press, 2002); and *Dr Golem: How To Think About Medicine* (with Harry Collins, University of Chicago Press, 2005). *Analog Days* was the winner of the 2003 Silver Award For Popular Culture, and "Book of the Year" of *Foreword* magazine. *The Golem: What You Should Know About Science* (with Harry Collins, Cambridge: Canto, 1998, 2nd ed.) was winner of the Robert Merton prize of the American Sociological Association.

Robert Prus, a professor of sociology at the University of Waterloo, is a symbolic interactionist, pragmatist ethnographer, and social theorist. Stressing the importance of connecting social theory with the study of human action in direct, experientially engaged terms, he has written extensively on the ways that people make sense of and deal with the life-worlds in which they find themselves. His publications include *Road Hustler* with C. R. D. Sharper; *Hookers, Rounders, and Desk Clerks* with Styllianoss Irini; *Making Sales*; *Pursuing Customers*; *Symbolic Interaction and Ethnographic Research*; *Subcultural Mosaics and Intersubjective Realities*; *Beyond the Power Mystique*; and *The Deviant Mystique* with Scott Grills. Working as an ethnohistorian and theorist, Robert Prus has been tracing the developmental flows of pragmatist thought from the classical Greek era (*c.* 700–300 BCE) to the present time. This transhistorical venture has taken him into a number of areas of Western social thought—including rhetoric, poetics, religious studies, history, education, politics, and philosophy.

Antony J. Puddephatt is Assistant Professor of Sociology at Lakehead University in Canada. He is interested in sociological theory, science and technology, and ethnographic research. He conducted a field study of amateur chess, and has written on G. H. Mead's neglected sociology of science.

Laurel Richardson is Professor Emeritus of Sociology at the Ohio State University. She specializes in qualitative methodology, gender, the sociology of knowledge, and arts-based research. She has published over 100 articles, among them the oft-cited "Writing as Method of Inquiry," in the *Handbook of Qualitative Research*. She is the co-editor of *Feminist Frontiers* (now in its sixth edition) and author of seven other books, including: the Cooley Award book, *Fields of Play: Constructing an Academic Life* (Rutgers University Press); *Travels with Ernest: Crossing the Literary/Sociological Divide* (Rowman and Littlefield, co-authored with the novelist Ernest Lockridge); and her most recent book, *Last Writes: A Daybook for a Dying Friend* (Left Coast Press), which was honored by the National Speech Association. Richardson is currently engaged in research practices that cross the boundaries between the visual arts and the ethnographic ones. She lives in Worthington, Ohio with her husband and her rescued Abyssinian cat.

Clinton R. Sanders is Professor in the Sociology Department at the University of Connecticut. His work focuses on cultural production, deviant behavior, ethnographic research, and sociozoology. In addition to *Customizing the Body: The Art and Culture of Tattooing* he is also the author of *Understanding Dogs: Living and Working with Canine Companions*, and co-author of *Regarding Animals* (with Arnold Arluke), both of which received the Charles Horton Cooley Award given by the Society for the Study of Symbolic Interaction. In 2004 Sanders was the recipient of the University of Connecticut Provost's Award for Research Excellence, and in 2006 he received the Distinguished Scholarship Award from the Animals and Society Section of the American Sociological Association. A revised and updated edition of *Customizing the Body* has just been published (2008, with D. Angus Vail) by Temple University Press.

William Shaffir is Professor of Sociology at McMaster University in Hamilton, Canada. He received his Ph.D. degree from McGill University. He is the author and co-author of books and journal articles in the areas of Hassidic Jewry, medical student socialization and professionalization, field research methods, ethnic violence, the social psychology of messianic revivalism, and religious affiliation and disaffiliation among newly-observant and formerly haredi (ultra-Orthodox) Jews. A recently completed study examined defeated politicians and how they cope with and rationalize defeat at the polls. Along with a colleague, he has conducted field research on a police service to examine the dynamics of racial profiling. His current research continues to focus on the challenges facing Hassidic Jewry as it confronts modernity.

Robert A. Stebbins, FRSC, is Faculty Professor and Professor Emeritus in the Department of Sociology, University of Calgary and Visiting Professor at the University of Bedfordshire. He received his Ph.D. in 1964 from the University of Minnesota. Stebbins has published or edited 34 books and written over 200 articles and chapters. He is author of *The Organizational*

Basis of Leisure Participation (Venture, 2002); *Between Work and Leisure: The Common Ground of Two Separate Worlds* (Transaction, 2004); *A Dictionary of Nonprofit Terms and Concepts* (Indiana University Press, 2006, with D. H. Smith and M. Dover); *Serious Leisure: A Perspective for Our Time* (Transaction, 2007); and *Personal Decisions in the Public Square: Beyond Problem-Solving into a Positive Sociology* (Transaction, 2008). Stebbins is presently writing a book entitled *Leisure and Consumption: Common Ground, Separate Worlds* (Palgrave Macmillan). Stebbins is an elected fellow of the Academy of Leisure Sciences and the Royal Society of Canada.

Will van den Hoonaard, Professor Emeritus, Department of Sociology, University of New Brunswick, Fredericton, Canada, has authored and edited seven volumes on a wide variety of topics, including the Dutch in New Brunswick, a fishing village in Iceland, the Baha'i Community of Canada, ethics, and qualitative methodology. He has also published or presented some 250 papers and book reviews in the areas of qualitative research, research ethics, culture, multiculturalism, crime in Iceland, sociology of religion, Baha'i studies, human rights, the world of map makers, and marine resource management. He is a founding member of the Canadian (Tri-Council) Inter-Agency Advisory Panel on Research Ethics, where he has also served as the first Chair of the Special Working Group on the Social Sciences and the Humanities on Ethics. He is a Woodrow Wilson Fellow and is recipient of the Global Citizen Award from the United Nations Association of Canada, the UNB Merit Award, the UNB President's Medal, and the Hasan M. Balyuzi Lectureship.

Loïc Wacquant is Professor of Sociology at the University of California, Berkeley, and Researcher at the Centre de Sociologie Européenne, Paris. His interests span incarnation, ethnoracial domination, urban inequality, penalization, and social theory. His recent books include *Body and Soul: Notebooks of an Apprentice Boxer* (2004); *Pierre Bourdieu and Democratic Politics: The Mystery of Ministry* (2005); *Urban Outcasts: A Comparative Sociology of Advanced Marginality* (2008); and *Punishing the Poor: The Neoliberal Government of Social Insecurity* (2009). He is a co-founder and past editor of the interdisciplinary journal *Ethnography* and recipient of the 2008 Lewis Coser Award of the American Sociological Association for "theoretical agenda-setting work."

PREFACE

The initial idea for this project was spurred on by the 2005 Symbolic Inter-action and Ethnographic Research Conference hosted in Pittsburgh, Pennsyl-vania. Bob Prus, a dear friend and colleague, was instrumental in organizing these meetings, and he included two thematic sessions titled "Ethnographies Revisited." The idea behind these sessions was refreshingly simple: Authors of ethnographies were invited to revisit their works to consider, in retrospect, what shaped their ideas and how the particular organization of their work unfolded. More broadly, authors would reflect on their mistakes and omissions, and consider their work with the hindsight of more recent developments.

The idea for this edited volume germinated a short time following these meetings. We definitely wanted authors to reflect on their ethnographic work, but decided this book needed a more pointed focus. There are already books on fieldwork reflections and general memoirs about the research experience, often centering on the emotional, ethical, personal, and methodological aspects of ethnography. We realized, however, that there was no serious body of literature where ethnographers reflect on the process of theoretical analy-sis as it unfolded. What a fresh idea it would be, we thought, to have some of the best researchers in sociological ethnography recount the major turning points of the conceptual aspects of their work. Fortuitously, the three of us were located in the Department of Sociology at McMaster University, which led to frequent conversations about the project, and a sharper crystallization of what we really had in mind.

But, we wondered, would prospective contributors to the volume be inter-ested? We sent out invitations to the best ethnographers we could think of, outlining the goals of our proposed volume. We explained that we wanted authors to reflect on the key concepts in their major book-length ethnographies, so as to teach students and researchers alike how to think creatively and thus research most productively in the field. We wanted authors to present real (as opposed to recipe-styled) accounts of how they struggled with different con-ceptual questions during their research. We asked them to structure the piece around a natural evolution of their work, using the lens of theory, rather than method, in telling the story of how their projects proceeded forward.

The large majority of people we invited responded favorably and enthusiastically. Many considered the project to be fun and rewarding; some said they were waiting to write a paper like this for years, but could never find the right venue. Others believed that they should contribute because this project is important and overdue; it is the first of its kind dedicated to reflexive, first-hand accounts of theory-work in ethnographic research. To say the least, we were delighted and charged up by the response.

As the papers began to stream in, we recognized this volume was a winner. We tried to be tough in our editorial work, and often pushed authors, perhaps too hard at times, to deliver on the conceptual focus we were aiming for. In response to our prodding, they were gracious and earnest in their efforts to give us the type of chapters we had in mind, and provided highly informative, and at times candid, insights into their thoughts and experiences as they unfolded. Needless to say, it was both educational and fulfilling to work with such a great cast of contributors; to see each unique conceptual puzzle presented, the frustration and perseverance toward solving it, and eventually, a creative answer. It is clear that the researchers in this volume are clever; but the real story here is the blood, sweat and tears required to tackle these puzzles from different angles. Like every other facet of social research, there is no substitute for hard work in theoretical matters either.

This volume is meant to move beyond traditional ethnographic collections that often detail the choice of research setting, problems of access, maintenance of social relations, matters of ethics, and other typical challenges facing field researchers. In contrast, our spotlight shines directly on conceptual and theoretical formulations: how they got started, were reconfigured, and possibly abandoned; and how new ideas emerged as the research proceeded forward. Undoubtedly, additional collections structured along similar or compatible lines await the efforts of enterprising students of the ethnographic craft. This book is intended as a first step.

We would like to thank our families and research colleagues for their encouragement, conversations, and support in putting this volume together. Further, we would like to thank our publisher, Gerhard Boomgaarden at Routledge, who was also enthusiastic about the project, and very professional in his dealings with us. As well, we are indebted to the Social Sciences and Humanities Research Council (SSHRC) for their help in funding the preparation of this volume. Most importantly, we would like to thank the authors, who have worked hard to demystify the process of theorizing in the field. We hope you enjoy the book.

Antony Puddephatt
William Shaffir
Steven Kleinknecht
November 1, 2008

INTRODUCTION
Exercises in reflexivity: situating theory in practice

Antony Puddephatt, William Shaffir and Steven Kleinknecht

Ethnographic methods, despite wars with the quantitative tradition over the years, have gained increasing legitimacy, well regarded by most segments of the discipline for their ability to offer fine grained descriptions of events and provide an in-depth examination of everyday situations. However, some critics still quip that ethnographers are often simply "poor journalists," who spend years working on projects that are conceptually bereft and no better than a weekly news documentary. Of course this is an unfair charge. At its best, ethnographic research provides concepts that extend beyond the particular case study in question and hold lasting value due to their elegance, insight, explanatory value, or broad application. As Gary Alan Fine (2008) put it in his keynote address at the recent 25th annual Qualitative Analysis Conference in New Brunswick, Canada, ethnographers differ from journalists mostly because of a six-letter word: theory.

Indeed, to the extent ethnographic work provides even one or two lasting theoretical concepts, it moves beyond the level of a faddish news story and becomes a more durable contribution to sociology, explaining or contextualizing social life in new and compelling ways. These ideas can then be used, challenged, or refined through future research by others. After all, how sociologically or analytically revealing is our writing if we do little more than journalists? Journalists typically tell a story better than we do, because they've been trained in ways that sociologists haven't been. They can cover a story far more quickly, and they can locate their sources of information with greater dispatch. One may be reminded of the community activist Saul Alinsky's musing that a sociology department "is the kind of institution that spends $100,000 on research projects to find the locations of houses of prostitution which a taxi driver could tell you for nothing" (quoted in Berson 1971: 141). Certainly, gaining an intimate familiarity with a locale often provides a better sense of how social life works, and where the most significant things to insiders are, in a more efficient manner. Still, familiarizing oneself with the ins and outs of a scene, and crafting a lasting work of sociology are not quite the same thing.

What makes ethnographic work special is that its authors are able to generate new theoretical concepts, identify the steps in a particular social process,

1

reveal the organizational principles of social groupings, identify explanatory mechanisms in social dynamics, and link these issues to broader theoretical frames of understanding. For example, ethnographers might study the career route of drug addicts, mental illnesses, religious conversions, professional socialization—in ways journalists do not, and cannot, since they have neither the training nor the time. Further, larger theoretical frames can often provide a context and a trained sociological eye to approach and interpret the social patterns, viewpoints, and behavior of the groups we observe in unique, imaginative, and penetrating ways. Key ideas, concepts, and theoretical statements are what make sociological careers, generate citations, furnish high-profile publications, and most importantly, provide the most lasting contributions to scholarship.

Think for example of Howard Becker's (1963) notion of a "deviant career," Edgerton's (1967) theory of a "cloak of competence," Everett Hughes' (1971) concepts of "dirty work," or "routine and emergency," Fred Davis' (1961) idea of "deviance disavowal," John Kitsuse's (1970) discussion of "people-processing institutions," Erving Goffman's (1961) description of "total institutions," and Anselm Strauss' (1978) formulation of the "negotiated order" found within organizational protocols. Consider also Sheldon Stryker's (1980) observations of a "salience hierarchy" in multiple role identities, Arlie Hochschild's (1983) insights into the hidden "emotional labour" of flight attendants, Lonnie Athens' (1980) notes on the "phantom communities" carried around by violent criminals, and Jack Katz's (1988) argument for the emotional attractions of crime. More recent examples include Dianne Vaughn's (1996) discovery of the organizational basis of risk in NASA, Elijah Anderson's (1999) depiction of local systems of justice in the "code of the street" of the inner city, and Gary Alan Fine's (2007) analysis of how scientists draw on incomplete information and uncertain data, yet manufacture predictions of certainty for the public, in his study of meteorologists. These examples surely only scratch the surface; the present volume contains a number of equally compelling examples of strong conceptual contributions in the ethnographic tradition. The point is simple; the more theoretically relevant a piece of ethnographic work is, the more it is able to travel from local community concerns and substantive areas to capture wider academic interest and make a more lasting contribution to scholarship. This book asks the authors of successful book-length ethnographies to reflect back on how they crafted winning ideas, to reveal the process of their own stages of "theory-work" as it unfolded in practice.

Unfortunately, the topic of theoretical development in ethnography has been badly neglected in the literature, in favor of orientations toward methodological concerns and research ethics. Of course, there are manuals that provide frameworks for conducting theoretical work in ethnography and qualitative research (Glaser and Strauss 1967; Blumer 1969; Strauss 1993; Prus 1996; 1997; Strauss and Corbin 1998; Clarke 2005; Charmaz 2006). Certainly, all

2

of these efforts to guide theory in ethnographic work are important, yet these are often presented as "top-down" approaches, in that, while they may draw on useful examples from their own work or those of others to bolster their theoretical points, the ideas are often discussed in rather abstract, and sometimes disconnected ways. In practice of course, theorizing is never as neat and tidy as many qualitative research manuals present it. General conceptual strategies, coding procedures, and rules of thumb are certainly helpful for novice researchers, but probably are not sufficient to truly know what it is to generate creative, dynamic concepts in the lived experience of ethnographic work. It is true that there have been a few valuable first-hand reflective accounts of theory-work in qualitative research, usually appearing as articles in journals for interpretive and qualitative research (e.g. Anderson 2003; Vaughan 2004). Still, these accounts are few and far between, and have never been collected and organized into one coherent volume.

This is the very purpose of this book. We invited leading ethnographic researchers to contribute original reflexive accounts about the conceptual decisions made in the midst of researching their major book-length ethnographies. We asked our contributors to think about and respond to the following questions: Did particular theoretical questions guide their research strategies, and if so, how? How did findings in the field disconfirm or challenge pre-existing principles, ideas, and frameworks initially introduced? How was a good conceptual "hook" for the study developed? When have outside sources and theoretical paradigms helped move the research forward, and when have they become a hindrance? How were new ideas linked not merely to the activities of the researcher immersed in the field, but also to the community of scholars in the broader exchange of academic ideas? These are the sorts of questions we hope this book takes first a step toward answering, by recounting real experiences from some of the most successful ethnographers in the field. It is important to draw on large numbers of such reflexive accounts of "theory-in-practice" if we are to learn about how conceptual work is actually accomplished in ethnographic research. And, by drawing these stories together and reflecting on the lessons gathered, we hope to take a step forward in trying to understand more about the creative process that accompanies successful research projects. In this sense, we hope this book has something very valuable to offer.

The ethnographic ambivalence to theory

Theory tends to hold an ambivalent place in ethnographic research. While it is true that some qualitative researchers embrace theoretical ideas both out of interest and to gain legitimacy, many prefer not to trouble themselves about theoretical issues, or treat theory as a general evil to be avoided. This ambivalence toward theory has likely been the culprit as to its somewhat difficult reputation as a method of social inquiry. If ethnographers can do no more than tell tales, or provide rich descriptions of social life, then what good is it as a social science? And on the part of ethnographers, if theory is a prerequisite for good social science, then why do so many ethnographers hold an antagonistic relationship to it? We argue the historical ambivalence of ethnography toward theory is a result of two major phases of interpretive scholarship: (a) ties to earlier movements that would legitimize qualitative research in the face of dominant quantitative approaches of the time; and (b) recent shifts in the ethnographic tradition toward postmodern scholarship as a result of the cultural turn, embracing non-totalizing, indeterminate, and situated modes of knowing, and moving away from universalizing language.

Early progenitors of qualitative modes of research were engaged in a war against positivism and the quantitative tradition of variable analysis, and the accompanying hypothetico-deductive theorizing this was associated with. In his paper "What is Wrong with Social Theory?" Herbert Blumer (1954) launched a full blown attack against the distorting quality of so called social theory as it is applied from the armchairs of professors who conduct survey-driven studies without any true grounding in the empirical reality of social groups. Blumer complained that hypothetico-deductive research designs use ill-fitting theoretical categories, measured by reliable but invalid survey questionnaires that were better at bending the empirical world to fit preformed categories than vice versa. Blumer's (1969) answer was to rid sociology of abstract theoretical frames altogether, and begin the hard work of creating new, clear, concepts that were closely fitted to the living, breathing, empirical world in question. Such concepts would not be generated overnight, but would accrue slowly, as researchers carefully fitted emergent concepts to the empirical social realities they would encounter. This exacting empirical scrutiny would be obtained not through survey measures, but rather, through the up-close examination of social life in the naturalistic instances in which it unfolds. In other words, through the use of largely qualitative, participant-observation designs, which would be executed in natural settings.

It is no secret that Blumer, basing his argument on the broader and long-standing tradition of the Chicago school tradition of pioneers such as Robert Park, Elsworth Faris, and contemporaries like Everett Hughes was largely responsible for "leading the charge" against positivistic sociology, giving a macho and gritty, but also an informed and scientific image to qualitative research (see Fine 1995). The fact that he posed the importance of interactionist-style field research against the grand, European-styled theoretical designs of people like Talcott Parsons left followers of the American interactionist tradition ideologically opposed to anything that sounds like theory. If Blumer was leading the charge of a pragmatist-inspired, distinctly American sociology, then grand, high-minded European social theory was the enemy.

This rejection of "armchair" theorizing also implied an embrace of concepts that had a more concrete connection to the language and meaning of everyday life according to the actors involved. What good is theory if it makes no sense to the people on the ground? For the interactionists, theory in the classical sense of the term was often a substitute for condescension and unnecessary abstraction – a language not introduced to better understand, but obfuscate, and distort, the social world. For example, instead of making room for the incorporation of traditional social theory in the analysis of ethnographic data, Prus (1996: 141–72) sets up categories termed "generic social processes" by which researchers are to explore the more mundane, generic elements of everyday life, flexible enough to be fitted to insiders' accounts of their experiences. For many classic symbolic interactionists, insider language and understanding should be as far as theory ought to go; to go beyond this would be undermining the research participants, treating people as though they are no more than "cultural dopes," or behaving in ways they cannot consciously control.

Blumer's charge against hypothetico-deductive theory was bolstered in the classic statements by Barney Glaser and Anselm Strauss (1967) in their watershed manual *The Discovery of Grounded Theory*. Here, they trumpet the necessity of exploratory, inductive designs in social analysis. By using the "constant comparative method," researchers would be able to make original theoretical discoveries in field research settings without the bias of the established wisdom of the scholarly literature getting in the way. While not completely abandoning the idea of using grounded theory to verify pre-existing ideas, Glaser and Strauss (p. 253) still warn that "to cover all the literature before commencing research, increases the probability of brutally destroying one's potentialities as a theorist." Instead of trying to prove previously held sociological understandings, students were expected to make constant analytic comparisons between emerging data. This fostered a broad and flexible approach for researchers to discover new things about the social world, and organize these findings into an analytical scheme that would be forged through an inductive, systematic method. Again, this methodology was radically opposed to the idea of merely testing old theories; originality and an open mind to discover new insights were seen to trump replication.[1] While certainly, the end-goal of this research protocol was to develop axiomatic theoretical statements derived from the data, in practice followers of this mantra would often use it as an excuse to ignore pre-existing theory and simply write about the people they encountered in their own way. They would justify this by the inductive argument that too much reading would only get in the way of originality.

Thus, traditional ideological commitments of ethnography are undoubtedly part of the problem contributing to the "a-theoretical" nature of qualitative research. One could argue that much the same argument against traditional social theory was being made in anthropology through the work of Clifford Geertz (1973). Geertz eschewed universal theories, favoring "thick descriptions" of social life that defy overly general, abstract accounts. It is probably Geertz who inspired more radical arguments against traditional

theory from authors like James Clifford. Clifford (1994) argues that all ethnographies carry moral or political allegories, and that researchers ought to
be honest that they are creating narratives or stories about local groups, and
be reflexive, that is, self-aware and honest about the ideological spins they
inevitably create. This is much in line with the general postmodernist appeal
to try and escape from universalizing and technocratic, imperialistic, and
dominating "meta-theory" and instead turn to fluid, indeterminate, situational, local narratives, giving more authorial voice to members of the
populations studied (Lyotard 1984; Denzin and Lincoln 2005; Seidman
2008). Traditional ethnography, in people's attempts to conduct statically
envisioned, categorical accounts of social life was seen by critical post-
modernists as too scientific and domineering (Hammersley 1990). Any
attempt to apply previously designed theory to subcultures of interest, or any
project that would try to link studies, or use ethnographies to advance
formal theoretical arguments, would be met with skepticism or scorn. For
the postmodernist wing of the discipline, placing people into pre-designed,
abstract theoretical boxes is not only too over-generalizing but is also dis-
empowering. Theory, at least in the old sense of the word, is often dismissed
as a relic of modernity.

Despite the best intentions of avoiding the use of universal theoretical
constructs for the reasons listed above, all researchers, postmodern or otherwise, must use some sort of abstract theory since that is the fundamental
basis of knowledge. *Some kind* of theorizing is germane to all social scientific
work, notwithstanding the various ranges of explanation, description, taxonomy, and the level of application intended. Blumer (1931) long ago asked
the question, "What is a science without concepts?" Without clear conceptual building blocks in place, Blumer argued that social science would
become "like a train without tracks, a skeleton without bones ... it would be
a fantastic creation" (pp. 115–16). Much of this ambivalence to theory comes
from a general confusion as to what theory actually refers to in the first
place. Gabriel Abend (2008) has recently differentiated seven present-day
semantic forms of theory, ranging from logically related general propositions,
to perspectival frameworks, to hermeneutic and situated "readings" of phenomena, and so on. If a more multifaceted understanding of what theory is
could be taken on, the problematic place of theory within ethnography might
move toward resolution. We will return to this idea later in the chapter.

We have tried to show that traditional sociological ethnography was legiti-
mated early on with a denunciation of classical deductive theorizing, sociological scientism in the form of positivist survey research, and European
intellectualism. Today, postmodern approaches rail against any attempt at
"meta-theory," and projects, ethnographic or otherwise, that place people
and actions into constrained, analytical categories. Instead, postmodern social
science attempts to provide narrative accounts, situated perspectives, and
entertaining and provocative imagery to challenge and waken the reader out

of routine arguments (Adler and Adler 2008). Thus, both traditional and postmodern ethnography are opposed to different sorts of theoretical approaches for different reasons; the result is similar however, as categorical claims about social life tend to be met with skepticism. Thus, while these two movements are clearly important and vital to the development of ethnography and qualitative research generally, there is no question they have also contributed to the ambivalence toward traditional conceptions of theory within the ethnographic tradition.

Are we constructing a problem, and trying to start a panic about something that doesn't really exist? Is theory vibrant and healthy in the practice of field research, despite this long-held antagonism we have painted? We certainly are not alone in thinking there is a problem. Hammersley (1992) stated that theory in ethnography does not often go far beyond the description of social life in the local terms of the participants, and often hides ideological bias on the part of the researcher by reproducing so-called "common-sense" accounts that implicitly support the status quo (for a more recent critique like this, see Wacquant 2002). For Hammersley, not only is more explicit theorizing required, beyond the level of detailed descriptive accounts, but more reflexive thought on the part of the researcher about the source and impact of these theories is needed as well. Robert Emerson (1987), reflecting back as then editor of the *Journal for Contemporary Ethnography*, argues that "weak conceptualization and analysis remain major problems confronting contemporary field research" (p. 73). Prus (1996) has also lamented the conceptual poverty of much of what passes as contemporary ethnography. He argues there is a disconnection of studies across different substantive areas, with little or no attempt to use abstract concepts to bridge them together.

Charmaz (2006) is also concerned with the weak state of field research under the auspices of "grounded theory," and is concerned with cultivating more theoretically driven, creative, and broader based ideas (see also Puddephatt 2006). Thus, she spends time showing students the benefits of "theoretical sampling" in research designs over and above traditional methodological approaches, so as to play up the importance of stronger, more theoretically relevant results. Snow et al. (2003) make a case for a greater elaboration of "analytical ethnography," which, in opposition to traditional ethnography and postmodern movements, tries to set up testable, logically connected statements from the field, which can be discovered, refined, or extended. These authors are also clearly concerned with the wings of the qualitative traditions that increasingly veer toward a-theoretical and thus, less sociologically relevant, accounts of social life. Instead, they envision amassing a literature of concepts that can be mutually built up and collectively refined for use by future generations.

Beyond the concerns, we have all seen and heard stories of graduate students embarking on ethnographic research projects, turning over little more than common-sense explanations of what they find. Is this the fault of the individual students? Or is it a larger problem in the way ethnographers share knowledge, which affects how students are taught? With so much of a focus on the methodology of research, such as "getting in," "passing ethics," "sampling," "developing rapport," and so forth, the whole aim of the research in the first place, that is, *developing a strong conceptual thesis*, is left by the wayside. We believe that this lack of conceptual focus, as well as the time constraints imposed on ethnography courses, leads to the problem of producing more ethnographers who gain Ph.D.s and conduct qualitative research, yet nevertheless avoid serious engagements with theory in the midst of their research. Exceptions probably had the benefit of a great personal mentor, excellent talent, or strong informal networks with like-minded others, since the literature provides very little concrete advice on how to develop concepts and maintain a theoretical focus in the field.

Hopefully, we have made the case so far that a stronger emphasis on theory is needed in ethnographic work generally, and that this topic has been neglected for specific historical reasons rather than fully rational ones. We also hope to have shown that at least part of the reason conceptual work in ethnography is in jeopardy is because there are few accounts of how to practically work on fostering strong theoretical arguments in existing qualitative research guides. This book aims to take a first step toward solving this problem by asking successful, established ethnographers to reflect back on their book-length studies, and recount the process by which they constructed their key concepts first-hand. We pushed these authors to be explicit, candid, and detailed about the process by which they generated theoretical ideas, by being as reflexive as possible about their engagement in the creative process as it happened.

Reflexivity and the ethnographic tradition

There has always been a fairly substantial discrepancy between how research ought to be done in an ideal world and how it has actually been accomplished in practice (Merton 1962). Thomas Kuhn's (1962) history of science brought forth a depiction of science as it was actually practiced vs. classical epistemology's traditional accounts of how science should be done. Scientists, Kuhn argued, are like the rest of us. They too are human beings, members of organized collectives that bring with them a host of theoretical biases in the way that the research is conducted and evidence is analyzed. Kuhn's argument has been bolstered in micro-sociological studies of scientific practice, which have left little doubt that there is a significant gap between the ideal visions of neat, textbook science of a slow accumulation of tentatively accepted facts vs. the sort of science that is actually accomplished "on the bench" (e.g. Collins 1985; Lynch 1985; Latour 1987; Collins and Pinch 1993). It seems that the traditional mystique and grandeur of science is challenged when the mundane, human, and error-prone quality of scientific work is examined first-hand. It is easy to sit back and speculate about how research ought to be done given ideal conditions; it is another matter entirely to uncover how research, social scientific or otherwise, is actually accomplished, warts and all, in real empirical instances.

It is in these empirical instances that science studies scholars would find that scientists were swayed in large part not only by the evidence at hand, but also how numerous social, institutional, and political influences would help shape the research agenda. Rather than trying to erase the researchers' connection to the social world and the interests that lead the research forward, scholars in science studies argued that a more radical reflexivity was in order, to draw the social-historical connections between politics and science explicitly. Thus, Steve Fuller (1988) argued for the development of a reflexive wing of science, where sociologists would be able to engage in an internal critique of the knowledge generated to keep the research more transparent and honest in its connection to political, social, and economic interests. Sandra Harding (1986) argued for the generation of a "standpoint episte-mology" for women and other minorities to conduct research while embracing the social position they occupy and the benefits that this marginal space provides. Haraway (1988) prefers the idea of reflexively coming to understand one's own unique social position that often defies traditional categories of gender or race, such that scholars can better account for the generation of their "partial perspective," which is far preferred over some falsely presented "God's eye" view of the world. Joseph Rouse (1993) sees cultural studies of science as a way to further engage with science reflexively, improving its practices by providing its practitioners with a fuller view of the relation between the knowledge produced and its wider context in society.

Of course, early on sociologists of science knew that if the sociological roots of the knowledge produced by the hard sciences could be uncovered, then certainly the same rule would have to apply to sociological knowledge as well (see Bloor 1991; Collins and Yearley 1992). Certainly sociologists are not immune to their own rules, and knowledge generated about social life is arguably more prone to the bias of socio-historical forces than the physical sciences are. At any rate, if an increased level of reflexivity was the goal for the natural sciences, surely the social sciences would benefit from a closer attention to the effects of their own research practices, theoretical preferences, and ideological loyalties in the knowledge claims they produce.

Along these lines, there has been much talk about the importance of reflexive practices in social science since at least the late 1970s, mainly originating from the aforementioned science studies literature, but also the anthropology of Clifford and Marcus (1986), as well as the critical sociology of Pierre Bourdieu (2001; see also Bourdieu and Wacquant 1992). A long-time critic of the institutional aspects of knowledge production in the university, Bourdieu realized it was important to turn these skills of criticism against himself, since he too, and the various movements he was connected to, would be prone to his own critiques against the academic establishment and the practice of science generally. Similar to Harding and Haraway, Bourdieu felt that a critical and thorough scrutiny of one's own science would actually help solidify, rather than undermine, the knowledge produced by it. In short, a reflexive approach to sociology was the only way to be critical about one's own work and present it with at least some insight into the social and political context in which it was created. Burawoy (2005) has also pushed for much needed reflexive exercises in sociology, arguing that internal critique, using the tools of science against itself, is essential to the fostering of a healthy discipline.

Within this discourse, one would think ethnographers and qualitative researchers to be the first in line to take the issue of reflexivity seriously; that is, recognizing one's own social and historical situation, political positioning, and practical contingencies in the research setting, and how these affect the claims and arguments made. In the way of field methods, ethnographers have been fairly forthcoming about the trial and error, uncertainty, and difficulty of field research as practiced. Publications emerged that offered a "down and dirty" accounting of the problems encountered, as well as how some of these difficulties were never overcome (e.g. Hammond 1964; Vidich et al. 1964; Shaffir et al. 1980; Shaffir and Stebbins 1991; Kleinman and Copp 1993). These volumes provided opportunities for readers to finally peer behind the scenes to see how field research was really done rather than idealized in traditional research methods manuals. In other words, these offered refreshing and honest accounts about the obstacles in place during the process of ethnographic work. Another key aspect in these accounts was that researchers more explicitly wrote about their feelings (Kleinman 1991). The subjective side of field research was paraded in the open, and we discovered how researchers' feelings impacted upon their experiences in the field, and on their conceptions about the group they studied.

Theoretical development, like all of field research practice, is not really organized as mechanically as accounts presented in the methods sections of research articles often suggest. It makes a difference if the researcher despises the people she follows, is disappointed in what she thought she would find, or if a researcher collaborator is lazy, incompetent, and unreliable (e.g. Barrett 1987; Kleinman 1991). Much like in the hard sciences, social science textbooks on methodology usually provide an idealized notion of how theoretical findings develop in the research journey. Only infrequently have sociologists, and field researchers in particular, reported on how the process of concept formation was actually accomplished in practice.[2] As most field researchers would admit, the so-called rules and canons of fieldwork, as well as the theoretical projects taken on, are frequently bent and twisted to accommodate the particular demands and requirements of the situation and the personal characteristics of the fieldworker. The following observations by

10

Howard Becker and Norman Denzin, respectively, reflect this view of the relationship between theory and research in ethnographic practice:

> As every researcher knows, there is more to doing research than is dreamt of in philosophies of science, and texts in methodology offer answers to only a fraction of the problems one encounters. The best laid research plans run up against unforeseen contingencies in the collection and analysis of data; the data one collects may prove to have little to do with the hypotheses one sets out to test; unexpected findings inspire new ideas.
>
> (Becker 1965: 602–3)

> My discussions of theory, measurement, instrumentation, sampling strategies, resolution of validity issues, and the generation of causal propositions by various methods proceed on the assumption that once the proper rules were learned, adequate theory would be forthcoming. Unfortunately, of course, this is seldom the case. Each theorist or methodologist takes rules of method and inference and molds them to fit his particular problem—and personality. Concepts do not automatically generate operational definitions, and theories do not fall into place once all the data are in. Rather, theoretical formulations arise from strange sources—often out of personal experiences, haphazard conversations with friends and colleagues. And many times these formulations bear only a distant relationship to data.
>
> (Denzin 1989: 249)

Despite this long awareness of the personal contingencies of social research, ethnographers have been reluctant to put forward honest, reflexive accounts of where and how their theory was generated in concrete terms. Why have we been so inattentive to our handling of theory in ethnographic work? To some degree, to be sure, our reluctance to focus on theoretical development reflects the imprecise tools in our conceptual arsenal that would make this effort less arduous. Attending to the ongoing nature by which our initial theoretical conceptualization becomes increasingly refined, or perhaps even substituted by another, is hard work, of which the results and pay-off may not be worth the effort. After all, how easy is it to embark upon a route of total introspection and fess up to an array of emotional baggage that may have shaped our decisions to follow one conceptual lead over another? For a variety of reasons, we are tentative about inviting outsiders to step into the most privileged of circles to actually witness how concepts or theories are formulated in the not-so-perfect world of practice. In this regard, our profession tends to reserve the right to share such secrets only with fellow members of the community, and often in less formal or official settings, such as drinks at the bar. In other words, the privileged status granted to insiders keeps the boundary to outsiders intact.

Perhaps it is okay that such reflexive accounts of theory and concept development are somewhat rare in the ethnographic literature. Were accounts of theoretical development shared among colleagues, one might invoke the Hebrew term *Dayeinu* (literally, it would have been enough for us), in that some element of sharing occurs regularly even if in a limited measure. The problem, however, is that attention to how concepts originate, develop, and are refined and applied is often not even shared within the closed circle of ethnographers. Since the conceptual and theoretical work that shapes, and is shaped by, the research process appears to be devoid of rigorous criteria, it is typically glossed over in our accounts as we reflect on the seemingly less arcane dimensions of research, such as ethics and sampling procedures. Perhaps this is done as a hope to preserve, if not salvage, the scientific credibility of our work, or maintain the illusion of individual genius in crafting our accounts of social life. One might call this the "theory-mystique," in that ethnographers are in no hurry to give up their well-kept magician's tricks, which they recognize full well are the pay-dirt of great sociological contributions in ethnography. To give away the fruits of their labor by presenting the mundane processes of how concepts and theories were formed almost takes away from the special contribution and individual achievement of the scholar in question.

For all of the above reasons, ethnographers are still somewhat sheepish about giving honest accounts of how their ideas evolved in the field. We know, however, that such final products are not manufactured *ex nihilo*, but necessarily involve a series of steps, throughout the research process, in which the researcher recognizes, identifies, and analyzes the data in the course of appreciating their relevance and meaning. There is every reason to encourage its practitioners to attend to, and reveal, how all aspects of the research process were accomplished; especially as it relates to the formulation of concepts and theories. This book is a first step toward this task. We have encouraged the authors to be as candid as possible in the many things that influenced and shaped their decisions in constructing the key concepts of their studies.

Critics of the current volume may argue that memory creates a problem in accounting for the realities of the research process, as scholars try to recall (or perhaps more to the point, construct) the so-called "eureka moments" of their field research projects. It is true that human memory often reveals more about the collective intentions of the present than it does about the objective content of the past (Mead 1932; Halbwachs 1992; Zerubavel 1997; Prus 2007). Thus, descriptions of past events as they relate directly to a project that researchers hold in high regard, and which is intimately connected to their symbolic capital as scholars, certainly raise questions about how obvious career interests might influence their respective cases. Trevor Pinch (this volume) questions the very possibility of escaping the fictional narrative of "theory-talk" that we ask contributors to engage in. Without getting into the extensive literature about the social construction of memory here, we recognize these concerns are real.[3] In place of perfect or accurate accounts of theory development in ethnographic work, the essays in this book capture the authors' experiences as best they can. Despite the shortcomings that undoubtedly accompany this exercise, we hope the results speak for themselves. We believe that despite the constructed nature of human memory, the contributions in this volume contain extremely valuable lessons for how to think conceptually while immersed in the field, and how to maintain a steady focus on the cultivation of strong theoretical propositions. It is here where the value of this collection rests.

Varieties of theory in ethnography

Part of the difficulty in discussing theoretical strategies in ethnographic work is that there are so many different styles of theory, which are often at odds with one another. Postmodern theory differs greatly from positivistic hypotheses, which differ still from ideographic historical explanations, and the list goes on. This variation has led some to distance themselves from theory entirely despite the fact that they are practicing it unknowingly all the time, and others to claim theory for themselves and label others as "a-theoretical." In short, theory has been subject to a great deal of academic politics and aggressive boundary work and policing, particularly within the discipline of sociology.

Is it true that there are different types of theory, which cannot be coherently grouped under the same categorical umbrella? Camic and Gross (1998) take this perspective as they lay out a basic typology of different types of theory, ranging from a construction of analytical tools, syntheses of approaches, refinements of existing knowledge, dialogues between competing perspectives, the expansion of theoretical approaches, the past analysis of theoretical ideas, the diagnosis of contemporary conditions in society, and the dissolution of universal generalizations. They do this explicitly as a way to avoid any overarching master definition of what theory ought to represent. Alexander (1982) also recognizes different types of theory, though he places these along a degree continuum between empirical and metaphysical poles. Abend (2008) has recently distinguished between seven different semantic meanings of the term "theory" as used in the practice of sociology, albeit in different wings of the discipline. Paraphrasing, Abend (pp. 177–81) lists the different meanings of theory as follows:

1 A general proposition or logically connected set of axioms
2 An explanation of some event or phenomenon
3 A hermeneutic interpretation or "reading" of some social phenomena

4 The study of early and/or famous sociological thinkers' ideas
5 A framework or general approach to understanding the social world
6 Normative prescriptions of how to improve the social world
7 An attempt to solve some specific problem germane to the field of sociology (e.g. the micro-macro problem).

We can see that the list accords somewhat with Camic and Gross' suggested categories, and agrees with Alexander's point that theory cannot be reduced to one thing, yet Abend's scheme seems cleaner and more analytically distinct. Using this as a starting point, Abend suggests that it is important to recognize that people often mean very different things when they talk about theory. Realizing this may lead some sociologists to lessen their general hostility to theory, or from the other side, to help quell the critics of so-called "a-theoretical work." Once these differences are understood, perhaps more room can be made for different theoretical approaches across the discipline. Ethnographers, as researchers who are well attuned to the importance of the multiplicity of meaning, ought to have a vested interest in the semantic differences surrounding theory. Still, we too have been guilty of not adequately allowing for different styles of theory in our discussions of the subject.

For Abend, a researcher who offers a narrative of an event is generating as much of a theoretical contribution, albeit of a different type, as someone trying to establish an axiomatic, conditional statement of human behavior. One should not necessarily be privileged over the other, since as they are of a different class of theory altogether, it would be like comparing apples to oranges. Of course, debates will continue that argue for a privileging of some of the theoretical types identified by Abend over others. Clearly, quantitative scholars would be most likely to privilege theory as axiomatic statements, while historians would favor ideographic explanations, and postmodern ethnographers would argue for the superiority of hermeneutic narratives. It is true that convincing sociologists to accept all forms of theory as relatively equal and different is not accomplished overnight, but will probably help people get along more harmoniously in the discipline in the long run. At the minimum, this view allows that theory cannot be monopolized by certain types of sociologists at the expense of others; theory lies at the core of all wings of sociology, qualitative field research being no exception.

It might be nice if despite the variation in theoretical types across the larger discipline, theorizing within ethnography was all of the same type (some might point to hermeneutical narratives as a common style in ethnography), but alas, ethnographers are allowed this luxury no more than your average sociologist. Snow et al. (2003) have tried to define theory in ethnography according to one set of definitional conditions, which are: (1) a set of logically related propositions; (2) an openness to empirical assessment; (3) an attempt to make events meaningful via conceptualization; and (4) a discourse that allows for the explanation of empirical events. While this definition seems safe enough on the surface, the problem is that not all notions of theory as practiced fit here. The authors concede that not all conditions need be met in all cases (and rarely are in ethnographic work), and that their conditions ought to be used as a rough guideline and definition. Even so, we argue that placing emphasis on these guidelines as the litmus test of whether work passes as "analytic ethnography" serves to privilege certain types of theory in ethnography over others.

For example, some ethnographers are looking explicitly for causal mechanisms in their field research, while others strive to gain insider meanings, while still others seek normative, ethical, and political solutions to perceived problems (see Puddephatt and Prus 2007; Adler and Adler 2008). Perhaps it is this reality of diversity, and the misunderstandings this diversity brings about, which leads to the ambivalence to "theory" in ethnography previously discussed. For example, Snow et al. (2003) recognize a diverse group of styles that are to be found in the interplay of theory and research. These are (a) theoretical discovery; (b) theoretical extension; and (c) theoretical refinement. While somewhat useful, the final two categories seem to be distinguished only in degree. One might argue we are left with a distinction between "grounded" and "theory-driven" ethnographic approaches. Similarly, Faulkner (this volume) has settled on an analytical typology to house what he calls "thin" and "thick" forms of theoretical "exploration" (grounded discovery) and "exploitation" (theory-driven application).

Peter and Patricia Adler (2008) have characterized four different rhetorical styles of ethnography, all of which adhere, roughly, to some sort of theoretical, ontological, and epistemological set of preferences. Roughly, they argue that the "four faces of ethnography" can be characterized by: (1) analytical ethnography, as seen in mainstream journals, often requiring some sort of logically interrelated conceptual apparatus at the core of the argument; (2) classical ethnography, which tells about the life of a group drawing heavily on their own meanings, language, and understanding; (3) postmodern narrative ethnography, which attempts to entertain, provoke, and moralize rather than provide scientific accounts; and finally (4) public ethnographies, which have a vested interest in carrying a normative message to audiences beyond their peers in academia. Here too, it is recognized that there are different ways to approach ethnography, and the resultant types of theories such studies are likely to make use of. While the authors favor of classically styled ethnography in the Chicago School tradition, they also show an openness and willingness to embrace other approaches, as they are valuable in different ways. The current volume aims to incorporate many different styles and approaches of handling theory in the ethnographic venture, and asks the reader to engage with this breadth and variety with an open mind. The more approaches to theory that we have access to, presented through the eyes of those individuals who spent countless hours knee-deep in successful ethnographic research, the more we stand to gain.

Contributions to the volume

We all have our own preferences (or prejudices) toward how to properly approach ethnographic work, as well as our own pet theories and styles of conceptualization. Nonetheless, learning other ways of putting things together, and alternate perspectives to both theory and research can only help to expand one's reservoir of tools, and awareness of what is available in generating concepts while in the field. As such, we have tried to gather a wide array of ethnographic styles and theoretical approaches for the present volume. As mentioned above, rather than favoring one theoretical style over another, we follow Abend (2008) in welcoming the diversity of conceptual approaches found throughout the ethnographic tradition.

We have attempted to set up conceptual sections according to a rough taxonomy of theoretical styles, placing papers into the categories we judged them to be most representative of. The authors were not consulted in this sorting process, and many of the papers could probably be placed in several of the categories. Nevertheless, and overlaps and blurred boundaries notwithstanding, we have tried to formulate a coherent set of categories for the volume, according to a variety of theoretical styles the range of papers seem to represent. While this undoubtedly distorts the unique contributions of each chapter, this approach provides a cohesive framework and allows us to discuss the diversity of approaches in a more straightforward way. Briefly, the styles of theory we have highlighted are the following: (1) generating grounded theory; (2) working with sensitizing concepts; (3) extending theoretical frames; (4) conceptualizing community and social organization; (5) challenging established wisdom; and, (6) theorizing from alternative data. We will first discuss each thematic section, and then give a brief synopsis of each of the contributions and how they fit into the particular theme in question.

Part I: Generating grounded theory

Glaser and Strauss (1967) contributed a landmark work in their argument for inductive, exploratory research designs that would flexibly generate new theory as a result of a close and persistent comparative method of emergent data gathered from the field. Many researchers have interpreted this strategy in such a way as to begin at the field-site rather than the library; to seek out a new scene or locale in an effort to uncover new theoretical insights. Perhaps this could be seen as the sociological equivalent of the anthropologist questing after the as-yet undiscovered tribe. Following this theoretical strategy, many researchers would advise that one simply "start where you are." Indeed, as Adler and Adler observe, it is a major benefit for researchers to research groups they are already familiar with, or embedded with, in that much of the work of understanding the dynamics of social organization, and the hidden meanings of the group, is well on the way to being accomplished. As such, an excellent strategy for students taking a seminar course on field methods is to choose a location they are relatively familiar with, cutting down drastically on the amount of preparation work required in fitting in with and coming to know the group in question. Certainly, grounded theory need not always begin in a familiar location, and hence, often a great deal of preliminary exploration is required.

As Kathy Charmaz (2006) makes evident, grounded theory today can mean a number of different things to a number of different people. To a traditionalist like Barney Glaser (1992; 2002), grounded theory involves actively resisting prior knowledge about a subject such that one can go into the field and process data in an effort to generate relatively bias-free knowledge about the social processes and mechanisms discovered. To abandon the purity of the constant comparative method in favor of pre-formed analytic constructs like Strauss and Corbin's (1998) "conditional matrix" is to lose the distinctive advantage of grounded theory over more generic qualitative data analysis approaches. Following the postmodern turn, Adele Clarke (2005) argues that the whole idea of reducing bias, or achieving the discovery of objective, externally acquired knowledge is a fiction; how researchers are situated in the setting to begin with, and what they bring along has a major role to play in the sorts of concepts they create. In line with this, Charmaz's (2006) program of "constructing grounded theory" emphasizes the relationship between the researcher and the participants, as well as the position and perspective the researcher brings into the field, which will be influenced by a host of factors, not least of which is a prior theoretical understanding. What connects the competing traditions of grounded theory, however, is a general aim of choosing a place or substantive topic, and emphasizing openness and flexibility over and above deductive testing. Thus, in general, the approach is case- or site-driven, and not theory- or concept-driven, despite the impossibility of removing or bracketing one's anticipations in this regard.

Each of the following contributions approaches the field using a relatively open agenda in mind, but each offers different lessons to take home about how to cultivate concepts from the ground up. David Karp offers the reader a fascinating description of the intellectual process behind the organization of *Speaking of Sadness* (1996)—an analysis of clinical depression from a symbolic interactionist perspective. Karp informs the reader that he has been grappling with a depression diagnosis since his early 30s. Indeed, this very personal experience with depression sparked and sustained his interest in deciphering the dynamics of mental illness and to offer the perspective—to give voice—to those whose encounters with depression were typically marginalized and even discounted. "How does an illness identity come into being and then evolve?" served as the underlying question guiding the research. In the process, Karp's volume attends to the dialectic of self and society, demonstrating that a grounded sociological take on the illness forcefully reveals that an appreciation of the cultural chemistry of depression is as relevant and vital as any analysis of the brain chemistry. Utilizing both his own experiences as a roadmap of the illness's trajectories, along with data from interviews with informants, Karp offers insights into the illness's "career," and the predictable consequences of "identity turning points." Situating the fulcrum of the analysis at the intersection of illness careers and identities, Karp is able to reveal remarkable connections between seemingly unrelated experiences; notably, the commitment and conversion processes connected to the use of, and thoughts about, medications and the similarities to comparable experiences in the realm of religion.

Kathy Charmaz recounts the intellectual research process of adopting grounded theory to interview people experiencing chronic illness for her 1991 book *Good Days, Bad Days: The Self in Chronic Illness and Time*. Charmaz recounts how her interest in this topic reflected both her experiences in dealing with chronic illness as a family member, and as an occupational therapist, before turning to academia. Her theoretical approach to the topic took into account the multiple perspectives that could be brought to bear, for example, between patients and healthcare practitioners as well as each other. Inspired by the philosophy of G. H. Mead (1932) as well as a novel by Thomas Mann (1929), there was an active curiosity at work of how the experience of time, and one's own interpretation of the past are linked closely to one's situation in the present. Charmaz shows convincingly how these intellectual, biographical, and professional precursors had a major bearing on the direction and conduct of the interviews she would collect in her portrayal of how the self and past is re-conceptualized as a mutually constitutive process by people experiencing chronic illness.

Clinton Sanders recalls that it was neither a theoretical motivation, nor a personal biographical reason that led him to study the tattooing culture, but rather, it was chance. The inspiration for his 1989 study *Customizing the Body: The Art and Culture of Tattooing*, began by his serendipitous introduction to the topic while killing time in San Francisco, which ended with him receiving a tattoo. From this experience, Sanders began to notice a number of sociologically relevant themes emerging, which provided the genesis for his 10-year study of the tattoo subculture. While Sanders agrees it is difficult to discard personal and academic presumptions upon entering the field, the attempt to do so is valuable, since theoretical research questions can often lead researchers astray, where focusing on the insights from first-hand experience would be much more fruitful. With this open-minded approach, Sanders pursued the themes deemed most relevant to the people who matter most, the insiders of the tattoo culture. Sanders recalls how each of these themes, from setting client typologies, to tattoos as social affiliations, to tattoos as an artistic practice, took precedence over stereotypical pop notions of what might be most relevant, such as regret, deviance, and so on.

The best way to determine what is most relevant is paying attention to insider meanings and being true to the issues present in the community itself, not popular discourse or even the academic literature.

Part II: Working with sensitizing concepts

Other researchers emphasize beginning the research process with an open mind as well, which is the main advantage of ethnographic data, yet argue for the use of starting concepts as a way to usefully guide the research process. As discussed, Herbert Blumer (1954) developed the notion of using flexible "sensitizing concepts" in empirical research rather than the sorts of reified social theories popular in sociology at the time. The emphasis was on entering the study with some direction and purpose, and a general idea of what was to be investigated, but a need to maintain an openness and flexibility to change the concept as the empirical reality of the case required. Thus, the researcher would enter into mutually dependent phases of "exploration and inspection," in which sensitizing concepts would take form and undergo testing against the "obdurate" nature of the group in question. The idea of using sensitizing concepts in field research has been inspirational to a number of other researchers, and has been explored in more depth by Will C. van den Hoonaard (1996). Van den Hoonaard pushes the point that sensitizing concepts are in place as a way to open up avenues of possibility, and attune the researcher toward vistas of possibility in the field. Thus, cultivating an openness to indeterminacy and multiple possibilities is a key feature of using sensitizing concepts. He contrasts this notion with the opposite tactic of invoking "desensitizing concepts"; defined as a way to close down, rather than open up, discourse into a contentious area, as is often used as a rhetorical tactic, for example, in politics.

All of the contributors in this section made use of sensitizing concepts either implicitly or more explicitly, using the particular cases at hand as examples. Each of the cases shows how entering the field with certain broadly formed ideas, rather than a blank slate, can be very helpful in accelerating the research process, and planting the seeds for the sorts of empirical data-gathering that may provide the most interesting results. In each case, early ideas were never quite right; but they served the purpose, in that they allowed the researcher to "get on with it" and gather useful data, even though the principle guiding that data collection strategy may have been, in hindsight, somewhat ill-advised. Thus, even though early conceptual notions may be imprecise, incomplete, or completely wrong-headed, they are useful in that they give direction and purpose to the study. Further, by proving themselves wrong in certain cases, better ideas and more refined or nuanced understandings often emerge as a result.

Robert Faulkner reflects on his 1983 ethnography *Music on Demand* to show the value of applying sensitizing concepts gained from the existing literature, as well as discovering unexpected contingencies in research practice, which often disrupts previous understandings or challenges academic wisdom, but also leads to good ideas. In considering the use of sensitizing concepts in field research, Faulkner develops a typology that characterizes the tension between "thin" and "thick" forms of what he calls theoretical "exploration" and "exploitation." Thin forms refer to the ideal, metaphysical end of the spectrum, meaning that the ideas in question may be well developed in the literature or in popular understandings, but are not adequately or thoroughly tested in the empirical data of the case in question. In contrast, thick forms refer to ideas that have been adequately grounded in the data, giving them more richness and local context. On the other continuum, exploration refers to inductive approaches to concepts as they emerge naturally from the case evidence, while exploitation leans toward the application of pre-formed theoretical frames or ideas. Faulkner argues that all of these approaches have pitfalls but at the same time are inevitable and useful for the genesis of ideas in the field.

Will C. van den Hoonaard recounts his 1992 study entitled *Reluctant Pioneers: Constraints and Opportunities in an Icelandic Fishing Community*. He provides examples of where his initial preconceptions, which served as sensitizing concepts to his approach to the study, were later discovered to be somewhat misguided. However, these misconceptions, once corrected, became a useful tool in crafting the writing and presenting the case in ways that would help to correct others' misunderstandings of the culture in question. As this process of reorientation unfolded, van den Hoonaard gained an ever increasing familiarity with the fishing culture, including important insider meanings and distinctions, social interdependencies, and power relationships and status hierarchies. Inspired by Everett Hughes, van den Hoonaard came to understand that the fisheries were increasingly losing the specificity of their local cultural identities through increased interaction with state-level science and governmental organizations. Hence, they began to develop a more nationalistic framework around their occupational identities.

In recollecting *Student Life and Exams* (1984), Daniel and Cheryl Albas tell of how they began their conceptual analysis by making use of what John Lofland (1976) referred to as "mini-concepts," or local, micro-level regularities in student behavior. Eventually these would be linked together to make more synthetic, "middle-range" statements (Merton 1957), which would in turn allow for larger "trans-situational" comparisons to other social contexts (Prus 1996). Once this was achieved, the Albases were able to link the observation of superstitious practices of students to the existing anthropological literature on magic, and their observations of face-work and concealment practices to many other social arenas, making for much broader theoretical contributions than would otherwise be possible.

Finally, Jaber Gubrium reflects back on his 1975 study *Living and Dying at Murray Manor*, and explains how this study effectively awakened him to the strong benefits afforded by ethnographic field research over his previous propensity for quantitative survey designs. Gubrium explains that many of the concepts with which he entered the nursing home setting echoed his past positivistic assumptions about variables and how they relate. More specifically, he was interested in better understanding the variation around "person-environment fit" according to different individual needs and different locations in the nursing home. Gubrium soon found that in speaking with the residents and staff, different people (often residents versus staff) would develop very different meanings for quality of care, time schedules, and how time was used. Thus, Gubrium linked these issues to the collision of different social worlds, and how these meanings would often conflict in the practices taking place in the nursing home setting.

Part III: Extending theoretical frames

While the previous group placed emphasis on particular concepts or ideas, others extol the virtue of using broader theoretical frames with which to organize the data encountered, bringing to bear a particular perspective or theoretical school of thought. Abend (2008) illustrates one semantic use of the word theory as the application of prior conceptual or paradigmatic frames, to contextualize and guide research into particular cases. Indeed, a very dominant conceptual strategy in ethnographic research is to apply a well developed perspective or theoretical frame to an object of study, creating the foundation but also the space for original theoretical arguments to be made about the topic at hand. One thinks, for example, of the unique insights gained through the labeling theory perspective in Lemert's (1962) study of paranoids, or Rosenhan's (1973) study of the diagnosis of patients in an insane asylum. Further, the neo-Marxist perspective has also been useful in highlighting the reproduction and reinforcement of social class in Burawoy's (1979) study of factory work, as well as Paul Willis' (1977) study of working class kids' orientation to the educational system. Applying a well established theoretical frame sets up the paradigmatic approach that precludes following all leads, which effectively constrains the focus in a way to direct the data collection and analysis in a more productive way. Once the frame is applied rigorously to the case at hand, the findings can be used to extend, qualify, refute, or bolster the major assumptions of the paradigm in question. This strategy also allows the researcher to build on previous studies that make use of the same conceptual framework for useful comparisons to other substantive areas.

Loïc Wacquant reflects on his study of an inner-city boxing club on Chicago's south side that was the basis of his book, *Body and Soul: Notebooks of an Apprentice Boxer* (2004). Wacquant recounts how his study can be seen as a sort an intersection of the conceptual frames provided by his teacher, Pierre Bourdieu, as well as his supervisor while in Chicago, William Julius

Wilson. Wilson's influence led him to analyze the social organization of the black ghetto through the boxing club in order to gain insight into this race- and class-based community as it is fostered by its own members. Bourdieu's theory of *habitus* led Wacquant to tie the social organization witnessed, and their shared practices, to emotional, carnal, and embodied dimensions of individual experience, such that the body is seen to be forged along with the will in the pugilistic discipline of boxing. Wacquant sees his own insider status as an apprentice boxer as a benefit, by feeling and experiencing the boxing gym first-hand in all of its gritty facets. However, such personal affective and embodied experience must be in constant dialogue with a more critical theoretical imagination and analysis, so as not to merely reproduce the folk wisdom of insider accounts. It is this reflexive ability to situate one's own deeply felt experiences within more systematic theoretical under- standings that is the foundation of Wacquant's approach, and the major difference, he argues, from traditional American ethnography.

Norman Denzin reflects on the research leading up to his major work (1987) *The Alcoholic Self,* and recalls how he applied the principles of his framework of postmodern ethnography to study *Alcoholics Anonymous* (AA). Rather than studying the topic in a neutral manner, Denzin firmly sides with the recovering alcoholics of AA, and, in so doing, challenges the efficacy of scientific models of alcoholism that tended to dominate at the time. Following Foucault, Denzin argues that rather than helping to "cure" alcoholics, the scientific, behaviorist approach to treatment only labels, stig- matizes, and brings more harm to those seeking treatment. Denzin shows that the AA philosophy is in good keeping with a postmodern approach to ethnography, in that members treat each other as equals, remain open to each other's experiences, and incorporate a holistic model of understanding that goes beyond logic and facts and connects at a deeply emotional level as well. It is this approach, Denzin argues, in contrast to more authoritarian and scientistic modes of practice, which allows members to heal and recover.

Robert Stebbins applied his own theoretical framework of "leisure theory," fostered over numerous studies throughout his career, to the case of three "nature challenge hobbies," in his 2005 book *Challenging Mountain Nature: Risk, Motive, and Lifestyle in Three Hobbyist Sports.* By linking the new cases to a prior established taxonomy of leisure theory, Stebbins illustrates how the facts collected could be more easily sorted into a coherent frame- work for analysis. While Stebbins was at each phase guided by the logic and existing knowledge of leisure pursuits provided by the framework, he argues that his research still uncovers unforeseen contributions. He discovered, for example, different perspectives on "risk" between insiders and outsiders, a closer appreciation of the process of self-fulfillment, and finally, the rela- tionship between "core" and more subsidiary leisure involvements of mem- bers, and the patterns observed therein. Stebbins shows that the key is to situate wide-ranging cases of leisure hobbies within the paradigmatic frame of leisure theory, so as to reinforce and bolster, but also expand and refine past understandings.

Finally, Trevor Pinch reflects on his 2002 book (researched and written along with Frank Trocco) *Analog Days: The Invention and Impact of the Moog Synthesizer*. Here, Pinch discusses how he placed his study of the Moog synthesizer within the theoretical frame provided by the social construction of science and technology (SCOT) approach. He first problematizes the very idea of generating an independent narrative of theory-construction, as a result of the difficulties within the inherent bias connected to professional memory. Nevertheless, Pinch recounts that drawing on the existing theoretical frame of SCOT not only helps set the research agenda, but also achieves a greater focus on which particular theorists, concepts, and facts uncovered in the Moog story would be most relevant. Beyond this, Pinch notes that most of the ideas that culminated from the intersection of prior theory-frames and the case at hand were also subsequently sifted and reshaped thanks to the various exchanges at professional conferences and informal consultations. Theorizing is not a lone activity, but a thoroughly collective process, which is largely tacit and difficult to pin down in retrospect.

Part IV: Conceptualizing community and social organization

Traditional exemplars of sociological ethnography, from Nels Anderson's (1923) account of the life of traveling hobos, to William F. Whyte's (1943) study of street corner society in an Italian slum, all centered around a general concern to capture the essence behind the social organization of the groups studied. How were people dispersed across the setting? What were the rules governing interaction, and how did the community work, often in informal ways, to accomplish the particular needs of its members? The earliest ethnographies staked out strategies to observe first-hand how social scenes were organized, and how members of these communities worked together in complex yet well integrated processes. The importance of this work has not faded, as we see contemporary ethnographies following much the same strategy today, such as Mitchell Duneier's (1999) study of the life of street vendors, as well as Elijah Anderson's (1999) analysis of moral rules in the culture of the inner city.

As long as there are groups of people who are not well understood, it is an important theoretical strategy to track their social organization and within this, uncover the meanings that members attribute to their social actions in relation to one another. Each of the contributions to follow places the researcher, at the outset, within a relatively foreign world that is to become familiar and eventually analyzed in some way. Faced with this daunting challenge, the contributors share the basic strategy of maintaining an openness to how the community in question is organized, slowly moving toward a more explicit analysis of the meanings that lay behind the practices of the members. Finally, more latent patterns of social organization are often highlighted, which often go beyond the immediate understandings of insiders. It is this last goal where the unique skills of the ethnographer to "solve the puzzle" or generate non-obvious explanations of social patterns come into play, and where the richest conceptual material is often generated.

Samuel Heilman bases his chapter on his 1993 ethnography titled *Defenders of the Faith: Inside Ultra-Orthodox Jewry*. In it, Heilman focuses on ultra-Orthodox Jews, or haredim as they are called, that appear to embody the Jewish past, the vanished world of one's European grandparents. He demonstrates, however, that unlike a relic of the past, ultra-Orthodox Jews are very much part of the contemporary landscape, far from untouched by, or effectively insulated from, modernity. The process of discovering the social organization of this religious community, including its lifestyle and mores regarding education, religion, marriage and sexual ethics, required that Heilman exercise an insider's advantage and a strong measure of cultural competence. This enabled him to recognize a series of critical insights as he moved analytically between the haredi and mainstream culture. Not denying the advantages of proceeding within the parameters of a conceptual framework to guide and structure one's data collection, Heilman, instead, chooses to rely on Lévi-Strauss' notion of "intellectual bricolage," a technique that frees him from any conceptual or theoretical straightjacket while allowing for improvisation—to make do "with whatever is at hand"—as the research unfolds.

In a closely related topic, William Shaffir recollects his early research experience in studying the social community of Hassidic Jews, which culminated in his major book-length ethnography, *Life in a Religious Community: The Lubavitcher Chassidim in Montreal* (1974). Unfamiliar with this segment of Orthodox Jewry, Shaffir was initially struck by the meticulous efforts at insulation adopted by the Hassidim to preserve their cherished and chosen way of life. This impression was at first based on conversations with Hassidim he encountered while visiting their summer colony and their houses of worship in Montreal. However, Shaffir could not initially reconcile the unusual proselytizing efforts of members of the Lubavitch Hassidic sect that appeared so at odds with measures adopted by the remainder of the sects; more specifically, while the latter eschewed all unnecessary contact with outsiders, the Lubavitcher organized an array of activities for the expressed purpose of contacting and inviting unobservant Jews to their activities and institutions. Shaffir discusses how this puzzling state of affairs was eventually resolved as he discovered that proselytizing efforts, when properly organized, indeed serve as an insulating mechanism resulting in identity consolidation.

Patricia and Peter Adler reflect on the genesis of their project that examines the social organization and power dynamics of school cliques in their ethnography *Peer Power: Preadolescent Culture and Identity* (1998). The Adlers recount how it was their role as parents and volunteers for their children that provided them access, and allowed them to study, the issues of peer dynamics among youth. Further, it was the compelling fascination and worry of watching their own children attempt to negotiate the terrain of the power-laden social norms of the peer community that provided much of the motivation to study this systematically. Patricia and Peter explain that while they started their research from a personal interest, they utilize a more top-down "gestalt analysis" rather than a traditional bottom-up approach of grounded theory, viewing their data through the frame of derived sociological viewpoints, which could be recast as necessary as new data emerged. They asked how stratification within and between peer groups happens in preadolescent culture, and how this might inform our conception of power in everyday life. It is the peer-group, they argue, not society or the individual that is the key to understanding stratification and conformity. The Adler's show the pressure facing even the most popular kids in cultivating careful boundaries of inclusion and exclusion within their peer-communities. Power is not fixed in the schoolyard, office building, or the street; rather, it is a thoroughly dynamic process negotiated actively by participants at all levels.

Finally, Robert Prus recounts his 1980 study (co-authored with Styllianos Irini) titled *Hookers, Rounders, and Desk Clerks*. In this chapter, Prus emphasizes that the point of his study was not to investigate whether hotel patrons of various stripes *had* a community, but rather, *how* that community worked as a relatively coherent set of shifting interests. The emphasis is on how different segments of the hotel community (con artists, strippers, hookers, bartenders, and others) would enter into exchange relations with each other to foster a relatively symbiotic community, for example, helping one another make money while at the same time avoiding the authorities, and coordinating legal and illicit ventures together in mutually supportive ways. Prus and Irini were not interested in testing any particular hunch or narrow conceptual issue. Rather, they undertook a systematic stock-taking of the social organization of the hotel community as they encountered it, utilizing the flexible approach of symbolic interactionist theory to do so.

Part V: Challenging established wisdom

Much of the motivation to conduct research is to challenge the established wisdom of either folk knowledge, or academic conventions. Nothing is better than conducting research and finding a radical departure from the established wisdom on a topic. The studies that we often find most interesting and compelling to read are those that "debunk," "unmask," and get past the popular appearances, or facades of everyday life, to uncover what is really going on. A hallmark of the contributions in this volume is that the reported research overturns people's assumptions about what they are doing and why it is they are doing it; that is, to look for the hidden meaning in what from a common-sense standpoint is inexplicable. We exist in a political world, in which prejudices and stereotyped opinions often die hard. One would like to think that academia is an exception to this, but here too one can find a good share of prejudice, as well as ingrained ways of thinking and knowing in the university that are not easily put to the side. There are political factions inside and outside of academia, and it is often an uphill struggle to make an argument against the grain. Still, the frustration of having to follow established wisdom when it no longer fits often provides exceptional motivation to proceed along an independent and sometimes contradictory path.

On the other hand, challenging established conventions or beliefs is not always the intention of researchers at the outset, but rather, it is the compelling and undeniable findings of the study that lead them to do so. This is probably the most accurate depiction of the four contributors to follow in this section. Some of these are heated and sensitive political issues, where public statements had to be made on a very fine line, and loyalties were jeopardized. Others simply found information that was largely contrary to the established wisdom of most outsiders to the activities and/or membership in question. At any rate, all tell a story of how they were surprised at what they found in their studies, and eventually realized they had a profound argument to make against the established wisdom of professional, academic and/or lay knowledge.

Based on his ethnography *Champions* (1988), and an article that won the American Sociological Association's Theory Section Prize (1989), Chambliss' contribution shows how his research on the stratification of competitive swimmers challenged the common-sense wisdom about these elite athletes. His implicit theory about excellence—that the top swimmers were the most talented, possessing a mysterious quality separating them from the rest—was necessarily transformed as he spent countless hours observing the swimmers in action. The magical discovery—seemingly so mundane for Chambliss—was that these top swimmers were simply people that swam fast. His initial preconceptions, gathered through a distorted media filter, required drastic modification: Great performance is far from innate and consists, rather, of a series of little particulars that are mastered to perfection. Challenging the established wisdom in Chambliss' case required jettisoning a series of misconceptions and learning to discover the various points where he had been wrong, all of which led to the realization that the "big secret" was that there was no "big secret."

Since ethnography is much like detective work, Donileen Loseke relies upon the mystery story genre to solve a riddle that, in effect, stymied her research at the "South Coast" shelter for battered women in her 1992 work *The Battered Woman and Shelters: The Social Construction of Wife Abuse*. More specifically, how was one to explain the seemingly inexplicable—that is, that staff workers failed to treat the residents equally and essentially divided the world into two categories of women, the "battered woman" and the "not battered woman." As Loseke discovered, unraveling this mystery required her to reconfigure her common-sense thinking about the shelter, and to focus on the characteristics of the women that would help explain workers' categorizations of them and account for their differential treatment. In the end, she emphasizes the importance of appreciating the cultural "tool kit" used by the workers to understand their conception of the ideal client frequenting the shelter, which involved specific characteristics that such clients would demonstrate, such as passivity, shyness, a plethora of fears and anxieties, devastation owing to victimization, and gratitude to the shelter.

Along similar lines, Jennifer L. Dunn discusses how her planned study of intimate stalking veered in a very different direction from what she originally planned in her ethnography that became *Courting Disaster: Intimate Stalking, Culture, and Criminal Justice* (2002). Expecting to write about the serious social problem of stalking, and how victims would situate it by drawing upon culturally and psychologically appropriate constructs rooted in the social structure, Dunn's focus and conceptualization shifted as she assumed a social constructionist perspective to understand that "stalking victim" was a label to be attached to women. Indeed, experiences in the field compelled her to alter her focus from interactions between stalkers and their victims to the centrality of interactions between victims and their audiences. Being labeled a victim of stalking was not conferred automatically but entailed a definitional process whereby victims learned how to mount a convincing self-presentation, while conforming to the normative expectations of victims' advocates. Stalkers' advocates felt sympathy for some of the victims but not for others and this was linked, to Dunn's surprise, with the victims' emotional presentation of self. Advocates, in other words, evaluated victims' self-presentation, which led them to define some victims differently from other victims. Contrary to common-sense wisdom, then, the victim role was one to be learned and perfected.

Harry Collins recounts the 30-year history of his ethnographic investigation of the practices and disputes of gravity wave scientists that led to his 2004 book *Gravity's Shadow: The Search for Gravitational Waves*. While Collins entered the field initially with the idea of trying to understand "knowledge diffusion" between groups in scientific networks, and decided to follow along groups who were trying to build a laser, a very difficult device to get working. Drawing on Wittgenstein, he found that the ability to learn how to build a laser correctly, much like how to set up a laboratory, is based largely on immersing oneself in the "form of life" of scientists so as to get the sort of tacit knowledge that is required over and above abstract diagrams and written accounts. He moved from following the construction of a laser to studying a budding scientific controversy (still not yet closed) surrounding the existence of gravitational waves. Following the dynamics of rival scientific groups in arguing about their experimental apparatus and professional competence, Collins found that experiments are rarely settled on the evidence alone because of the logic of what he calls the "experimenter's regress," in that the grounds for whether or not an experiment is seen to work cannot be removed from prior theoretical judgments of what ought to be found if it works correctly.

Hence, scientific disputes are not closed, as often popularly assumed, by rationality and evidence alone, but also by myriad social factors such as one's professional reputation among the "core set" of scientific networks. Collins argues that the test of good ethnographic concepts, in the end, ought to be whether they successfully go beyond mere insider understandings, and contribute ideas that are both unforeseen and useful to the group studied.

Part VI: Theorizing from alternative data: documentary, historical, and autobiographical sources

Often the inspiration for great theories, as many of the contributors have expressed throughout the volume, comes from odd places. Indeed, the seeds of ideas may be generated from life experiences, accidental happenstance occurrences, and may lead the researcher to non-traditional ethnographic sources of data. The following are tales of researchers who work from the ethnographic tradition yet who found themselves pulled in different directions because of the compelling nature of some sort of data linked tightly to an emerging interest and enduring curiosity. While the sources of data drawn on may be deemed by some to fall outside the proper definition of ethnography, the authors to follow emphasize how their alternative data are explored and used in ways that are true to the ethnographic tradition. The reader can decide whether or not these "count" as ethnographic projects or not. More important is that readers pay attention to the use of varied data forms as they become defined as essential through emergent theoretical activity. By following one's nose, often in unexpected ways, researchers sometimes need to free themselves of participant observation and interviews in order to best answer particular theoretical questions in the most direct way possible, drawing on evidence of other kinds.

Laurel Richardson reflects on the rather serendipitous process whereby she came to write *Last Writes: A Daybook for a Dying Friend* (2007). In this reflexive portrait of this work, Richardson makes it evident that she didn't realize she was writing theory until long after she had started the process of personal writing in her day book. What started out as deeply personal notes to herself about her changing relationship and feelings in regard to her dying friend, turned into an excursus about long-term relationships, and the reflection of significant others in one's own self at various stages of life. By working through her diary notes and attempting to find the latent meanings therein, she began to piece together the potential meanings of her personal journey and the theoretical implications to follow. Her chapter is a fascinating account of how theory can take root from our own personal lives and experiences, and how the creative process does not necessarily begin, nor end, with a formal research cycle. One hopes that the reader appreciates how ideas can be cultivated from unforeseen locations, which is a helpful lesson to put to use in traditional ethnographic designs as well.

Dorothy Pawluch recounts the conceptual process behind *The New Pediatrics: A Profession in Transition* (1996). Unlike Richardson, Pawluch began her project as a traditional ethnography, but was drawn by her theoretical curiosity more and more into written records and document sources. Following Glaser and Strauss, Pawluch argues that such library sources provide a rich source of data and allow the researcher to obtain the many "voices begging to be heard" on an issue. While she did bolster her study of the changing nature of the pediatrics profession with some interviews and observations, her theoretical questions led her to analyze documents first and foremost. It was in these documentary sources where Pawluch could follow along the debates and claims-making activities of various segments of the pediatric field to better understand how the profession was being redefined in response to various threats. Through this research process, Pawluch explains that what started out as an inquiry into medicalization quickly turned into an investigation of a profession in process, of how the "new pediatrics" was able to create a formula for revitalization during a period where its relevance was coming under more scrutiny as a result of competition with general practitioners. Pawluch emphasizes in her case that the mess and chaos of data is part and parcel of the ethnographic venture; with time, patience, and persistence, the right themes will emerge and crystallize.

Nachman Ben-Yehuda reflects on the development of what he refers to as an "historical ethnography," in his 1995 work *The Masada Myth: Collective Memory and Mythmaking in Israel.* The ethnography itself started as a personal historical dispute between the author and a historian as to the happenings at Masada between Jewish fighters and the Roman Imperial army in 70 AD. The traditional history written from the time period in question paints a rather grim and depressing tale of the Jewish group as ruthless assassins, while the mythical contemporary history, almost 2,000 years later, regards them as brave and noble freedom fighters. Ben Yehuda immediately became interested in his own ideological indoctrination of the mythical story and how the story helps to form a conception of Jewish and Israeli identity. As such, he began an ethnography to investigate how such myths are propagated in the present through various sites including the science of archeological studies, the myths presented on guided tours of Masada, and the work of intellectuals in their textbook (re)writing of history. Ben Yehuda tells how he utilized all of these forms of evidence so as to understand how the past is reconstructed by powerful groups so as to serve various needs related to culture and identity.

Notes

1 For contemporary statements on the grounded theory method, see Strauss and Corbin (1998), Glaser (2004; 2007), Clarke (2005) and Charmaz (2006).
2 See for example Anderson (2003) and Vaughan (2004).

3 It is for this reason that we encourage those doing ethnographic research now to keep a detailed diary of their experiences, paying careful attention to day-to-day decisions, especially those that are theoretically and conceptually relevant. Not only will this allow researchers to be more aware and conscious of the intellectual decisions they make during the research process, leading to better work in the end; it will also provide a more stable account for valuable, reflexive essays as to concept formation in ethnographic work. The more essays of this kind we can accumulate, the more concrete lessons for young ethnographers and students of the craft.

References

Abend, G. (2008) "The Meaning of Theory," *Sociological Theory*, 26: 173–99.

Adler, P. and Adler, P. (1998) *Peer Power: preadolescent culture and identity*, New Brunswick, NJ: Rutgers University Press.

——(2008) "Of Rhetoric and Representation: the four faces of ethnography," *The Sociological Quarterly*, 49: 1–30.

Albas, D. and Albas, C. (1984) *Student Life and Exams: stresses and coping strategies*, Dubuque, IN: Kendall/Hunt.

Alexander, J. (1982) *Theoretical Logic in Sociology*, Berkeley, CA: University of California Press.

Anderson, E. (1999) *Code of the Street: decency, violence, and the moral life of the inner city*, New York: Norton-Wiley.

——(2003) "Distinguished Lecture: Jelly's Place: an ethnographic memoir," *Symbolic Interaction*, 26: 217–37.

Anderson, N. (1923) *The Hobo: the sociology of the homeless man*, Chicago: University of Chicago Press.

Athens, L. (1980) *Violent Criminal Acts and Actors: a symbolic interactionist study*, Boston, MA: Routledge and Kegan Paul.

Barrett, S. (1987) *Is God a Racist? The wing in Canada*, Toronto, ON: University of Toronto Press.

Becker, H. (1963) *Outsiders: studies in the sociology of deviance*, London: Free Press of Glencoe.

——(1965) "Review of Sociologists at Work," *American Sociological Review*, 30: 602–3.

Ben-Yehuda, N. (1995) *The Masada Myth: collective memory and mythmaking in Israel*, Madison: University of Wisconsin Press.

Berson, L. (1971) *The Negroes and the Jews*, New York: Random House.

Bloor, D. (1991) "The Strong Programme in the Sociology of Knowledge," in *Knowledge and Social Imagery*, 2nd ed. (pp. 4–23), Chicago: University of Chicago Press.

Blumer, H. (1931) "Science without Concepts," *American Journal of Sociology*, 56: 515–33.

——(1954) "What's Wrong with Social Theory?" *American Sociological Review*, 19: 3–10.

——(1969) *Symbolic Interactionism: perspective and method*, Berkeley, CA: University of California Press.

Bourdieu, P. (2001) *Science of Science and Reflexivity*, Chicago: University of Chicago Press.

Bourdieu, P. and Wacquant, L. J. D. (1992) *An Invitation to Reflexive Sociology*, Chicago: University of Chicago Press.

Burawoy, M. (1979) *Manufacturing Consent: changes in the labor process under monopoly capitalism*, Chicago: University of Chicago Press.

——(2005) "2004 ASA Presidential Address: For Public Sociology," *American Sociological Review*, 70: 4–28.

Camic, C. and Gross, N. (1998) "Contemporary Developments in Sociological Theory: current projects and conditions of possibility," *Annual Review of Sociology*, 24: 453–76.

Chambliss, D. (1988) *Champions: the making of Olympic swimmers*, New York: William Morrow and Company.

——(1989) "The Mundanity of Excellence: an ethnographic report on stratification and Olympic athletes," *Sociological Theory*, 7: 1.

Charmaz, K. (1991) *Good Days, Bad Days: the self in chronic illness and time*, New Brunswick, NJ: Rutgers University Press.

——(2006) *Constructing Grounded Theory: a practical guide through qualitative analysis*, Thousand Oaks, CA: Sage.

Clarke, A. (2005) *Situational Analysis: grounded theory after the postmodern turn*, Thousand Oaks, CA: Sage.

Clifford, J. (1994) "On Ethnographic Allegory," in S. Seidman (ed.) *The Postmodern Turn: new perspectives on social theory* (pp. 205–28), Cambridge, MA: Cambridge University Press.

Clifford, J. and Marcus, G. E. (1986) *Writing Culture: the poetics and politics of ethnography*, Berkeley, CA: University of California Press.

Collins, H. (1985) *Changing Order: replication and induction in scientific practice*, Beverley Hills, CA: Sage.

——(2004) *Gravity's Shadow: the search for gravitational waves*, Chicago: University of Chicago Press.

Collins, H. and Pinch, T. (1993) *The Golem: what you should know about science*, New York: Cambridge University Press.

Collins, H. and Yearley, S. (1992) "Epistemological Chicken," in A. Pickering (ed.) *Science as Practice and Culture* (pp. 301–26), Chicago: University of Chicago Press.

Davis, F. (1961) "Deviance Disavowal: the management of strained interaction by the visibly physically handicapped," *Social Problems*, 9: 120–32.

Denzin, N. (1987) *The Alcoholic Self*, Newbury Park, CA: Sage.

——(1989) *The Research Act*, 3rd ed., Englewood Cliffs, NJ: Prentice Hall.

Denzin, N. and Lincoln, Y. (eds.) (2005) *Sage Handbook of Qualitative Research*, 3rd ed., Thousand Oaks, CA: Sage.

Duneier, M. (1999) *Sidewalk*, New York: Farrar, Strauss and Giroux.

Dunn, J. L. (2002) *Courting Disaster: intimate stalking, culture, and criminal justice*, New York: Aldine de Gruyter.

Edgerton, R. (1967) *The Cloak of Competence: stigma in the lives of the mentally retarded*, Berkeley, CA: University of California Press.

Emerson, R. (1987) "Four Ways to Improve the Craft of Fieldwork," *Journal of Contemporary Ethnography*, 16: 69–89.

Faulkner, R. (1983) *Music on Demand: composers and careers in the Hollywood film industry*, New Brunswick, NJ: Transaction Books.

Fine, G. (1995) "Introduction," in G. Fine (ed.) *A Second Chicago School? The development of a postwar American sociology* (pp. 1–16), Chicago: University of Chicago Press.

——(2007) *Authors of the Storm: meteorologists and the culture of prediction*, Chicago: University of Chicago Press.

——(2008) "Ten Myths of Ethnography Revisited," The Nels Andersen Plenary Address for the 25th Annual Qualitative Analysis Conference, University of New Brunswick, Fredericton, NB, May 22.

Fuller, S. (1988) *Social Epistemology*, Bloomington: Indiana University Press.

Geertz, C. (1973) *Interpretation of Cultures: selected essays*, New York: Basic Books.

Glaser, B. (1992) *Basics of Grounded Theory Analysis*, Mill Valley, CA: The Sociology Press.

——(2002) "Constructivist Grounded Theory?" *Forum: Qualitative Social Research*, 3. Online. Available at www.qualitative-research.net/fqs-texte/3-02/3–02glaser-e.htm (accessed October 15, 2006).

——(2004) "Remodeling Grounded Theory," *Forum: Qualitative Social Research*, 5. Online. Available at www.qualitative-research.net/index.php/fqs/article/view/607/ 1316 (accessed July 10, 2008).

——(2007) "Constructivist Grounded Theory?" *Historical Social Research*, 19: 93–105.

Glaser, B. and Strauss, A. (1967) *The Discovery of Grounded Theory*, Chicago: Aldine Publishing.

Goffman, E. (1961) *Asylums*, New York: Anchor.

Gubrium, J. ([1975] 1997) *Living and Dying at Murray Manor*, Charlottesville: University of Virginia Press.

Halbwachs, M. (1992) *On Collective Memory*, Chicago: University of Chicago Press.

Hammersley, M. (1990) *Reading Ethnographic Research: a critical guide*, New York: Longman.

——(1992) *What's Wrong with Ethnography?* New York: Routledge.

Hammond, P. E. (1964) *Sociologists at Work: essays on the craft of social research*, New York: Basic Books.

Haraway, D. (1988) "Situated Knowledges: the science question in feminism and the privilege of partial perspective," *Feminist Studies*, 14: 575–99.

Harding, S. (1986) *The Science Question in Feminism*, Ithaca, NY: Cornell University Press.

Heilman, S. (1993) *Defenders of the Faith: Inside Ultra-Orthodox Jewry*, New York: Schocken.

Hochschild, A. (1983) *The Managed Heart: the commercialization of human feeling*, Berkeley, CA: University of California Press.

Hughes, E. (1971) *The Sociological Eye: selected papers*, Chicago: Aldine.

Karp, D. (1996) *Speaking of Sadness: depression, disconnection, and the meanings of illness*, New York: Oxford University Press.

Katz, J. (1988) *Seductions of Crime: moral and sensual attractions of doing evil*, New York: Basic Books.

Kitsuse, J. (1970) "Editor's Preface," *American Behavioral Scientist*, 14: 163–65.

Kleinman, S. (1991) "Field-Workers' Feelings: who we are, how we analyze," in W. Shaffir and Stebbins, R. (eds.) *Experiencing Fieldwork: an inside view of qualitative research* (pp. 184–95), Newbury Park, CA: Sage.

Kleinman, S. and Copp, M. (1993) *Emotions and Fieldwork*, Newbury Park, CA: Sage.

Kuhn, T. S. (1962) *The Structure of Scientific Revolutions*, Chicago: University of Chicago Press.

Latour, B. (1987) *Science in Action: how to follow scientists and engineers through society*, Cambridge, MA: Harvard University Press.

Lemert, E. (1962) "Paranoia and the Dynamics of Exclusion," *Sociometry*, 25: 2–20.

Lofland, J. (1976) *Doing Social Life*, New York: Wiley Interscience.

Loseke, D. (1992) *The Battered Woman and Shelters: the social construction of wife abuse*, Albany, NY: State University of New York Press.

Lynch, M. (1985) *Art and Artifact in Laboratory Science: a study of shop work and shop talk in a research laboratory*, London: Routledge.

Lyotard, J-F. (1984) *The Postmodern Condition: a report on knowledge*, Minneapolis: University of Minnesota Press.

Mann, T. ([1929] 1952) *The Magic Mountain*, New York: Knopf.

Mead, G. H. (1932) *The Philosophy of the Present*, Chicago: University of Chicago Press.

Merton, R. K. (1957) *Social theory and Social Structure*, New York: Free Press.

——(1962) "Foreword," in B. Barber (ed.) *Science and the Social Order*, New York: Collier Books.

Pawluch, D. (1996) *The New Pediatrics: a profession in transition*, Hawthorne, NY: Aldine de Gruyter.

Pinch, T. and Trocco, F. (2002) *Analog Days: the invention and impact of the Moog Synthesizer*, Cambridge, MA: Harvard University Press.

Prus, R. (1996) *Symbolic Interaction and Ethnographic Research*, New York: SUNY Press.

——(1997) *Subcultural Mosaics and Intersubjective Realities*, New York: SUNY Press.

——(2007) "Human Memory, Social Process, and the Pragmatist Metamorphosis," *Journal of Contemporary Ethnography*, 36: 378–437.

Prus, R. and Irini, S. (1980) *Hookers, Rounders, and Desk Clerks: the social organization of the hotel community*, Toronto, ON: Gage.

Puddephatt, A. (2006) "Special: An Interview with Kathy Charmaz: on constructing grounded theory," *Qualitative Sociological Review*, 2: 6–20.

Puddephatt, A. and Prus, R. (2007) "Causality, Agency, and Reality: Plato and Aristotle meet George Herbert Mead and Herbert Blumer," *Sociological Focus*, 40: 265–86.

Richardson, L. (2007) *Last Writes: a daybook for a dying friend*, Walnut Creek, CA: Left Coast Press.

Rosenhan, D. L. (1973) "On Being Sane in Insane Places," *Science*, 179: 250–58.

Rouse, J. (1993) "What are Cultural Studies of Knowledge?" *Configurations*, 1: 57–94.

Sanders, C. (1989) *Customizing the Body: the art and culture of tattooing*, Philadelphia, PA: Temple University Press.

Seidman, S. (2008) *Contested Knowledge: social theory today*, 4th ed., Malden, MA: Blackwell Publishing.

Shaffir, W. (1974) *Life in a Religious Community: the Lubavitcher Chassidim in Montreal*, Toronto: Holt, Rinehart and Winston of Canada.

Shaffir, W., Stebbins, R., and Turowetz, A. (eds) (1980) *Fieldwork Experience*, New York: St. Martin's Press.

Shaffir, W. and Stebbins, R. (eds.) (1991) *Experiencing Fieldwork: an inside view of qualitative research*, Newbury Park, CA: Sage.

Snow, D., Morrill, C., and Anderson, L. (2003) "Elaborating Analytic Ethnography: linking fieldwork and theory," *Ethnography*, 4: 181–200.

Stebbins, R. (2005) *Challenging Mountain Nature: risk, motive, and lifestyle in three hobbyist sports*, Calgary, AB: Detselig.

Strauss, A. (1978) *Negotiations: varieties, contexts, processes and social order*, San Francisco, CA: Jossey-Bass.

——(1993) *Continual Permutations of Action*, New York: Aldine de Gruyter.

Strauss, A. and Corbin, J. (1998) *Basics of Qualitative Research: techniques and procedures for developing grounded theory*, 2nd ed., Thousand Oaks, CA: Sage.

Stryker, S. (1980) *Symbolic Interaction: a social structural version*, Menlo Park, CA: Benjamin/Cummings Publishing Co.

van den Hoonaard, W. (1992) *Reluctant Pioneers: constraints and opportunities in an Icelandic fishing community*, New York: Peter Lang.

——(1996) *Working with Sensitizing Concepts: analytical field research*, Thousand Oaks, CA: Sage.

Vaughan, D. (1996) *The Challenger Launch Decision: risky technology, culture, and deviance at NASA*, Chicago: University of Chicago Press.

——(2004) "Theorizing Disaster: analogy, historical ethnography, and the Challenger accident," *Ethnography*, 5: 315–47.

Vidich, A., Bensman, J., and Stein, M. (1964) *Reflections on Community Studies*, New York: Wiley.

Wacquant, L. (2002) "Scrutinizing the Street: poverty, morality, and the pitfalls of urban ethnography," *American Journal of Sociology*, 107: 1468–532.

——(2004) *Body and Soul: notebook of an apprentice boxer*, New York: Oxford University Press.

Whyte, W. F. (1943) *Street Corner Society*, Chicago: University of Chicago Press.

Willis, P. (1977) *Learning to Labor: how working class kids get working class jobs*, New York: Columbia University Press.

Zerubavel, E. (1997) *Social Mindscapes: invitation to cognitive sociology*, Cambridge, MA: Harvard University Press.

Part I

GENERATING GROUNDED THEORY

1

LEARNING HOW TO SPEAK
OF SADNESS

David A. Karp

One of the great joys of sociology is the freedom it provides to periodically reinvent oneself. Over the course of nearly 40 years I have explored a variety of topics. My doctoral dissertation involved participant observation in New York's Times Square (Karp 1973). As a newly minted assistant professor I co-authored books on urban social psychology (Karp et al. 1991) and the "sociology of everyday life" (Karp et al. 2004). Then, as I approached mid-life my attention turned to questions of aging. That personal interest led to another book (Clair et al. 1993) and, in turn, to a several-year interview study of people between 50 and 60 years old (see, for example, Karp 1989). Along the way I have been intrigued by such matters as student participation in college classrooms (Karp and Yoels 1976) and what happens in upper middle-class families during the year that a child applies to college (see, for example, Karp et al. 1998). Since the early 1990s my abiding interest has been to decipher the experiences of mental illness (Karp 1996; 2000; 2006).

Such a peripatetic research history might lead to the conclusion that there is little consistency to my sociological thinking. However, I maintain that all of my writing has been driven by a few global theoretical questions. Shortly after entering graduate school I was introduced to the works of those who were shaping a distinctive sociological social psychology which came to be labeled "symbolic interaction theory" (Blumer 1969). Nearly instantly I felt an affinity with this emerging perspective and its principal idea that there are no intrinsic meanings to objects, events, and situations. Rather, human beings collectively invest their daily worlds with meaning. Such a view leads social psychologists of my stripe to ask, "How do people make sense of complicated life circumstances and how are their behaviors, emotions, and attitudes linked to such interpretive processes?" This is the fundamental question that motivates and animates all my writing.

Diagnosed with depression in my early 30s, I have been grappling for more than 30 years with the meanings and consequences of emotional illness. Since I am an ardent believer in C. Wright Mills' (1959) injunction that

DAVID A. KARP

social scientists should "translate private troubles into public issues," I began to explore the possibility of writing a book on depression in the late 1980s. As any researcher would, I initially plugged the words "clinical depression" into several databases. I learned that social scientists had by that time written hundreds of articles on depression. However, nearly all of them were survey research efforts linking the incidence of depression to an enormous array of variables. It struck me as an exceedingly odd omission that researchers were writing about a feeling disorder and yet rarely did I hear the feelings of those with the disorder. In this respect, the starting point for *Speaking of Sadness* was an urge to fulfill one of sociology's most enduring mandates—to give voice to those whose experiences are typically marginalized or discounted altogether. I also had the hope that by listening to others' narratives I might gain greater insight into my own life difficulties.

These days, a growing number of sociologists practice "auto-ethnography" (see, for example, Ellis and Bochner 2002). Effectively, these colleagues are writing sociologically informed biographical narratives. They are using their own experiences to reflect on generic social processes. In retrospect I find it interesting that one of the pre-publication reviewers of *Speaking of Sadness* commented that "Perhaps a book such as this could not have been written a decade ago, but today, with the introduction of the 'postmodern impulse' in ethnography, we are permitted greater liberty in using ourselves, subjectively, as characters in our own science." It may indeed be that postmodern intellectual currents influenced the decision to tell parts of my own story at the beginning of *Speaking of Sadness*. However, I simply thought that sharing my struggles with depression was the most honest thing to do. After all, "when we discuss others, we are always talking about ourselves" (Krieger 1991: 4). It was only fair that readers understand how my own experiences shaped my biases, intersected with my theoretical sensibilities, and potentially influenced my interpretations of the 50 in-depth interviews at the heart of the book. In the end, though, good social science requires that the interpretations and analyses offered be strictly disciplined by the data collected. Researchers ought to creatively use their own experiences as long as they "let the world speak back" (Blumer 1969).

My awkward dance with depression over many years also powerfully articulated with my interests as a social psychologist. As I grew more serious about the project and began to think about how I might approach things conceptually, one phrase in particular—"negotiating ambiguity"—became a constant part of my internal dialogues. Ongoing reflection on my own illness path reminded me how confusing and opaque my depression journey had been to that point. It took years before I could/would attach the word depression to my feelings. People do not typically wake up one morning and tell themselves, "I'm a person suffering from a disease called depression. Therefore, I better get myself to a psycho-pharmacologist who will give me an antidepressant to correct a serotonin imbalance in my brain."

Nearly every interviewee eventually confirmed that depression can remain for years a pain without a name. By the end of the study I had heard dozens of comments like these: "During my sophomore year in high school, when I'd wake up depressed and drag myself to school ... I didn't know what it was. I just knew that I had an awful time getting out of bed and ... a hard time, you know, getting myself to school ... I kind of just had the feeling that something wasn't right." Another person said, "I really can't pinpoint the moment [when I was aware that I was depressed] ... It was just something that I felt I was living with or had to live through ... " The more I thought about the social dimensions of mental illness and heard comments like these, the more persuaded I became that, apart from my personal stake in the matter, the subject would allow me to illuminate an important question; namely, "How does an illness identity come into being and then evolve?"

Along with the personally compelling nature of the subject matter, I saw a study of depression as providing a unique opportunity to display the power and utility of a sociological angle of vision. When I told people that I was contemplating a book on depression they often responded by saying, "But you're a sociologist. Isn't depression something that psychologists, doctors, or biologists ought to be studying?" I tried to explain to questioners my skepticism about the triumph of biological thinking in psychiatry. I expressed to them my discomfort with the prevailing medical notion that depression is solely the product of broken brains. I maintained, rather, that there is an inseparable link between culture and even our innermost thoughts and feelings, including, of course, the deeply troubling thoughts and feelings we label as depression. To be sure, every chapter in *Speaking of Sadness* deals with the dialectic of self and society, thereby demonstrating that a full understanding of depression depends as much on cultural chemistry as it does on brain chemistry.

A paradox of depression is that sufferers yearn for social connection even as they withdraw from others. Depression is an illness of isolation. Feeling the urge to be alone when interaction becomes increasingly arduous, individuals retreat from social life. Such a choice provides short-term gains, but ultimately withdrawal only deepens the anguish of depression. Here again there was impressive regularity in the stories I heard. A female graduate student explained the dynamic: "It's a real catch-22 because you feel bad and you feel that if you see your friends you're going to make them feel bad too ... So then you just want to stay by yourself, but if you stay by yourself it just gets worse and worse and worse." As social psychologists explain, the self reflects the bond between the person and the social world. Consequently, when the pain of depression moves people to withdraw from social life, the self loses its foundation and begins to wither. It is in the vicious feedback loop of withdrawal, the erosion of self, a greater sense of hopelessness, and further withdrawal that we witness in its most powerful form the negative dialectic of self and society.

I often tell graduate students at Boston College that if their aim is to finish a doctoral dissertation as quickly as possible they do well to avoid problems requiring qualitative data collection. Studies involving participant observation or in-depth interviewing are extremely labor-intensive. Additionally, success with such ventures requires that researchers have an enormous tolerance for ambiguity. While qualitative researchers begin their work with a *preliminary* conceptual agenda, there is no easy formula for discovering important patterns in thousands of pages of interview materials. Certainly, though, the likelihood of making such discoveries is intimately connected to the richness of one's data. Someone once said that a significant function of data is as "an aid to a sluggish imagination." Although I have worked hard to cultivate a sociological imagination, I never leap into a multi-year study until I have reasonable faith that my interviews will yield powerful, poignant, and theoretically provocative materials.

During the years leading up to this project I had been attending a support group nearly every Wednesday evening at McLean's Hospital in Belmont, Massachusetts. The stories that I heard at MDDA (Manic Depressive and Depressive Association) meetings staggered me. They were unfathomably complex, revealed the nearly unimaginable pain of depression, illustrated the sheer confusion generated by mental illness, and spoke to the extraordinary heroism of sufferers. Once I became serious about offering a sociologically informed analysis of the depression experience, my role in the group shifted. As previously, I sought solace each week in the company of fellow travelers. Equally, though, I now arrived as an ethnographer listening carefully for themes in the words of my comrades. In 1992 the *Journal of Contemporary Ethnography* published a paper based on my observations (Karp 1992). Entitled "Illness Ambiguity and the Search for Meaning," this writing helped to solidify both my thinking on depression and my commitment to a more extended project.

An obvious first step in an interview study is to get straight the questions you want to ask people. I recognize from reading and private conversations that sociologists have different ideas about the value of interview guides. In the spirit of eliciting thoroughly unfettered narratives, some researchers conduct interviews with very few prepared questions. While understanding the logic of their approach, I spend considerable time constructing a guide. I consider work on the interview guide as far more than a purely methodological exercise. It is yet another point in the research process when I try to clarify the analytical motifs and ambitions of my work. An interview guide plainly sets out my "domains of inquiry." Certainly, I respect the idea that a well done interview is an artful conversation that often moves in unexpected directions. And while a researcher's questions inevitably change over the course of an investigation, I think long and hard about the fundamental issues that I want to cover during each interview.

As I scoured my first 10 or so interviews I increasingly thought of my respondents as following a distinctive illness "career." In turning to the career notion I plainly owe a debt to sociologists like Everett Hughes (1958) and Howard Becker (1963) who previously employed the career concept to think about such diverse groups as medical students and marihuana smokers. Although we normally associate careers with such professionals as lawyers, businesspeople, doctors and teachers, the sociological turn of mind also appreciates that criminals, lovers, prisoners, and patients follow predictable career paths. Moreover, just as each stage in a "conventional" career generates new identities, so also should we expect that a predictable "depression career" will spawn a succession of new identities. Thus, at a less abstract theoretical level than described by the basic premises of symbolic interaction, I placed the fulcrum of my analysis at the intersection of illness careers and identities. Comments of the following sort bolstered this choice:

> You know, I was a mental patient. That was my identity ... Depression is very private. Then all of a sudden it becomes public and I was a mental patient ... It's no longer just my own pain. I am a mental patient. I am a depressive. *I am a depressive* (said slowly and with intensity). This is my identity. I can't separate myself from that. When people know me they'll have to know about my psychiatric history, because that's who I am.

I was further persuaded by additional data collection that depressed people typically move through a predictable sequence of "identity turning points" (Strauss 1992). Consequently, in chapter 2 of the book, called "Illness and Identity," I tried to capture how my interviewees viewed themselves and their problem over time. Should you turn to the book, you will find that I describe *a period of inchoate feelings* during which people lack the vocabulary to label their experiences as depression. This is followed by a phase during which individuals reluctantly come to the conclusion that *something is really wrong with me*. Then, a *crisis* thrusts these same persons into a world of therapeutic experts. Finally, nearly everyone interviewed had to *come to grips with their new illness identity*. This last career moment nearly invariably involves embracing a bio-medical explanation of their difficulty. The chapter, in short, details how each of these predictable junctures requires reformulations of self and sickness.

Years ago the sociologist Stanislav Andreski (1972: 108) wrote that "The so-called methods of induction ... tell us how to test hypotheses but not how to arrive at them. Indeed, the latter process is just as much a mystery as it was in the days of Socrates. All that is known is that in order to conceive fruitful original ideas one must have talent, must immerse oneself in the available knowledge, and think very hard." Rather than reading Andreski's comment in a deterministic way—you either see things or you don't—I would prefer to see his words as a commentary on the magic of research and writing; a statement on the pleasures of intellectual work in general. If we knew what would come from our data before collecting them there would not be much point in doing research. I love those moments when I suddenly see a new way to understand my data and, thus, to frame an analysis. Chapter 4 on the "Meanings of Medication" illustrates how this sometimes happens.

As a preface to the way that chapter 4 took form, I want to comment on how I organize and work with data. Should you read the literature on qualitative methods you will find substantial discussions on data coding and computer-assisted analysis. Perhaps I am hopelessly old fashioned and altogether too set in my ways, but I do very little coding and find computer programs for analyzing qualitative data too mechanical. My preference is to create "data books" on general topics that I expect to be the basis for book chapters or significant sections of chapters. Recognizing that it would be impossible to write about depression without substantial attention to the role of psychiatric drugs, I systematically collated from all interviews every conversation related to medication use. The result was a document of several hundred pages that detailed the medication talk in each of my 50 interviews. At this point my methodology was simple. I lived with those pages over several weeks, yet again noting patterns in the words of the interviewees and identifying especially powerful statements. As always, the critical question was, "How will I do theoretical justice to these materials?"

One day I noticed that a number of people were saying things about medication that had virtually a religious tone. While it would be misleading to say that claims of drug miracles were the norm in my sample, I was certainly struck by those who described finding the right medication as a "revelation," as a "spiritual awakening," as an "ecstatic" experience. For example, listen to these words: "All I can tell you is, 'Oh my God, you know when you are on the right medication.' It was the most incredible thing. And I would say that I had a spiritual experience." Or, "I was a convert to Prozac, and I was like, 'This stuff is incredible.' I was thinking, 'This stuff is just the greatest stuff I've ever taken in the world.' I mean, 'This is a miracle.'" And later, when the Prozac stopped working this same person told me, "Now I have a somewhat more balanced view of the Prozac ... It's not a miracle drug. It hasn't saved me ... I did for a while think, 'I am going to be cured.' It was the ultimate disappointment. You know, it was connected with an intense sense of loss and redemption."

For several days words like those above rolled around in my head. They were, of course, part of a mental mix containing many diverse ideas. However, the thought that people on psychiatric medications might go through something like a conversion process kept returning to the front of my mind. I kept thinking, "Might there be analogies between commitment to a biomedical version of reality and commitment to religious faith?" I often preach in my classes that the essence of both good art and science lies in making connections between things that at first seem thoroughly unrelated. Therefore, the idea of an analogy between commitment to medical and religious realities had appeal for me. Because the idea persisted, I eventually found myself at the library reading sociological literature on religious conversion. I am not a student of religion and days earlier could never have predicted that I would be immersed in studies of cults and conversion. Like life itself, research takes you to wholly unexpected places.

I was struck by how closely the stages of religious conversion described in the literature paralleled the commitment process to medications. While there is no absolute equation between the two processes, it is nevertheless plain that "commitment" and "conversion" assume common forms in quite different social arenas. The notion of a conversion process provided a novel way to look at the medication experience over time, even for those who felt deeply uncertain about the efficacy of psychiatric drugs. Thus, I made a choice for ordering my medication data that could never have been envisioned at the outset of my work. Chapter 4 describes how patients move through four predictable consciousness shifts in their shared medication career: resistance, trial commitment, conversion, and disenchantment.

While I surely feel obliged to collect data as carefully as possible, my mission in *Speaking of Sadness* was not to reveal definitive and unchanging truths about the experience of depression. My research begins with the presumption that social life is a very messy affair and that the most realistic goal for sociologists is to write trenchant contemporary history—to provide incisive interpretations of important social phenomena. Given this aspiration, the "conversion framework" for chapter 4 was only one plausible way to interpret my data. As an alternative, I toyed with the possibility of centering the chapter on Howard Becker's (1960) notion of "side bets." Becker makes the astute observation that commitments are rarely made consciously at a given moment in time. Rather, they are the cumulative result of a series of decisions (side bets) that seem inconsequential at the moment we make them. I could likely have organized the data in terms of the typical side bets leading to patients' commitment to biological explanations of depression and, thus, to long-term use of psychiatric medications. My broader point here, though, is that multiple frameworks can be fruitfully applied to the same data; that a writer's commitment to a particular set of ideas for ordering data is itself the product of side bets.

Earlier I made a strong pitch for the importance of carefully constructing an interview guide. The guide, I maintain, is a kind of research map that outlines the general boundaries of the whole enterprise and provides the first image of possible book chapters. The guide also helps one to anticipate the likely contours of conversations with study participants. At the same time, early maps of the research process are inevitably crude, since the actual geography of a study's terrain cannot be formalized until researchers "hit the ground," as it were; until they get to know the natives who then take them on expeditions of their worlds' hidden dimensions. Maps must also be periodically redrawn to accommodate elements of the social landscape that are often uncovered accidentally. For me, one such surprising discovery was the critical role of spirituality in the lives of many depressed people. It wasn't until I had conducted about 15 interviews that spirituality became an important feature of my cognitive map.

Sociologists routinely ask a number of basic demographic questions, usually at the beginning of an interview. We want to know, for example, each person's age, occupation, family background, marital status, ethnicity, and religion. While such information may later become important as researchers interpret attitudinal or experiential differences within their samples, these background questions are usually covered quickly and ritualistically. However, after a few interviews I began to notice that my routine question on religious background produced surprising answers. Over and again I would hear, "Well, I was born Jewish (or Catholic, Protestant, Baptist, etc.), but I no longer practice that religion. I am, though, a very spiritual person." At a certain point enough people spoke about spirituality that I began to ask everyone about it. Certainly, there were some who had little to say, but the question more often elicited an outpouring of talk. A simple demographic question had opened up a totally new vista to explore.

As it turned out, these conversations about spirituality significantly shaped my writing decisions. The ideas I heard became central to a chapter on "Coping and Adapting." There, I explained how my respondents moved through yet another patterned sequence of consciousness changes about the meanings of illness. When depression first arrives, people often engage in a variety of behaviors (partying, exercising, drinking) to divert attention away from their pain. At a point it becomes impossible to sustain the definition of their pain as normal. With this recognition individuals set out to "fix" the problem. They might try to resolve things by modifying their lives in terms of their own theories about the source of their sadness. Eventually, they turn reluctantly to therapeutic experts with the expectation that they will solve the problem. When the best efforts of healers often fail, depression pilgrims frequently conclude that their problem may never be fixed once and for all. Such a new consciousness requires a different approach to suffering. As the reality of pain's permanence sinks in, their goal shifts from eradicating depression to living with it. Many move away from the medical language of cure and toward the spiritual idiom of transformation. A 41-year-old female travel agent spoke for many when she said:

> You know, people say, "Would you like to have a different life?" I say, "Absolutely not. I'd live it all over again." But I think it takes a while to get there; to see some of [the pain] as a real gift ... As horrible as it was, I don't see how I could be what I am without it. So, in a Buddhist sense I embrace it when it comes to this stuff. The dark side, all the awful stuff has to be just as much part of my life [as the good stuff]. The yin and the yang can't exist without each other.

My unexpected excursion into the connections between spirituality and coping also reminded me how carefully writers must choose their words. Often the subtlety of theorizing turns on the words used to describe data patterns. Reading and re-reading how individuals redefined the meaning, significance, and place of depression in their lives, I experimented with different words to capture the phenomenon. At first, the tone of their comments seemed "fatalistic," but this word did not quite work since fatalism connotes a kind of helpless capitulation. I considered the word "surrender," but this also seemed too passive and defeatist. I considered "embrace" as a possibility. But this word didn't exactly fit either. In the end, since respondents' "post fix-it orientation" contained elements of both acceptance and resistance, the word "incorporation" seemed most appropriate. Their new approach involves fighting against depression as best they can while constructing a life based on its continuing presence. Analysis of how incorporation is achieved became central to chapter 5 as well as to a short appendix in the book entitled, "Sociology, Spirituality, and Suffering."

To this point, I have commented on the substance of a few chapters in *Speaking of Sadness* to convey how my sociological ideas were shaped and expressed. Despite my own long history with depression, I had to learn from others how best to speak sociologically about sadness. I want readers to understand that a book's success depends on having a core "problem"—here, how illness identities come into being and change over time—which gives coherence to the whole endeavor. Each chapter, then, must somehow illuminate an important facet of that problem. At the same time, each chapter must have a distinctive message that can stand on its own. I would like to add that all of this should be accomplished without resorting to heavy prose or jargon. Sociologists should never confuse the complexity and importance of their ideas with obscure writing. In this regard, let me borrow one more time from C. Wright Mills (1959: 240) who advised that "To overcome the academic pose you first have to overcome the academic prose."

A short essay like this one forces me to be radically selective in my description of the intellectual processes behind the production of *Speaking of Sadness*. I could end this essay with a more complete explanation of why the book is subtitled, "Depression, *Disconnection*, and the Meanings of Illness." Neither have I explained my treatment of the views expressed by a smaller number of people in a chapter called "Family and Friends." Finally, I could specify how the larger society is implicated in America's current depression pandemic. Hopefully, you will be moved to read the book if you are interested in these matters. Instead of turning to these features of the book, I want to end by telling you why, along with the intrinsic gratification of academic work, I am willing to spend several years working on a book like *Speaking of Sadness*.

I believe that all genres of sociological work have important value and serve distinctive ends. I have, after all, written textbooks for classroom use, journal articles meant primarily to reach my professional colleagues, books synthesizing available literature in an area like aging, and retrospective essays like this one. However, my last three books, beginning with *Speaking of Sadness,* have been, in the lingo of publishing companies, "trade" books. Trade books are meant to reach a general audience of literate readers. Certainly I want to write sociology that my colleagues will applaud. As well, though, I want my work to be read by those dealing with depression and those who care for and about them.

Among the most exhilarating results of my writing are the many e-mails, letters, and phone calls from people who want me to know that they feel less alone after reading my work and understand their own situations more deeply as a result of my analysis. I began this essay by saying that one of sociology's many joys is the chance to study whatever animates you intellectually. I have been privileged to write about things that I find deeply meaningful, are profoundly important to readers, and can make a difference in people's lives. One reviewer of my most recent book on psychiatric medications, Professor Barbara Schneider, kindly writes (2006: 528), "Karp has mastered the delicate art of straddling the line between academia and the 'outside' world ... His analysis is no less rigorous and insightful for being accessible to a general readership ... Could an academic author hope to do any better than to have people reading and finding meaning in his work?"

Professor Schneider understands completely the fuel that has energized my efforts to render depressive illness sociologically intelligible.

References

Andreski, S. (1972) *Social Sciences as Sorcery,* New York: St. Martin's Press.
Becker, H. (1960) "Notes on the Concept of Commitment," *American Journal of Sociology,* 66: 32–40.
——(1963) *Outsiders: studies in the sociology of deviance,* New York: Free Press.
Blumer, H. (1969) *Symbolic Interaction: perspective and method,* Englewood Cliffs, NJ: Prentice-Hall.
Clair, J., Karp, D., and Yoels, W. (1993) *Experiencing the Life Cycle,* 2nd ed., Springfield, IL: Charles Thomas.
Ellis, C. and Bochner, A. (eds.) (2002) *Ethnographically Speaking: autoethnography, literature, and aesthetics,* Walnut Creek, CA: AltaMira.
Hughes, E. (1958) *Men and their Work,* New York: Free Press.
Karp, D. (1973) "Hiding in Pornographic Bookstores: a reconsideration of the nature of urban anonymity," *Urban Life and Culture,* 1: 427–51.
——(1989) "A Decade of Reminders: changing consciousness between fifty and sixty years old," *The Gerontologist,* 28: 727–38.
——(1992) "Illness Ambiguity and the Search for Meaning: a case study of a self-help group for affective disorders," *Journal of Contemporary Ethnography,* 21: 139–70.
——(1996) *Speaking of Sadness: depression, disconnection, and the meanings of illness,* New York: Oxford University Press.

——(2000) *The Burden of Sympathy: how families cope with mental illness*, New York: Oxford University Press.

——(2006) *Is It Me or My Meds? Living with antidepressants*, Cambridge, MA: Harvard University Press.

Karp, D. and Yoels, W. (1976) "The College Classroom: some observations on the meanings of student participation," *Sociology and Social Research*, 60: 421–39.

Karp, D., Holmstrom, L., and Gray, P. (1998) "Leaving Home for College: expectations for selective reconstruction of self," *Symbolic Interaction*, 21: 253–76.

Karp, D., Stone, G., and Yoels, W. (1991) *Being Urban: a sociology of city life*, 2nd ed., New York: Praeger Publishers.

Karp, D., Yoels, W., and Vann, B. (2004) *Sociology in Everyday Life*, 3rd ed., Prospect Heights, IL: Waveland.

Krieger, S. (1991) *Social Science and the Self*, New Brunswick, NJ: Rutgers University Press.

Mills, C. W. (1959) *The Sociological Imagination*, New York: Oxford University Press.

Schneider, B. (2006) "Review of 'Is It Me or My Meds? Living with antidepressants'," *Health*, 10: 526–28.

Strauss, A. (1992) "Turning Points in Identity," in C. Clark and Robboy, H. (eds.) *Social Interaction*, New York: St. Martin's Press.

2

RECOLLECTING GOOD AND BAD DAYS

Kathy Charmaz

> The intercalation of periods of change and novelty is the only means by which
> we can refresh our sense of time, strengthen, retard, and rejuvenate it, and
> therewith renew our perception of life itself.
>
> (Thomas Mann 1952: 107)

The theoretical antecedents of my study, *Good Days, Bad Days: The Self in Chronic Illness and Time*, are woven through the fabric of my life.[1] The ideas in this study arose as a natural consequence of my earlier experiences and previous studies and have continued to engage me years after publication of the book. As I look back, I draw on George Herbert Mead's (1932; 1934) insights about time and action. The past informs our thinking in the present, the present informs our reconstructions of the past. Both time and action are emergent phenomena. Thus, what we bring to our studies frames but does not determine what we learn from them. Similarly, how we theorize reflects our interactions before we begin and those occuring within and beyond the field. Theorizing arises through analytic thinking about our field experiences, not merely recording and synthesizing them.

Good Days, Bad Days is more than a discrete study of 115 interviews.[2] Rather, it also evolved from views and questions that had long concerned me. Specifically, this study returned to my dissertation research on experiencing chronic illness and the reconstruction of self (Charmaz 1973). More generally, *Good Days, Bad Days* represents multiple standpoints and accumulated understandings from which I had viewed illness throughout my life.

I grew up in the shadows of illness and disability. As a small child, constant upper respiratory infections and hemorrhaging after a tonsillectomy taught me something about the "sick role" (Parsons 1953). My only grandmother's wooden leg stood alone and unused in a corner of her bedroom but sparked the awe and fascination of a five-year-old. As a teenager, the advent of a beloved uncle's and then my father's serious heart disease reinforced earlier lessons about the fragility of life. Like my sister and cousins, I pursued a degree in the health professions and graduated with a Bachelor's of Science in occupational therapy, an unusual degree to be granted by a department of design in a school of fine arts.

The theoretical direction of my later research emerged several years before I knew anything about sociology, much less about symbolic interactionism. During my sojourn as an occupational therapist, I witnessed revealing incidents that evoked my interest in patients' perspectives and awakened a nascent sociological awareness. While working in physical disabilities, I observed instances of staff blaming patients for their lack of progress, inadequate motivation, denial of their disabilities, and I attended several patient-staff conferences that dissolved into degradation ceremonies equal to anything that Harold Garfinkel (1967) could have imagined. I saw firsthand the powerful consequences of professionals' derogatory definitions of patients whose views of their situations clashed with staff's. And I realized that staff and patients lived in separate worlds.

Other pivotal events led to further realizations and fostered my sensitivity to the social psychology of illness and disability. I became good friends with a young woman who had used a wheelchair since childhood. During a shopping trip one day, we parked under a tree. As I helped my friend get out of the car, a branch suddenly broke off. It slammed against the arm of her chair but did not touch her body. She exclaimed in hurt surprise, "It *hit* me!" The meaning of her response struck me. I recall thinking, how fascinating; the wheelchair has become part of her self-concept. Her tone as well as her words revealed that she viewed the incident as meaning more than an intrusion on her personal space.

After several years of working in physical rehabilitation, I decided to pursue a master's degree to qualify me for teaching occupational therapy students. I aimed to broaden my background and thus began studying sociology but remained involved in rehabilitation through conducting field research. Again I witnessed how power differentials between staff and patients were played out and affected patients' identities and subsequent lives. My interests in intersections between time and identity grew while conducting an ethnographic study in a large rehabilitation facility for the poor. I watched residents struggle against anonymity as they attempted to create identities in the institution (Calkins 1970; Charmaz 2000b). I learned how slowed-down institutional time contradicted the incremental, progressive movement of rehabilitation time directed toward returning patients to their former lives. This ethnographic experience sparked enduring interests in identity and time that I pursued later in my research about living with chronic illness.

Good Days, Bad Days rests on having lived in these multiple realities, having had this range of experiences. All supported developing the theoretical implications of my study. Moreover, I had gained an epistemological perspective and a certain theoretical sensitivity about my past before pursuing my research for *Good Days, Bad Days*. This epistemological perspective formed a foundation for my research, and grounded theory methods encouraged conducting it with theoretical sensitivity. The imprint of my epistemology foreshadowed specific concepts in the book. Because of its overriding but implicit influence, I emphasize the place of my epistemological perspective in the following research story.

Pages from the past

People, places, and points in time find their way into our studies. I learned grounded theory from Barney Glaser in the late 1960s but shared pragmatist assumptions about reality, knowledge, and truth with my dissertation chair, Anselm Strauss (Charmaz 2008a). Then as now, Glaser argued for researchers discovering original ideas from their data and argued against importing preconceived ideas into their analyses. At a time when abstract theory reigned, I understood Glaser's logic and commended his commitment to inductive theorizing. The notion of the researcher as a *tabula rasa*, however, sounded absurd to me in 1969 and still does.[3]

Rather than denying our pasts and removing ourselves from theoretical conversations of the present, we need to scrutinize how our experiences and disciplinary ideas have influenced us and what we find in the empirical world. We can construct fresh interpretations about the world without ignoring earlier knowledge. Granted, it means balancing openness to the empirical world, conceptual innovation about it, *and* acknowledgment of scholarly literatures. Building inductive analyses precludes merely applying extant ideas.

To which traditions did I attend? Studies in medical sociology and social psychology that dealt with time and becoming processes influenced my thinking. These works included *Timetables* (Roth 1963), *Passage Though Crisis* (Davis 1963), *Time for Dying* (Glaser and Strauss 1968), "The Moral Career of the Mental Patient" in *Asylums* (Goffman 1961), as well as *The Presentation of Self in Everyday Life* (Goffman 1959), *Stigma* (Goffman 1963), *The Silent Dialogue* (Olesen and Whittaker 1968), and *Mirrors and Masks* (Strauss 1969). Merleau-Ponty's (1962) views of perception and Mead's (1932) analysis of the past greatly interested me. And later, on reading Thomas Mann's *The Magic Mountain* (1952), I realized how several key ideas in my study echoed themes in his exquisite exegesis on the seeds of time.

Yet my initial interest in the relativity of time—of life—stemmed from different sources. I had read a fair amount of philosophy of science before becoming acquainted with any of the classic statements above. An epistemology requirement for my master's program enabled me to articulate presuppositions that I had long held: Standpoints matter; the viewer is part of what is viewed; fact and value are inseparable; objectivity rests on definition and consensus, not on givens of distance and neutrality. Like many graduate students of my era, reading Thomas S. Kuhn's *The Structure of Scientific Revolutions* (1962) and an array of physical theorists captivated me and refocused my worldview. My impassioned epistemology seminar papers questioned conventional scientific conceptions of method, objectivity, and truth in 1966. The relativist epistemology of a fledgling graduate student now decades past has shaped my work since then (see, for example, Bryant and Charmaz 2007; Charmaz 1973; 1990; 2000a; 2006; 2009).

A relativist epistemology resonated with Schutz's (1962–66) concept of multiple realities and remained far more congruent with social constructionist empirical research than 1960s and early 1970s positivist renderings of reality. Relativism formed the epistemological foundation for my dissertation research and its continuation in *Good Days, Bad Days*. My dissertation, "Time and Identity: The Shaping of Selves of the Chronically Ill" (1973), focused on relativity of experience and standpoint in the lives of people with chronic illness. I aimed to tease out relationships between the subjective experience of time and the reconstruction of self. I believed that the experiences of people with chronic illness could tell us something about the intersections between meanings of time and self-construction. I reasoned that their lives and hardships might illuminate otherwise invisible experiences occurring throughout adult life. My studies treated chronic illness as a particular type of experience in which time and self became problematic. How did people with chronic illness experience time? Under which conditions did their perspective on time change? To what extent, if any, did their experience of time and troubles due to illness spur changes of self? I pursued these questions in my dissertation and took them up again in *Good Days, Bad Days*.

Implications of data collection for theorizing

Methodological decisions are consequential. Writing practices are, too. Studying my form of inquiry as well as its content fostered theorizing in new ways. I also aimed to make my conceptualizations of time and identity accessible. My dissertation had simultaneously achieved the heights of Glaserian (1978) theoretical density and the depths of Teutonic inaccessibility.[4] It contained numerous fresh ideas encased in a writing style equal to the worst of sociological scribes.

By the time I finished my degree, possible venues for publishing dissertations had shrunk. Publishers had increasingly turned to textbooks and medical sociology lists turned to health policy. I attended to teaching and wrote a textbook, but planned to revise the dissertation later for publication. When I returned to the project in 1979, I brought a chapter to my multidisciplinary writing group. One of the nursing postdoctoral students pronounced, "You haven't got enough data." She was right. Although I had conducted 55 interviews, they were often thin and haphazard. In true Barney Glaser fashion, I had been instructed to take notes rather than tape-record these interviews.[5] But notes simply did not cover all that transpired.[6] Notes could not sufficiently preserve the participants' tone and tempo, silences and statements, and the form and flow of questions and responses. My notes not only erased many situational details, but also much of the construction of the interview.

Clues about the form and content of theorizing reside within data-gathering methods—and the researcher's experiences. My dissertation was theoretical *despite* rather than *because of* the quality of my data. The range and depth of my experience in this area of study had provided the foundation from which I conceptualized my dissertation data.[7] By using notes instead of transcripts, I moved quickly to abstract theoretical concepts but lost rich details that would have enlivened the abstractions. Herein resides a major difference between conventional grounded theory (Glaser 1978; 1998; 2001; 2006), and the kind of theorizing to which I aspired. Conventional grounded theory starts with the studied reality as a given; it does not take it apart. Like an aerial photograph, conventional grounded theory maps the boundaries of experience from a distanced view. My approach relied on getting close to the experience and learning how it developed from the ground up. I wanted the explorer's engagement with the terrain.

Both my research objectives and my colleague's pronouncement spurred me to gather more data with clearer sampling criteria, better interview questions, and participant referrals that came through multiple sources in addition to health professionals. In my earlier studies, health professionals often relied on their concerns when making interview referrals, whether or not these concerns coincided with my research objectives. Thus, I had occasionally interviewed people whom their practitioners saw as amusing, troublesome, non-compliant, or in need of a visitor but who did not fit my study. The new interviews for *Good Days, Bad Days* began in 1979 and initiated research relationships with my participants, some of which still continue today.

By 1980, the literature in qualitative research methods offered a growing array of resources and I had honed my interviewing skills. I adopted but adapted Lofland and Lofland's (1984) definition of an interview and thus saw it as a directed conversation, but a lightly directed one. I had decided long before embarking on my study that minimizing my participants' discomfort took precedence over asking intrusive questions to obtain compelling data. Talking about having a serious illness and facing uncertainty can evoke participants' unanticipated realizations and unstated ruminations. Interviewing in this area may proceed on shaky grounds. Worries about financial survival, loss of autonomy, possible abandonment—and death—all surface.

To complicate matters, I wanted to explore how my research participants experienced time, what it meant to them, and how periods of illness affected their views of themselves. My background as an occupational therapist gave me special knowledge of living with disabilities. By drawing on my past, I better understood their present. Did my past preconceive what I saw and heard? Not exactly. I still brought sociological questions to the data and let fresh theoretical understandings of them emerge, but my background sensitized me to my participants' experiences in ways that other social scientists might not share. When I entered the worlds of people whose former lives had slowed or halted, I understood the symbolic significance of slowing my pace to match theirs. I slowed my words and let time stretch, putting aside the busyness and cacophony of my world to experience the stillness and silent rhythms of theirs. I also understood that illness altered relationships between time, space, and body movement. It wasn't simply a matter of everything taking longer. Serious illness challenged people to integrate and coordinate the minutiae of their lives in new ways and, at times, to reinvent themselves. Thus, I caught nuances of meaning they voiced about the logistics of their daily lives from getting ready for the day to getting through the tasks before them. Having been an occupational therapist not only directed me to issues to theorize, but also expedited my practice of theorizing.

How much direction I gave an interview depended on how well I knew the participant, his or her relative ease in handling questions, my reading of cues about trouble spots and last, what I hoped to learn.[8] The following conversation occurred in an interview with Patricia Kennedy, who had multiple sclerosis. Perhaps because I had come to know her quite well and appreciated her willingness to talk about her situation, Patricia appeared to be comfortable both with talking about elusive experiences and answering occasional probing questions. During such moments, my interview style became more direct. Once in a while I would crystallize a point in a summary statement as I did below. When I asked Patricia about what taking prednisone did to the other symptoms she was having, she added the following comments to a lengthy reply:

PATRICIA: ... Over a period of months, I just got better and better and stronger and stronger. But I worked at it—I—you know, it just didn't happen. *It would be real easy to just give into. Not for me, but I could see that is the course of least resistance, is just to give into it.* [My emphasis]

KATHY: What would giving into it do?

PATRICIA: To me?

KATHY: Well to other people or yourself, as you see it?

PATRICIA: Oh, to me it would be that the disease would win.

KATHY: And?

PATRICIA: And I'd lose.

KATHY: You'd lose.

PATRICIA: Yeah, I'd lose a lot of things that are of value to me.

KATHY: Such as?

PATRICIA: Such as, you know, the—the freedom to move around. You, know, the—the ability, you know to be independent.

KATHY: So you think it would be real easy to let the disease be the foreground in your life.

My interests in forging theoretical connections between experiencing a serious chronic illness and identity, self, and time informed the line of questions I took in this excerpt. Patricia Kennedy's response allowed me to direct her attention to "giving in" and subsequently make telling comments about the potential effects of illness on self and identity. Her metaphor of winning and losing implies a certain stance toward illness with crucial identity stakes arising during pivotal periods in the course of illness.

Throughout the interviews, I tried to read my participants' responses and take lines of questions only so far as they seemed comfortable, while simultaneously opening spaces for them to broach discomforting topics, if they wished. These spaces allow unforeseen questions and intuitions to surface—for the research participant as well as the interviewer. Conducting multiple interviews allows both researcher and participant to continue directions in earlier interviews. During the same interview with Patricia Kennedy as in the previous excerpt, I followed up on an earlier conversation about locating oneself in time. I asked her where she now located herself in time. Note how I follow her statements and return to key points that she raised.

PATRICIA: I'm in the present.
KATHY: You're in the present.
PATRICIA: Oh yeah.
KATHY: And that's a change, isn't it?
PATRICIA: Where was I before?
KATHY: In the future.
PATRICIA: Future. Yeah. Yeah. [said thoughtfully] I'm right here—today.
KATHY: And has all this [what we had talked about in the preceding hour and a half] brought you to today?
PATRICIA: The whole process? Yeah.
KATHY: And what does tomorrow look like?
PATRICIA: Tomorrow's hopeful.
KATHY: How much of tomorrow do you see today with you [being] right here today?
PATRICIA: I see some. I can see quite a bit of tomorrow, I think. But what I see is that part ... I feel like because I—I have much more control over my—my life today that tomorrow will be better as a direct result of how I live today. But I also know that there's a great deal of unknown in there. But I think there are a lot of unknowns for a lot of people, for everybody. And that I have the advantage over everybody else because I'll be able to deal with it.
KATHY: Hmm, that's interesting. And your today is, when your self is in today, what does that mean to you?
PATRICIA: When myself is in today, what I'm probably saying about today is, *today*—actually today.

Framing questions about time raised some knotty problems. Because we don't have much of a language to talk about time, I realized that asking participants questions about time might leave them feeling bewildered and embarrassed. In the excerpt above, Patricia and I had already started a frame to talk about the self in time. Interestingly, she seemed comfortable with the question although she had forgotten her earlier statement.

This kind of framing emerged during the interview process. In contrast, when I began collecting data or added a new participant, I first concentrated on their experiences with illness and inserted questions about time at opportune points. I asked only one or two general questions that spoke directly to time, such as the following question that I asked after getting a sense of the participant's experience: "As you look back on your illness, were there any other events that stand out in your mind?" I started with a handful of interview questions and followed the leads in participants' responses. Mostly I listened and their views took shape and their stories unfolded. They watched me as I observed and listened to them. My slowed questions imparted my interest in participants' views and defused potential sparks of interrogation. The above exchange proceeded in a slow tempo that allowed Patricia Kennedy's words to form. I became a safe confidante for people I interviewed numerous times. Safety, slowness, and a space for reflection opened possibilities for exploring meanings and experiences of time.

With transcribed interviews, I could closely attend to my symbolic inter-actionist dictum: Pay attention to language. I pieced together liminal meanings of time. When interviews proceeded in a slow reflective pace, I could insert a question to explore time. Mike Reilly had had a massive heart attack while in his early 40s. During an interview, he said, "Memorial Day, was my anniversary [of his heart attack] ... " I asked, "What did the anniversary mean to you?" This question directed me toward a theoretical line of inquiry while it guided Mike's reflection. The implications of interviews for constructing theory have not been fully explored. Where, when, and how we ask questions in the field matters, as well as which questions we ask, whether we go into the field as ethnographers or interviewers.[9]

Constructing concepts

The iterative strategies of grounded theory transformed inquiry on experiencing time from an elusive search to a manageable project. I could respond with immediate questions as I listened in an interview, as I did above, or questions that struck me as I coded my data. Throughout the process, I gained new insights and saw when I needed more detailed views or further information.

Constructing concepts for *Good Days, Bad Days* meant simultaneously constructing a *method of analysis* while developing my emergent content and categories (Charmaz 2007; 2009). True to my epistemological position, I did not stand outside the studied process but was an integral part of it. I was part of the concepts that I constructed. Yet interaction built the foundation for their construction (Charmaz 2006; 2009).

Both the topic and my participants' situations fostered a reflexive stance about my research relationships and nascent analysis before reflexivity became a focus in discussions of methods. I scrutinized what occurred during the times I spent with participants. In which ways did I affect what I was seeing and hearing? What reciprocities could I offer participants for sharing their stories? How did the development of our interactions shape my evolving analysis? When should the interview recede into the background and the relationship move into the foreground? Times shared with participants, in conversation, in silent recognition, molded my days, shaped my ideas, and transformed me. Those times reverberated in my consciousness long after I had left the scene.

Still, my interactions took another form. Grounded theory methods engaged me in active analytic interaction with data, codes of the data, and preliminary writing about data and codes in memos. Grounded theory is a comparative method so at each level of inductive analysis, I compared people in similar and different situations, responses from the same individual at different times, data with codes, codes with codes, codes with categories, and categories with categories. These comparisons kept me interacting with my materials and engaged in the analytic process. Coding my material increased my awareness of implicit meanings in the interviews, and sequential interviews often made these meanings explicit without my asking. I had believed that Mark Reinertsen, who had kidney disease, pushed himself to maintain a frenetic pace so that he could live a packed although foreshortened life. His many endeavors and the pace at which he pursued them buttressed his sense of self while he experienced a devastating illness. At that time, he fit my category of situating the self in "the filled present." I defined this category as "a present crammed with activities and events. Activity and speed distinguish the filled present, rather than emotional involvement. A sense of rapid succession of present events validates the self" (Charmaz 1991: 241).

After Mark Reinertsen received a kidney transplant, he felt he had received a reprieve from his death sentence and could hope for a future. A glimpse of a future changed the relationship between his self and time. The chance of having a future meant he could live now. Time slowed. By this time Mark's illness had forced him to relinquish his packed schedule but he intensely experienced his remaining involvements. He exchanged quantity of endeavors for quality of experiences. With this exchange, Mark showed how shifts in situating the self may occur because he now fit my category of "the self in the intense present."

The grist for constructing conceptions sometimes arose explicitly during the interview. My straightforward question above to Mike Reilly about the anniversary of his heart attack elicited depths of subjective meaning. He said:

Oh, time for reflection again. In fact, I went on a bicycle ride. I went half the route that I did go on when I had my heart attack. I wasn't strong enough to go the full 25–50 miles so I just did half. I went around to where I had the heart attack, just to see that I could do it. What was I feeling? I don't know—time for reflection—because a lot went on in my life those last two years, you know, economically, health-wise, strain on the family, ah, so—yeah—a lot. How lucky I was [to survive] ...

Memorial Day will always mean a time of reflection to me. It always had since Vietnam. Now with the heart attack, more so. I shall never forget Memorial Day.

(Charmaz 1991: 196)

Mike Reilly's response to my question gave me a clear analytic direction to pursue. In short, the analytic direction here resides in the interview account itself. But would another researcher at that time follow this direction? Probably not. In the 1980s, managing illness provided a guiding metaphor for understanding how people experienced chronic illness. My theoretical bent, however, led me to pursue other analytic leads in the interview and my epistemological position led me to look for the relativity of these leads. In this case, Mike Reilly's statement placed the event in his chronology of illness as well as the flow of his life. It suggested how events take on enlarged meaning in the lives of those who experience them. I then turned to address comparative and analytic questions:

What makes some events timemarkers and turning points, but not others? Which events do ill people highlight as part of their chronologies of illness? Which events foreshadow an altered self?

(Charmaz 1991: 197)

Throughout the analytic process, I looked for tacit meanings as well as explicit ideas and actions. The question I posed to Mike Reilly helped to explicate the personal meaning that the anniversary held for him. Although such anniversaries can connote important time markers, not everyone remembered or observed them. By addressing the analytic questions above, I moved into a more implicit level of meaning. Subsequently, I needed to piece together bits of data and test my emerging ideas against new data. The iterative nature of grounded theory kept me moving between data and analysis.

The immediate meaning of an illness anniversary lay close to the surface for those who marked them. Other terms entered a general lexicon of illness although their meanings still remained tacit. Hence, I sought the tacit meanings of terms that many participants used.[10] Among them were ill people's conceptions of "good" and "bad" days. Everyone recognized them. Everyone had them. But what did they mean? To ferret out such meanings I typically asked participants about what good and bad days covered and how they differed. Then I checked their views across the responses of a number of other participants. In that way, I defined the properties of each and moreover showed how earlier bad days became good days as people's illnesses progressed.

The properties of common-sense terms such as a "good day" at first seem obvious. A good day was one in which a person's illness did not intrude on his or her life.[11] My definition reads: "A good day means minimal intrusiveness of illness, maximal control over mind, body, and actions, and greater choice of activities" (Charmaz 1991: 50). Note that I brought control and autonomy into the definition and made their place explicit. Beliefs in having control and autonomy support assumptions about what it means to be a functioning adult. Losses in these areas symbolize crucial encroachments on the self. These encroachments then illuminate an implicit link between time and self.

The terms, good and bad days, suggested more than measures of a day. These terms also implied possible temporal horizons. Not just now, but for the future. What did a good day mean for self? What did a bad day portend? Concerned faces, fleeting comments, and murmured asides gave me cues. By piecing together their views and the assumptions supporting these views to form the following analytic connection with self:

> Definitions of a good day derive from a sense of being in character, being the self one recognizes and acknowledges. On a good day, ill people have more opportunity to be the selves they wish to be. In addition, on a good day, the earlier jarring questions about present self, the doubts, the eroded confidence, and the nagging fears about the future all recede into the past, or may be completely forgotten.
>
> (Charmaz 1991: 51)

Returning to the writing

Last, a note about writing. When I returned to rework my dissertation, I had vowed to make the book interesting and accessible. My immersion in the research and involvement in learning to write occurred simultaneously. The analysis proceeded into the writing and occasionally the writing sent me back to the field in order to check and refine my ideas. My focus shifted, too.

My main theoretical interests resided in analyses of time and self; the book is ostensibly about illness. Why the shift? I reasoned that highlighting illness gave readers some familiar signposts to which they could tie the analysis. Moving from the mundane reality of illness to time would ready them for the esoteric analysis of time. On a larger scale, I wished to construct progressively theoretical concepts about time in successive books. At that time, I envisioned a three-volume set with the first book on illness; the second on self, identity, and the body; and the third and most theoretical, on time.

58

Most of the analysis in *Good Days, Bad Days* resulted from conceptualizing the new data I collected and developing fresh terms in the analysis. Three major themes, however, largely remained from my dissertation because these themes reflected my participants' simultaneous experience of illness and time. I had originally categorized the range of experiences of illness time as "Interrupted Time," "Intrusive Time," and "Encapsulated Time" (Charmaz 1973). In the book, these categories became "Chronic Illness as Interruption," "Intrusive Illness," and "Immersion in Illness." The categories not only showed that people experienced chronic illness in other ways than only disruption (cf. Bury 1982) but also revealed how people moved from one category to the next as illness progressed.

Grounded theory favors theoretical analysis over narrative coherence and completion. Hence, the emphasis on properties, processes, causes, conditions, and consequences, and the like. Such writing risks removing the analysis from human experience and thereby creating abstract disembodied theories separated from the contexts and situations that gave rise to them. I aimed for a coherent analytic story without sacrificing the richness and diversity of my participants' lives. I wove their stories throughout the narrative yet their stories stand in service of the analytic tale. As I strove to make this tale engaging, my simple terms and clear accounts belied the complexity of a dense analysis. In attempting to move away from grounded theorists' scientistic exposition, perhaps paradoxically, I made my theorizing more grounded and, like Patricia Kennedy, increased my readers' awareness of the unknowns.

Acknowledgments

Writing this chapter elicited many memories of days long past. I thank the editors for inviting me to contribute to this volume. I very much appreciate Antony Puddephatt and William Shaffir's careful reading of an earlier draft of my paper and useful comments on it. I also am grateful for comments on the previous version from Jennifer Nance and the following members of the Sonoma State University Faculty Writing Program: Dorothy Freidel, Diana Grant, and Richard Senghas.

Notes

1 First a caveat. I conducted intensive interviews, not traditional ethnographic research, to collect data. I interviewed a subset of my research participants multiple times and attended some special occasions marking their lives and deaths.
2 My approach to the study reflects a way of working through empirical and theoretical problems. I build on past questions and emphases, but start from a new or revised standpoint. My writings on qualitative methods show a similar iterative approach. I attempt to articulate other researchers'—and my own—taken-for-granted assumptions and strategies and re-evaluate them (see Bryant and Charmaz 2007; Charmaz 1983; 1990; 2000a; 2003; 2006; 2007a; 2007b; 2008; 2009).

3 In retrospect, it seems that several arguments Strauss (see Glaser and Strauss 1967; Strauss and Corbin 1994) mounted for rhetorical reasons, Glaser (1978; 1998; 2001) endorsed as methodological prescriptions.

4 See Glaser's (1978) later explication of his version of grounded theory. Glaser emphasized developing a dense theoretical explanation of the data through subjecting it to rigorous inductive analysis. He fought against leaving qualitative research at the descriptive level. I learned how to raise theoretical questions and to raise the abstract level of my analysis. In doing so, I managed to make my writing as turgid and uninviting as many sociological tomes of the day.

5 Decades later, Glaser (2001) still advocates taking notes rather than transcribing interviews. He believes that the interviewer will record the main points and not be distracted by extraneous details and subsequently will quicken the pace of analytic development. I realized then that taking notes caused me to miss significant, not merely extraneous, details.

6 See also Fine (1993) who demonstrates that researchers' recall fades rapidly after observing an event that different researchers may vary on what they record.

7 The theoretical level of the dissertation caused a bit of a rumpus during my defense. One department member expressed disbelief that anyone could—or would—develop such an abstract analysis from 55 interviews. Barney Glaser agreed but pointed out that the dissertation represented my entire life, not just 55 interviews. I appreciated his insight then and still do although its irony did not escape me. Glaser (1978; 1998; Glaser and Strauss 1967) has always been a strident critic of any hint of researchers preconceiving their analyses by looking at them through the lens of past theories or experience.

8 This type of interviewing can also elicit reflections on receiving, of gratitude. I found this response particularly with older men who felt that they had neglected their marriages during their careers but whose wives had nonetheless remained steadfast caregivers.

9 Some critics see interviews as artificial situations that "manufacture data" (Silverman 2007). Artificial? Not necessarily. True, participants may manage their self-presentations yet we may also witness their attempts at impression-management dissolve. An interview can be a special situation that allows everything from inchoate feelings to reconstructed stories to emerge. Interviews elicit accounts; that's obvious. Nonetheless interviews may also elicit participants' immediate thoughts and enduring concerns. From a grounded theory perspective, the accuracy of the content of a specific interview holds less significance than the patterns found by comparing data in many interviews.

10 I have detailed the logic of this kind of analysis in Charmaz (2006).

11 Exploring meanings of good and bad days provides one example of areas in which I tread lightly. I tried to seek further views from those whose composure indicated that they could handle talking about these areas.

References

Bryant, A. and Charmaz, K. (2007) "Grounded Theory in Historical Perspective: an epistemological account," in A. Bryant and Charmaz, K. (eds.) *The Handbook of Grounded Theory* (pp. 31–57), London: Sage.

Bury, M. (1982) "Chronic Illness as Disruption," *Sociology of Health and Illness*, 4: 167–82.

Calkins, K. (1970) "Time: perspectives, marking and styles of usage," *Social Problems*, 17: 487–510.

Charmaz, K. (1973) "Time and Identity: the shaping of selves of the chronically ill," Ph.D. dissertation, University of California, San Francisco.

——(1983) "The Grounded Theory Method: an explication and interpretation," in R. M. Emerson (ed.) *Contemporary Field Research* (pp. 109–26), Boston, MA: Little, Brown.

——(1990) "Discovering Chronic Illness: using grounded theory," *Social Science and Medicine*, 30: 1161–72.

——(1991) *Good Days, Bad Days: the self in chronic illness and time*, New Brunswick, NJ: Rutgers University Press.

——(2000a) "Constructivist and Objectivist Grounded Theory," in N. K. Denzin and Lincoln, Y. (eds.) *Handbook of Qualitative Research*, 2nd ed. (pp. 509–35), Thousand Oaks, CA: Sage.

——(2000b). "Looking Backward, Moving Forward: expanding sociological horizons in the twenty-first century," *Sociological Perspectives*, 43: 527–49.

——(2006) *Constructing Grounded Theory: a practical guide through qualitative analysis*, London: Sage.

——(2007a) "Constructionism and Grounded Theory," in J. A. Holstein and Gubrium, J. F. (eds.) *Handbook of Constructionist Research* (pp. 319–412), New York: Guilford Press.

——(2007b) "Tensions in Qualitative Research," *Sociologisk Forskning*, 2: 76–85.

——(2008) "The Legacy of Anselm Strauss for Constructivist Grounded Theory," in N. K. Denzin, Salvo, J. and Washington, M. (eds.) *Studies in Symbolic Interaction*, 32: 125–39, Bingley, U.K.: Emerald Publishing Group.

——(2009) "Shifting the Grounds: constructivist grounded theory methods for the twenty-first century," in J. Morse, P. Stern, J. Corbin, B. Bowers, K. Charmaz, and A. Clarke, *Developing Grounded Theory: the second generation* (pp. 127–54), Walnut Creek, CA: Left Coast Press.

Davis, F. (1963) *Passage Through Crisis: polio victims and their families*, Indianapolis IN: Bobbs-Merrill.

Fine, G. A. (1993) "Ten Lies of Ethnography," *Journal of Contemporary Ethnography*, 22: 267–97.

Garfinkel, H. (1967) *Studies in Ethnomethodology*, Englewood Cliffs, NJ: Prentice-Hall.

Glaser, B. G. (1978) *Theoretical Sensitivity*, Mill Valley, CA: Sociology Press.

——(1998) *Doing Grounded Theory: issues and discussions*, Mill Valley, CA: Sociology Press.

——(2001) *The Grounded Theory Perspective: conceptualization contrasted with description*, Mill Valley, CA: Sociology Press.

——(2006) *Doing Formal Grounded Theory: a proposal*, Mill Valley, CA: Sociology Press.

Glaser, B. G. and Strauss, A. L. (1967) *The Discovery of Grounded Theory: strategies for qualitative research*, Chicago: Aldine.

——(1968) *Time for Dying*, Chicago: Aldine.

Goffman, E. (1959) *The Presentation of Self in Everyday Life*, Garden City, NY: Doubleday Anchor Books.

——(1961) *Asylums*, Garden City, NY: Doubleday.

——(1963) *Stigma*, Englewood Cliffs, NJ: Prentice Hall.

Lofland, J. and Lofland, L. (1984) *Analyzing Social Settings: a guide to qualitative observation and analysis*, Belmont, CA: Wadsworth.

Kuhn, T. S. (1962) *The Structure of Scientific Revolutions*, Chicago: University of Chicago Press.

Mann, T. ([1929] 1952) *The Magic Mountain*, New York: A.A. Knopf.

Mead, G. H. (1932) *The Philosophy of the Present*, La Salle, IL: Open Court.

——(1934) *Mind, Self, and Society*, Chicago: University of Chicago Press.

Merleau-Ponty, M. (1962) *Phenomenology of Perception*, New York: Humanities Press.

Olesen, V. L. and Whittaker, E. W. (1968) *The Silent Dialogue: the social psychology of professional socialization*, San Francisco: Jossey Bass.

Parsons, T. (1953) *The Social System*, Glencoe, IL: Free Press.

Roth, J. A. (1963) *Timetables*, New York: Bobbs-Merrill.

Schutz, A. (1962–66) *Collected Papers*, 3 vols., The Hague, The Netherlands: M. Nijhoff.

Silverman, D. (2007) *A Very Short, Fairly Interesting and Reasonably Cheap Book about Qualitative Research*, London: Sage.

Strauss, A. L. ([1959] 1969) *Mirrors and Masks*, Mill Valley, CA: Sociology Press.

Strauss, A. L. and Corbin, J. (1994) "Grounded Theory Methodology: an overview," in N. K. Denzin and Lincoln, Y. (eds.) *Handbook of Qualitative Research* (pp. 273–85), Newbury Park, CA: Sage.

3

COLORFUL WRITING

Conducting and living with a tattoo ethnography

Clinton R. Sanders

There are three basic routes by which ethnographers enter into major research projects. Some investigations start with a theoretical concern and the researcher searches for and enters a field setting in which emotional management, identity construction, stigmatization, or other issues of sociological interest are obviously central. Most studies, however, start rather more modestly. In some cases, the researcher is involved with a particular group or activity in his or her "private life" and comes to recognize the value of "starting where you are" (Lofland et al. 2006). Here access is not a problem, some measure of rapport has been established, and he or she has already "learned the ropes" (Shaffir et al. 1980: 111–84) that, in a major way, shape the collective action within the setting. The third way in which ethnographic studies get started is through simple chance. The (soon to be) researcher happens to encounter a group or setting that is interesting, interactionally rich, and, preferably, relatively unexplored by sociologists.

I entered the social world of tattooing and began the project which eventually culminated in *Customizing the Body: The Art and Culture of Tattooing* (Sanders 1989) by this third route. In the late 1970s I found myself in San Francisco for a week with few obligations to constrain my time and attention. I looked at the listing in the Yellow Pages under "Museums" and eventually found myself climbing the dingy stairs leading to the Tattoo Art Museum. Tattooing was a phenomenon about which I knew absolutely nothing. I had never been in a tattoo shop and had no acquaintances who wore tattoos. I spent some time looking through the collection of "flash" (sheets of designs available in commercial tattoo establishments, see Paul Rogers Tattoo Research Center 1994), the photos of tattooed sideshow attractions (see Adams 2001; Bogdan 1988), and an array of machines and other equipment used in the tattooing process. I was fascinated and, like (as I was to later discover) many first-time tattooees, I went into the tattoo studio conveniently attached to the museum, impulsively chose a small tattoo off the wall flash, and had the burly tattooist (about whom I knew nothing) permanently alter my right forearm.

I learned quite a bit from this first foray into what was to become a decade-long research endeavor. First, I learned that, yes, getting a tattoo *does* hurt. Never having been fond of needles, I became somewhat queasy during the initial process of inscribing the outline of the tattoo and asked the tattooer to stop for a bit until I regained my equilibrium.[1] I also realized that the social and occupational world of tattooing was shrouded with secrecy, though, as I was later to discover, this secrecy was entirely unnecessary since the materials necessary to inscribe tattoos were and are relatively easy to acquire and the basic technical knowledge needed to do tattooing is easily learned. The tattooist was entirely unwilling to answer what I thought were the most innocuous of questions such as whether the ink was made solely for tattooing, how he obtained his equipment, and how he had learned to tattoo.[2]

The third major lesson was that having a tattoo has some impact on how one is treated by others. The people with whom I had close relationships initially greeted the revelation of my new tattoo with various degrees of shock, amusement, or disbelief. They did not see me as "the kind of person" who got a tattoo. While visiting my partner's family and, later, my own parents, I concealed the small tattoo with a bandage and explained that I had suffered a burn that needed to be kept covered. I was unwilling to confront the show of parental distaste that I knew would result from my tattoo revelation. As I was later to discover, this issue of to whom and when to show one's tattoos and the consequent responses to this revelation were matters of central importance to tattooees and eventually to my discussion of becoming and being a tattooed person.

Having had both my professional and personal curiosity piqued by my encounter with tattooing, upon my return to the East Coast I once again consulted the Yellow Pages and discovered that there was a tattoo shop not far from my office. After classes one afternoon I summoned up my courage and drove to the small street shop. After looking at flash and the photos of the artists' work for a few minutes, I introduced myself to the owner of the shop and the tattooist who worked for him. I showed them the tattoo I had acquired in San Francisco (they did not seem terribly impressed) and asked if they would mind if I dropped by occasionally since I might be interested in "writing a book" about tattooing[3] work. Having someone with a modicum of social status—an author, university professor, sociologist, scientist—interested in writing a book about you and what you do is, for most people (at least those in the middle of the social status ladder or lower), quite rewarding. After I further assured them that I had no intention of attempting to learn how to tattoo, I was afforded somewhat less than entirely enthusiastic entrée and began frequenting the shop two or three times a week.[4]

Clearly, the ethnographic work that eventually resulted in *Customizing the Body* was not initiated because of my desire to explore a particular sociological issue or answer a somewhat abstract "research question." My basic assumption is that when people get together routinely to do something—to engage in collective action—what they are involved in is sociologically interest-ing. As Howard Becker has observed, focusing, at least early on, on abstract issues potentially can divert attention away from that which is most important:

> We often turn collective activity—people doing things together—into abstract nouns whose connection to people doing things together is tenuous. We then typically lose interest in the more mundane things people are actually doing. We ignore what we see because it is not abstract, and chase after the invisible "forces" and "conditions" we have learned to think sociology is all about.
>
> (1991: 190)

Although the symbolic interactionist perspective is central to the conceptual organization of my work and provides the lens through which I see all social phenomena, I do not start my research projects with any theoretical or con-ceptual commitments. I am interested in exploring people doing things toge-ther and, like Becker (1993), I tend to regard theory as an inconvenient and potentially distracting necessity. This being said, I certainly do not advocate throwing out the analytic baby with the ethnographic bath water. I do not see my tasks to be giving voice to the oppressed; describing in great detail my own thoughts, feelings, experiences, and problems; or constructing enter-taining or emotionally evocative stories, poems, or playlets as advocated by some contemporary ethnographers.[5] Concepts, theories, research questions, hypotheses, and other abstract intellectual scaffolding arise from the experi-ences I share with people in the field and the things they tell me. Starting out with any presumption, even one so vague as a "research question," has always struck me as a way of backing into the ethnographic process and to hold the potential of leading one astray. Preconceptions can be difficult for social scientists to discard, though nothing is as persuasive as the immediate and long-term experience central to ethnographic research.

There was at this time rather little literature, either popular or academic, to which I could refer. There were a few anthropological works on body modification practices in non-Western cultures (e.g. Brain 1979) but the most common source for "serious" discussions of tattooing was found in the medico-psychological and criminological literature. Typically, based on research with tattooed people in mental hospitals, prisons, or other total institutions, these materials offered a rather dim view of tattooing and pre-sented it as symptomatic of various forms of psychopathology or anti-social tendencies (e.g. Briggs 1958; Grumet 1983; Haines and Huffman 1958). The primary value of these works was to demonstrate the definedly deviant character of tattooing.[6] The most useful academic discussion I uncovered—one which was comprehensive, serious, and not derogatory—was *Art, Sex and Symbol: The Mystery of Tattooing* (1974) by R. W. B. Scutt and Chris-topher Gotch. Written primarily by a Royal Navy surgeon, though somewhat dated and overly devoted to the presumed sexual connections of tattooing, the book offered a wealth of information on the cultural roots and history of tattooing, medical issues related to tattooing, and tattooing as both a working-class practice and a fad within the upper classes and European royalty.

Of course, no one initiates a field study, or any other type of research project, without pre-existing interests, presumptions, and questions. I entered the field carrying some fairly commonsensical conceptual baggage. I assumed that pain was something of an issue. I was interested in answering the standard question "why does someone get tattooed?" I wanted to discover what impact a tattoo had on the recipient's personal and social identities. I wondered how frequently people regretted getting tattooed and what actions their feelings of regret prompted. I was more or less successful in gaining insight into these matters. People get tattooed for a variety of reasons related to their desires to indelibly communicate their connections to activities, groups, individuals, or a presented self. Pain is a factor that, most importantly, shapes the interaction between the tattooist and his or her client. Tattoo regret is relatively uncommon and is prompted more by the inferior quality of the tattoo than the fact of having acquired a tattoo.

The emergence of themes and concepts

Tattooing as service work

As is typical in ethnographic research, a number of unanticipated issues became important as the data collection proceeded. As I spent more time hanging out in the local tattoo shop, listened to the tattooists talk about their experiences, and watched them interact with customers, I came to realize that their work life had much in common with that of taxi drivers, accountants, prostitutes, waitresses, and other service workers. Tattooists, like service workers generally, confronted the central issue of how to maximize their profit while minimizing the problems inherent in dealing with clients. I began to think about the tattooist as a service worker who had to find effective ways to define and interact with customers so that this central element of the occupation proceeded more or less smoothly.

This recognition of the service work character of tattooing came initially from my first-hand observations of tattooists in the shop but also arose and gained structure by a somewhat serendipitous encounter with a particular journal article. I had been thinking about submitting an early paper to the journal *Work and Occupations* focusing on the occupational careers of tattooists.[7] In preparation, I looked through back issues of the journal to see what had appeared that had potential utility for my own discussion (I have often found that the extant sociological literature can help lead to new avenues for analysis and, besides, citing articles from the journal to which one is submitting is always an advisable tactic). I soon encountered what is now a classic article and a discussion that had considerable impact on the way I thought and wrote about tattooing. Lewis Mennerick's (1974) "Client Typologies: A Method of Coping with Conflict in the Service Worker-Client Relationship" uses the author's research with social welfare workers to detail the factors service personnel use to define customers as either "good" (unproblematic) or "bad" (troublesome) and offers a basic typology of the characteristics that generally threaten the worker's interest in getting as much money in as short a time and as unproblematically as possible.[8] Armed with this useful categorization system I went back to look at my field notes and began to focus more carefully on how the tattooists talked about and dealt with problematic tattoo recipients. I found that, from the perspective of the tattooist, good clients had light, fine-textured, unblemished skin; did not bleed profusely, squirm in pain, or pass out during the tattooing process; chose a place on the body that was easily tattooed and did not require the tattooist to handle intimate parts of the recipient's anatomy; was not dirty or intoxicated; and chose a tattoo design that was unlike the routine, often cartoonish, images displayed on the "flash sheets" that adorned the shop walls. Clearly, these were client features that helped make the tattooist's interactions with clients, and consequently his or her work life, less problematic and, once I began to look specifically for the typological elements suggested by Mennerick's paper, I routinely encountered incidents and statements that highlighted the central importance of how clients are defined and handled.[9]

Beginning to look at the relationship between tattooing and other, more conventional, commercial endeavors, prompted me to think about the tattoo as a consumer product. I had a close friend in the business school who encouraged me to explore the consumer research literature with which I was almost entirely unfamiliar. I soon became aware that this academic sub-field was dominated by economic or psychological perspectives and focused, almost exclusively, on dealers in and buyers/users of conventional consumer products and services. I prepared a paper on tattooing as a stigmatized consumer product that was accepted for presentation at the meetings of the Association for Consumer Research. What I had to say was not enthusiastically received. The audience was composed mostly of men in suits and women in standard business attire and they clearly appeared to be puzzled by my focus on consumption as a form of social interaction and the tattoo as a consumer good that moved through an identifiable "product life-cycle" like a washing machine or winter coat. The discussant in the session, a well known senior scholar in the field, saved his comments on my presentation to the end of his remarks and simply said, "As for the paper on tattooing ... I have no idea who would be interested in this sort of thing." At that moment I realized two things—that I was probably wasting my time trying to make connections with such a conventional group and that, as sex researchers sometimes observe, one's area of substantive academic interest has clear impact on how one is identified and dealt with. The disvalued character of tattooing was so pervasive that even those who studied it were regarded as deviants and their work was seen as having little value or relevance to the larger world of sociology.[10]

The tattoo as a mark of affiliation

Given my training, experience, and substantive interests, I initially conceived of my work on tattooing as an investigation of deviant behavior. As it eventually emerged, *Customizing the Body* is, in fact, a study in the sociology of deviance. It employs key ideas from the labeling theory of deviance and Erving Goffman's (1963) work on stigma to highlight the impact of having a tattoo on a person's relationship with others. Though initially focused primarily on the "negative" social consequences of having a tattoo—the body alteration as what I refer to as a "mark of disaffiliation"—I came to be more interested in the other side of the stigma equation. Largely because of its power to generate some measure of "conspicuous outrage" within conventional social circles, the tattoo acted as a source of cohesion for tattooed people. Tattoos were symbolic of membership in a collectivity ("tattooed people") and marked a connection to a particular self-concept and significant others. The tattoo was, I discovered, a powerful "mark of affiliation."[11]

This view of the tattoo's power to bind people together and act as a symbol of collective membership and identity had various sources. For decades the sociology of deviance has stressed how the problems shared by people who are socially disvalued push them together into protective subcultures (see, for example, Arnold 1970; Jones et al. 1984). During the 1980s when being tattooed—especially extensively tattooed—was still seen as unconventional and indicative of other, more threatening, forms of rule-breaking, being permanently decorated in this way presented certain problems. These shared problems, as the deviance literature stresses, pushed tattooed people together.[12]

Deviance theory was, however, not the major source of my emphasis on the tattoo as an affiliative mark. Both daily experience and the field situations in which I placed myself provided the most convincing evidence. As I went about my ordinary life I started (understandably) to notice other people's tattoos. Though initially hesitant, I soon began stopping tattooed people on the street to ask about their marks, how they chose that design, where the work was done, and so forth. As my own tattoo collection grew I reciprocated by showing my own work. What was most striking about these casual encounters is that we, as obvious members of the "tattoo community," would routinely touch each other's skin—a form of interaction that is strongly condemned in the public encounters of strangers. The people I talked with and touched during these brief exchanges almost never refused to speak with me or objected when I touched their tattoo to judge the quality of the craftsmanship.

Another development prompted me to appreciate the affiliative power of the tattoo. Fairly early in the research process I learned of the formation of a formal organization for both tattooists and tattoo "fans." I was an early (and enthusiastic) member of the National Tattoo Association. I attended a number of the organization's conferences, collected both interview and questionnaire data during these get-togethers, and even presented some of my early findings at a lecture session that also included a dermatologist. It did not require particularly acute observational and analytic skills to see that the organization, with its lectures, equipment displays, banquets, contests, and awards, was a committed collectivity bound together by its members' shared involvement in creating and collecting tattoos.

One incident stands out as having brought home to me the importance of seeing the tattoo as symbolically both drawing people together and setting them apart from others. I was attending one of the National Tattoo Association conventions. As usual, it was held in a major city (this one was in Philadelphia) at a facility large enough to accommodate a sizeable number of attendees and short-term visitors (this convention met in a Holiday Inn). I was riding in the elevator with some heavily tattooed people and some tourists who had come to Philadelphia to see the Liberty Bell and other sights. Heavily tattooed people are relatively unconcerned about public exposure of their bodies and two of the elevator riders dropped their pants to display the latest pieces in their collections. The tourists clearly were shocked and, as I followed behind them after they exited the elevator, I heard them talking about how they had heard that a convention for "devil worshipers" was being held in the hotel. For the tattooed people on the elevator their marks were sources of pride, appreciative interaction, and status. For the "outsiders" the behavior of the wearers was inappropriate and the tattoos were shocking in themselves and indicated the generally deviant character of those who displayed them.

Tattooing as an artistic practice

So, out of what I initially saw as a study of a form of deviance emerged both a study of a service occupation and the mechanisms by which people display their connections to others. But another important central issue emerged from the data after I had left the field and had a chance to more carefully review my notes and interviews. I was struck by how tattooing was now beginning to have characteristics previously seen primarily in conventionally recognized artistic practices. Tattooists were "tattoo artists"; tattoo shops were "studios"; tattoos were referred to by insiders as "pieces," "work," or tattoo "art."[13] Recalling Becker's (1974) classic discussion "Art as Collective Action," I began to think more seriously about tattooing as a productive activity surrounded and sustained by a unique "art world." This basic idea led me to look into the literature related to the "institutional theory of art" (e.g. Becker 1982; Dickie 1974)—a perspective that emphasizes that "art" is a social designation applied by certain members of a particular social world. Eventually, I used tattooing to explore the important issue of what factors increase or decrease the likelihood that a form of cultural production will be regarded as "art" and the producers given the honorific and legitimating label of "artist." Eventually, the factors I came to see as being most definitionally important were whether or not the cultural product could be seen as having an identifiable history, was regarded as having aesthetic features, demonstrated some measure of skill or talent on the part of the producer, was displayed in museums or galleries, was the focus of serious academic discussion, and had some commercial value as a collectable investment.

My perspective on tattooing as an art form—at least as a potential art form—flowed from and was enhanced by what I see as a key ethnographic question. Throughout the data collection and analysis (which are never separate endeavors), I am consistently asking myself, "What is this (phenomenon, perspective, problem, relationship, and so forth) like?" This comparative process is central to the generation of concepts and theoretical generalizations. In this specific instance, for example, I kept asking myself what other forms of accepted or candidate art forms carried the same disadvantages as did tattooing. Tattooing does not result in an easily collectible material commodity but neither does conceptual art. The process of creating a tattoo entails physical pain but so does ballet. Tattooing has its roots in the fringes of conventional society and is a disvalued practice but so is graffiti art. The creative pursuit of connections to other worlds of social action and very different collective phenomena is what moves the analytic process forward.

Like my realization that tattooing was as much an affiliative practice as one that separated unconventionally marked people from "ordinary" society, my focus on tattooing as an art form came from my experience in the field. After having published an initial article (Sanders 1988) and speaking at various academic conferences (e.g. the International Congress of Anthropological and Ethnological Sciences in 1983 and the International Congress of the International Union of Prehistoric and Protohistoric Sciences in 1986) my research on tattooing began to generate a modest amount of media attention. One day I received a call from the producer of a New York City "magazine" program. She said that she was putting together a segment on tattooing and asked if I would like to appear on camera. I agreed and suggested it would be good to also have a tattooist on the program. She asked if I could recommend anyone in the New York area. I had just read an interview with a tattooist in New Jersey in the National Tattoo Association newsletter. Shotsie Gorman seemed considerably more articulate and thoughtful than the run-of-the-mill tattooist and I suggested that she contact him. A few weeks later I met Shotsie in the studio before the taping, and the seed of my emphasis upon tattooing as a candidate art form was planted. Gorman was highly experienced, had apprenticed with one of the best known (and most notorious) East Coast tattooists, and had an art school background. His unique talent and training were reflected in the tattoos he produced, which ranged from photorealistic portraits through detailed nature scenes to colorful abstract pieces. He spoke of his work as art, his "studio" looked like the sort of setting in which art is created, and he had well-developed aesthetic concepts underlying his work and practice.[14] As I spent many hours in Shotsie's studio talking with him, watching him work on and interact with clients, and having him inscribe a number of pieces on my own body it became obvious that tattooing at this level was more about art than craft, more about aesthetics than deviance, more about collecting than nose thumbing.

As a "candidate" art form tattooing highlighted the definitional elements that were central to the larger art world but the prospects for its acceptance were limited by certain characteristics. The tattoo process involved some measure of pain (but so did ballet and some forms of conceptual art) and, while relatively expensive, tattoos had no resale value. Tattooing, on the other hand, had clear cross-cultural roots and an identifiable history in the West. Tattoo exhibits increasingly were being organized in established galleries and museums, tattooing and tattoo artists were discussed in key art world publications such as *Art Forum*, large-format and expensive "coffee-table" books of tattoo photographs were now available, and academics (especially social scientists, aestheticians, and art historians) were paying professional attention to tattooing.

I came, then, to see my investigation of tattooing as having to do as much with the sociology of art as it did with the sociology of deviance. But it soon became clear that the exotic world of tattooing was far more appealing to journalists, reviewers, and readers than was the issue of what constitutes art. Post-publication reviews of *Customizing the Body* were generally positive though there was some griping in reviews directed specifically at the body alteration subculture about the sociological concepts and language. For example, a well-known British figure in the body modification world was decidedly ambivalent when he reviewed my book for the specialized publication *Body Art* (issue 6, 1989, p. 40):

> [T]he book is not without its problems. In particular, Sanders' use of the sort of writing style which afflicts most academic sociologists will cause many a reader ... to exclaim "What Bullshit!" and hurl the book across the room ... Nevertheless, I strongly urge anyone interested in this ... occupational world to stick with it ... because, despite its jargon, sociology does have a way of putting an interesting slant on things which will surprise even those who have been involved with tattoos all their lives. And ... because the numerous quotes from tattooists and their customers are so often spot on and delightful.

Exotica can always be counted on to draw media attention and I soon found myself interviewed by journalists for a wide variety of publications from

Newsweek and *Esquire* to *Chemical and Engineering News*. Press attention to my work led to appearances on mainstream media outlets such as the Learning Channel, NBC, and the Discovery Channel. These appearances, in turn, led to additional media exposure and more interview requests from journalists. Although this media attention was initially ego-gratifying and helped to boost book sales, it soon became tiresome. Despite having moved on to other research projects and very different substantive issues, I found myself confined in the kind of identity trap encountered by many social scientists that study sex workers, violent criminals, adherents of fringe religions, right-wing separatists, and other marginal members of society. I also tired of answering the same routine questions; "Why does someone get tattooed?" "What should a parent tell a child who wants to get a tattoo?" "Do you have tattoos yourself?" Eventually, I began to pass journalistic inquiries on to younger colleagues who were more interested and actively involved in the world of body modification than I was.

As I said, I had come to see *Customizing the Body* as being as much about cultural production and the social construction of art as it was about stigma and deviant identity. Consequently, I was, and continue to be, disappointed that my work received virtually no attention within the literature on the sociology of art. This is understandable since those most involved in the sociology of art tend to focus their attention on what are conventionally regarded as the "fine" or "high" arts. I suspect that this rather elitist focus has kept those who are most active in the sociological study of the arts from paying much attention to an ethnography of such a plebeian practice as tattooing.

Conclusion

A few years ago while reading a student's field notes I encountered a wonderfully descriptive phrase that succinctly summarizes a major joy of doing ethnography. The student and I had recently been talking about an issue she was encountering that seemed to hold special promise. I advised her to look carefully for instances of this issue being played out as participants interacted and listen closely when those she was observing talked about the issue. In her field notes she recounted a conversation in which a participant explicitly made reference to the matters we had identified as significant. She described her inner response to finding this nugget of useful information as "my brain smiled."

My exploration of the social world surrounding tattooing offered many situations, relationships, encounters, and conversations that generated the sort of experience described by my student. On the other hand, doing the ethnography put me in daily contact with some people I would have happily avoided and placed me in situations that were alternatively boring, annoying, and frightening.[15] There were many ways in which this decade of rather mixed experience was worth it. It resulted in a book that turned out to pave the way for the work of a number of young sociologists, it led to a number of close friendships, it provided me with the opportunity to put together a personal tattoo collection composed of the work of some major artists, and it reminded me of a key feature of social life and the research process that requires direct involvement in it. I realized yet again that, no matter how marginal, exotic, or bizarre a social group seems, the concerns of the members of that group are the same concerns as those of people involved in far more conventional associations. The central issue confronted by social beings—be they tattoo consumers or insurance agents—is how to establish, pass on, and maintain the shared understandings that act as the foundation for collective action.

But, at its core, a good ethnography is a good story told by someone who has lived with the people and shared the experiences that are central to that story. It opens up a world with which the reader is unfamiliar or helps him or her to see a familiar world in a new way. Theory and abstract concepts provide a necessary structure for the story but, in the end, I agree with Clifford Geertz when he says:

> The capacity to persuade readers ... that what they are reading is an authentic account by someone personally acquainted with how life proceeds in some place, at some time, among some group, is the basis upon which anything else ethnography seeks to do—analyze, explain, amuse, disconcert, celebrate, edify, excuse, astonish, subvert—finally rests.
>
> (1988: 143–44)

Notes

1 I have undergone many hours of tattooing since this first encounter with the needle and each time I get more "work" done I have the initial realization that the experience is not all that pleasant. Fortunately, as I discuss in *Customizing the Body* (Sanders 1989: 80–81, 136–38), the pain the recipient experiences typically decreases as the body produces endorphins—a phenomenon tattooists refer to as "settling to the needle."

2 It wasn't long before I learned that tattooists regarded these kinds of questions with considerable suspicion. Commonplace, street-shop, tattooing is relatively easy to do, the standard designs—typically taken from commercially available flash—are widely available, and, given tattooers of equal competence, it is difficult to tell who did most tattoos. Consequently, tattooists were (and to a lesser degree continue to be) very wary of competition. Unless one is highly talented, well known in the tattoo world, and creates expensive custom work sought after by serious "collectors" (Vail 1999), the tattooist's ability to earn a living at his or her craft is seriously threatened by competition for customers seeking standard, typically small-scale, tattoos.

3 The door-opening power of "writing a book about X" is a major ethnographic resource (in most, but not all, research settings—see Sanders 2006: 150–53).

4 For a more detailed discussion of method and field experience see Sanders (1989: 165–78).

5 These issues related to such trends as institutional ethnography, autoethnography, postmodern ethnography, the "crisis of representation," and so forth have been debated at great length. For a taste of this debate see Denzin (2003); DeVault and McCoy (2002); Ellis and Bochner (1996); and the exchange on autoethnography in the 2006 issue of the *Journal of Contemporary Ethnography* (vol. 35, no. 4). For critiques of some of these trends see Prus (1996) and Sanders (1995).

6 This derogation of tattooing and other forms of voluntary body modification as pathological or symptomatic of underlying pathologies continues. For example, see Ceniceros (1998); Houghton et al. (1996); and Lorimer and Werner (1992).

7 The editor of the journal quickly rejected my submitted article on the grounds that its subject-matter was "inappropriate" for the journal.

8 Basically, Mennerick (1974) emphasizes that the differentiation between problematic and unproblematic clients is based on whether the client (1) assists or hinders the service worker's activities, (2) allows the worker to control the service exchange, (3) does not behave in ways that cost time and money, (4) does not present a physical or psychological threat, and (5) appears to be more or less morally responsible.

9 I later encountered Neal Shover's (1975) article on "tarnished goods and services" and found that it fit nicely with the basic ideas I was trying to develop about the mixture of conventional and unconventional features of tattooing.

10 For related discussions of how the study of popular culture and those who study it are treated with some disdain in academic circles see Browne (1989) and Ross (1989).

11 It is important to note that during the 1980s when the data for *Customizing the Body* were being collected, tattooing was far less common than it is today. Standard estimates at the time were that somewhere around 5–10 percent of the adult population were tattooed (e.g. Anderson 1992). More recent research (e.g. Laumann and Derick 2006) indicates that about a quarter of American adults now wear tattoos.

12 The anthropological literature on tattooing, piercing, cutting, branding, and other forms of permanent body modification as practiced in non-Western tribal cultures emphasizes the importance of these processes as demonstrations of social connection, social position, and ritual movement from one status to another (see, for example, Sanders 1989: 6–13; Simmons 1986; Vlahos 1979).

13 Along with learning and coming to use conventional terms and labels as a key element of doing ethnography, the field researcher also must learn the terms that, while they may be common in certain circles, are seen, within the culture of particular interest, as being illegitimate and indicative of not being knowledgeable. I soon learned, for example, that calling a tattoo machine a "gun," calling a tattoo "piece" a "tat" or "tatty," and referring to a shop (or studio) as a "tattoo parlor" marked one as being outside the tattoo subculture.

14 For a more detailed description of Gorman and his work see Sanders (1985). The fact that this article is published in an accepted art journal is of considerable significance.

15 One of my key informants, a highly talented and widely experienced fine art tattooist, described the world of tattooing quite succinctly. He said, "One of the real problems with the 'tattoo community' is that so many of the people in it are thugs."

References

Adams, R. (2001) *Sideshow U.S.A.*, Chicago: University of Chicago Press.

Anderson, R. (1992) "Tattooing Should be Regulated," *New England Journal of Medicine*, 326: 207.

Arnold, D. (ed.) (1970) *The Sociology of Subcultures*, Berkeley, CA: Glendessary Press.

Becker, H. (1974) "Art as Collective Action," *American Sociological Review*, 39: 767–76.
——(1982) *Art Worlds*, Berkeley, CA: University of California Press.
——(1991) *Outsiders*, New York: Free Press.
——(1993) "Theory: the necessary evil," in D. Flinders and Mills, G. (eds.) *Theory and Concepts in Qualitative Research*, New York: Teacher's College Press.
Bogdan, R. (1988) *Freak Show*, Chicago: University of Chicago Press.
Brain, D. (1979) *The Decorated Body*, New York: Harper and Row.
Briggs, J. (1958) "Tattooing," *Medical Times*, 87: 1030–39.
Browne, R. B. (1989) *Against Academia*, Bowling Green, OH: Bowling Green State University Popular Press.
Ceniceros, S. (1998) "Tattooing, Body Piercing, and Russian Roulette," *Journal of Nervous and Mental Disease*, 186: 503–4.
Denzin, N. (2003) *Performance Ethnography*, Thousand Oaks, CA: Sage.
DeVault, M. and McCoy, L. (2002) "Institutional Ethnography: using interviews to investigate ruling relations," in J. Gubrium and Holstein, J. (eds.) *Handbook of Interview Research*, Thousand Oaks, CA: Sage.
Dickie, G. (1974) *Art and the Aesthetic: an institutional analysis*, Ithaca, NY: Cornell University Press.
Ellis, C. and Bochner, A. (1996) *Composing Ethnography*, Walnut Creek, CA: Alta Mira.
Geertz, C. (1988) *Works and Lives*, Stanford, CA: Stanford University Press.
Goffman, E. (1963) *Stigma*, Englewood Cliffs, NJ: Prentice Hall.
Grumet, G. (1983) "Psychodynamic Implications of Tattoos," *Journal of Orthopsychiatry*, 53: 482–92.
Haines, W. and Huffman, A. (1958) "Tattoos Found in a Prison Environment," *Journal of Social Therapy*, 4: 104–13.
Houghton, S., Durkin, K., Parry, E., Turbet, Y., and Odgers, P. (1996) "Amateur Tattooing Practices and Beliefs Among High-School Adolescents," *Journal of Adolescent Health*, 19: 420–25.
Jones, E., Farina, A., Hostorf, A., Markus, H., Miller, D., and Scott, R. (1984) *Social Stigma: the psychology of marked relationships*, New York: Freeman.
Laumann, A. and Derick, A. (2006) "Tattoos and Body Piercings in the United States: a national data set," *Journal of the American Academy of Dermatology*, 55: 413–21.
Lofland, J., Snow, D., Anderson, L., and Lofland, L. (2006) *Analyzing Social Settings*, 4th ed., Belmont, CA: Wadsworth/Thompson.
Lorimer, N. and Werner, E. (1992) "Tattoos and High Risk Behavior Among Drug Addicts," *Medical Law*, 11: 167–74.
Mennerick, L. (1974) "Client Typologies: a method of coping with conflict in the service worker-client relationship," *Sociology of Work and Occupations*, 1: 396–418.
Paul Rogers Tattoo Research Center (1994) *Flash from the Past: classic American tattoo designs 1890–1965*, Honolulu, HI: Hardy Marks.
Prus, R. (1996) *Symbolic Interaction and Ethnographic Research*, Albany: State University of New York Press.
Ross, A. (1989) *No Respect: intellectuals and popular culture*, New York: Routledge.
Sanders, C. (1985) "Tattooing as Fine Art and Client Work: the art/work of Carl (Shotsie) Gorman," *Appearances*, fall/winter: 12–13.
——(1988) "Marks of Mischief: becoming and being a tattooed person," *Journal of Contemporary Ethnography*, 16: 395–432.

——(1989) *Customizing the Body: the art and culture of tattooing*, Philadelphia, PA: Temple University Press.

——(1995) "Stranger than Fiction: insights and pitfalls in post-modern ethnography," *Studies in Symbolic Interaction*, 7: 89–104.

——(2006) "The Dog you Deserve: ambivalence in the K-9 officer/patrol dog relationship," *Journal of Contemporary Ethnography*, 35: 148–72.

Scutt, R. and Gotch, C. (1974) *Art, Sex and Symbol: the mystery of tattooing*, New York: Barnes.

Shaffir, W., Stebbins, R., and Turowetz, A. (eds.) (1980) *Fieldwork Experience*, New York: St. Martins Press.

Shover, N. (1975) "Tarnished Goods and Services in the Market Place," *Urban Life and Culture*, 3: 471–88.

Simmons, D. R. (1986) *Ta Moko: the art of Maori tattoo*, Auckland, New Zealand: Reed Methuen.

Vail, D. A. (1999) "Tattoos are Like Potato Chips ... You Can't Have Just One: the process of becoming and being a collector," *Deviant Behavior*, 20: 261–76.

Vlahos, O. (1979) *Body: the ultimate symbol*, New York: Lippincott.

Part II

WORKING WITH SENSITIZING CONCEPTS

4

IMPROVISING ON SENSITIZING CONCEPTS[1]

Robert R. Faulkner

William James complained that critics of the concept of pragmatism used the "stock phrase ... 'what is new is not true, and what is true is not new'" (quoted in Merton 1967: 21–22). The "stock phrase" he quotes captures an important fact for ethnographers: To count as a valuable contribution, ethnography should be both true *and* new—and ideally, if originality (the new) is conveyed through vivid, credible, plausible, and trustworthy detail (the true). This joining or coupling of the new and the true is "thick empiricism."

Qualitative researchers are wedded to "thick empiricism." From Blumer's "exploration" and "inspection" of the social world (1954) to Becker's "inference and proof in participant observation" (1958) through Geertz's "thick-description ethnography" (1973: 26) and Schatzman and Strauss's protocols for "intensive observation" (1973), to Glaser and Strauss's "grounded theory" (1967), scholars underline the importance of joining close observation and accurate recording with the shaping, reshaping, and refining of concepts. More recently, Tilly (1994) following Stinchcombe (1978) takes up the uses of the thick/thin metaphor to characterize "thick history" and time in/of historical events as "drenched with causes that inhere in sequence, accumulation, contingency, and proximity" (Tilly 1994: 270).

"Sensitizing concepts" are central organizing ideas in field research. Where do they come from? How do they affect the research questions being asked? How are they affected by what the investigator discovers during the fieldwork (interviews, observations, and examination of archival data)? As the ethnography unfolds, how are these "sensitizing concepts" assembled and reassembled as the research problem changes? How are research problems defined and redefined during the course of the investigation? (On the temporal ordering of research problems, see Kuhn 1970: 171–72, 198–200, 209–10.)

Certain conditions foster or suppress the new and true in specific contexts. Ethnographers have many ideas that could be considered sensitizing concepts, but most of them don't qualify. We have an idea, we try it out, and nothing comes of using it, nothing interesting anyway, so we try another one.

79

We improvise on concepts. This is disciplined imagination (Becker and Faulkner 2006; Faulkner 2006; Faulkner and Becker forthcoming). The elements of discipline and organization, the rational and the routine, are on one side of the equation. The elements of improvisation and imagination, the spontaneous and the indeterminate, are on the other side. Ethnographers have ideas they develop. They go into the field, talk to people, collect running records of events, and observe and record observations with care and precision. They improvise, try out new ideas and see what happens. If nothing interesting happens, the ideas are forgotten. If something does happen, ethnographers keep following it out to see where it goes. They work with it and on it. The task that is hard for our more "scientistic" colleagues is where a good sensitizing concept takes hold, and where it does not take hold is often completely divorced from the original idea and the initial intention. Ethnographers welcome this, through learning plus adapting. There is interplay between *taking* sensitizing concepts and *making* sensitizing concepts.

There are two sources of sensitizing concepts and two outcomes. *Concept exploration* involves improvisation, experimentation, and the discovery of new knowledge. *Concept exploitation* involves receiving, refining, and extending existing knowledge. The two outcomes are the coupling or decoupling of concept and evidence. Ethnographic coupling is the tight alignment and interweaving of in-depth fieldwork evidence with the sensitizing concept. In the write up, "thick descriptions" are closely aligned with hard won empirical data. Decoupling, by way of contrast, is characterized by a gap between concept and measurement. To illustrate the interplay of exploration versus exploitation and tight and loose coupling, I draw on *Music on Demand* (Faulkner 1983), an inquiry into the careers of freelance composers in the Hollywood feature-film industry.

The sensitizing concept

Over 50 years ago, Herbert Blumer introduced the evocative idea of "sensitizing concept." "Sensitizing concepts" emerge when the observer discovers something worth problematizing, "addressing" the concept to the objects of investigation, producing precise and accurate evidence of chosen phenomena. He discusses how "sensitizing concepts" (1954) may be *"attached"* to events in the empirical world, suggesting "exploration" and "inspection" as the tools to deploy in the attachment process (1956; 1969). But he leaves the issue of how "sensitizing concepts" actually become aligned with evidence and proof unanswered.

Blumer habitually exhorted sociologists to relinquish their commitment to received concepts and theory testing. Better to get out into the thick of things. He distinguishes between agency *of* the idea—a concept's ability to act on the sociologist—and agency *over* the concept—the sociologist's ability to act upon the concept (see Latour 1987). In this interplay, Blumer prefers control *over* the concepts emerging from engagement. However, the reader is left adrift with vague ideas about a "careful and imaginative study of the stubborn world to which such concepts are addressed" (1954: 150). We need a more precise and detailed explanation. Where Blumer's recommendations for assembling and shaping "sensitizing concepts" drift into abstractions lacking clear empirical referents (Becker 1988), Bruno Latour (1987) shows the contingent and temporal nature of the research problem and how scientists at work develop rhetorical strategies to mobilize constituencies and shape understandings. Agency of the idea and agency over the idea can be seen as infusing the work of Latour (1987: 23–29), who situates interpretative strategies and condensing symbols as key objects or "actants" in scientific inquiry and collective action. Erving Goffman speaks of "the serious ethnographic task of assembling the various ways in which the individual is treated and treats others, and deducing what is implied about him through this treatment" (Goffman 1971: 342).

Ethnographic studies commonly assume that something new or unusual will be discovered with participation in social life. Less value, however, is attached to the precision with which it is known. The pairings are evocative: "thick" versus "thin," "deep" versus "shallow," or "drenched" versus "arid." Thick empiricism is not only preferred, it is an ideal. The ethnography is supposed to be infused with detail and packaged as a whole; it is supposed to be empirically grounded and, moreover, move from thin to thick. In addition, thin ethnography is written by social science academics who care more about whether ideas (and concepts) are new, and interesting, than whether they are true. Combining both new and true, thick empiricism is the essential criterion in our judgment of ethnography.

Shaping the sensitizing concept

I use two key dimensions to examine the use of sensitizing concepts. As noted above, the first distinguishes *exploitation* from *exploration*; each considered by whether it leads to tight coupling or loose coupling between ideas, evidence, and proof in fieldwork. Exploitation uses existing concepts, and refines, deepens, and extends our knowledge of them. Exploration discovers new concepts, developing new, nuanced interpretations. Exploitation works on the known, the conceptually tried and true, with anticipated results; exploration involves adventure and unanticipated findings. The second distinguishes *thick* versus *thin* ethnography. Researchers shape sensitizing concepts through "assembling and deducing." Thick assembly is a tight coupling of the concept with strong evidence close at hand. Thin assembly is loose coupling of the concept with suggested evidence, more an assumption than a repeatedly demonstrated fact. There are four scenarios.

These are ideal types and there is mutual intertwining of them as the data collection and analysis takes place. The richest measures of ethnography

81

(new and true) are generally to be found in "thick exploration." In this case we discover and establish that the phenomenon actually exists, and that it is enough of a regularity to require and to allow explanation. Other styles and forms are absolutely essential as they trigger and generate potential in this area. "Thick exploitation" is important and worthwhile in framing concepts, in selecting, amplifying, and condensing sensitizing concepts for study. Sometimes concepts are thin but need not necessarily be abandoned, as they are useful in providing background for framing careers and markets rather than as foreground concepts. In practice, there is interplay across these ideal types as the ethnographer uncovers and locates strategic research sites, objects, and events that exhibit the phenomena to be explained or interpreted. For brevity, hereafter the proper citations appear in the reference section.

Thick exploitation

Thick exploitation, as exemplified in my study of composers, markets and careers in Hollywood, starts with a checklist of known concepts: for instance, career, career contingency, client control, and clash of perspectives, orienting concepts from the Chicago school of occupational and institutional sociology. It was summer in Hollywood and I started calling composers and setting up interviews. I had met some composers in connection with my earlier study on freelance musicians. My early interviews immediately revealed the tensions and clashes of perspectives between composers (the artists) and the producers and directors who are their clients. After a dozen I focused on the meanings and activities of "recurring networks." This was one defining concept in the then developing area of the study of "art worlds." The focus was on the production features of art markets that are the suppliers, buyers, rivals, reviewers, and regulators who are involved in the making of cultural products.

Devotees of film scour the credits looking for insights and connections. The adventure surrounding the documentation of "recurring networks" and "career dynamics" in art worlds entailed experimentation and play on the distinctive detail of the film as a project in a labor market. Each film is a market event for all those involved in its production; a film is a point or node in a career. "Career contingencies" was a sensitizing concept in the work of the Chicago School of occupational sociology. Careers are contingent on the accumulation of credits and connections. Careers are contingent on moving into "the thick of things." In the film business this means access to more work, better work, being considered by higher-status clients, getting some control over your career, and denser associations with diverse film producers and directors. I started drawing up filmographies of each of my interviewees. This list facilitated focus in the face-to-face interview. I took each interviewee through his or her career asking how each project came about, how it was to work with the producer and/or director, problems encountered, and relationships established. I wanted to get at the quality and quantity of relationships between composers and others in the market. I exploited the concept of "contingency," showing the factors upon which mobility, access, and reputation depend, thereby extending and deepening one of the central insights of occupational sociology.

Making use of this theoretical orientation, I learned how disparaging language used by professionals about their clients tells you something about what they are trying to maximize in their relations with those people. The early interviews with composers taught me the value of "a clash of perspectives," especially in a setting in which control and power is in the hands of the film producers and directors. Composers stressed the variety of people they have to work with, indicating the importance of being able to "read the values of the film," "deal with producers," and "try to understand what *they* are trying to achieve in a film," and then to write a score that satisfies everyone involved in the project. I wrote up a couple of chapters on this concept of clash, tension, and resolution. On the ethnographic side, the project involves exploring the actual work transactions in this market, tying each idea to composers' statements and stories about their work with producers and directors on specific projects. I saw that the composer's career is oriented not only to particular transactions and film projects but also to a web of social relationships and their controllers.

I had to decipher a large network of linkages between producers/directors and the composers they hired to score feature films. I want to challenge the black-box conceptualization of the market itself and show how career attainment was linked to market behavior between buyers (Hollywood producers and directors) and sellers of professional talent (composers). I mean "decipher" in an almost "a-theoretical" sense of being able to represent the level and direction of recurrence among buyers and sellers in a feature film labor market, to discern its major outlines.

Another sensitizing concept emerged during the course of the interviews. It was an idea that I thought was straightforward and mundane, but which eventually linked the master sensitizing concepts: reputation. This refers to the difficulty everyone in the film business has in measuring the specific contributions of composers as artists to the quality of an aesthetic object, such as a film. There is little consensus about what constitutes competence among creative personnel. There is also little understanding about what makes a film a hit or not. Films and their makers—directors, producers, screenwriters, and composers—are assessed post hoc, based on the commercial success of the products they work on. One respondent told me, "It is better to be a shit in a hit, than a hit in a shit." It is a matter of the success of the whole project shaping the judgment of the specific contribution. In the film market, the most tangible sign of a composer's future productivity is his or her association with prior successful film projects ("shit in a hit") regardless of the artistic merits of the film score ("hit in a shit"). A career line is a succession of temporary projects embodied in an identifiable line of credits and reputation-seeking films. This market is a system of codes and conduct; where skill and productivity are not easily measured, market status or reputation is a signal of a freelance composer's standing and worth to clients. Identifiable projects send strong signals to the buyer side of the market. This is called "a typecast." The concept of "typecasting" unexpectedly came out of "reputation" and was confirmed again in the field as an industry-wide cultural framework for understanding "how the business works."

"Typecasting" as a social process had a double-edged nature: "It's good, because at least people make a link between the composer [and his film score in a film]. It's bad, because producers and directors tend to confuse what a composer *does* with what he *can* do." In Hollywood, film market producers and directors evaluate and buy professional talent by hiring composers, their decisions shaped by cumulative credits, reputation, and typecasting of the composers. "Typecasting" as an extreme form of status attribution by buyers in the market introduces limitations on the composer's identity. It is experienced as only loosely related to one's true talent, but at least it carries the recognition necessary for securing future work and a potential line of credits.

Thin exploitation

Existing sensitizing concepts don't always work. When existing concepts are initially imported, but then found to be ill-fitted to the empirical world, we have thin exploitation. This happened three times. In the first case, a powerful concept from labor economics called "market interaction" called for detailed labor market histories with panel data, tracking possible candidates for jobs through the bids they receive, the offers they seriously consider, and the jobs they take. In order to exploit this concept, I needed information on all offers (or bids for composer services) and all completed market transactions (or done deals or films scored). This meant I had to ask each interviewee about these events. This idea is difficult to document through interviews. Composers politely refused to talk about the jobs they didn't get or jobs they didn't take. By continuing to ask these questions, I undermined my credibility with composers. Therefore, I replaced the sensitizing concept of "market interaction" by another concept called "consummated market exchange" or "transactions." Transactions are the completed film productions, and this became a leading concept in my study. In this case, sensitizing concepts that don't work can sharpen the data collection and analysis.

The second concept was "age-grading," in which age *and* cohort effects are critical in understanding labor markets and career attainment. The concepts are important for understanding the market matching of composers and clients by their respective ages. Hollywood composers told me that "the wheel turns" and that younger producers and directors want to work with younger composers. A key informant said, "Young directors want to work with someone they can talk to, not revere." In order to develop convincing evidence about careers and cohorts—and the interdependence of aging and career—I needed voluminous data on participants on both sides of the labor market. I thought about working up a sample of directors and composers by age and film credits. This would have taken me into another, different, type of ethnography. I chose not to proceed. In this case, sensitizing concepts that don't work can be distractions.

The third case is complicated. The sensitizing concepts were "reciprocity" and "gift giving" in market behavior. For example, some composer-respondents said they attempted to pursue a career strategy of working with one or two directors or producers in hopes of building strong and lasting relationships. They wanted to build up "the accumulation of loyalty 'chits,'" in which free-lancers hope producers or directors would reciprocate that goodwill, offering generous prices for their artistic services. Both would move "up" in the business, getting called to work on more and better film productions. "You help them out and they help you out," said a composer. When gratitude is not reciprocated, anger and frustration ensues. Composers talked about how some producers or directors "trade up." "Trading up" reveals the hierarchy of work in Hollywood when a heretofore loyal client chooses a more prestigious composer on his next film project. The former composer is abandoned. Non-reciprocation is important for what it reveals about clients and their preferences.

The sensitizing idea of "trading up" and non-reciprocation was thin. I had difficulty documenting it across all the interviewees. Still, respondents were incensed at the "lack of loyalty" by clients. I collected many anecdotes of this from composers. Interviews with producers and directors would help in understanding the reasons behind their hiring decisions; however, that kind of data collection would be the start of another, different, occupational ethnography. I went ahead and used "lack of gratitude" or "lack of reciprocity" in market exchange as a storytelling device. In this case, thin sensitizing concepts can enhance the storyline and the appeal of the theory of markets as transactions.

Thick exploration

All ethnographers observe with the anticipation of discovery. Thick description refers to new concepts and ideas that emerge from detailed data collected from a close, intimate immersion in the social world studied. Initially, I wanted to discover the contingencies of a freelance career, that is, the factors upon which career advancement and success depend. I knew something about the idiosyncratic nature of Hollywood film production, and a lot about scoring and recording film music. I was unprepared for the wide range of film projects that the composers worked on, and the diversity of the demands they faced.

I started to understand how film credits accumulated into reputations. The emerging sensitizing idea is straightforward: career was a succession of temporary projects embodied in an identifiable line of film credits. The trick was to see that many, many composers never experience the "succession." Small armies work on one film and never work on another. There is a small circle of very busy, and even famous, composers who do many films. The industry is clearly segmented. "Segmented careers" emerged as a major sensitizing concept. In interviews I learned that building a career line is an uncertain and often erratic process. While analyzing credits, I discovered that 20 percent of the composers did over 80 percent of the films. The same percentages occurred in the occupations of producers, directors, screenwriters, and cinematographers. There was a huge dispersion of market outcomes in (a) the continuity of films as transactions over a period of time, (b) the range of recurrent ties with many *and* different kinds of producers and directors on the buyer side of the market, and (c) the trust and problem solving that result from these market alliances. A central idea became the network "span" or range of connections. The re-sensitized concept became the network-resourced career.

Halfway through the project, I discovered that interviewees believed that the content and arrangement of connections with producers and directors affected their careers. I started improvising on the idea of "credit history" and "identity profile," developing career profiles for each composer and asking them about "close" and "collaborative" clients work versus "one shot" projects or arm's-length "business connections" on the other. The former are stronger market ties, the latter are weaker market ties. Interviewees told me about how they wanted to work repeatedly with some directors and producers. They said: "They become your partners," "you work closely with them on a number of films," and "you collaborate with them." Composers could point to exemplary relationships in the industry: Blake Edwards and Henry Mancini, Alfred Hitchcock and Bernard Hermann, and Steven Spielberg and John Williams. One composer told me that he had recently talked with other colleagues and they agreed that "everyone who has had a successful career in this business had a father," and "a father" referred to stable and enduring relationships between client (producer or director) and composer. I learned that special market relationships were characterized by mutual trust, respect, and joint problem solving between composer and client.

Having these strong, partner-like, collaborative relationships was essential for career advancement. Strategy is at work by these composers. I developed another concept: "the career portfolio." Diversification of ties to clients increases career chances in the freelance labor market. A composer needs a combination of repeat collaborative partnerships versus one-shot relationships with a wide range of directors and producers. I focused in on the careers of the 20 percent who scored 80 percent of the films. A diverse portfolio of ties, a hybrid pattern, maximizes access to the buyer side of the market, increases information flow, and reduces dependence on only one or two clients. I conducted my analysis by counting repeated collaborative ties, and then dividing the number of unique or one-shot project ties between composer and client. I also continued interviewing the interplay of repeat versus non-repeat ties to clients. One important discovery was that repeated collaboration in an *early career* might exert the strongest influence on ultimate success in a Hollywood career.

Along with the portfolio or hybrid pattern is the concept of market-matching. Markets are social structures. There is a pattern of mutual attention and hiring of buyers and sellers who have accumulated similar career profiles. The two sides of the freelance labor arrangement pay close attention to one another. Hollywood begins to reveal a looking glass market in which sellers or artists are searching for buyers and both are involved in the joint social construction of matching through film productions. They share a common orientation by observing each other's strategies and evaluative criteria regarding success in this market. I continued to explore this discovery.

In interviews I knew that composers believed that the highly productive and busy directors work with the highly productive and busy composers. I developed a running record and sorted the credits. The respective points on the inverted J-shape curve or differential distribution are side by side. The one-shot directors—with only one credit—are jointly linked on this curve to the one-shot composers. This became a brute force display of how the concept of career interdependence and client control was enriched through respondent and informant interviews combined with a huge data set drawn from tangible ties among the market actors.

What networks emerged at the very busy center of this market? To help explain this, I used the concept of "structural equivalence" taken from network analysis. I had two results, one anticipated and one totally unanticipated. The anticipated result was a spreadsheet of composers by producers and directors—a "map" representing the blocks of homogeneous composers who are alike in their pattern of connections to the other side of the market. The unanticipated result was a tight clustering of segments in the ecology of careers. I called this the "echelon" configuration. This was a network of affiliations comprised by over 100 nodes (62 buyers or producers/directors) × 40 sellers (film composers) with hundreds of films as consummated market transactions. This is the center of the recurrent tier of both buyers *and* sellers. I mapped the center of the market and the intersection of clients and careers. In this case, I followed my discovery of matching the two sides of the market, used archival documents to track the running records of the two sides, and displayed a network of the results. In practice, "thick exploration" (of seller-side dynamics) leads back to "thick exploitation" (of network concepts, joining buyers and sellers in a matrix). And then the "thick exploitation" of block modeling and markets bolsters new insights into markets. It was one of the first empirical studies of markets as tangible social structures.

Thin exploration

Instead of the ethnographer addressing a sensitizing concept *to* the social world, sometimes the social world addresses a sensitizing concept to the ethnographer. Thin exploration refers to concepts provided by the insiders of social worlds, although they are not necessarily well fitted to the actual empirical situation. Nonetheless, because these concepts are reified within cultures, they become powerful meanings for people to draw on as they construct lines of action and engage in patterned behavior. The concept was "the blockbuster," known in the film industry as "the blockbuster strategy," making huge budget, multiple release productions. This type of film changed the rules of filmmaking and influenced the growth and decline of various role combinations: producer, director, and screenwriter. I learned that the rules of filmmaking were changing. Interviewees started to talk about it. The press reported it. Academics wrote about it. The era of my data collection became known as the "era of the blockbuster film." I interviewed composers who worked on these kinds of films. I wrote about the impact of blockbusters on careers but put aside a thorough treatment of stochastic processes for another time. I had a book to finish. I took up the task of blockbusters and role combinations a few years later. It wasn't so much that the concepts didn't work but rather I didn't have the time to launch a thorough study of these market processes. Sensitizing concepts have attractions; they can also turn into distractions. That is, every ethnography is, in principle, endless. There are always new avenues to explore, new discoveries to be made. I learned that when not to use sensitizing concepts is as strategic as when to use them.

Instead of abandoning "blockbuster" as a sensitizing concept, I wrote a memo on how filmmakers were "adapting" to the rise of the blockbuster. I thought I could focus on how they were shifting into combinatorial forms better able to solve organizational and technical problems. I saw imitation at work in Hollywood. Clients imitated the combinatorial forms that were associated with successful blockbusters as part of an appeal to emerging norms about the "right ingredients" for producing and directing money-making movies. It was a neo-institutional approach to the client side of the market. I pitched this idea to a close colleague who was also working on the social organization of markets. We eventually went to work on it.

The sensitizing concepts of "blockbuster" and "imitation" led us to investigate two trends: the rise of the specialized producer role, and the rise of the consolidated artistic roles. It was eventually published in a leading journal. In this way, sensitizing concepts are vehicles for collaboration, symbols to be shared at work, resources to be assembled and shaped, and products to be diffused through a population of readers and potential adopters. Throughout the process of sharing and shaping, sensitizing concepts have to be treated with care. As I have noted, some work, some do not.

Some should be abandoned and forgotten. Others deserve to be put on the shelf to be resurrected later.

Concluding observations

"Thick empiricism" is typically invoked as a disciplinary rallying cry, rather than as a construct subject to close inspection. Improvising on sensitizing concepts can break new ground and dig deeper into old. In ethnographic writing some sensitizing concepts give off robust signals. Other sensitizing concepts do not. Some are alive and (used) well. Others are alive and used incorrectly. Sensitizing concepts can be *desensitizing* as the original idea becomes excessively condensed or shortened, highly focused or sharpened, over-assimilated or hyper-amplified (in the fashion long since established in the study of rumor).

Who remembers and, more importantly, correctly implements the concepts of "looking glass self," "marginal man," or "the race relations cycle"? Beyond honorific citation and slogan, these concepts are dead and gone. When concepts are going concerns, on the other hand, they can be strongly imprinted or attached to their authors. Sensitizing concepts and their authors—*and* authors and their concepts—have careers. Both careers rise and fall, or live and die. Expressed in the patois of demography, *both* concepts and their creators experience differential rates of transition, convergence, interdependence, and hazard (i.e. from time of birth until death, or from inception through decay until they are forgotten).

Thus, concepts have successful or unsuccessful careers. Witness the success combined with the current mis-specification of "mimetic isomorphism," one of the conceptual foundations of a neo-institutional theory of organizational similarity. Then there is the drift of the original "diffusion of innovation" away from "any innovation" into its current use as "good innovation." The mechanisms underlying the founding and successive implementation of sensitizing concepts are ill understood. Ethnographers need a demography of concepts. They also need an analysis of the mechanisms underlying the rise and fall of sensitizing concepts. This volume offers a source book, and a beginning.

Knowledge and mastery of existing sensitizing concepts is a constituent feature of occupational socialization in sociology, and other social sciences. To know concepts is to be armed with a repertoire of (symbolic) resources. To know how to use them is another matter. To know how to improvise on them is the mark of a seasoned ethnographer. That includes the intuition regarding when to deploy, or postpone, or even avoid sensitizing concepts. It means disciplined imagination, knowing when to do things superficially and when not to, and how to pay attention to your elders' ideas and how to discard them (with reverence and etiquette, of course). In sum, knowledge, use, and shaping of novel combinations of sensitizing concepts is a repertoire for creativity in ethnographic writing.

Coda

Not much is known about the factors that influence the reception of sensitizing concepts and their affects on the careers of their creators. Space limitations prohibit a discussion of this theme. But as a spur to improvisation, here are some concepts in the sociology of careers and markets, a few of which have informed the argument of this chapter. Can you name one of the leading sociological authors connected to the concept?

a. "Career contingency"
b. "client control"
c. "unanticipated consequences"
d. "art world"
e. "moral career"
f. "career stages"
g. "embeddedness"
h. "structural hole"
i. "mimetic isomorphism"
j. "sphere of influence"
k. "typecasting"
l. "market interface"
m. "network closure"
n. "career portfolio"
o. "career flow"
p. "block-modeling"

(*Answers on page 91*)

Note

1 My debt to Howard Becker, Laura Faulkner, Margaret Malone, Gerald Platt, and A. J. Puddephatt for giving my work an incalculable amount of time and intellectual energy, and for assisting me, intellectually and practically, in bringing this chapter to completion. They have contributed immensely to whatever clarity this chapter may have.

References

Becker, H. S. (1958) "Problems of Inference and Proof in Participant Observation Research," *American Sociological Review*, 23: 625–60.
——(1988) "Herbert Blumer's Conceptual Impact," *Symbolic Interaction*, 11: 13–22.
Becker, H. S. and Faulkner, R. R. (2006) "Le Repertoire de Jazz," in J. Uzel (ed.) *Enonciation Artistique et Socialite* (pp. 243–48), Paris: L'Harmattan.
Blumer, H. (1954) "What is Wrong with Social Theory?," *American Sociological Review*, 19: 146–58.

——(1956) "Sociological Analysis and the Variable," *American Sociological Review*, 21: 683–90.

——(1969) *Symbolic Interactionism: perspective and method*, Englewood Cliffs, NJ: Prentice-Hall.

Faulkner, R. R. (1983) *Music on Demand: composers and careers in the Hollywood film industry*, New Brunswick, NJ: Transaction Books.

——(2006) "Shedding Culture," in H. S. Becker, Faulkner, R. R. and Kirshenblatt-Gimblett, B. (eds.) *Art from Start to Finish: jazz, painting, writing, and other improvisations* (pp. 91–117), Chicago: University of Chicago Press.

Faulkner, R. R. and Becker, H. S. (forthcoming) *Do You Know? Jazz repertoire in action*, Chicago: University of Chicago Press.

Geertz, C. (1973) *The Interpretation of Cultures*, New York: Basic Books.

Glaser, B. G. and Strauss, A. L. (1967) *The Discovery of Grounded Theory: strategies for qualitative research*, Chicago: Aldine.

Goffman, E. (1971) *Relations in Public*, New York: Basic Books.

Kuhn, T. ([1962] 1970) *The Structure of Scientific Revolutions*, 2nd ed., Chicago: University of Chicago Press.

Latour, B. (1987) *Science in Action*, Cambridge, MA: Harvard University Press.

Merton, R. (1967) *On Theoretical Sociology*, New York: Free Press.

Schatzman, L. and Strauss, A. (1973) *Field Research: strategies for a natural sociology*, Englewood Cliffs, NJ: Prentice Hall.

Stinchcombe, A. L. (1978) *Theoretical Methods in Social History*, New York: Academic Press.

Tilly, C. (1994) "The Time of States," *Social Research*, 61: 269–95.

The Coda Quiz answers

a. H. S. Becker

b. E. Freidson

c. R. K. Merton

d. H. S. Becker

e. E. Goffman

f. O. Hall

g. M. Granovetter

h. R. S. Burt

i. P. DiMaggio and W. Powell

j. J. Levine

k. R. R. Faulkner

l. W. E. Baker

m. J. S. Coleman

n. R. R. Faulkner

o. H. S. Becker and A. L. Strauss

p. H. C. White, S. A. Boorman, and R. L. Breiger

5

ON DEVELOPING AND USING CONCEPTS IN AN ICELANDIC FIELD-RESEARCH SETTING[1]

Will C. van den Hoonaard

As soon as I became acquainted with ethnographic research as an undergraduate student, I felt a strong desire to conduct fieldwork in a very remote setting. I eventually boiled my choice down to Anticosti Island or Iceland. Both settings evoked startling images and neither, as far as I knew, had had anthropologists or sociologists visit the area for field research. Anticosti Island (in the St. Lawrence Seaway and part of Quebec) proved to be inaccessible—a pulp and paper mill had leased the whole island and did not permit entry by those who did not work for the mill. Iceland, however, had a different story, and I felt compelled to follow through on my one remaining option to conduct fieldwork there.

Between 1970 and 1983, I undertook four research trips to Iceland. The first study took place in Árborg (a fictitious name), a southern village where I explored local–state relations; the second trip (1973–74) placed me in a northwest community where I developed an interest in studying the shrimpers (van den Hoonaard 1977); the third research stint occurred in 1980 when I returned to update empirical data for a book on these shrimpers (van den Hoonaard 1992); the fourth research stay, in 1983, concerned itself with crime in Iceland (van den Hoonaard 1991). However, it was my second research visit to Iceland that yielded fruitful and interesting conceptual developments— as it still does even 36 years after having completed this research.

Located in the northern North Atlantic, Iceland finds itself surrounded by some of the richest fishing grounds in the world which, at the time of my research, supplied 85 per cent of Iceland's GNP. A country with a homogeneous population of 235,000 (in 1973), it has among the highest living standards in the world, including a long life expectancy and very low infant mortality rate. Its 226 towns and villages are spread around the edge of the country, while its inlands consist of glaciers, lava fields, and sub-arctic deserts. My first locale of research (Árborg) had a rural population of 500;

my second locale that constitutes the subject of this chapter is situated in the extreme northwest, surrounded by magnificent and visually stunning fjords facing Greenland, just 150 miles away. The fjords contain an abundance of sealife, especially shrimp. The town (Kaupeyri, a fictitious name) is home to 3,100 people who rely principally on the fisheries. This chapter focuses on the shrimp fishermen in this community whose catches constitute 58–65 per cent of all shrimp catches in Iceland.

This chapter highlights some conceptual developments while conducting field research among the shrimp fishermen in Kaupeyri. It outlines a number of misconceptions I entered the field with in northwest Iceland, and suggests that once I jettisoned those misconceptions I was able to see my way more clearly in developing useful concepts. I had initially failed to see the inter-dependence of all the fisheries in the locale and certainly did not understand the impact of increasing shrimp catches on the traditional, larger fisheries. Only after I began to understand the social, technological, and ecological context of the shrimp fishery in Kaupeyri was I able to make progress in developing concepts. The chapter dwells on how the shrimp fishery was positioned as a low-status occupation and how insights from the literature on the sociology of work provided meaningful concepts. The chapter high-lights some of these concepts, especially those that analyze the way the occupational group of shrimpers relates to the outside world, whether pro-moting their hierarchy of skills, sending delegates to centralist institutions to effect policy changes, or engaging in a discourse that sought to undermine the scientific work of the marine biologists. My research relied on using sen-sitizing concepts to learn what the shrimpers themselves were thinking and saying about these relationships to the outside world.

Whereas my research in Árborg spoke about local–state relations as a matter of governance among administrative, governing bodies (van den Hoonaard 1972), I decided in my next research stay to look at the fisheries themselves (rather than at administrative bodies). Within the fisheries, I concentrated my research on the community of 77 shrimpers on 42 boats, a compact fishery that, on the surface, appeared to be far less complex than if I were to study the far more pervasive traditional trawlers and longliners.

Not knowing what to expect in the way of data or concepts in the new locale, I immersed myself in the usual manner of any field researcher. I hung out on fishing boats, in the local library, at meetings of the fishery associa-tions and unions, and in any other gatherings open to me, including the Saturday night dances. I maintained regular contact with a dozen shrimper families. I consulted 25 Icelandic books on local history and was able to use the mayor's office, the local sheriff's office, the manager of the ship-to-shore radio station, and local and national newspapers to find valuable informa-tion on vessel ownership, purchasing patterns, crew composition, catch records, and whereabouts of boats, among others. I extensively used historical and statistical data provided by the Fisheries Association of Iceland.

Veils of misconceptions

It was only after I had removed particular veils from my eyes that I was able to engage in developing concepts. It was essential for me to realize that the shrimp fishery was not an autonomous fishery, and that it occupied a fringe status in the community. My realization of these two facts pushed my analysis in a very different direction.

The interdependence of fisheries

Despite my relative openness to the research topic, I had not counted on having particular misconceptions about small fisheries which I had carried over from my first research stay in this locale. While studying local–state relations in Árborg, I had cast a superficial eye on its local lobster fishery. And because I had not studied the lobster fishery, I assumed that such small fisheries as the lobster fishery were autonomous operations, not connected to other sectors. However, after a few months of fieldwork in Kaupeyri, I realized that the shrimp fishery was intimately connected to the other fisheries in the area.

The gathering of data from interviews and participant observation showed a steady migration of manpower between the shrimp fishery and the other fisheries. In collecting data about the movements of all the men, I learned that by the time a fisher owned his own shrimp boat later in life, he would have worked on between nine and as many as 21 different vessels. Typically, it was the relatively older men who moved from work on trawlers and longliners to the shrimp fishery, acquiring their own boats and becoming "their own master," as they would say. When individuals did not succeed in the shrimp fishery, there was a movement back to the trawlers or longliners. There was also an ecological connection of the shrimp fishery to the other fisheries.

The prevalence of accidents in the shrimp fishery was responsible for my gaining an understanding of the unique social features of the shrimp fishery. Simon Schama in his brilliant work, *The Embarrassment of Riches* (1989), pointed out that the Dutch were particularly prone to hearing about disasters, especially those out at sea. Although transposed to various countries, I, as a Dutchman, continued to carry this fascination with disasters in Kaupeyri (e.g. there were 51 accidents out at sea between 1930 and 1945, with 176 men perishing (van den Hoonaard 1977: 107–8)). This fascination became a clue in my own research and led me to conceptualize the shrimp fishery in altogether different ways, either in terms of crew composition (to minimize the impact of disasters on families), the relationship between weather and going out for shrimp fishing, perceptions about weather and one's status in the community, the dangers of going out in the small shrimp vessels, the lengthy time of repairs, the push to establish a training program for skipper certificates, the role of accidents in moving men back to the (safer) traditional fisheries, and the value placed on the hierarchy of skills among the shrimpers. To run the risk of a pun, my cultural fascination with accidents was an accidental aspect of my research that opened many conceptual doors.

Shrimp as a different species

My second misconception was borne out of the fact that I had innocently lumped together all marine species on equal terms. Cod, redfish, lumpsuckers, shrimp, and so on were, in my estimation, "similar" from the perspective of the fishers. To paraphrase *Star Trek*'s Dr. McCoy, "I am a sociologist, not a fisherman!" Of course, from the perspective of those familiar with life in the oceans, there are crucial differences among the species. Many traditional fishermen, in fact, would dispute that shrimpers are "fishers." Shrimp are crustaceans, a feeder stock for fish, especially cod upon which depended the traditional fisheries. This distinction between crustaceans and fish, as this chapter will later show, proved to be a critical dimension in the way I would interpret the occupational culture of the shrimpers. While the shrimp fishery could easily be considered marginal by the amount of catch it brought in relation to all the catches in Kaupeyri (5.4 per cent in 1978), its fringe status is better understood as a relational matter: increased catches of shrimp threatened the cod stocks. Conflict was not uncommon. However, there were also other characteristics that situated the shrimp fishermen in the whole community.

Lowly social status of shrimper community

A conceptual understanding of the shrimper community proceeded from grasping certain empirical touchstones, including the relationships among the fisheries and the fact that shrimp is a crustacean upon which depends the life of mainstream fisheries. Moreover, in the early 1970s in Iceland, shrimp was not necessarily seen as food fit for humans, not occupying the same solidly meritorious status as fish. However, there were also technological and social characteristics that reinforced the lowly status of the shrimpers. Technologically, the shrimpers operated smaller boats (12–15 BRT) which set them apart from those working on the new gleaming trawlers and on the established, traditional longliners. According to the traditional fishermen, shrimp fishing requires "less commitment," and in 1963 the Association of Westfjord Vessel Owners decided to exclude shrimp fishermen from its membership. During my own fieldwork stay, I heard a public lecture given by a manager of one of the local fish plants which, in his words, dealt with "all" aspects of fishing in Kaupeyri. Not once did he refer to the shrimp fishermen.

Socially, the daily life of shrimpers offered a sharp contrast to the routines associated with life on trawlers and longliners. The shrimpers were "family men," who were able to steam home every day and be with their families, as opposed to other crews' staying out for many days at a time. They, moreover, tended to be older than the men on the trawlers and longliners. Ageism pervaded the stereotypical perspective issuing from the younger crews in the other fisheries.

All of these elements of the shrimp fishery—ecological, technological, and social—indicated a community of low status relative to the mainstream fisheries. These elements also created a distinct occupational culture that became worthy of further sociological exploration.

The ethnographic study of an occupation

Everett C. Hughes (1958) had already drawn a conceptual sketch of occupations. He averred that occupations consist of a culture (i.e. its internal social aspects), and of "techniques" (i.e. relations to the wider community). I had already expected to do an ethnographic study of the shrimper community/culture and had been hoping to use Habenstein's work (1962) on funeral directors, incumbents of low-status occupations who formed a set of self-interests, creating organizations, careers, training, and norms. It was Hughes' ideas, however, that provided the realization that I had to study also the external relations of the community of shrimpers if I were to make deeper sociological sense of that community. It was not enough to simply study the internal dynamics of the community. From that moment on, I realized, however, that the occupational culture and norms of the shrimpers were not only defined by them, but also notably by other occupational groups with whom they regularly interacted, especially the marine biologists. An occupational culture does not stand on its own and a proper study would have to include its incumbents' interactions between that group and other groups. As the weight of the study shifted from focussing on the dynamics *within* a single occupational culture to its interactions with other cultures, I realized that I needed a better appraisal of the occupational culture itself and this would guide my conceptual scheme for the remainder of my research stay.

When I discovered that I should deal with the external relations (Hughes called them "techniques") of a low-status occupation, I began to see the relevance of what other sociologists were saying about such relations. Drawing on George Ritzer (1972: 57), E. A. Krause (1971: 76), Jeffrey Reimer (1976), and Theodore Caplow (1964), I made a list of issues that define external relations of low-status occupations. Those occupations would (1) make essential distinctions between co-workers and laypeople, (2) develop and maintain an occupational image, often "mythical," (3) use ideologies, and (4) make claims that public interests are promoted by the occupational grouping. Although any reader would note that these "techniques" could apply to any occupational group, including those with high status, I suggest that they are particularly relevant to low-status occupations that have everything to gain or lose depending on whether or not they pursue these techniques. The larger community, or the public, would not legitimize them on its own accord; it would be left to the low-status group to take the initiative. How much more so for the shrimpers, who were not only low-status but who were also beleaguered by encroachments from the traditional fisheries and by external marine-resource management policies.

Space does not allow me to consider the many facets of such external relations. As a consequence, I am focussing only on the shrimpers' relations with marine biologists. It is one thing for shrimpers to define themselves in relation to other local groups (such as the traditional fisheries), but it is an entirely different issue when attempts at defining themselves involved groups external to the community. It was no longer the traditional fisheries and community groups that defined the social identity of the shrimpers, but it was outsiders—the marine biologists—who would now have a hand in defining their social identity.

The shrimp fishery gained interest from the marine biologists for a variety of reasons. First, as Icelandic marine law prohibits the use of trawls within twelve miles of the coast, the shrimpers' use of trawls drew forth continuing criticism, especially by marine biologists. The Ministry of Fisheries relied extensively on the advice of the marine biologists, especially when the fishery was new and where gaps in biological information were still so evident. To safeguard the shrimp stocks, marine biologists were occupied in setting new quotas, the number of shrimp vessels the fleet was allowed to have, and the start and closing dates of the season. Marine biologists played thus a pre-eminent role in the welfare of the shrimp fishing community. Therefore, the shrimpers directed most of their external relations work toward the biologists.

Using sensitizing concepts to explore external relations

To fully grasp the nature of those external relations, I had to abandon the idea of finding data based on theoretical constructs (however valuable they were in initially conceiving the sociological problem) and, instead, find out what shrimpers themselves and those with whom they had those external connections were saying about those connections. To that end, I found the sensitizing concept an extremely valuable tool.

The sensitizing concept[2] is a logical, and even an essential, methodological consequence of Blumer's ideas about symbolic interactionist research. It has a meaning that naturally arises among the people we study, allowing us to see those meanings that people attach to the world around them:

> [A sensitizing concept] gives the user a general sense of reference and guidance in approaching empirical instances ... [and] merely suggest[s] directions along which to look.
>
> (Blumer 1954: 7)[3]

What better way of capturing such meanings than by using the sensitizing concept which, if properly constructed, contains the words and thoughts that research subjects attach to their world? The sensitizing concept is a construct derived from the research participant's perspective, uses their language or expression, and sensitizes the researcher to possible lines of enquiry.[4] The sensitizing concept suggest "directions along which to look" (Blumer 1954: 7). The sensitizing concept is also a "second-order" concept which is one more step removed from the data, but using, as much as warranted, the perspective of the research participants. As a "construct of constructs" sociologists use the sensitizing concept as a deliberate ploy to generate theory (van den Hoonaard, 1997).

Through this process of analyzing the data, it occurred to me that there were at least three concepts that seemed relevant to understanding how the shrimp fishermen related to the outside world, namely a "hierarchy of skills," "going south," and "desk science." I did not generate these concepts *ex nihilo*, but literally took note of what people were saying, deriving the concepts from data which emanated from conversations with fishermen, from relevant correspondence between the shrimp fishermen and the marine biologists, and from official documents. The question remains, "how did the sensitizing concepts emerge over time?" Although the first term, "hierarchy of skills," related more directly to the occupation's "prescribed activity of the individuals within toward each other" (Hughes 1958: 35), it bore indirectly on the shrimpers' relations to marine biologists. The latter two concepts ("going south" and "desk science"), however, underscored the distinctive features of the shrimper community to the larger world and to the marine biologists in particular.

"Hierarchy of skills"

A shrimper's belief that finding shrimp denoted cleverness pervaded the ideology of the shrimper culture. Although a shrimper had to take into account the vagaries of nature—he had to show a healthy respect for it— the community of shrimpers placed considerable emphasis on skills, both imputed and demonstrated. While there were two sorts of places where shrimp could be trawled, the best skippers trawled in the area known as *upp i kant,* along the edge, where one meter in trawling could make all the difference between an excellent or a very poor catch; it is a scraggy area filled with underwater boulders which could do untold damage to trawl equipment. If successful, however, catches were plentiful and could be harvested in less time than out in the more-distant flat areas of the fjords (*i dypinu*) where shrimp were more easily trawled, but where the amount was more readily overfished.

The difficulty of the "edge," according to the shrimpers, had to be matched by *áræði* (daring) and *dugnadur* (clever) trawling. By daring too much, you could lose a trawl, and by not daring enough your catch would be low. The skill of the top skippers involved the use of smaller trawls with lighter doors and fewer leadweights. The larger the vessel, the more difficult it became to maneuver in this area. A judicious combination of size of boat, engine, and gear spelled success. The larger the vessel, the more conspicuous the honor that accrued to the top skippers if the catch was high. Still, skippers entertain many doubts, even if they need to balance being out in bad weather versus maintaining reputation in the community. As one skipper stated:

> The skipper has great responsibilities to honour the law [on safety]. He is often in conflict in his own mind. For example, shall I not finish dragging the line or trawl in stormy weather? Maybe the other boats are finishing their dragging. Shall I be blamed for stopping now, or shall I not come home with all my lines? Will people say I have little courage? Why haven't we done anything before [to prevent accidents]? Are we thinking too much about getting more and more fish?—Too much about money?

Despite the threat imposed by bad weather (or perhaps because of it?), the best skippers tend to stay out longer in the fjords than the more average skippers. According to the information provided by the local radio center (Talstoðin), 83 percent of the top skippers tended to stay out in bad weather, while only 44 percent of the average skippers did so (van den Hoonaard 1977: 86).

Only 10 or 12 skippers (out of 42) achieved this rank; they were deemed to possess the highly prized traits of individualism, cleverness, and independence.[5] The following transcriptions taken from conversations underscore this desire for independence:

> May we not be free after so many years out at sea?
> I have always wanted to be my own master.
> It's no good to be under someone else.

My field notes, moreover, state that "some shrimpers even resent having to make the mandatory reporting of their location to the radio station in Kaupeyri. One boat actually never reports."

However, independence is fragile and some men do give up on shrimp fishing. My field notes convey a high sense of disappointment when a shrimpfisherman gives up:

- "A 34-year-old shrimper has quit shrimping because 'we can't handle large boats,' and has sold his boat and is now taking a course for II degree bo's'n."
- "It 'went bad' for a 29-year-old man because he is not used to working on shrimp boats."

- "An illness of a 38-year-old shrimper has forced the man to give up his vessel and shrimping."
- "Another shrimper, 41, has had 'bad luck' and 'is not a good skipper.' He joined his brother on another shrimpboat."

The hierarchy of skills was not only meaningful in terms of the shrimpers' interrelationships and emulative identity for all in the occupation, but, as I began to see, played a significant role in the occupation's relationship to the outside world and to marine biologists in particular. What emerged was a group of top skippers who stressed their own skills as highly-valued assets of the occupation as a whole. They were able to trawl in less time, find fatter shrimp closer to port, and fill their quota in a matter of days (rather than taking a whole week to match their quota). This time-saving was so significant that it permitted members of this top group to have the time to travel to the capital city and negotiate resource-management policies with marine biologists. Not unexpectedly, the steady application of more incursive shrimp-fishery controls had a graver impact on the crews who were less skilled at fishing for shrimp. For example, the top skippers were more talented in catching larger shrimp and avoiding catching shrimp which were below the size stipulated by government controls.

It is significant to note that the marine biologists, politicians, and the larger community looked up to the top skippers who became the authoritative voice that everyone sought out. With more time on their hands, the top shrimpers could organize visits to Reykjavik to meet with marine biologists and politicians.

"Going south"

As a relatively recent fishery, the shrimp fishery in the late 1960s was not as clearly regulated as the more traditional fisheries. Each new advance in technology or in commerce in the shrimp fishery created contradictory decisions and policies. In 1967, for example, there was a disagreement about whether one ought to be a member of the local Shrimp Boat Owners' Association to secure a licence. In the same year, a new trawl was introduced which had not yet received approval. The traditional fishermen accused the shrimpers of killing young fish and, in 1970, sought limits by pressing marine biologists to effect new rules. This lobbying effort received considerable publicity on the state radio. The shrimp fishermen were forced to act and initiated a number of regular trips of their own to Reykjavik.

One concept that emerged from the data is "going south" (að fara suður). As I see it, this concept,

> signifies a specific type pf action between political and administrative institutions in Reykjavik on one hand and interest groups

outside the Capital, on the other hand. It is the personal visit of a party of representatives hoping to effect some decision to benefit the group.

(van den Hoonaard 1992: 101–2)

It made perfect sense for the shrimpers to describe this policy-shifting process as "going south," because they lived in northwest Iceland, and Reykjavik was in the south of the country. However, when I discovered that even communities south of Reykjavik itself spoke about "going south" to effect changes, I realized the fundamental role and place of centralist institutions that called Reykjavik home. Once I understood the importance of this phenomenon, I began soliciting copies of letters and documents produced by the shrimpers and the marine biologists. I then realized that the events related to "going south" only took place at the initiative of those coming from the periphery, that a crisis situation was usually the precipitating factor, and that marginal groups resorted to it only when all other methods of changing policy had proven fruitless.

This analysis also opened the way to my understanding the nature of the relationship between peripheral groups and the "center." My findings about the interactions between the shrimpers and the marine biologists echoed the wider characteristics of a society which must constantly deal with the periphery and the center.

"Desk" science

In my conversations with the top skippers (as well as inspecting the letters and documents exchanged among them, the marine biologists, and politicians), it became clear that the skippers took the "hierarchy of skills" argument to a higher level. Were they not, in fact, responsible for finding the shrimp that the marine biologists had difficulty in finding? Through their daily contact with the shrimp, were they not intimately familiar with the habits of the shrimp? Were their high catches not proof that they knew what they were doing? Was shrimping not a practical science based on empirical observations and testing? Indeed, if science were about empirical observations, were they, the shrimpers, not the real scientists to begin with?

It soon became clear that the shrimpers defined their relationship to marine biologists in terms of how they defined science. One top skipper articulated this position in this way:

Our scientists may now draw conclusions from statistical material they only work with in the South, in Reykjavík. They [marine biologists] must also become familiar with the problems in the real world. Thus, they would be able to arrive at scientific conclusions.

(van den Hoonaard 1992: 113)

The definition of science had thus become a contested terrain. Marine biologists, they argued, practiced science from figures and statistics, remote from (shrimp) areas. Shrimpers, however, saw their work as more closely in tune with the animating purpose of science, i.e. to do *empirical* work. For the shrimpers, it became a question of their doing pragmatic and "real" science, whereas the marine biologists were conducting "desk science." These terms clearly established whose "science" was legitimate and whose was not.

The consequence of the marine biologists' not finding new shrimp was an act of "injustice." If marine biologists had their way, the shrimpers would be kept away from the shrimp stocks which "they and the nation are entitled to." The shrimpers employ numerous other rationalizations, virtually reversing the blame: yes, shrimp is a feeder-stock, but it is the foreign trawlers, not the shrimpers, that have wiped out the traditional fisheries. A shrimper expressed this rationalization as follows:

> We've been forced to fish for these highly specialized species by the foreign trawler fleets which have wiped out our main cod stocks.

Conclusion

In the case of my research among the shrimpers in northwest Iceland, I had to dispel some misconceptions about the empirical reality of the world of the shrimpers in order to proceed with developing concepts. Fundamental to revising the subject of my research was acknowledging the relational nature of the shrimp fishery in the locale. Not only did I find a constant flow of manpower among all the fisheries, but there was also an important ecological connection between the shrimp and such species as the cod (which spilled out into conflict between the traditional and the shrimp fisheries).

Once I understood that the shrimp fishery occupied, in effect, a relatively low status in the setting, I brought to bear the sociological literature on low-status occupations. This literature highlighted the significance of studying the way an occupational group relates to the outside world. The shrimpers articulated a hierarchy of skills as one of the defining characteristics of their occupation, emulating the accomplishments of the top skippers. This hierarchy provided the top skippers with opportunities to engage in contact with the larger world and with the marine biologists, in particular, to change policies to their benefit. One of the strategies involved traveling "south," that is to Reyjavik, which they also used to discredit the "desk" science of the marine biologists by turning the table on empiricism. From the perspective of the shrimp fishers, "true" science could only be practised by shrimpers. After all, it was the shrimpers who were practiced observers of the shrimp and who were familiar with the habitat of the shrimp. These efforts established the legitimacy and social identity of the shrimpers as a worthy fishers. To inspect the thoughts and words of the shrimpers about these relations with the larger world, I used sensitizing concepts.

As their fishery came under increasing scrutiny and control by marine biologists and state-level decision makers, it became a question for the shrimpers to articulate their social identity vis-à-vis these outsiders. The framework of their identity was no longer local, but became national.

Notes

1 I wish to acknowledge the financial support of the Social Sciences and Humanities Research Council of Canada (formerly Canada Council) which provided a doctoral fellowship and, later, a Standard Research Grant.
2 I must confess though that it took me 25 years to realize that these expressions were, in fact, sensitizing concepts. As a fieldworker committed to working around data as the source of concepts, I was, however, not familiar with the literature related to the role of sensitizing concepts in research. I chanced upon the idea of sensitizing concepts when I was taking field notes about speech therapy sessions and quite coincidentally revisited Herbert G. Blumer's discussion of sensitizing concepts (1954).
3 *Symbolic Interactionism: Perspective and Method* (1969) contains Blumer's important articles dealing with sensitizing concepts (but also with his approach and methodology involving symbolic interactionism).
4 I should mention that as I experienced considerable social isolation in my first research setting in Árborg I had the extra time to explore linguistic expressions in Icelandic. This exploration, as it turned out, became a boon in developing concepts during my second research stay in that country.
5 The transcripts of my interviews and conversations with the shrimpers contain at least 16 different expressions in Icelandic to denote the "high-catchers," or top skippers (van den Hoonaard 1992: 139, fn. 30).

References

Blumer, H. G. (1954) "What is Wrong with Social Theory?," *American Sociological Review*, 19: 3–10.
——(1969) *Symbolic Interactionism*, Englewood Cliffs, NJ: Prentice-Hall.
Caplow, T. (1964) *The Sociology of Work*, New York: McGraw-Hill.
Habenstein, R. W. (1962) "Sociology of Occupations: the case of the American funeral director," in A. M. Rose (ed.) *Human Behavior and Social Processes: an interactionist approach* (pp. 225–46), London: Routledge and Kegan Paul.
Hughes, E. C. (1958) *Men and Their Work*, Glencoe, IL: Free Press.
Krause, E. A. (1971) *The Sociology of Occupations*, Boston, MA: Little, Brown, and Co.
Reimer, J. W. (1976) "'Deviance' as Fun: a case of building construction workers at work," paper presented at the 71st Annual Meeting of the American Sociological Association, New York, August 30 to September 3.
Ritzer, G. (1972) *Man and His Work: conflict and change*, New York: Appleton-Century-Crofts.
Schama, S. (1989) *The Embarrassment of Riches: an interpretation of Dutch culture in the golden age*, Toronto: HarperCollins.
van den Hoonaard, W. C. (1972) "Local-level Autonomy: a case study of an Icelandic fishing community," M.A. thesis, Memorial University of Newfoundland, St. John's, Newfoundland.

——(1977) "Social Context and Evaluation of an Occupational Culture: a case study of [a shrimp-fishing community] in Iceland," Ph.D. dissertation, University of Manchester, Manchester, U.K.

——(1991) "A Nation's Innocence: myth and reality of crime in Iceland," *Scandinavian-Canadian Studies*, 4: 97–114.

——(1992) *Reluctant Pioneers: constraints and opportunities in an Icelandic fishing community*, New York: Peter Lang.

——(1997) *Working with Sensitizing Concepts: analytical field research*, Thousand Oaks, CA: Sage.

6

BEHIND THE CONCEPTUAL SCENE
OF *STUDENT LIFE AND EXAMS*

Daniel Albas and Cheryl Albas

John Lofland (1970; 1976) in his overview of ethnographic research states that sociologists are too casual in their development of theoretical concepts. He concedes that they make use of "encompassing conceptions" such as impression management but do not delineate what he calls "mini-concepts" as micro regularities and the way they are interrelated so as to constitute what he says Merton (1957) calls "theories of the middle range." Accordingly, we will attempt to demonstrate how we went about delineating the mini-concepts constituting impression management in the settings we studied and suggest a theoretical understanding of how these mini-concepts are related to each other in a logical fashion to constitute theory. The mini-concepts (e.g. repressed bubbling, subtle concealment, motive mannerisms, etc.) not only help elucidate behavior in exam-related contexts but, as shown below, are widely applicable to other contexts such as international border crossings, work settings, driver behavior, shopping, courtship, and even behavior in funeral homes. When we are mindful of the trans-situational properties of concepts (mini- or otherwise) they become, as Prus asserts, "like 'magic carpets' or 'open sesames' ... [enabling] researchers to [move] quickly, easily, and productively from one setting to another" (1994: 395).

Initial ideas leading to the study

The objective of the study was forcibly pressed upon us by the universal attitude of students from the first day of class to find out how they would be evaluated. Almost inevitably, exams constituted a major portion of the evaluation which in turn led to questions about their frequency, their nature (essay, short answers, or multiple choice), whether questions would be mainly from the lectures, assigned readings or a combination of both. The latter point gets careful attention because a "combination" response requires class attendance or at least obtaining a decent set of notes! A "secondary" aspect of student questions based on responses to the previous ones invariably concerns whether or not copies of exams from previous years are available to "study from," whether there is a study guide to accompany the major text, and if it is "worth the while" to purchase it.

These particular evaluation questions related directly to exams (as opposed to those with an "intellectual," "distinguishing" basis which cause many students to heap scorn upon the few "eager beavers" who pose them) are widely approved of as being commendable because they help to reduce uncertainty and hence anxiety for *all* students in the class.

These student ways of thinking and acting were very obvious and relevant to us when we embarked on this long-term study in the 1970s because we were still involved in graduate studies ourselves and, as such, still highly sensitized to the exam ordeal. We were beginning academic careers and were motivated to learn as much as possible about students' ways of life so as to draw from them their own best academic efforts as well as play our own roles most effectively.

Research strategies and relevant research literature

To capture student perspectives and maximize conceptualization for ourselves we gathered student "logs" (their own written experiences of university student life), carried out interviews, engaged in participant observation (including some photographs) and Garfinkling (breaching experiments), collected unobtrusive measures, and acquainted ourselves with relevant research literature. At that time (in the early 1970s) most research was of a "quantitative" nature and did not answer specific questions we wanted to pursue within a symbolic interactional frame which "emphasizes the ways that people experience and accomplish activities, interchanges and relationships that are so integral to the education process" (Prus 2007: 113). There were few qualitative studies (Becker et al. 1961; 1968; Haas and Shaffir 1977; Mechanic 1962) relevant specifically to our interest in university student experiences of exams, their difficulties with them, the questions they ask and how they cope.

In *Boys in White: Student Culture in Medical School* Becker et al. (1961) document how incoming medical students begin with a strong sense of idealism and high purpose, but when they find themselves confronted by various obstacles to achieving success—the greatest of which are exams—they collectively develop strategies of coping. In so doing they pool their "prophetic" talents regarding what will be on the exams and largely *limit their studying accordingly*. Specifically, in the beginning, talented students who do not participate in "collective strategy development" sessions are typically ostracized by others. However, the demands of exams are so overwhelming that the idealism of both groups is overridden and replaced by a more utilitarian, practical pragmatism. Eventually, as graduation day approaches, a more knowledgeable and informed idealism begins to emerge as students begin to contemplate their futures as medical doctors.

In *Making the Grade: The Academic Side of College Life*, Becker et al. (1968) focus this time not on medical students, but general undergraduates at the same institution. Becker et al. see a close analogy between the academic side of college life where students exchange work for grades with the work world, where workers exchange work for money. Similarly, in both cases, the rewards (grades or money) tend to be regarded as more important than what is put into the effort to achieve them. Just as in the work world where there are pressures placed on "rate busters" (Roethlisberger and Dickson 1961) to reduce production, among students there are pressures placed on students who study too much and who become labeled as "brown-nosers" and "damned average raisers."

In *Students Under Stress: A Study in the Social Psychology of Adaptation*, Mechanic (1962) focuses on Ph.D. students preparing for comprehensive examinations. One coping strategy he notes was the use of a talisman by one student. The significance of this finding becomes apparent in relation to our studies of student magic that we discuss later.

In "The Professionalization of Medical Students: Developing Competence and a Cloak of Competence" Haas and Shaffir (1977) study the medical student experience and its relation to examinations. In this innovative form of medical training students are subject to a novel mode of exams. Students do not "sit down and write an exam" but rather are divided into groups of five. Each group is supervised by a tutor who conducts them on rounds through the wards. The tutor asks questions of the students and they, in turn, can ask questions of the tutor to clarify and/or elaborate on relevant topics they experience in the process. This continual open-ended, back-and-forth questioning creates continual uncertainty and insecurity for students, who, if they are going to survive, must develop coping skills. The students' response to this challenge is to envelop themselves in a "cloak of competence." One such technique is to steer the conversation into areas with which they are already familiar and even ask questions to which they already know the answers, just in case the question is returned—a strategy ethnomethodologists call "the question-answer" chain rule (Speier, 1973).

All of these studies seem to indicate that the strategies students use help to reduce uncertainties and concomitant anxiety associated with exams. Our monograph *Student Life and Exams: Stresses and Coping Strategies* (1984) also addresses this theme. Our studies of student magic (1989a) and emotion work (1988c) add to Mechanic's (1962) observations on the topic. Our study on post-exam impression management strategies (1988b) attempts to elaborate upon Haas and Shaffir's (1977) study on strategies of ego defense and ego enhancement. Our studies on the institutional staging of exams (1988a), student responses to the staging of examinations (1989b), and disclaimer mannerisms (1993) are further elaborations of this impression management theme. Finally our work on studying students studying (1994) attempts to elaborate specifically on Mechanic's (1962) study and in some measure more generally on all the above studies.

In our work we have always attempted to maximize conceptual development. From the onset we have been influenced by Strauss' (1967) "practical strategies" which suggest studying the "unstudied" and the "unusual." Strauss says that a study done by one of his students of a Chinese laundry and laundry workers was one of the richest sources for conceptual development of his own theory of urban life because it forced him to examine it from a completely new and unusual point of view. For us, student magic served a similar purpose. In this context, Charmaz (2006) stresses the necessity for "rich data." One source we found especially rich in data of this kind was the personal diaries (logs) we asked student volunteers to keep. Diaries were basically non-directed; however, we did ask for a focus on their student lives including descriptions of thoughts, emotions, and behavior they considered significant from the first day of classes up to and including the return of final examination grades. Over time logs were collected from approximately 300 students of all ages, and grade performance levels, and a variety of social backgrounds. These records served as a valuable source of information about the inner lives of students and other aspects we were in no position to observe.

The logs also enriched our insights into features of student life (e.g. the significance of magic and its role) of which we were previously unaware. In addition, we combined student logs with other data-gathering methods and brought them together in a "triangulated" manner. In sum, the procedures we employed came to influence each other and became increased (i.e. produced a synergetic effect). For example, the logs sensitized our observations to the presence of what we came to recognize as "magic" which, in turn, served to "sharpen" our interviewing and led us to probe and investigate more detailed aspects of student life that we will discuss later.

Three specific studies of university student life and exams

In our review of the relevant literature we saw that Mechanic (1962) mentioned that some students made use of magic; however, he did not go on to make a systematic study of it. Accordingly, this is the first theme we will deal with. John Lofland (1970) in his critique of symbolic interactional research states that "encompassing conceptions" such as "perspective," "negotiated social order," and "impression management" are well represented but that "there is very little attempt to develop limited and precise notions of microscopic social processes ... articulate depictions of little rivulets of constancy in the flux of social life" (Lofland 1970: 37, 43). These he terms "mini-concepts" that should be developed to remedy the "conceptual poverty" of the field. This we attempt to do when we discuss impression management in the following two sections of this chapter.

"Student magic" as a strategy to cope with uncertainty

One of the most fascinating yet difficult features of the study to understand was the existence of, and extent to which students employed, magical rituals and charms. As noted earlier, we kept coming across seemingly irrational and bizarre behavior, for example, the student who reported that she always studied in the presence of one of her torn-off toenails which she also took to the exam because it "brought her good luck." Such thinking, Marcel Mauss (2001) and Lévy-Bruhl (1931) declared, was characteristic of people in pre-scientific cultures. We therefore dismissed the cases students reported to us in the logs as idiosyncrasies and as such non-significant. At conferences we informally discussed these cases and were warned to be cautious because students might just be "pulling your leg." However, one colleague mentioned that Mechanic (1962) in his study of Ph.D. students under stress noted an incident where one student on the way to write a comprehensive exam lost a treasured talisman which was most important for "good luck" and refused to leave home without finding it, even at the cost of being late for the exam. Thus the significance of a seemingly trivial superstition. This led us to start collecting, classifying, and evaluating the occurrences our students told us about as to whether they were material items (e.g. lucky sweaters) or beha-vior (e.g. ritual formulae or prayer) prescribed for luck or to be avoided (e.g. don't let anyone wish you "good luck" or don't sit near anyone wearing something pink). On the basis of this analysis, we found that at least one-quarter to one-third reported engaging in such practices. This seemed to be a significant finding and reinforced what Malinowski (1954) previously indi-cated when he observed that fishers when fishing in their outrigger canoes outside of the safety of the lagoons employed magic to protect themselves from the various dangers of the high seas. Before departing they gathered together to perform in a formal manner the elaborate magical rites passed down to them by their ancestors. Malinowski suggests that when the objec-tive is highly valued but, at the same time, potentially dangerous, then people practise magic. In the case of our students, we suggest that the danger of not achieving a desired grade is what leads them to employ magic. Thus, we defined magic as action directed to the achievement of an outcome with no logical relationship between the action and the outcome itself.

A further review of relevant literature revealed that magic was regularly employed by soldiers in battle, miners, gamblers, stage actors, professional athletes, and a variety of other groups. In all cases they did not fully control the outcomes of their activity and thus experienced some degree of anxiety. One of our students who hoped to gain entrance into medical school and so needed to maintain a straight A or A+ average in all courses reported that every time he entered an exam room he felt as if he was "going into battle. The prof's the enemy and the questions the bullets ... you never know when a stray one is going to get you" (i.e. you might end up with a grade of B or less). His magical ritual was that at breakfast on exam days he meticulously stirred his coffee for exactly the number of times as the number of final grade "As" he needed for entrance to medical school.

While we did provide an explanation of why students in contemporary society employ magic, it did not convince the reviewers for the *Journal of Contemporary Ethnography* to publish it in their journal. One reviewer stated that "it convincingly shows how students use magic in ways Malinowski argued" in preliterate societies "but it breaks no new theoretical ground." Another added "its significance in providing insight into other groups and cultures is not conveyed clearly." The journal editors suggested that such theoretical insight "might be found in pursuing the societal context: namely groups, era, or some other relevant sociological dimension of this (magical) behavior." Accordingly, we set out to delineate and offer explanations for the major differences between "preliterate" and "contemporary student" (and other contemporary) groups.

A "historical" or "era" comparison of preliterate groups with contemporary students revealed that their forms of magic differed in a variety of ways: (1) preliterate people mostly perform rituals publicly whereas our students carried them out secretly; (2) preliterate people pass down their magical rituals to their next generation, whereas our students invented their own; (3) the meaning of the ritual is widely shared by preliterate people, whereas there is little or no agreement on its meaning by students; (4) the details of rituals are stylized and meticulously followed by preliterate people, whereas among students they are varying (i.e. no official prescriptions other than the whim of the practitioner). We concluded that the particular aspects of student magic which are atypical of magical rituals in the past and, in some ways, inexplicable might be at least partially explained in terms of: (1) increasing societal complexity and heterogeneity, as well as; (2) shifts in cultural values from a collectivity-orientation to self-orientation.

A "homogeneity," "cooperation" comparison of preliterate people, groups of actors, soldiers, etc. in contemporary society, with our students revealed that the actors and soldiers fell somewhere between the other two groups and probably closer to students since they are both exposed to the same degree of societal heterogeneity and complexity. The main difference with students seems to be that actors, soldiers and athletes share a larger bulk of cultural meanings. For example, actors have a taboo against mentioning Macbeth while on stage, their good luck is implied in the phrase "break a leg," and baseball players do not mention a winning streak while a game is in progress. Students do not share a culture of magical practices and exhibit a much higher degree of self-invention, idiosyncrasy, and even contradiction (e.g. a shirt of the same color may mean "good luck" for one, "bad luck" for another, or even "good luck" at one point in time but later be a symbol of "bad luck" for the same person). These differences make sense when we realize that soldiers, actors, and baseball players must, of necessity cooperate with others in their own group for their performances and as such will have more of a collective orientation than students who compete with one another, but less than the collective orientation found among members of preliterate societies.

In sum, we employed basic concepts and their relationships to show how group "homogeneity" or "heterogeneity" in the division of labor in society and the form of interaction in which they engage—"cooperation" (among soldiers) or the "competition" (between students), provides an explanation for the variations in the types of magic they employ.

Impression management: strategies students employ to maintain a positive self-image when graded exams are returned

To this point we have discussed how students use magic to cope with "pre-exam" stress. Post-exam circumstances create their own stresses for students who must find ways to cope: (1) In the case of a superior performance students face the dilemma of wanting to "have one's cake and eating it too." That is, they know that it is immodest and that they will be branded as "conceited" if they talk too much about their good grade but if they are too modest they might not get the praise they're looking for. (2) On the other hand, a failing or low grade calls for a series of strategies to protect the self from disgrace and the scorn and pity of others.

Reading student logs, doing interviews, and making our own observations provided a basis on which we came to recognize a number of strategies students employ to protect an ever changing and ever vulnerable self-image. The most relevant concept here is probably Goffman's (1959) "impression management," which details the strategies we use to influence the probability that others will see us and judge us in the best possible light. Sometimes we fail. A "negative case" occurred and a student was left looking, not modest, but impossibly arrogant and boastful:

> In Grade 12 our teacher told us we'd better study hard for our next math exam because it would give us a taste of what university was like ... For the first time in my life I really studied and got a much higher mark than I was used to. When my friend asked me what it was like I said it was "easy ... I crushed it. I got 92%." She bombed it and in an angry, disgusted tone she replied "Oh God, you're so full of yourself ... it wasn't that easy." I felt extremely guilty and apologized.

On the other hand, students might be shrewd enough to reveal their high grade in such a way, without seeming conceited as to have the "cake" of approval even though they have "eaten" it. For example, when the professor returned tests in class one student discovered that he had received a higher grade than his friend who usually beat him! He said that he let the test paper with the grade clearly visible on it "accidentally" fall in front of his friend and thus he could reveal the high grade without boasting. This strategy we termed "accidental revelation."

Students who fail exams or do very poorly engage in other impression management strategies to avoid embarrassment such as "absenteeism" by simply not showing up for class when exams are returned, or, if they do, they lie about their grades. These examples are representative of hundreds of illustrations of either revelation by top exam performing "Aces" or concealment by low performing "Bombers." We sifted, sorted, and classified these illustrations into seven categories of revelation and five categories of concealment[1] and attached to each several seemingly generic labels that appeared to us as apt. We then interviewed students who had practiced these types of revelations or concealments to check the aptness of these labels with them and settled on the term which seemed to resonate most strongly and aptly with them. For example, we suggested a number of different terms to describe their inability to conceal their self satisfaction, obvious pride, and great satisfaction when they received an unexpectedly high mark and found that the label universally agreed to was "repressed bubbling" over other alternatives such as "suppressed exhilaration" or "emotional repression." This conceptualization of categories and the names attached to them served as what van den Hoonaard (1997) terms "sensitizing concepts" and provided the basis for further explorations of them in other areas of everyday life (Albas and Albas 2007).

Strategies of revelation

"Repressed bubbling" calls for concealment but despite the actor's best efforts revelation breaks through. Repressed bubbling occurs in a vast array of social settings. In one instance a young woman who discovered at her bachelor uncle's funeral that she was "richly left by him in his will" relates that "despite my best efforts the joy just leaked out of me ... my best friend didn't know what had happened ... she said 'What's up with you? ... You look like the cat that just swallowed the canary.'" In Goffman's terms this is an impression "given off" (involuntarily) as opposed to the case mentioned previously when the star student "accidentally" dropped his high grade paper intentionally (i.e. impression given) or when a newly engaged woman finds many more things than usual to do with her left hand so that others can see the new shiny diamond ring and note her change in social status without "rubbing it in the face of your friends who are still single."

"Passive persuasion" is another technique which allows people to reveal their superior performances to others while at the same time maintaining a decent aura of modesty for themselves. "Ace" students who assume unusual mannerisms (e.g. a jaunty walk) may provoke others to ask "What's up?" which provides the opportunity to reveal their good fortune (e.g. high grades). In a "generic" sense a similar scenario was played out by a young man who, when walking home late one night, noticed a house he was passing was on fire. He rushed inside to warn the residents and actually rescued one of the children who was sleeping upstairs. Proud of his accomplishment but knowing that it is not proper to brag openly about it, his act of passive persuasion was to develop a rather marked cough so that when others would ask sympathetically about its origins he could "modestly" respond and reveal his "heroism" to them.

The strategy of "active persuasion" involves more actively soliciting a response from others than does "passive persuasion." In the case of "active persuasion" the persuaders actively solicit responses from others by such actions as "catching their eyes," raising their own eyebrows in a manner that unmistakably asks how others fared and "incidentally" inviting a request from others as to how they themselves did. Outside the classroom context the same strategy of active persuasion occurs when a person philosophically states "Life is good" which actively encourages others to inquire what is good about it and thus provides the individual an opportunity to describe a recent success or feat.

An extension of "active persuasion" and another strategy is the "question and answer chain rule." Ethnomethodological (e.g. Speier 1973) studies of interactional sequencing revealed that not only are questions and answers tightly paired (i.e. every question demands an answer) but that, in turn, the respondent is constrained to return the question which again compels an answer. In effect, it involves a series of questions rather than a single one. As one student put it "It's common knowledge that when you ask others about their grade on a test, they almost always answer ... and then return the question." Given that an existing term to describe this strategy already exists there was no need for us to offer another.

A strategy of revelation that fits Freedman and Fraser's (1966) pre-existing definition of "foot in the door" wherein initiators "move in" gradually to elicit their desired outcome, is demonstrated, for example, when students don't immediately ask others what their total score was but usually only how many points they achieved on a particular question. The ensuing discussion of a particular question not unusually expands to include the whole exam and grade ending with the question to the initiator of " ... and how did you do?" This is precisely what initiators have been waiting for and sets the stage for them to answer "modestly"!

The last strategy of revelation is "selective revelation," wherein actors reveal their achievements (e.g. high grade, pay raise) not to rivals but rather to significant others such as parents and best friends.

Strategies of concealment

Strategies of revelation are employed principally by Aces and not surprisingly strategies of concealment are confined mostly to Bombers. We have already discussed two strategies of concealment—"absenteeism" and "lying." A third strategy of concealment, "emphatic concealment," occurs when actors employ dramatic shows of avoidance of others by, for example, maintaining a tight jaw, rigid posture, or pulling up a "hoodie" to cover the head to avoid possible contact or communication. This strategy also plays itself out in many other areas of social life, for example, at a party a female may avoid an approaching undesirable male who wants to dance with her by turning her body away and making conversation with others.

A fourth strategy of concealment is termed "subtle concealment." In this case, for example, students might "accidentally" place an elbow on the exam paper in such a way as to conceal the mark or "accidentally" lose the paper in the shuffle of other papers and thus avoid the possible appearance of willfully hiding a low or failing grade. This strategy also plays itself out in other settings when shoppers conceal condoms, female hygiene products, or junk food under magazines or piles of "innocent" groceries.

A fifth and last strategy of concealment is studied "nonchalance" over what might be expected to be a severe disappointment or hurt feelings. In this instance actors adopt an air of "couldn't care less," "it really doesn't matter," as was the case of one jilted lover who stated "there are plenty more fish in the sea."

In sum, in these studies of student life we have attempted to develop what Lofland (1970; 1976) termed "mini-concepts" by searching out the full range of ways people cope with a generically conceived problematic situation, classifying them into what appear to be generic strategies, then naming and presenting them in an ordered and preferably numbered manner. To do any less he states is to engage in "analytic interruptus."

Toward a theory

Concepts depict particular slices of reality and are the building blocks for theory which is "an organized set of statements expressing relationships among concepts" (Hewitt 2003: 36). In our case we sought to identify the factors that might be associated with variations in impression management among our respondents and distill them into a set of theoretical propositions that might move us, in some small way to realize the promise in Glaser and Strauss' (1967) classic work *The Discovery of Grounded Theory.* Miller (2000) states "Although grounded theory ... is often involved as a methodological strategy, ironically too little grounded theory is actually done" (p. 700). Similarly, Charmaz (2006) observes that "theory generation continues to be the unfilled promise potential of grounded theory" (p. 35).

In the case of our student respondents we noticed that efforts at impression management varied systematically with the status relationships of the interactants. Interaction among students who "aced" the exam (Ace–Ace encounters) tended to occur in an open and positive atmosphere where they could "rejoice in their shared sense of accomplishment." As one Ace noted "It's much easier to admit a high mark to someone who has done better than you, or at least as well." Students who "bomb" (Bomber–Bomber encounters) also tend to be ready to share their mark with others who look as miserable as they feel. Fellow feeling, as the adage goes, "makes us wondrous kind." Bombers tend to share their disappointment in get-togethers they (and others) often call "pity parties."

On the other hand, in Ace–Bomber encounters each tends to be more self-conscious and wary while in the presence of the other. Bombers express a greater desire to avoid such encounters (absenteeism) than do Aces because Bombers "end up looking like the dumb one" or "you feel like you are lazy or unreliable." Both are more reluctant to reveal their exact grade, preferring instead to employ circumlocutions such as "let's say I passed" or "I did OK." It is not unusual for Bombers to inflate their grade (lying) and, though not as often, for Aces to deflate theirs.

Many Bombers experience feelings of antagonism toward Aces. In one instance, a student said that when he was in grade 4 he actually kicked a girl in her shins (hard) when she too openly and proudly announced that she got the highest grade on a test! Most Bombers, however, squelch such urges and try to be gracious and even congratulatory toward Aces. In turn Aces, often feel that Bombers get what they deserve, especially when they openly skip classes and talk to others about non-class material during class (e.g. wild parties and love life). However, most Aces usually say they feel compelled to commiserate with Bombers if they have to interact with them: "You try to help them find excuses ... or say 'I had a lot of time to study' or 'I just got lucky.'"

In sum, efforts at impression management will be intensified when there is a clash between the struggle for achievement and ascendancy on one hand and a strain for community and congeniality on the other. The ascendancy component emerges from the competitive nature of exams and the individual differences between students in ability and effort. The strain toward community comes from the communal norm of courtesy and its expectation that we help others "save face." Thus, in situations where there are marked status differences in achievement as well as pressures toward community and congeniality there will be a high incidence of impression management (as in Ace–Bomber encounters). The least amount of impression management occurs when status differences between interactants is lowest (as in Ace–Ace or Bomber–Bomber encounters).

This proposition can be used to interpret, if not explain, observations made in other settings such as workplaces where employees at the same level in the organization are awarded differential merit pay, in effect, generating an Ace–Bomber difference.

"Motive mannerisms" as aligning explanations for questionable behavior

As C. W. Mills (1940) says, whenever there are problems in interaction between groups (e.g. Aces and Bombers) there are established ways of coping (e.g. vocabularies of motives) which are typical of the status and situation (e.g. religious or secular) of the interactants. For example, Aces are ready to offer excuses not only for themselves (e.g. "I was just lucky") but for Bombers as well (e.g. "the test was tricky"). These explanatory excuses, justifications, etc., Mills (1940) calls "motive talk." Scott and Lyman (1968: 46) call them "accounts" and intend them to have a restorative role in that they seem to "repair the broken and restore the estranged." Hewitt and Stokes (1975) introduce the term "disclaimers" to describe the words people use to neutralize possible negative effects of their forthcoming behavior. In effect, the distinction between accounts and disclaimers is chronological—the former has a retrospective reference and the latter a prospective one. All such motive givings are verbal. However, in the exam setting which is the specific focus of this study, vocalization is *verboten*. Accordingly, alternative terms are necessary to refer to strategies used to explain and justify questionable behavior. Such strategies must, of necessity, be nonverbal and in what Stone (1981) terms the "universe of appearance" rather than the "universe of discourse." The term we coined is "motive mannerisms." Motive mannerisms involve the choice or avoidance of particular locations, body language, and other visible symbols to convey a guiltless, excusable, or even virtuous identity when our own identity or someone else's identity is threatened.

In order to respect the distinction of accounts for past behavior from disclaiming guilt for what we might be about to do in the universe of appearance, we introduced the terms "account mannerisms" and "disclaimer mannerisms" respectively. In sum, we built on the classic concepts developed by Mills, Scott, and Lyman, as well as Hewitt and Stokes and offered our own terminology (i.e. motive mannerisms, account mannerisms, and disclaimer mannerisms) to describe and analyze motive-giving during exams so as to avoid the impression of guilt.[2] In other studies (e.g. Albas and Albas 2007) we were able to show how these concepts applied to other areas of social life such as international border crossings, driver behavior, and shopping. Thus, in any situation where talk is not appropriate or possible there is potential for "label liability." For example, professors patrolling during exams or overly vigilant customs agents make us feel potentially guilty, so we respond with disclaimer mannerisms rather than verbal disclaimers.

In our observations of hundreds of exams we noted that suspicion avoidance was conveyed nonverbally and principally by disclaimer mannerisms given before problems arise. For example, students who take a break from exam writing gaze at the ceiling or the invigilator—but not at another student's exam paper. People at border crossings take off their sunglasses when they are being processed to avoid being typed as "shady." Both these cases describe the control of eyes to avoid the suspicion of guilt and can be labeled as "actions avoided." A second aspect of "actions avoided" is the "avoidance of temptation" by removing items that might cause suspicion (e.g. course-relevant textbooks and notes by students or purses and backpacks by shoppers) to where they cannot be readily accessed. A third aspect of "actions avoided" is staying away from places and situations (e.g. students avoid areas where cheaters and troublemakers gather or, on the other hand, where Aces gather so they cannot be accused of trying to cheat off of them). In wider society, male shoppers often avoid sections of department stores that sell lingerie for women; shoppers also often avoid "pornographic" or "sexual" sections of bookstores. Glassner and Corzine (1978) refer to this practice of avoidance as respecting the "morality of place."

"Actions taken," on the other hand, include "exaggerated shows of over conformity with regulations" when students deliberately push their hair back and away from their faces to reveal their eyes and eye movements or turn their cap peaks to the back for the same reasons. Such displays of "rectitude" also happen among drivers. As one stated, "whenever the police are watching I always sit up very straight and place my hands at the 10/2 position on the steering wheel so I look like a good, safe driver ... and a law abiding citizen."

A second "action taken" we termed "the expressions of repression of creature releases." These refer to those body actions (e.g. itches, yawns) that slip through our self-control and momentarily assert our animal nature (Goffman 1963). For example, students who need to make use of the toilet during an exam will often make exaggerated gestures (i.e. press their thighs together) to impress upon the professor that their situation is urgent and to dispel any implication that they may be trying to cheat. A third "action taken" we called "exaggerated shows of innocence." Students say that a lack of activity might be interpreted as a lack of preparation on their part and thus "a greater need to cheat." As a consequence, when they are not actually writing they may resort to dumb shows of diligence by underlining or circling phrases or words on the exam sheet. Similarly, shoppers often take self-conscious precautions to avoid looking suspicious by, for example, tying a knot at the top of every bag they are carrying to give the message that nothing else is being added.

The objective of this chapter was to study and document some of the salient features of student life—particularly in regard to examinations. One of the most important was students' use of magic. Another major concept related to the many strategies students used to reveal modestly a superior performance or subtly conceal a poor one after graded exams were returned in class. In this case we followed Lofland's (1970) recommendation that encompassing conceptions like impression management should be broken down into "mini-concepts." We showed how we developed most of the ones we talked about ourselves (e.g. "repressed bubbling," "accidental" disclosure, etc.). Some others (e.g. the "question-answer chain rule" and "foot in the door") were borrowed from the existing literature. We followed the same methodology in regard to student behavior during the actual exam where acts that could be seen as problematic to an invigilator were openly dramatized as innocent through the use of disclaimer mannerisms (e.g. exaggerated shows of over conformity with regulations by turning one's baseball cap backward to more openly reveal the innocence of one's eyes).

The mini-concepts we developed in the study of exams provided for us what van den Hoonaard (1997: 30) found to be the case when he says, "when I am able to apply concepts in a research setting other than the original one, I find that my enthusiasm for sociology is rekindled." So it is hoped will happen here.

Notes

1 Initially we attempted to categorize all post-exam impression management strategies but found so many "middle" types that it made a full categorization of them in a single paper cumbersome, so we left them for a subsequent project.
2 Originally we were not sufficiently explicit in making disclaimer mannerisms the central focus of the paper; in fact we called it "The Underpersonalized Concept of the Labeled." We used Becker's (1963) labeling theory, especially his observation that people can be labeled even though they are not guilty and once labeled may become deviant in fact. Critics have charged Becker with being a determinist. Gouldner, for example, states that "the deviant [is seen] as a passive nonentity" (1968: 106). This is what Dennis Wrong (1961) would call "an oversocialized" concept of the deviant. We suggested that if labeling theorists broadened their focus to include what happens before labeling occurs, especially in label-prone situations such as exams, they would see actors engaged in a wide variety of gestures to ward off being labeled. These we called disclaimer mannerisms. A focus on them would perhaps correct the passive underpersonalized concept of the deviant for which critics blamed Becker. Reviewers for the *Canadian Review of Sociology and Anthropology* agreed that the "avoidance of being labeled for the first time as in some way 'deviant' is rarely studied." However, another reviewer stated that the authors failed to realize "the significance of their own theoretical contributions ... disclaimers as body language or symbolic gestures and not 'vocabularies of motives' that has been the focus thus far."

References

Albas, C. and Albas, D. (1988c) "Emotion Work and Emotion Rules: the case of exams," *Qualitative Sociology*, 11: 259–74.
——(1994) "Studying Students Studying: perspective, identity and activity," in M. L. Dietz, Shaffir, W., and Prus, R. (eds.) *Doing Everyday Life: ethnography as human lived experience* (pp. 273–89), Toronto: Copp Clark Longman.
Albas, D. and Albas, C. (1984) *Student Life and Exams: stresses and coping strategies*, Dubuque, IN: Kendall/Hunt.
——(1988a) "The Institutional Staging of an Examination," *The Canadian Journal of Higher Education*, 18: 65–74.
——(1988b) "Aces and Bombers: the post-exam impression management strategies of students," *Symbolic Interaction*, 11: 289–302.
——(1989a) "Modern Magic: the case of exams," *The Sociological Quarterly*, 30: 603–13.

——(1989b) "The Staging of Examinations: a student response to the institutional perspective," *Canadian Journal of Higher Education*, 18: 69–81.

——(1993) "Disclaimer Mannerisms: how to avoid being labeled as cheaters," *Canadian Review of Sociology and Anthropology*, 30: 451–68.

——(2007) "Modesty: a case for revelation and concealment," paper presented at Annual Meetings of the Society for the Study of Symbolic Interaction, New York, August.

Becker, H. S. (1963) *Outsiders: studies in the sociology of deviance*, New York: Free Press.

Becker, H. S., Geer, B., and Hughes, E. C. (1968) *Making the Grade: the academic side of college life*, New York: Wiley.

Becker, H. S., Geer, B., Hughes, E. C., and Strauss, A. (1961) *Boys in White: student culture in medical school*, Chicago: University of Chicago Press.

Charmaz, K. (2006) *Constructing Grounded Theory: a practical guide through qualitative analysis*, Thousand Oaks, CA: Sage.

Freedman, J. L. and Fraser, S. C. (1966) "Compliance Without Pressure: the foot-in-the-door technique," *Journal of Personality and Social Psychology*, 4: 195–202.

Glaser, B. and Strauss, A. (1967) *The Discovery of Grounded Theory*, Chicago: Aldine.

Glassner, B. and Corzine, J. (1978) "Can Labeling Theory Be Saved?" *Symbolic Interaction*, 1: 74–89.

Goffman, E. (1959) *The Presentation of Self in Everyday Life*, Garden City, NY: Doubleday.

——(1963) *Behavior in Public Places: notes on the social organization of gatherings*, Glencoe, IL: Free Press.

Gouldner, A. (1968) "The Sociologist as a Partisan: sociology and the welfare state," *The American Sociologist*, 3: 103–16.

Haas, J. and Shaffir, W. (1977) "The Professionalization of Medical Students: developing competence and a cloak of competence," *Symbolic Interaction*, 1: 71–88.

Hewitt, J. (2003) *Self and Society: a symbolic interactionist social psychology*, New York: Allyn & Bacon.

Hewitt, J. and Stokes, R. (1975) "Disclaimers," *American Sociological Review*, 40: 1–11.

Lévy-Bruhl, L. ([1931] 1973) *Primitives and the Supernatural* (Le surnaturel et la nature dans la mentalité primitive), New York: Haskell House

Lofland, J. (1970) "Interactionist Imaginary and Analytic Interruptus," in T. Shibutani (ed.) *Human Nature and Collective Behavior: papers in honor of Herbert Blumer*, Englewood Cliffs, NJ: Prentice Hall.

——(1976) *Doing Social Life*, New York: Wiley Interscience.

Malinowski, B. (1954) *Magic, Science, Religion*, New York: Doubleday.

Mauss, M. (2001) *A General Theory of Magic* trans. Robert Bain, New York: Routledge.

Mechanic, D. (1962) *Students Under Stress: a study in the social psychology of adaptation*, New York: Macmillan.

Merton, R. K. (1957) *Social Theory and Social Structure*, New York: Free Press.

Miller, D. (2000) "Mathematical Dimensions of Qualitative Research," *Symbolic Interaction*, 23: 399–402.

Mills, C. W. (1940) "Situated Actions and Vocabularies of Motive," *American Sociological Review*, 5: 904–13.

Prus, R. (1994) "Generic Social Processes: intersubjectivity and transcontextuality in the social sciences," in M. L. Dietz, Shaffir, W. and Prus, R. (eds.) *Doing Everyday*

DANIEL ALBAS AND CHERYL ALBAS

Life: ethnography as human lived experience (pp. 393–412), Toronto: Copp Clark Longman.

——(2007) "Activities and Interdependencies in the Education Process: an interactionist approach to student venture in learning," in L. Tepperman and Dickinson, H. (eds.) *Reading Sociology: Canadian perspectives*, Don Mills, ON: Oxford.

Roethlisberger, F. J. and Dickson, W. J. (1961) *Management and The Worker: an account of a research program conducted by the Western Electric Company, Hawthorne Works*, 12th ed., Cambridge, MA: Harvard University Press.

Scott, M. B. and Lyman, S. (1968) "Accounts," *American Sociological Review*, 33: 46–62.

Speier, M. (1973) *How to Observe Face-to-Face Communication: a sociological introduction*, Pacific Palisades, CA: Goodyear.

Stone, G. P. (1981) "Appearance," in G. P. Stone and Farberman, H. A. (eds.) *Social Psychology through Social Interaction* (pp. 101–13), New York: Wiley.

Strauss, A. (1967) "Strategies for Discovering Urban Theory," in L. Schnore and Fagin, H. (eds.) *Urban Research and Policy Planning* (pp. 79–98), Beverly Hills, CA: Sage.

van den Hoonaard, W. C. (1997) *Working with Sensitizing Concepts: analytical field research*, Thousand Oaks, CA: Sage.

Wrong, D. (1961) "The Oversocialized Conception of Man in Modern Sociology," *American Sociological Review*, 26: 183–93.

7

HOW MURRAY MANOR BECAME AN ETHNOGRAPHY

Jaber F. Gubrium

Living and Dying at Murray Manor (Gubrium [1975]1997) is the first book-length ethnography of a nursing home. It is the touchstone for similar contributions dealing with what came to be called the "culture of long-term care" (Henderson & Vesperi 1995). In revisiting the Murray Manor project, I'll describe how the research began, especially how I thought about the nursing home experience before the fieldwork started, and what led me to conceptualize how the organization of life and work in the nursing home was ethnographically accessible.

In the spirit of this collection, I focus on the developing analytic framework. While many memories of the Murray Manor fieldwork are personal and I'll touch on this, it is the evolution of a way of thinking about institutional life that eventually made the research and the book what they became. What will be apparent in my account is the increasing realization of the shortcomings of preconceived categories in coming to grips with the complexity of everyday life. Murray Manor became the site of ethnographic fieldwork and formed my ethnographic skills, as much from a shift in analytic perspective, as from a developing interest in the aging experience.

Beforehand

I was trained as a survey researcher. My dissertation, completed in 1970, dealt with the relationship between personal needs in old age and the resources available to elderly residents of varied living environments. I was especially concerned with the fit between needs and resources and how various combinations affected the quality of life. I was working with a person-environment fit model, which was popular in the late 1960s. The plan was to interview elderly men and women to see how different residential settings affected the quality of their lives. Despite the positivistic character of the project, even at that time I aimed to gather data about the quality of life as it was understood by the elderly themselves. I wanted to move beyond what standard modes of assessment produced. So, while the intent was to survey residents in different settings, there was an inkling of interest in subjective understanding. Missing was an appropriate way of thinking about this and a method of procedure suitable to the task.

The dissertation research eventually was completed and led to articles whose frequencies, percentages, and cross-tabulations (remember this was the 1960s) displayed the results. Taking a job in 1970 as an assistant professor of sociology at Marquette University in Milwaukee, I was ready to extend the approach and my research skills to additional settings. I hadn't done interviews in care facilities and was curious about what I might find there about elderly residents' views of the quality of their lives. I started to develop a grant application based on my dissertation research and aimed to apply the model I'd been using together with survey methodology. The administrators of various nursing homes in the area were contacted to see if they'd participate in the study, which now centered on how residents viewed the quality of care as well as the quality of their lives in nursing homes. Until then, these factors were assessed by service providers, not by those who were provided the services. So I was about to enter new territory.

I did complete such a study, but not until twenty years later. Fortunately, my interpretive inclinations were better developed and more appropriate research skills were in place by then (Gubrium 1993). Meanwhile, back in my early Marquette years, I was aiming to construct an interview instrument that would fit the experience and circumstances of nursing home residents. It occurred to me that I had never been in a nursing home nor did I know anyone who lived in one. How was I to ask sensible questions in my interviews? None of the elderly residents I'd interviewed for the dissertation research was seriously ill and none appeared to be dying. Many had lived in their homes, apartments, or retirement communities for years, if not decades.

The quality life and of care for nursing home residents raised questions I wasn't prepared to handle. All residents had left their own homes and most faced the prospect of never returning to them. Many were seriously ill, disabled, or demented, and if they weren't sick, they interacted daily with others who were. All of them to some degree were cared for by others, not themselves. The plain fact of the matter was that the key terms I was using—life, care, quality—to formulate the new project would flag a dramatically different circumstance when it came to person-environment fit. One question was how was this nursing home "person" to be understood in relation to the nursing home "environment," given that discontinuity in personhood for many residents would probably be an issue? And what could "fit" mean in the context of an environment that I guessed would, at best, be only home-like?

Enter Murray Manor

With such questions in view, I figured I should get a working sense of what nursing home life was like before I went any further. Several of the nursing home administrators I'd contacted were willing to participate in the study, would facilitate access to residents, and expressed interest in the results. One, in particular, the administrator of Murray Manor, was disturbed by the continuing "bad press," as he called it, that nursing homes were getting locally and across the nation. He viewed his facility as exemplary and was eager for the Manor to be the testing ground for an unbiased view. He didn't want anyone to "whitewash" what nursing home care was like, and added that, indeed, there were many "hellish" facilities, terms he used. In his opinion, a more balanced picture was needed. This administrator eventually became the Mr. Filstead featured in *Living and Dying at Murray Manor*. When I asked him whether I might casually talk to residents and staff members and get the feel of nursing home life before I started my project, he welcomed me aboard.

So I took time to hang around Murray Manor. Filstead eased my entry in many ways. He introduced me enthusiastically to those I eventually called the "top staff," which included the medical director, director of nursing, charge nurses on various floors, the dietitian, the social worker, and the activity director. They, in turn, introduced me to employees I called the "floor staff" (frontline workers), which included RNs (registered nurses), LPNs (licensed practical nurses), and NAs or nurses' aides. All helped with introductions to the residents. The introductions and the staff's continuing support were extraordinarily helpful in adjusting to the premises and in building rapport.

I was now ensconced in what eventually would become my field site, but with old analytic lenses. I figured that Filstead's welcome and the staff's follow-through would be points of departure for what I still planned to be a survey of the quality of life, and now also the quality of care. In anticipation of that, I would be getting to know about the nursing home as a living environment, how my future respondents figured in, and how the broad contours of life and care in nursing homes as opposed to other environments related to that. Becoming familiar with Murray Manor was to be a learning experience preliminary to the actual study I would conduct and the conclusions I would reach about person-environment fit in general.

There is a noteworthy lesson in this about the relationship between an analytic perspective and a method of procedure, which will become clearer as I move along. The lesson wasn't apparent then, and couldn't have been because I needed another viewpoint to recognize it. The lesson is marked by the words and categories I was using at the time to describe my research plans. That lesson is that the working language we use to refer to what we are doing is related to one's perspective on empirical material (Gubrium and Holstein 1997).

Let me explain. Murray Manor wasn't yet a field site and I didn't refer to it as such. Rather, I spoke of it as a source of background information. What I was doing wasn't fieldwork, but instead familiarizing myself with things before the real (survey) research began. I wasn't yet using ethnographic language to describe my activities, even while I was located in a kind of field and conducting a form of empirical work within it. Systematic participant observation was as far from my mind as the moon. Social interaction on the premises and the contexts of meaning-making were, as yet, mostly uninteresting and certainly undocumented. Instead, the language of variables and co-relationships was leading the way.

Enter ethnography

Little did I know that what I was doing would lead to another form of analysis and a different method of procedure. Instead and understandably, as I got a feel for nursing home life, I thought ahead about how what I was learning could be applied in my survey interviewing. Rather than ask residents directly about the quality of life, I would be able to specify, if needed, to what aspects of daily life that could pertain. It seemed reasonable to do this, because I began to learn that the residents and staff members would be likely to have particular things in mind when they talked about the qualities of care and of life at the Manor.

Listening to, and speaking with, residents and staff, I was gaining a more nuanced understanding of what words such as "quality," "life," and "care" connoted in the context of the nursing home. "Care," "caregiving," and "caring," in particular, were categories whose meanings seemed to shift, depending on the circumstances. I was awed and rather dismayed at the same time that the very words I was prepared to apply in formulating interview questions were like semantic chameleons—changing contexts gave way to complex practical meanings absent in other living environments.

These realizations didn't immediately change my conceptualization of the project I was planning. Initially, awe signaled methodological difficulties and empirical complexity. My concern was with how I was to formulate interview items that would be validly sensitive to what I was hearing and observing at the Manor. I considered that perhaps more open-ended interviewing might help. Structured and forced-choice response options would only hide or marginalize variations in meaning, some of which would likely even contradict others. I later came to know that without built-in context-specifying mechanisms, differences in responses to the same question were likely to be coded as contradictions by default. Looking back thirty-five years later, I'm surprised at how analytically tenacious I was. Then again, I suppose most serious researchers would be. One's methodological training and analytic framework don't simply disappear when the going gets tough. One refines, repairs, and adjusts one's understandings as well as one's skills for dealing with the issues. Add to that the research track record in place, which appropriately provides both direction and experience as a basis for continuing with one's work. My published articles were based on survey material and I expected future articles to be, which together would reflect an unfolding program of research.

Still, certain personal factors were starting to work against this commitment, which eventually would lead to a reconceptualization of the project. One was that, throughout my undergraduate college years, I had been fascinated by ethnographic fieldwork, both anthropological and sociological. Especially close to my heart was William Foote Whyte's (1943) book *Street Corner Society*, which is an ethnographic study of Cornerville, an Italian slum district in Boston. I regularly talked about it in class. I came alive with enthusiasm, as did my students, as I detailed the research's challenges for Whyte, its intellectual context, and its discoveries. I have to admit that I always was a closet constructionist, as I urged my students to think about how social life is assembled, structured, and sustained, and approached colleagues' work in the same manner. I had read Peter Berger and Thomas Luckmann's (1966) book *The Social Construction of Reality*, which in its own way contributed to a change in analytic commitment.

I don't recall having had a grand conversion to an ethnographic view. If anything, I slowly eased into what initially was only a whiff of fieldwork, done for ancillary purposes. Several weeks into this preliminary period, I remember Filstead stopping me just as I finished making the rounds of several residents' rooms with an aide I'd befriended. He asked how things were going and whether what I was finding was useful to me. He was a wonderfully curious and insightful man, eager to learn and open to a variety of perspectives. I had his full confidence and felt comfortable talking with him about my work. Not everything we shared bore directly on the Manor. He knew and appreciated that I was interested in the quality of life of elderly persons in general. We did talk about everyday life for residents, however, and what the quality of care meant from their point of view. I didn't know at the time that this was a nascent constructionist concern, one that eventually would ratchet upward conceptually into a project on the social organization of meaning in nursing homes.

Filstead encouraged me to become comfortable with the residents and staff members, and to nonjudgmentally seek to understand how they respectively fit into the scheme of things on the premises. (Neither of us knew it, but his use of the term "fit" was closer to my later sense of it than the person-environment fit model designated.) He reminded me that the transition to nursing home living was a challenge to most residents, but effectively working with them was a challenge to staff members as well. He kept noting that I mustn't forget that everyone, both the residents and the staff, were up against issues of quality care. Unknowingly, he was pointing me to the social context of quality, most especially to the institution in which all concerned were being brought together in different ways in this regard.

I started to think about institutional life, returned to earlier interests in local cultures, and continued to read related gerontological literature. Increasingly telling was how often I was saying to myself and to anyone who was curious about what I was doing, "that's not how it works" and "it's really more complicated than that." This loomed in importance as I thought about how perspective and social organization figured in matters of caregiving and the quality of life. I thought this way especially when stereotypic explanations were forthcoming, which were often individually focused. Bad care, for example, was commonly construed as a matter of bad care workers. I also realized that the model that had informed my gerontological research to date—person-environment fit—was too simple to capture what it means for anything to fit with anything else in various circumstances. Time and again, I noticed that the connotation of fitting itself was influenced by diverse sentiments and subject to negotiation in practice.

I started to realize that the "bad worker" couldn't be figured in relation to fixed criteria. Just as the "good worker" did, bad and good shifted in meaning depending on one's point of view. For example, if for some the bad worker was inefficient and didn't conform to established care regimens, the same characteristics could signal good work to a resident, say, who wanted a familiar face to "stay and visit for a spell." These were initially anecdotal noticings and only became analytically pertinent later as the fieldwork unfolded and the organizational dimensions of the quality of care grew in importance.

Then there was the matter of grant support; this, too, influenced my turn to ethnography. Preliminary discussions with funding agents were discouraging. Standard survey methodology was de rigueur in those days, especially for sociologists. My explanations about the complex and fluid meanings of the quality of life pretty much fell on deaf ears, or ears that acknowledged the issues but were uncertain whether such research was fundable. What broke the camel's back in this regard and pushed me over the edge was the sarcastic remark of one funding agent with whom I was acquainted. Following a rather tiresome conversation, he blurted, "No one's going to pay you, Jay, for just hanging around a nursing home."

It was clear that I wouldn't be funded for undertaking what I was increasingly comfortable doing and enthusiastic about, for seriously putting into place what I would eventually call an "everyday life" perspective in my observations. Summer was approaching and I was looking forward to the free time it would offer for research. In a moment of inspiration—which the combination of challenges I've just described certainly encouraged—I happened by Filstead's office and asked whether he'd be interested in my doing an ethnographic study of the Manor. I explained, "Kind of study it like a small society and write a book about it." I pointed out that no one had done such a study before. I felt confident that the results would help set the record straight about the complex world of the nursing home.

He was immediately receptive to the idea and asked me to come in and talk about it. I was quite open with my thoughts and intentions. What I proposed certainly wouldn't be an exposé, but serious research of the kind our continuing conversations implied was needed. I mentioned that everything I wrote about the Manor would be anonymous and that, in that sense, the Manor and its people wouldn't get credit for what was produced. At the same time, in as much as the social organization of the Manor reflected the organization of everyday life and work in similar facilities, an ethnography of the Manor would be a contribution to general knowledge about residential care. I recall him saying something like "My blessings, Jay. Full-speed ahead and all the best in this endeavor."

Shifting gears

It was time to shift gears on two fronts. One was a shift in the way I was keeping track of my observations. Initially, I was pretty haphazard about this, because I figured that what I was learning was not data as such, but in support of the data I would collect. Whatever was written down about what I learned, it certainly wasn't thought of as fieldnotes. If anything, it was a laundry list of things to take into account in formulating good interview questions. Now I needed to keep careful and systematic track of what I was viewing and hearing, as well as of my developing perspective. It was only then that I began to take proper fieldnotes, and refer to them in this way.

The early 1970s was still a time when fieldnotes took the form of written accounts in notebooks, which were completed later in the day after the researcher left the field. The current distinction between jottings, which are brief mnemonic notes written in the field, and full-blown fieldnotes, which are extended descriptions of the day's thoughts and events, was nonexistent (see Emerson *et al.* 1995). The representational issues that arose much later in social research, centered on the relationship between empirical matters, jottings, fieldnotes, and ethnographic writing, were yet to be raised (see Clifford and Marcus 1986). Mostly, like other ethnographic fieldworkers, I took fieldnotes to be an experience-near means of collecting the empirical material I would use to present my findings. I hardly reflected on them, their precursors, or what followed in any way other than to assume that the better notes I had, the more valid and compelling my presentations and publications would be.

This accompanied another, more analytic shift. Pen in hand, paper at the ready, typewriter available when I returned home, were not enough. I saw and heard many things as I wandered Manor hallways, sat in rooms and chatted with residents, shadowed nurses and aides on their rounds, visited in lounges and ate with residents in the dining room, interacted with families, and participated in staff meetings called "patient care conferences." What was it about all of these things I should record in my jottings and later elaborate upon in fieldnotes? What was significant about them? What wasn't significant and needn't be viewed as empirically relevant? I was facing one of the most important problems any observational researcher encounters as he or she settles into the field. That is the problem of needing a framework to give direction to one's observations and notetaking, and to provide a way of understanding results.

It's one thing to be in the thick of things and be able to hear different voices and observe interaction as it unfolds; it's quite another to have some basis for sorting what is significant from what is not. Was extended time spent by an aide in a resident's room a form of malingering and work inefficiency? Or was it an informal sign of the quality of care? Was how I heard staff members describe residents in patient care conferences a matter of being more or less accurate about caregiving? Or did what staff members say relate as much to their accountability to superiors, families, other agencies, and the public at large? The meaning of what I was observing and hearing up-close wasn't obvious, even while I was a direct witness to everything. I needed analytic guidance, some way of determining what was and what wasn't important in the scheme of things.

After several weeks of taking voluminous fieldnotes without direction, the analytic shift I needed came when I started to concertedly consider that matters such as quality, life, and care had distinctive terms of reference and practical sensibilities from the points of view of those concerned. To move from seeing things "from their points of view" as being a matter of rapport and preliminary to asking locally relevant questions, to conceiving viewpoints as having separate social bearings, was a leap in analytic imagination. It was exactly what I was looking for. It was a way of moving beyond empathetic observation to conceptual understanding.

A new analytic framework

The new analytic framework took shape as I started to take notice of, and to take fieldnotes about, the particular words and associated meanings that various groups used to refer to matters of quality in life and care. I couldn't altogether leave my initial terms of reference behind, because I needed them in order to relate to an informing literature and to research colleagues. But I did start to catalog the ordinary connotations of quality and their accompanying points of reference. I became especially interested in the events and circumstances residents, staff members, and relatives referred to when they described and offered judgments about the quality of life and of care. This was now analytically important, not just window-dressing. I was fascinated that, at times, good care could be referenced in terms of how "sweet" an aide was because the aide bothered to ask about an enlisted son's framed photograph on a resident's bureau. To the resident, this could mean that the aide was taking a personal interest in her and wasn't just "running around with her head chopped off," as it was sometimes put.

While aides who spent time with residents instead of "running around with their heads chopped off" were appreciated by the residents, it was just as clear that it could make quite different sense to the aides and their supervisors. The aides weren't just caregivers, but also held jobs in a service organization. They were accountable not only to residents for the quality of their work, but simultaneously to the administrative staff who evaluated quality in their own terms, such as job completion. The floor staff not only offered care, but were paid to do so. In the context of work, the quality of care was as much a matter of time given over to assigned tasks, as it was a matter of caring for those in need of caregiving.

An important activity for the floor staff was keeping the premises neat and orderly and the residents clean. I coined a catchy term for this, calling it "bed-and-body work." It was a handy way of referring to what floor staff were up against in matters of quality care. If, to residents, "staying a spell" and otherwise being attuned to personal needs signaled good care, the nurses' and aides' bed-and-body work was equally at the forefront for them. Keeping bedding clean and odor-free, keeping beds made and the surroundings otherwise attractive, keeping residents' skins and clothing free of bodily wastes and their appearance attractive—these were important signs of good care for everyone. According to the administrative staff, families, and those residents who could care about it, follow-through on this front surely improved the quality of residential life.

But it wasn't so much these dimensions of care in their own right that differentiated staff, family, and residents' understandings. Rather, the working sense of for whom these were being accomplished was always in view. For example, when residents perceived bed-and-body work as being a matter of getting the work done as opposed to contributing to the quality of the residents' care, it was viewed negatively by residents. No set of quality criteria worked under all circumstances, because circumstances could shift the meaning of quality indicators when various points of view and purposes were taken into account.

Alternative senses of time were an important ingredient of such differences. Time for residents largely centered on passing time, which related to endless daily cycles of sleeping, waking, eating, walking, sitting, watching, visiting, and talking about the mundane happenings of residential life. Residents didn't so much keep time, which the staff certainly did, as their lives drifted along with the recurrent rhythms of life on the premises. Time wasn't so much kept, as it moved along, mostly unnoticed and ungauged. It was beholden to nothing other than itself—its passing paces. This contrasted sharply with staff's sense of time, which related to job descriptions, work shifts, and caregiving loads, among other dimensions of employment, all of which were noticeable and metered, sometimes excruciatingly.

In this context, when a resident asked an aide to "come sit for a spell," for the resident it referred to a very slow form of time, which was enjoyed and evaluated in terms of its simply passing along in the often silently attentive company of someone else. The aide who indulged this risked running out of the time organizationally allocated to her. To the resident, as time ran out for the staff member, it was easy for "sitting a spell" to leap into the perception of the staff member as "running around with your head chopped off." On the other hand, "running around" doing one's job could lapse into a staff member "sitting a spell," which risked drifting too far into the *world* of passing time. Simple as these ordinary expressions and related sentiments were, they grew in importance as I systematically took note of how they related to different perspectives on the quality of life and of care, which would otherwise seem to have similar ingredients to everyone. I emphasize the word "world" because, as I'll soon explain, the idea that the ordinary could be embedded in distinctively different social logics was just on the horizon for me.

Regular reviews of my fieldnotes and ongoing participant observation made it evident that it wasn't just the ingredients of care, work, and quality that I needed to document, but what meanings were being assigned to them and how these operated from varied points of view. Looking ahead at the time, I decided I needed to document how common terms of reference figured in practice in the scheme of things. Regularly looking ahead actually became a useful way of systematically pushing the analysis forward. As I moved along, I asked myself over and over what would I need to write an article or a book or to present to an interested audience that demonstrated the importance of meaning and circumstance as these related to common terms of reference? How did one's standpoint figure in discerning the quality of life and of care in a nursing home? How did social interaction and circumstances work to bring about different versions of the "same" things?

What I initially referred to as the "scheme of things" was a short step away from referring to the social organization of everyday life. Common terms of reference needed to be connected with what those using them were indicating and what the consequences for them were of reckoning things the way they did. What I was observing day-in and day-out in many telling circumstances was how much the application of different frames of reference and related purposes sorted the meaning of things in distinctive ways. I started to document how terms of reference in their varied social contexts took on their meanings, formed particular understandings, related to alternative interests, and spawned separate consequences.

At just about this time, an otherwise mundane incident combined with an emerging way of thinking to clarify my analytic framework. In most nursing homes, the day shift starts at 7am. It is the responsibility of night-shift staff, who leave at 7:30am or thereabouts, to begin waking up the residents, getting them out of bed, and ready for the day before they leave work and the day shift starts. Bed-and-body work features much of this, even while breakfasting and the distribution of medications are part of the process. On one occasion, a resident who was returning from breakfast, stopped by the nurses' station to chat with me and said that she was really tired that morning, she hadn't slept well, and just wanted to take a "cozy nap" in her room.

I knew that the staff on the floor was shorthanded that day, which wasn't especially unusual at the Manor, nor for that matter in most nursing homes. The resident's bed had been made for the day, or so it was assumed by the aide assigned to the resident's room. When the aide later discovered that the resident was sleeping not on, but in, the bed, with the covers in disarray, it caused quite a stir. The aide complained that she "didn't need this," because remaking the bed and tidying things up took time away from her other duties. To aides and overseeing charge nurses, made beds were sure signs of work completed, and of quality care. A distinctive moral order was in effect for the aide in the circumstances and was now casting her negatively.

Soon enough, another moral order informed the audibly annoyed resident who, according to the resident, had been "very rudely" thrown out of her room as a result. I recall the resident shouting at the nurses' station something like, "That's my room. That's my bed. And I have a right to sleep in it whenever I please. I pay a lot here and I'm going to report it!" A contrasting standard for the quality of care was at stake for the resident. She valued cleanliness and tidiness as much as anyone, but the circumstances had altered their meaning for her. If the moral order deployed by the aide and nursing staff was presented in the language of tidiness and work completed, it was now deployed by the resident in the language of rights and privacy.

Events such as this made visible the complex working meanings of common terms of reference. It seemed as if terms of reference for the quality of care and life were part of different social worlds, all operating within a single setting. Yes, Murray Manor was one nursing home. It was a discernible institution, had an organizational chart, and job descriptions. One could imagine that accountability within an organization would center on a more or less uniform set of standards or expectations. But endless, ethnographically witnessable events such as those that took place in the untidy room incident provided evidence for a contrasting view. Apparent contradictions in terms of usage and application in various situations seemed consistent and reasonable from their separate viewpoints, but inconsistent and at considerable odds from a uniform organizational perspective.

What finally capped the study and the ethnography analytically was the concept of "social worlds," which Anselm Strauss (1978) and his research associates were developing. I had started to informally use the term before that to highlight differences in everyday understanding, but it became the way I eventually would formally conceptualize living and dying at Murray Manor. Well into the fieldwork, I began to view the Manor as an organization that deployed distinctive social worlds. What was important in practice about the quality of care and of life was that these matters couldn't be understood separate from the moral orders of their respective social worlds. It wasn't this or that particular ingredient of quality that was important, so much as it was how social worlds and the circumstances of everyday life related to it.

These social worlds had distinct operating logics, their own senses of justice, and particular consequences for those concerned. The title of science fiction writers Philip Gordon Wylie and Edwin Balmer's book *When Worlds Collide* helped me to understand conflict and contention between social worlds as they operated in the setting. As long as the Manor's indigenous social worlds were separate and didn't collide, there was relative peace on the premises. When social worlds collided, as they did in the untidy room incident, issues of the quality of care and of life came to a head, boldly exposing the seen but unnoticed social organization of the nursing home. It is something a survey with its uniform coding practices could never reveal and that interviews, as open-ended as they might be, could only hint at.

I don't mean to suggest that there is no room for improvement in the quality of care as a result, but only that social worlds need to be taken into account in quality improvement decisions. Surely, being kept personally clean, the premises odor-free, and otherwise tidy and attractive are valued by everyone. Any survey would reveal as much. At the same time, the competing demands and definitions of various social worlds come into play as interpretive challenges. Orientations to uniform meaning, such as approaching quality in terms of formal standards, don't take social worlds into account and risk becoming undone in the everyday scheme of things.

Conclusion

Analytically, the Murray Manor project was a long road traveled. It was an amazingly enriching research experience, as it turned my attention to the dead ends that come with preconceived and uniformly coded empirical material. My fieldwork opened to view varied possibilities for the meaning of the matters with which I was concerned. I'm glad that I took the opportunity to think differently, because it launched my career as an ethnographer and as a constructionist. In time, *Living and Dying at Murray Manor* became part of the literature supporting the venerable view that experience can be put together in many ways and that researchers might very well try to examine how these operate and relate to each other in order to understand the complex worlds of everyday life.

References

Berger, P.L. and Thomas L. (1966) *The Social Construction of Reality*, Garden City, NY: Doubleday.

Clifford, J. and Marcus, G.E. (1986) *Writing Culture: the poetics and politics of ethnography*. Berkeley: University of California Press.

Emerson, R.M., Fretz R.L. and Shaw L.L. (1995) *Writing Ethnographic Fieldnotes*, Chicago: University of Chicago Press.

Gubrium, J.F. (1993) *Speaking of Life: horizons of meaning for nursing home residents*, New York: Aldine de Gruyter.

——([1975]1997) *Living and Dying at Murray Manor*, Charlottesville, VA: University of Virginia Press.

Gubrium, J.F. and Holstein, J.A. (1997) *The New Language of Qualitative Method*, New York: Oxford University Press.

Henderson, J.N. and Vesperi, M.D. (1995) *The Culture of Long Term Care: Nursing home ethnography*, Westport, CT: Bergin & Garvey.

Strauss, A.L. (1978) "A Social World Perspective," in N.K. Denzin (ed.) *Studies in Symbolic Interaction* (pp, 119–28), Greenwich, CT: JAI Press.

Whyte, W.F. (1943) *Street Corner Society*, Chicago: University of Chicago Press.

Part III

EXTENDING THEORETICAL FRAMES

8

HABITUS AS TOPIC AND TOOL
Reflections on becoming a prizefighter

Loïc Wacquant

In this essay, I recount how I took up the ethnographic craft; stumbled upon the Chicago boxing gym that is the main scene and character of my ethnography of prizefighting in the black American ghetto; and designed the book *Body and Soul* that reports on its findings so as to both deploy methodologically and elaborate empirically Pierre Bourdieu's signal concept of habitus (Wacquant 2004a). I draw out some of the biographical, intellectual and analytic connections between this research project on a plebeian bodily craft, the theoretical framework that informs it, and the macro-comparative inquiry into urban marginality of which it is an unplanned offshoot. I sketch how the practicalities of fieldwork led me from the ghetto as implement of ethnoracial domination to embodiment as a problem and resource for social inquiry. Through this reflection on becoming a prizefighter, I argue for the use of fieldwork as an instrument of theoretical construction, the potency of carnal knowledge, and the imperative of epistemic reflexivity, as well as stress the need to expand the textual genres and styles of ethnography so as to better capture the *Sturm und Drang* of social action as it is manufactured and lived.

The concept of habitus supplied at once the anchor, the compass, and the course of the ethnographic journey recapped in *Body and Soul*. It is the *topic* of investigation: the book dissects the forging of the corporeal and mental dispositions that make up the competent boxer in the crucible of the gym. But it is also the *tool* of investigation: the practical acquisition of those dispositions by the analyst serves as technical vehicle for better penetrating their social production and assembly. In other words, the apprenticeship of the sociologist is a methodological mirror of the apprenticeship undergone by the empirical subjects of the study; the former is mined to dig deeper into the latter and unearth its inner logic and subterranean properties; and both in turn test the robustness and fruitfulness of habitus as guide for probing the springs of social conduct. Contrary to a commonly held view that it is a vague notion that mechanically replicates social structures, effaces history, and operates as a "black box" that obviates observation and confounds explanation (see Jenkins 1991 for a standard regurgitation of these nostrums), it emerges that Bourdieu's sociological reworking of this classic philosophical concept is a powerful tool to steer social inquiry and trace out operant social mechanisms. Properly used, habitus not only illuminates the variegated logics of social action; it also grounds the distinctive virtues of deep immersion in and carnal entanglement with the object of ethnographic inquiry.

From the South Pacific to the South Side of Chicago

Since the notion of habitus proposes that human agents are historical animals who carry within their bodies acquired sensibilities and categories that are the sedimented products of their past social experiences, it is useful to begin with how I came to ethnographic research and what intellectual interests and expectations I brought with me to the South Side of Chicago. My initiation to fieldwork predates my entry in graduate school at the University of Chicago in 1985. To fulfill my military duties (as every French male had to do back then), by a stroke of luck, I was assigned to do a civilian service in the South Pacific as a sociologist in a research center of ORSTOM, France's former "office of colonial research." So I spent two years in New Caledonia, a French island northeast of New Zealand, in a small research team—there were only three of us—at the time of the Kanak uprising of November 1984. This means that I lived and worked in a very brutal and archaic colonial society, because New Caledonia in the 1980s was a colony of the nineteenth-century type that had survived virtually intact to the end of the twentieth century (see Bensa 1995 for an account). It was an extraordinary social experience for an apprentice sociologist to carry out research on the school system, urbanization, and social change in the context of an insurrection, under a state of emergency, and to observe in real time the struggles between the colonials and the independence forces, and to have to reflect in a concrete way about the civic role of social science. For instance, I was privileged to participate in a closed congress of the Kanak Socialist National Liberation Front in Canala at the height of the clash, and I also traveled all the way around the "Grande Terre" (the main island) and made several sojourns in Lifou island at the home of friends who were long-time Kanak militants at a time when practically no one was moving about in the territory.

The New Caledonian crucible sensitized me to ethnoracial inequality and to spatial consignment as a vector of social control—the Kanaks were largely relegated to isolated rural reservations and hypersegregated neighborhoods in the capital city of Nouméa. It also alerted me to the variegated workings of rigid hierarchies of color and honor in everyday life and to the crucial place of the body as a target, receptacle, and fount of asymmetric power relations. And it exposed me to extreme forms of deprecative racial imagery: the native Melanesians were typically pictured as "super-primitives" devoid of culture and history, even as they were rising to seize their historical fate

(Bourdieu and Bensa 1985). All of this would prove immensely useful later, on the South Side of Chicago, where germane treatments of African Americans were current. It is in New Caledonia that I read the classics of ethnology, Mauss, Mead, Malinowski, Radcliffe-Brown, Bateson, etc. (especially works on the South Pacific: the Trobriand Islands were just nearby) and that I kept my first field notebooks. The very first was scribbled among the tribe of Luecilla, in the Bay of Wé, at Christmas of 1983, about a year before the independentist uprising (its highlight was a section on going bat-hunting and having to eat the roasted proceeds of our expedition at dinner that evening). Field notations found their way into my first publications on educational inequality, colonial conflict, and the transformation of Melanesian communities under the press of capitalist expansion and French rule.

At the close of my Caledonian sojourn, I got a four-year fellowship to go do my doctorate at the University of Chicago, the cradle of U.S. sociology and home of the main tradition of urban ethnography. When I arrived in Upton Sinclair's town, my intention was to work on a historical anthropology of colonial domination in New Caledonia, but I got unexpectedly derailed and detoured into America's dark ghetto. On the one side, the New Caledonian gates were abruptly shut after I filed a complaint against the mediocre bureaucrat who was my supervisor in Nouméa and had forced his name as co-author of a monograph on the school system that I had carried out by myself (Wacquant 1985). The directors of the Institute in Paris hastened to cover up for the cheater and effectively banned me from the island. On the other side, I found myself confronted day-to-day with the gruesome reality of Chicago's ghetto, or what was left of it. I was assigned the last student-housing unit available on campus, the one nobody had wanted, and so lived on 61st Street, at the edge of the poor black district of Woodlaw. It was a constant tremor and puzzlement to have right under my window this quasi-lunar urban landscape, with its unbelievable decay, misery, and violence, backed by a totally hermetic separation between the white, prosperous and privileged world of the university and the abandoned African-American neighborhoods all around it. Coming from Western Europe. where such levels of urban blight, material destitution and ethnic segregation are unknown, this challenged me profoundly on a quotidian level, intellectually and politically. It is at this point that the second decisive encounter of my intellectual life took place, the one with William Julius Wilson (the first was with Pierre Bourdieu, five years earlier, when I decided to convert from economics to sociology after hearing a public lecture by him, see Wacquant 2002a).

Wilson is the most eminent African-American sociologist of the second half of the twentieth century and the foremost expert on the nexus of race and class in the United States—his analysis of "Blacks and American Institutions" in *The Declining Significance of Race* (Wilson 1978) set the parameters for that subfield of social research in 1978. He was one of the faculty who had initially attracted me to Chicago, and so when he asked me to work with him on the big research project on urban poverty he had just started (roughly, the agenda marked out by his book *The Truly Disadvantaged*, Wilson 1987), I jumped at the chance, and I quickly became his close collaborator and co-author. This afforded me the opportunity to get straight to the core of the subject and also to get a close-up look at how this scientific and policy debate operated at the highest level, especially in the philanthropic foundations and think tanks that shaped the resurgence of the problematic of race, class and poverty in the inner city. That is how I started my investigations, first as an acolyte of Wilson and then by myself, on the transformation of the dark ghetto after the riots of the 1960s, by striving to break with the pathologizing vision that pervaded and distorted research on the question.

I owe a huge personal and intellectual debt to Bill Wilson, who was a mentor at once demanding and generous: he stimulated and supported me, and he also gave me the freedom to diverge from his analyses, and at times to go in a direction diametrically opposed to his. By example, he taught me intellectual courage: to pursue the big picture, to dig deep into the details, to ask the hard questions, even when this entails ruffling a few social and academic feathers along the way. He also invited Pierre Bourdieu to speak to his research team on his Algerian research on urbanization and proletarianization from the early 1960s (Bourdieu et al. 1963). As it turns out, Bourdieu had tried to get *The Declining Significance of Race* translated into French a few years earlier. This meeting and the ensuing discussion solidified my sense that I could make a link between Bourdieu's early anthropological inquiries into the lifepaths of Algerian sub-proletarians and the contemporary predicament of the residents of Chicago's black ghetto which preoccupied Wilson. But I did not know just how yet.

Ethnography played a pivotal role at that juncture, on two counts. On the one hand, I took more anthropology than sociology courses because the sociology department at the University of Chicago was very dull intellectually and because I was viscerally committed to a unitary conception of social science inherited from my French training. The courses, works, and encouragements of John and Jean Comaroff, Marshall Sahlins, Bernard Cohn and Raymond Smith pushed me toward fieldwork. On the other hand, I wanted to quickly find a direct observation post inside the ghetto because the existing literature on the topic was the product of a "gaze from afar" that seemed to me fundamentally biased if not blind (Wacquant 1997). That literature was dominated by the statistical approach, deployed from on high, by researchers who most often had no first-hand or even second-hand knowledge of what makes the ordinary reality of the dispossessed neighborhoods of the Black Belt, and who fill this gap with stereotypes drawn from common sense, journalistic or academic. I wanted to reconstruct the question of the ghetto from the ground up, based on a precise observation of the everyday activities and relations of the residents of that *terra non grata* and for this very reason, *incognita* (see Wacquant [1992] 1998a for an early effort).

I deemed it epistemologically and morally impossible to do research on the ghetto without gaining serious first-hand knowledge of it, because it was right there, literally at my doorstep (in the summertime, you could hear gunfire going off at night on the other side of the street), and because the established works seemed to me to be full of implausible or pernicious academic notions, starting with the scholarly myth of the "underclass" which was a veritable intellectual cottage industry in those years (see Katz 1993 and Gans 1995 for critical accounts and Wacquant 1996 for a conceptual dissection). As a white Frenchman, my formative social and intellectual experiences made me a complete foreigner to this milieu and intensified the need I felt to acquire some practical familiarity with it. After a few aborted attempts, by accident I found a boxing gym in Woodlawn, some three blocks from my apartment, and I signed up saying that I wanted to learn how to box, quite simply because there was nothing else to do in this context. In reality, I had absolutely no curiosity about or interest in the pugilistic world in itself (but I did want to get good exercise). The gym was to be just a platform for observation in the ghetto, a place to meet potential informants.

Habitus comes to the gym

But, very quickly, that gym turned out to be, not only a wonderful window into the daily life of young men in the neighborhood, but also a complex microcosm with a history, a culture, and a very intense and rich social, aesthetic, emotional, and moral life of its own. In a matter of months, I formed a very strong, carnal, bond with the regulars of the club and with the old coach, DeeDee Armour, who became a sort of adoptive father to me. Gradually I found myself attracted by the magnetism of the "Sweet Science" to the point where I spent most of my time in and around the gym. After about a year, the idea grew on me to dig into a second research subject, namely the social logic of a bodily craft. What is it that thrills boxers? Why do they commit themselves to this harshest and most destructive of all trades? How do they acquire the desire and the skills necessary to last in it? What is the role of the gym, the street, the surrounding violence and racial contempt, of self-interest and pleasure, and of the collective belief in personal transcendence in all this? How does one create a social competency that is an embodied competency, transmitted through a silent pedagogy of organisms in action? In short, how is the *pugilistic habitus* fabricated and deployed? That is how I found myself working on two connected projects simultaneously—two projects ostensibly very different from each other but in fact tightly linked: a carnal microsociology of the apprenticeship of boxing as sub-proletarian bodily craft *in the ghetto*, which offers a particular "slice" of this universe from below and from inside (Wacquant 2004a); and a historical and theoretical macrosociology *of the ghetto* as instrument of racial closure and social domination, providing a generalizing perspective from above and from the outside (Wacquant 2008).

141

I had started writing a field diary after every training session from my first afternoon at the gym, initially to overcome the overpowering sense of being out of place on the pugilistic scene on so many levels and not knowing really what I would do with these notes. Now I shifted to taking systematic notes and to exploring the various facets of the Sweet Science. The notion of habitus immediately came to me as a conceptual device to make sense of my personal experiences as a boxing apprentice and a scaffold to organize my ongoing observation of pugilistic pedagogy. I had read Bourdieu's anthropological works front to back during my Caledonia years. So I was fully familiar with his elaboration of the notion, intended to overcome the antinomy between an objectivism that reduces practice to the mechanical precipitate of structural necessities and a subjectivism that confuses the personal will and intentions of the agent with the spring of her action (Bourdieu [1980] 1990; see Wacquant 2004b for a genealogy and exegesis of the notion). The author of *Outline of a Theory of Practice* had retrieved habitus from a long line of philosophers, stretching from Aristotle to Aquinas to Husserl, to develop a dispositional theory of action recognizing that social agents are not passive beings pulled and pushed about by external forces, but skillful creatures who actively construct social reality through "categories of perception, appreciation and action." But, unlike phenomenology, Bourdieu insists that, while being resilient and shared, these categories are not universal (or transcendental, in the language of Kantian philosophy), and that the generative matrix they compose is not unchanging. Rather, as the embodied sediments of individual and collective history, they are themselves socially constructed.

> As the product of history, habitus produces individual and collective practices, and thus history, in accordance with the schemata engendered by history. It ensures the active presence of past experiences which, deposited in each organism in the form of schemata of thought and action, more surely than all formal rules and all explicit norms, to guarantee the conformity of practices and their constancy across time.
>
> (Bourdieu [1980] 1990: 54)

Four properties of the concept of habitus suggested its direct relevancy for disclosing the social making of prizefighters. First, habitus is a set of *acquired* dispositions, and no one is born a boxer (least of all, me!): the training of fighters consists precisely in physical drills, ascetic rules of life (concerning the management of food, time, emotions, and sexual desire), and social games geared toward instilling in them new abilities, categories, and desires, those specific to the pugilistic cosmos (Wacquant 1998b). Second, habitus holds that practical mastery operates *beneath the level of consciousness and discourse*, and this matches perfectly with a commanding feature of the experience of pugilistic learning, in which mental understanding is of little help (and can even be a serious hindrance in the ring) so long as one has not grasped boxing technique with one's body (Wacquant 1995a). Third, habitus indicates that sets of dispositions *vary by social location and trajectory*: individuals with different life experiences will have gained varied ways of thinking, feeling, and acting; their primary dispositions will be more or less distant from those required by the Sweet Science; and thus they will more or less be invested in and adept at picking up the craft. This certainly accorded with my personal experience and notations on the disparate behaviors of my gym mates over time, as they tangled with the competing lure of the street and the gym, adapted to the authority of our coach, and sought to remake their self in accordance to the exacting demands of the trade. Fourth, the socially constituted conative and cognitive structures that make up habitus are malleable and transmissible because they result from *pedagogical work*. If you want to pry into habitus, then study the organized *practices of inculcation* through which it is layered (Wacquant 1995b).

The "magical moment" of fieldwork that crystallized this theoretical hunch and turned what was initially a side activity into a full blown inquiry into the social logics of incarnation, was a rather inglorious one: it was getting my nose broken in sparring in May of 1989, about nine months into my novitiate. This injury forced me to take a long "time out" away from the ring, during which Bourdieu urged me to write a field report on my initiation for a thematic issue of *Actes de la recherche en sciences sociales* in preparation on "The Space of Sports." The result was a long article that showed me that it was both feasible and fruitful to convert the theory of action encapsulated by the notion of habitus into an empirical experiment on the practical production of prizefighters at the Woodlawn gym (Wacquant 1989; 2002a). This article was soon augmented by more direct engagement with habitus on the theoretical front.

While I was carrying out my investigations on boxing and on the ghetto, I was in permanent contact with Pierre Bourdieu, who encouraged and guided me. Upon learning that I had signed up to learn how to box at the Woodlawn Boys Club, he had written me a note that said essentially, "Stick it out, you will learn more about the ghetto in this gym than you can from all the surveys in the world." (Later on, as I got deeper into my immersion, he got a bit scared and tried to get me to pull back. When I signed up to fight in the Chicago Golden Gloves, he first threatened to disown me as he feared that I would get hurt, before realizing that there was no need to panic: I was well prepared for this trial by fire.) Bourdieu came to Chicago several times, visited the gym, and met DeeDee and my boxer friends (I introduced him to them as "the Mike Tyson of sociology"). During one of these visits, we hatched the project of a book that would explicate the theoretical core of his work, aimed at the Anglo-American readership, since it was on this front that there were the strongest distortions and obstacles to a fertile grasp of his

143

models. We devoted three years to writing this book across the Atlantic (by fax, phone, letters and meetings every few months), entitled *An Invitation to Reflexive Sociology* (Bourdieu and Wacquant 1992), in which we disentangle the nexus of habitus, capital, and field. During those years, I led a sort of Jekyll-and-Hyde existence, boxing by day and writing social theory by night. In the afternoon, I would go to the gym, train, hang out with my buddies, and "conversate" on end with our coach DeeDee before driving him home at closing time. And, later that evening, after having typed my fieldnotes, I would turn to the book manuscript with Bourdieu. It was in turns intoxicating, invigorating, and exhausting. But the daytime sessions as a student of pugilism offered both a respite from theoretical cogitation and powerful stimuli for thinking through the abstract issues tackled in the book in very mundane empirical terms. The sociology of the ghetto (which I had extended to encompass a comparison with the postindustrial transformation of the French urban periphery), the carnal ethnography of the skilled body, and theoretical work with Bourdieu: all of these strands were elaborated together and at the same time, and they are all woven together.

The boxing project is an ethnography in a very classic mold in terms of its parameters, a sort of village study like the ones British anthropologists conducted in the 1940s, except that my village is the boxing gym and its extensions, and my tribe the fighters and their entourage. I retained this structural and functional unity because it encloses the boxers and carves out a specific temporal, relational, mental, emotional and aesthetic horizon which sets the pugilist apart, pushes him to "heroize" his lifeworld, and thereby raises him above his ordinary environs (Wacquant 1995c). I wanted, first of all, to dissect the cloven relation of "symbiotic opposition" between the ghetto and the gym, the street and the ring. Next, I wanted to show how the social and symbolic structure of the gym governs the transmission of the techniques of the "Manly Art" and the production of collective belief in the pugilistic *illusio*. And, finally, I wished to penetrate the practical logic of a corporeal practice that operates at the very limits of practice by means of a long-term apprenticeship in "the first person." For three years, I melted into the local landscape and got caught up in the game. I learned how to box and participated in all phases of the preparation of the pugilist, all the way to fighting in the big amateur tournament of the Golden Gloves. I followed my gym buddies in their personal and professional peregrinations. And I dealt on a routine basis with trainers, managers, promoters, etc., who make the planet of boxing turn and share in the spoils of this "show-business with blood" (Wacquant 1998c). In so doing, I was sucked into the sensuous and moral coils of pugilism, to the point where I seriously envisaged interrupting my academic trajectory to turn professional.

But, as the foregoing should have made clear, the object and method of this inquiry were not of the classic mold. *Body and Soul* offers an *empirical and methodological radicalization of Bourdieu's theory of habitus*. On the one hand, I open the "black box" of the pugilistic habitus by disclosing the production and assembly of the cognitive categories, bodily skills and desires which together define the competence and appetence specific to the boxer. On the other hand, I deploy habitus as a methodological device, that is, I place myself in the local vortex of action in order to acquire through practice, in real time, the dispositions of the boxer with the aim of elucidating the magnetism proper to the pugilistic cosmos. This allows me to disclose the powerful allure of the combination of craft, sensuality, and morality that binds the pugilist to his trade as well as impresses the embodied notions of risk and redemption that enable him to overcome the turbid sense of being superexploited (Wacquant 2001). The method thus tests the theory of action which informs the analysis according to a recursive and reflexive research design.

The idea that guided me here was to push the logic of participant observation to the point where it becomes inverted and turns into *observant participation*. In the Anglo-American tradition, when anthropology students first go into the field, they are cautioned, "Don't go native." In the French tradition, radical immersion is admissible—think of Jeanne Favret-Saada's ([1978] 1980) *Deadly Words*—but only on condition that it be coupled with a subjectivist epistemology which gets us lost in the inner depths of the anthropologist-subject. My position, on the contrary, is to say, "go native, but *go native armed*," that is, equipped with your theoretical and methodological tools, with the full store of problematics inherited from your discipline, with your capacity for reflexivity and analysis, and guided by a constant effort, once you have passed the ordeal of initiation, *to objectivize this experience and construct the object*, instead of allowing yourself to be naively embraced and constructed by it. Go ahead, go native, but come back a sociologist! In my case, the concept of habitus served both as a bridge to enter into the factory of pugilistic know-how and methodically parse the texture of the work(ing) world of the pugilist, and as a shield against the lure of the subjectivist rollover of social analysis into narcissistic story-telling.

From flesh to text

Some of my critics, conflating the narrative form of the book with its analytic contents and mistaking my work for an extension of the "study of occupations" in the style of the second Chicago School (Hughes 1994), did not even notice the double role which the concept of habitus played in the inquiry and even complained about the absence of theory in the book (Wacquant 2005b). In fact, theory and method are joined to the point of fusion in the very empirical object whose elaboration they make possible.

Body and Soul is an *experimental ethnography* in the originary meaning of the term, in that the researcher is one of the socialized bodies thrown into the sociomoral and sensuous alembic of the boxing gym, one of bodies-in-action whose transmutation will be traced to penetrate the alchemy by which boxers are fabricated. Apprenticeship is here the means of acquiring a practical mastery, a visceral knowledge of the universe under scrutiny, a way of elucidating the praxeology of the agents under examination, as recommended by Erving Goffman (1989) in a famous talk on fieldwork—and not the means of entering into the subjectivity of the researcher. It is absolutely not a fall into the bottomless well of subjectivism into which "auto-ethnography" joyfully throws itself (Reed-Danahay 1997), quite the opposite: it relies on the most intimate experience, that of the desiring and suffering body, to grasp *in vivo* the collective manufacturing of the schemata of pugilistic perception, appreciation, and action that are shared, to varying degrees, by all boxers, whatever their origins, their trajectory, and their standing in the sporting hierarchy (Wacquant 2005a). The central character of the story is neither "Busy" Louie, nor this or that boxer, and not even DeeDee the old coach, in spite of his central position as conductor: it is the gym as a social and moral forge.

Indeed, I hold that, with this project, I did in an explicit, methodical, and above all *extreme* manner that which every good ethnographer does, namely, to give herself a practical, tactile, sensorial grasp of the prosaic reality she studies in order to shed light on the categories and relations that organize the ordinary conduct and sentiments of her subjects. Except that, usually, this is done without talking about it or without thematizing the role of "co-presence" with the phenomenon being studied, or by making (herself and others) believe that this is a mental process, and not a bodily and sensual apprenticeship which proceeds beneath the level of consciousness before it becomes mediated by language. *Body and Soul* offers a demonstration in action of the distinctive possibilities and virtues of a *carnal sociology* which fully recounts the fact that the social agent is a suffering animal, a being of flesh and blood, nerves and viscera, inhabited by passions and endowed with embodied knowledges and skills—by opposition to the *animal symbolicum* of the neo-Kantian tradition, refurbished by Clifford Geertz (1973) and the followers of interpretive anthropology, on the one hand, and by Herbert Blumer (1969) and the symbolic interactionists, on the other—and that *this is just as true of the sociologist*. This implies that we must bring the body of the sociologist back into play and treat her intelligent organism, not as an obstacle to understanding, as the intellectualism drilled into our folk conception of intellectual practice would have it, but as a vector of knowledge of the social world.

Body and Soul is not an exercise in reflexive anthropology in the sense intended by what is called "poststructuralist" or "postmodern" anthropology, for which the return of the analytic gaze is directed either on to the knowing subject in her personal intimacy or on to the text that she delivers to her peers and the circuits of power-knowledge in which it travels, in a contradictory and self-destructive embrace of relativism (Hastrup 1995; Marcus

1998). Those forms of reflexivity, narcissistic and discursive, are rather super-ficial; they certainly constitute a useful moment in a research undertaking by helping to curb the play of the crudest biases (rooted in one's identity and trajectory, affects, rhetorical effects, etc.). But they stop the movement of critique at the very point where it should start, through the constant questioning of the categories and techniques of sociological analysis and of the relationship to the world these presuppose. It is this return to the *instruments of construction of the object*, as opposed to the subject of objectivation, which is the hallmark of what one may call *epistemic reflexivity* (Bourdieu and Wacquant 1992: 36–46; Bourdieu 2002). And here is another difference with the "egological" or textual reflexivity of the subjectivist anthropologists: epistemic reflexivity is deployed, not at the end of the project, *ex post*, when it comes to drafting the final research report, but *durante*, at every stage in the investigation. It targets the totality of the most routine research operations, from the selection of the site and the recruitment of informants to the choice of questions to pose or to avoid, as well as the engagement of theoretic schemata, methodological tools and display techniques, at the moment when they are implemented.

So *Body and Soul* is a reflexive book in the sense that the very design of the inquiry forced me to constantly reflect on the suitability of the means of investigation to its ends, on the difference between the practical mastery and the theoretical mastery of a practice, on the gap between sensorial infatuation and analytic comprehension, on the hiatus between the visceral and the mental, the *ethos* and the *logos* of pugilism as well as of sociology. Likewise, *Urban Outcasts* (Wacquant 2008), the companion book of macrosociology which draws up the comparison of the structure and experience of urban relegation in the Black American ghetto and the French urban periphery, is a work of reflexive urban sociology because it ceaselessly interrogates the very categories it puts into question and into play—"underclass," "inner city," "banlieues," hyperghetto, anti-ghetto, precariat—to think the novel configurations of marginality in the city. And because it rests on a clear-cut demarcation between folk categories and analytic categories, which is for me the plinth of reflexivity.

Epistemic reflexivity is all the more urgently needed by ethnographers as everything conspires to invite them to submit to the preconstructions of common sense, lay or scholarly. By methodological duty, they must be attentive to the agents they study and take seriously their "point of view." If they do their job well, they also find themselves bound to these agents by affective ties that encourage identification and transference (for an astute analysis of the methodological use of transference in *Body and Soul*, see Manning 2005). Finally, the public image of ethnography (including, regrettably, in the eyes of other social scientists) likens it to story-telling, diary-writing, if not to epic. So much to say that the anthropologist or sociologist who relies on fieldwork must *double the dose of reflexivity*. This is what I tried to demonstrate in "Scrutinizing the Street" about recent trends and foibles in U.S. urban ethnography (Wacquant 2002b). The considered target of my critique is not the three books on race and urban poverty that I subject to a meticulous analytic dissection (and still less their authors, who are here simply points in academic space, or their political positions, to which I am completely indifferent), but a certain epistemological posture of unreflective surrender to folk apperceptions, to ordinary moralism, to the seductions of official thought and to the rules of academic decorum. This posture is the fount of serious scientific errors, as these errors are systematic and have both ordinary and scholarly common sense on their side.

To enable the reader to experience the thrills of the apprentice boxer and make palpable both the logic of the fieldwork and its end-product required adopting a quasi-theatrical mode of writing. How to go from the guts to the intellect, from the comprehension of the flesh to the knowledge of the text? Here is a real problem of concrete epistemology about which we have not sufficiently reflected, and which for a long time seemed to me nearly irresolvable (notwithstanding the varied attempts at and discussions of formal innovation and poetic construction among anthropologists). To restitute the carnal dimension of ordinary existence and the bodily anchoring of the practical knowledge constitutive of pugilism—but also of every practice, even the least "bodily" in appearance, including sociological analysis—requires indeed a complete overhaul of our way of writing social science. In the case at hand, I had to find a style breaking with the monological, monochromatic, linear writing of the classic research account from which the ethnographer has withdrawn and elaborate a multifaceted writing that mixed styles and genres, so as to capture and convey "the taste and ache of action" to the reader (Wacquant 2004a: vii–xii).

Body and Soul is written against subjectivism, against the narcissism and irrationalism that undergird so-called "postmodern" literary theory, but that does not mean that we should for that deprive ourselves of the literary techniques and instruments of dramatic exposition that this tradition gives us. That is why the book mixes three types of writing, intertwined with each other, but each given priority in one of the three parts, so that the reader slides smoothly from concept to percept, from analysis to experience. The first part anchors a classic sociological style in an analytic mold that identifies at the outset structures and mechanisms so as to give the reader the tools necessary for explaining and understanding of what is going on. The tone of the second part is set by ethnographic writing in the strict sense, that is, a dense depiction of the ways of being, thinking, feeling, and acting proper to the milieu under consideration, where one encounters again these mechanisms but in action, through the effects they produce. The experiential moment comes in the third part, in the form of "sociological novella" that delivers felt action, the lived experience of a subject who also happens to be the analyst.

The weighed combination of these three modalities of writing—the sociological, the ethnographic, and the literary—according to proportions that become gradually inverted as the book progresses, aims to enable the reader to feel emotionally and understand rationally the springs and turns of pugilistic action. For this, the text weaves together an analytic lattice, stretches of closely edited fieldnotes, counterpoints composed by portraits of key protagonists and excerpts from interviews, as well as photographs whose role is to foster a synthetic grasp of the dynamic interplay of the factors and forms inventoried in the analysis, to give the reader a chance to "touch with her own eyes" the beating pulse of pugilism. Here again, everything hangs together: the theory of habitus, the use of apprenticeship as technique of investigation, the place accorded to the sentient body as vector of knowledge, and formal innovation in writing. Indeed, there is no point in carrying out a carnal sociology backed by practical initiation if what it reveals about the sensorimotor magnetism of the universe in question ends up disappearing later in the writing, on the pretext that one must abide by the textual canons dictated by Humean positivism or neo-Kantian cognitivism.

Many social researchers view theory as a set of abstract notions that either float high up in the pure sky of ideas, disconnected from the nitty-gritty of the conduct of inquiry, or constitute responses to the empirical questions that the latter raises, to be discovered in the real world, as in the approach labeled "grounded theory." This is a misconstrual of the relationship of theory and research, and ethnography in particular. Whether the investigator is aware of it or not, theory is always driving field inquiry because, as Gaston Bachelard (1971) taught us, "the vector of knowledge goes from the rational to the real," and not the other way around. And it must of necessity engage observation in order to convert itself into propositions about an empirically existing entity. This applies to habitus, which, like every concept, is not an answer to a research question but an organized manner of asking questions about the social world—in the case recounted here, a methodical plan to vivisect the social fabrication of pugilists in their workaday environment.

References

Bachelard, G. (1971) *Epistémologie*, Paris: Presses Universitaires de France.
Bensa, A. (1995) *Chroniques Kanak. L'ethnologie en marche*, Paris: Ethnies.
Blumer, H. (1969) *Symbolic Interaction*, Englewood Cliffs, NJ: Prentice-Hall.
Bourdieu, P. ([1980] 1990) *The Logic of Practice*, Cambridge: Polity Press.
——(2002) "Participant Objectivation: the Huxley Medal lecture," *Journal of the Royal Anthropological Institute*, 9: 281–94.
Bourdieu, P. and Bensa, A. (1985) "Quand les Canaques prennent la parole," *Actes de la recherche en sciences sociales*, 56: 69–85.
Bourdieu, P., Darbel, A., Rivet, J., and Seibel, C. (1963) *Travail et travailleurs en Algérie*, Paris and The Hague: Mouton.

LOÏC WACQUANT

Bourdieu, P. and Wacquant, L. (1992) *An Invitation to Reflexive Sociology*, Chicago: University of Chicago Press and Cambridge: Polity Press.

Favret-Saada, J. ([1978] 1980) *Deadly Words: witchcraft in the bocage*, Cambridge: Cambridge University Press.

Gans, H. (1995) *The War Against the Poor*, New York: Pantheon.

Geertz, C. (1973) *The Interpretation of Cultures*, New York: Basic Books.

Goffman, E. (1989) "On Fieldwork," *Journal of Contemporary Ethnography*, 18: 123–32.

Hastrup, K. (1995) *A Passage to Anthropology: between experience and theory*, London: Routledge.

Hughes, E. C. (1994) *On Work, Race, and the Sociological Imagination*, ed. L. A. Coser, Chicago: University of Chicago Press.

Jenkins, R. (1991) *Pierre Bourdieu*, London: Routledge.

Katz, M. B. (ed.) (1993) *The "Underclass" Debate: views from history*, Princeton, NJ: Princeton University Press.

Manning, P. (2005) *Freud and American Sociology*, Cambridge: Polity Press.

Marcus, G. (1998) *Ethnography through Thick and Thin*, Princeton, NJ: Princeton University Press.

Reed-Danahay, D. (ed.) (1997) *Auto/Ethnography: rewriting the self and the social*, New York: Berg.

Wacquant, L. (1985) *L'École inégale. Éléments de sociologie de l'enseignement en Nouvelle-Calédonie*, Paris and Nouméa: Editions de l'ORSTOM with the Institut Culturel Mélanésien.

——(1989) "Corps et âme: notes ethnographiques d'un apprenti-boxeur," *Actes de la recherche en sciences sociales*, 80: 33–67.

——(1995a) "The Pugilistic Point of View: how boxers think and feel about their trade," *Theory and Society*, 24: 489–535.

——(1995b) "Pugs at Work: bodily capital and bodily labor among professional boxers," *Body and Society*, 1: 65–94.

——(1995c) "Protection, discipline et honneur: une salle de boxe dans le ghetto américain," *Sociologie et sociétés*, 27: 75–89.

——(1996) "L''underclass' urbaine dans l'imaginaire social et scientifique américain," in S. Paugam (ed.) *L'Exclusion: l'état des savoirs* (pp. 248–62), Paris: Editions La Découverte.

——(1997) "Three Pernicious Premises in the Study of the American Ghetto," *International Journal of Urban and Regional Research*, 21, "Events and Debate": 341–53.

——([1992] 1998a) "Inside the Zone: the social art of the hustler in the black American ghetto," *Theory, Culture and Society*, 15: 1–36.

——(1998b) "The Prizefighter's Three Bodies," *Ethnos: Journal of Anthropology*, 63: 325–52.

——(1998c) "A Fleshpeddler at Work: power, pain, and profit in the prizefighting economy," *Theory and Society*, 27: 1–42.

——(2001) "Whores, Slaves, and Stallions: languages of exploitation and accommodation among professional fighters," *Body and Society*, special issue on "Commodifying Bodies," 7: 181–94.

——(2002a) "Taking Bourdieu into the Field," *Berkeley Journal of Sociology*, 46: 180–86.

——(2002b) "Scrutinizing the Street: poverty, morality, and the pitfalls of urban ethnography," *American Journal of Sociology*, 107: 1468–532.

——([2000] 2004a) *Body and Soul: notebooks of an apprentice boxer*, New York and Oxford: Oxford University Press.

——(2004b) "Habitus," in J. Beckert and Zafirovski, M. (eds.) *International Encyclopedia of Economic Sociology* (pp. 315–19), London: Routledge.

——(2005a) "Carnal Connections: on embodiment, membership and apprenticeship," *Qualitative Sociology*, 28: 445–71 (response to the special issue on "Body and Soul," 28, no. 3).

——(2005b) "Shadowboxing with Ethnographic Ghosts: a rejoinder," *Symbolic Interaction*, 28: 441–47 (response to the symposium on "Body and Soul").

——(2008) *Urban Outcasts: a comparative sociology of advanced marginality*, Cambridge: Polity Press.

Wilson, W. J. (1978) *The Declining Significance of Race: blacks and changing American institutions*, Chicago: University of Chicago Press.

——(1987) *The Truly Disadvantaged: the inner city, the underclass, and public policy*, Chicago: University of Chicago Press.

9

RESEARCHING ALCOHOLICS AND ALCOHOLISM IN AMERICAN SOCIETY

Norman K. Denzin

Introduction

This chapter revisits a nearly 30-year-old ethnographic project. Since 1981 I have been studying alcoholism in treatment centers across the country, and in Alcoholics Anonymous (AA). In this chapter I discuss the theoretical underpinnings of this project, and how they came to be. My argument unfolds in three parts. I begin with a discussion of the scientific literature on alcoholism, including scientific theories of alcoholism. I then take up my AA study, showing how it became a critique of this literature. This propelled me, via postmodern ethnography, toward a more holistic, emotional, and non-reductionist analysis of alcoholics and alcoholism in American society. I then discuss the generation of the key concepts that emerged through my research: AA and science, AA's theory of alcoholism, the AA group as an interactional site, and AA's modes of understanding. I show how AA provides the context for self-help groups to develop their own modes of social control and empowerment. I contrast, in this regard, science's theory of alcoholism and the alcoholic with AA's theory.

My research resulted in four publications: *The Alcoholic Self*; *The Recovering Alcoholic*; *Treating Alcoholism: An Alcoholic's Anonymous Approach*; and *The Acoholic Society: Addiction and Recovery of the Self* (Denzin 1987a; 1987b; 1987c; 1993). *Treating Alcoholism* was explicitly written for alcoholics, their families, and for alcoholism counselors. Hence, from the outset, these works have been identified with the AA approach, and antithetical to the behavioral view that dominates in this field. In *The Alcoholic Self* and *The Recovering Alcoholic* I developed a Foucault-like critique of positivism, behavior modification theories of treatment, and the institutional models of control that exist in modern alcoholism treatment centers. While grounding my text in the major findings of the research, I write through the lens of theory. A multi-voiced interpretive postmodern ethnography should take sides, examine lived experience, uncover the models of truth and discourse that operate in the research site, and privilege the languages of emotionality.

I examine the origins of AA's theory in medicine, science, religion, and pragmatic philosophy. I compare the structures of AA's "local knowledge" (Geertz 1983) of alcoholism, to the scientific discourse on treatment. I then suggest that a postmodern ethnography of the "alcoholism" experience in American society must deal with the structures of experience modern science has created. Such a work must also speak to the interactional experiences of alcoholics who recover through AA. Postmodern, interpretive ethnography (Denzin 1997; 2001; 2003) writes the interpretive theories of the oppressed, "diseased" subject that modern, emancipatory science has helped create (see Clifford and Marcus 1986; Turner and Bruner 1986; Geertz 1988). Hopefully such work will allow these subjects to gain greater control over their own lives.

Scientific theories of alcoholism

Upon beginning my study, there was already a burgeoning scientific literature that presented explanations for alcoholism. A common set of assumptions and biases organize the several theories that have been developed to account for alcoholism, including the psychoanalytic, the psychological, the sociological, the anthropological, the genetic, and the biological. This set of assumptions assumes that the mind and the body of the alcoholic can be objectively studied as a stonelike thing, independent of lived experience. It leads to investigations that measure the effects of alcohol intake on the body while they attempt to identify the objective symptoms that do or not define who an alcoholic is. This science orients itself to the phenomenon of alcoholism from a position that is normative, controlling, and rational.

These studies attempt to control the uses and abuses of alcohol in human society. They do so from a normative stance that regards drinking as normal and good, if properly controlled. Elsewhere (Denzin 1987a: 62), I have termed this the objective thesis of alcoholism, alcohol, and the alcoholic. This objectivist thesis suffers from a number of flaws. It is genderless, and often ahistorical. It fails to consider the larger political economy that controls alcohol production and consumption. It seldom studies the lived experiences of the problem drinker.

The alcoholic subject that science has created comes in several varieties: skidrow; chronic; alcohol or chemical dependent; dual addicted; problem drinker; black; white; American Indian; Asian; Irish; Jewish; Catholic; Protestant; male; female; teenage; elderly; upper-, middle-, and lower-class; rural; urban; gay and lesbian (Denzin 1987a: 32). This subject's alcoholism is understood to be a progressive, multidimensional illness, or disease, which is brought on by excessive alcohol consumption. The disease may or may not be inherited, and it may represent a failure of will. While there is some disagreement over whether or not an alcoholic personality exists, it is generally conceded that alcoholics have the following characteristics: (1) high anxiety in interpersonal relationships; (2) emotional immaturity; (3) ambivalence toward authority; (4) low self-esteem; (5) low tolerance of frustration; (6) feelings of isolationism, perfectionism, and guilt; (7) compulsiveness; (8) sex-role confusion; and (9) grandiosity, defiance, narcissism, resentment, and anger (see Denzin 1987a: 31 for a review of the literature on the alcoholic personality).

Given such a view of the alcoholic, it is not surprising to read the following statements which describe the alcoholic's drinking patterns, and his or her alcoholism:

[Alcoholic drinking] is learned behavior, maintained as a function of its consequences.

(Sobell and Sobell 1978: 33)

The [alcoholic] subject's performance was [not] coming under stimulus control as would be expected in the usual performance on a multiple chain schedule from a sophisticated pigeon.

(Mello 1972: 228)

Men who have accentuated needs for personal power drink excessively.

(McClelland et al. 1972)

The alcoholic has a permanently unfilled desire for dependency, but is ashamed to admit this need.

(Williams 1976)

This appeal to an objectively definable personality type, which includes the attempt to locate needs and biological predispositions within the alcoholic personality, presumes an "essentialist" view of human nature. It assumes that "there is an essential structure to alcoholic human nature that precedes alcoholic existence" (Denzin 1987a: 31). Such an essentialist view ignores the situated, interactional dimensions of the alcoholic's existence. It ignores the fact that a "normal" personality type has never been identified. Yet such a position rests on the assumption that the alcoholic, like the mentally ill and the criminal subject, have inside themselves character flaws that make them deviant and abnormal (see Foucault 1975).

This search for an invariant personality type attempts to inscribe the scientifically identified characteristics of alcoholism on the body and in the mind of the alcoholic. The alcoholic, like the madman or madwoman of the seventeenth and eighteenth centuries, is made into a walking objectification of his disease. On this point Foucault (1973: 159) observes that "The madman's body was regarded as the visible and solid presence of his disease: whence those physical cures whose meaning was borrowed from a moral perception and a moral therapeutics of the body."

The scientific and clinical treatment of alcoholism

Treatment centers compete for patients. In 1987, during the time I was doing my original research, over 1 million Americans were treated for alcoholism, in over 1,000 clinics at a cost of over $15 billion. Two dominant theories governed the treatment of alcoholics in the United States in the late 1980s. The first takes its orientation from behaviorism and from the "disputed" discovery in the early 1960s that certain kinds of alcoholics could be reso-cialized to become successful social drinkers (see Cahalan 1987 and Stock-well and Clement 1987 for reviews of these studies). Treatment programs for such drinkers involve complex behavioral reinforcement schedules derived from Skinnerian psychology. Their success has been hotly debated (see Denzin 1987a: 38–54; Pendery et al. 1982).

The second, more traditional approach to the treatment of alcoholism has followed the AA 12-Step Program, which advocates abstinence for the alcoholic. A majority of American treatment centers follow AA's program. Many add family counseling, ongoing group therapy, aftercare, various forms of psychodrama, Reality Therapy, confrontational therapy, pastoral counseling, nutritional and recreational therapy, occupational rehabilitation, and individual psychiatric counseling (see Denzin 1987b: 23).

Reading treatment

Six observations need to be made about these treatment approaches. First, as Foucault (1973) noted with the treatment of mental illness, current institutional practices regard the alcoholic's mind and body as concrete expressions of the illness called alcoholism. By individualizing the illness in the alcoholic's body, these institutional practices make the subject responsible for his disease. This move legitimates the creation of a particular kind of sick subject—the willful alcoholic who cannot control alcohol. Science and the micro-power treatment structures of society thus produce large classes of individuals whose "abnormality" concretizes the need for the very control structures and regimes of knowledge that create these individualities in the first place.

Second, the power of modern positivist, psychological science, and psychiatry increases as they impose themselves upon the institutional care and treatment of the alcoholic. They become the arbitrators of the treatment of this illness, while they define what "recovery" and "normality" will be. They do this by locating the illness in the alcoholic, by putting in place programs that simultaneously purify the alcoholic's body and mind, while they condition him to either not drink, or drink in a controlled fashion.

Third, the birth of the modern alcoholism treatment center, which dates from the early 1970s (Denzin 1987b: 180), like the birth of the medical clinic in the eighteenth and nineteenth centuries (Foucault 1975), brings the alcoholic

155

subject into a facility where he is under the "treatment gaze" of a new class of professional, the alcoholic counselor. This individual, often a recovering alcoholic, is now given the task of treating (curing) large classes of individuals who have been defined by their peers, their families, and the courts as alcoholics. This new professional works hand-in-hand with the theories of alcoholism and normality that AA, behavioral science, psychiatry, medicine, recreational, and occupational therapists, and pastoral counselors have developed. Lay theories of recovery and treatment are coupled with the languages of alcoholism that science has created. The result is the production of large groups of individuals who may or may not call themselves alcoholics, but who find that they have been so defined by others.

Fourth, this new clinic alienates alcoholics from society while it groups them together in a milieu where their socially defined, individual illness is now defined and treated as a collective phenomenon. An alcoholism counselor speaking to a group of repeat offenders states:

> It's been decided on high ... that you Repeaters need special treatment ... this is your Group. ... Group is not just here in this room two hours a day five days a week. ... Treatment goes on every minute you're awake. ... Everyone of you is on trial; if you don't show definite progress by the end of three weeks, you're out.
>
> (Berryman 1973: 42–43)

The milieu of the modern alcoholism clinic transforms alcoholics into persons who treat each other's illness. In a swift, paradoxical move, society and its agents have made individuals responsible for their alcoholic illness, while demanding that each person, now in treatment, treat not only himself, but other persons in the group as well.

Fifth, the patient–counselor relationship stands at the center of this treatment process. The counselor remains, like the psychiatrist in the mental hospital, the key to treatment (Foucault 1973: 278). The counselor unravels the individual's alcoholism, prescribes treatment, unlocks the inner mental life of the alcoholic that led to excessive drinking, encourages talk, makes judgments about treatment progress, and, in many cases, ultimately decides when the alcoholic is ready to leave the clinic.

Sixth, by turning treatment over to recovering alcoholics, science and treatment centers admit that there resides in the self-help group something that they alone (and together) cannot provide; namely, recovery from this disease called alcoholism. Yet these two micropower structures (treatment centers and the sciences of alcoholism) refuse to relinquish control over this illness that they have created. They control access to, and the structures of, these self-help groups as they operate in the clinic. They define who has recovered, who is a successful social drinker, who is a repeater, and who is a chronic alcoholic.

Scientific, objective vs. subjective stocks of knowledge

Modern behavioral science and the alcoholism clinic have turned alcoholism into a thinglike, static structure, which can be objectively manipulated by the tools and techniques of AA, medicine, pharmacy, behaviorism, psychiatry, the law, the courts, and the clinics. This body of knowledge documents the complex interplay and effects of genetic, physiological, neurophysiological, behavioral, cognitive, emotional, personal, social, and cultural processes on the alcoholic's conduct. Knowledge of the effects of these factors is present, in some form, in the mind of the individual who perceives him- or herself as having problems with alcohol. The existence of scientific knowledge on alcoholism constitutes a stock of knowledge (Schutz and Luckmann 1973: 243–60) or horizon against which the drinker judges his or her personal experiences. This "objective" stock of knowledge becomes a "subjective stock of knowledge" that is fitted by individuals to their theory of their problematic experiences with alcohol.

As I began my research and began interviewing alcoholics, it became apparent that the clients' subjective stocks of knowledge in relation to this objective, scientific literature, were also important to take account of. Here is a recovering alcoholic who is describing her drinking patterns to a group of AA members. Her statement draws on what she has learned about alcoholism from a popular cultural text:

> I never drank in the morning. I only drank on the weekends and when my husband was out of town. I read about a scientific study that said alcoholics were morning drinkers. I read it in Reader's Digest. Since I didn't drink in the morning, I couldn't be an alcoholic.

Another AA member reacts to the disease concept of alcoholism:

> When I was an undergraduate I took a course on alcoholism. My father was an alcoholic. That was back in the early 1960s. It was about the time Jellinek's book on the disease concept came out. My instructor, who is a leader in the field, spent the entire course (as I remember it) rejecting Jellinek. When I began having problems drinking I could never bring myself to believe I had a disease. I knew the scientific meaning of disease and AA's wasn't scientific. I thought I could control it myself. I nearly drank myself to death trying to control it.

The next individual speaks to the genetic, inherited conception of alcoholism.

> My father died of alcoholism. I believed it was inherited and that I had no choice over the matter. I did not think people could recover from alcoholism. I was also taught that alcoholism was a matter of self-control and that alcoholics lacked will power and moral strength.

157

In these statements, alcoholics frame their experiences against, and in terms of, what modern science has to say about their problems with alcohol. It was this resistance and discomfort with the scientific treatment of this problem on the part of clients that helped to frame the importance of my own unique research approach.

Writing postmodern ethnography

In my research I attempted to capture and interpret problematic experiences that are shaped and molded by the micropower structures of late post-modern society (Denzin 1986; 1988b; 2003). This version of postmodern ethnography may also be termed the anthropology of existential experience. The following list of principles helps to show the reader what assumptions I was utilizing as I approached the research project. This undoubtedly influenced the questions deemed relevant to ask, and the approach to dealing with respondents in the study.

1 *The researcher takes sides*: After Becker I assume that it is not possible to do research "uncontaminated by personal and political sympathies" (1967: 239). The question is not "whether we should take sides ... but rather whose side are we on" (Becker 1967: 239). I took the side of AA. I went native, to use the term of current parlance. I made the following statement in *The Recovering Alcoholic*:

> This work may be controversial or problematic for certain experts in the field of alcoholism studies. It is, in a sense, "pro-Alcoholics Anonymous." I am of the opinion that one's biases should be immediately placed in front of the reader. I have seen AA work and I have seen individuals die from "alcoholism" after they were taught to be normal social drinkers.
>
> (Denzin 1987b: 12)

2 *Experiences that are biographically meaningful for the researcher are studied*: The researcher, informed by the postmodern sociological imagination (Mills 1959), studies experiences that connect personal troubles to public issues. Investigators connect these troubles, as issues, to the institutions and groups that address those problems. The topic of alcoholism is biographically meaningful to me since I have alcoholics in my family. I wanted to make sense out of what it meant to live in an alcoholic family. I wanted to know how alcoholics experienced treatment and how they came to terms with their own problems with alcohol.

3 *Attention is directed to the pivotal turning point experiences in the lives of those who are studied*: Some experiences and their expressions are more important than others. For existential anthropologists (see Turner 1986:

41), and interpretive interactionists (see Denzin 1988a: chs. 1 and 7) the focus is on those social episodes (dramas) which display the liminal phase of experience (Turner 1986: 41). In these moments the mundane, ordinary world of experience is exploded and the threshold between the past and the future is illuminated, often in frightening detail, with existential consequence for the person and his fellows. These turning point experiences are epiphanies; in them character is revealed, and lives are turned around (see Denzin 1988a: ch. 7). In my studies I focused on those moments when alcoholics surrendered and entered treatment, when they slipped and relapsed, when they took on sponsors and started sponsoring others, and when they fell into despair and killed themselves.

4 *The models of truth, accuracy, and authenticity that operate in these worlds are uncovered and displayed*: Within any social world, multiple structures of truth, authenticity, and accuracy operate, although one set of criteria will typically predominate. The criteria may be taken from the norms of rationality that organize scientific work and involve concepts like validity and reliability. They may involve models of health and curing, as in modern medicine, that is: Does this prescription or treatment cure a patient? The researcher must uncover these discourse structures and determine how persons in the settings studied judge the accuracy and truthfulness of each other's statements and actions.

5 *The researcher privileges the languages of emotionality and feelings over the analytic languages of rationality and scientific explanation*: I have argued elsewhere (Denzin 1984) that the languages of emotionality in any social world express the deep, underlying feelings of self that give rise to authentically, meaningful experience. The researcher is charged with uncovering these structures of emotionality. I followed this argument in my AA study.

The models of truth, accuracy, and authenticity that operate in AA involve two criteria: (1) sobriety time, and (2) the expression of one's feelings in a way that allows sobriety to be maintained. A truthful statement in AA is one that does not give a member more sobriety than he has. An authentic statement in AA expresses the member's feelings and emotions. I learned that emotionality and the expression of feelings was central to the AA experience and that treatment centers called alcoholism an emotional disease (Denzin 1987b: ch. 2). In AA, members are shown how to express negative emotions. They are taught that resentment can get them drunk. Hence, AA talk privileges emotionality and discourse about feelings over analytic interpretations of experience.

6 *The researcher attempts to uncover the multiple discourse structures that organize experience in the settings studied*: Multiple forms of talk and discourse will be present within any social world. Depending on the setting, these will range from talk about work and family, to discussions of health, illness, sexuality, appearance, world politics, religion, popular culture, and similar related topics. These forms of discourse will shape

and define how personal experience is organized. The researcher must grasp, record, and present these multiple forms of talk. He must connect these forms of discourse to the larger culture-making institutions that give rise to and structure the topics that are discussed and experienced.

In AA, the voices of old-timers and newcomers, of treatment counselors, of men, women, young people, gays and lesbians, and dual addicts can be heard. Talk about family, work, failed marriages, problem children, relapses, and victories over alcohol is everywhere to be heard. Also present are discourses learned in treatment centers, discussions about AA history (both local and national), and controversies over new scientific treatments for alcoholism. I attempted to capture and record these multiple discourse structures. In so doing I privileged these discourses over my "interpretive" text (see Tyler 1986: 126).

7 *A multivoiced, polyphonic text is written and includes the researcher's experiences*: Postmodern ethnographic texts are multivoiced and polyphonic (Tyler 1986: 127). This means that no single voice has more authority than another. The researcher has no vaulted place in the text. The idea of writing an authoritative, abstract, analytic account of a culture is foreign to the postmodern impulse. The groups that are studied already write themselves through the stories their members tell one another (see Clifford 1986: 118). It is the investigator's task to create the spaces that allow this discourse to appear and articulate itself. This, by necessity, makes the written text multivoiced, conflictual, open-ended, descriptive, and rhetorical, only when the native's voice is rhetorical.

8 *The text that is written is decentered and then deconstructed*: There is no center to the text that is produced. Several implications follow from this assertion. First, the interpretive stance toward the text is "simultaneously exterior and interior" (Frank 1987: 109). The author's voice is both in the narratives that are spoken by the natives, and in the interpretive text that leads up to, and follows, the presentation of the native's text. It is exterior to those voices, but part of them. An opposition is established; "the intelligibility of either term depends on the continuing opposition of the other" (Frank 1987: 110; see also Derrida 1976). Second, there is no single voice that directs discourse and interpretation. There is no hierarchy in the text. Minimalist interpretations are written. Third, it is not that the ethnographer writes an "authorless" text; rather, the traditional position of authority that ethnographers have appropriated for themselves is relinquished. In the *Alcoholic Self* I attempted to minimize my voice and privilege the voices of AA members. I created the spaces for the articulation of their theories of treatment, sobriety, slips, and relapses. I recorded what recovery meant to them, in their words. At the same time I attempted to deconstruct the AA version of recovery and show how it did not work for certain alcoholics.

9 *Readers create their own versions of the texts that ethnographers write*: Readers bring their own meanings to the texts that are written. This means

that the author's place in the text will be displaced (decentered) by the reader's interpretive acts. The act of reading anchors the reader in the structures of experience written by the author. Recovering alcoholics who have read my books have looked for themselves in the stories I recorded. They have pointed to persons who have stories like their own. They have caught errors and called my attention to how the practices of AA in their area differ from the groups that I studied. As biographically informed readers, they took over the meanings of these books.

To summarize, the anthropology of experience rejects the traditional, received conceptions of fieldwork and ethnography. Terms like observer role (overt, covert), role relations, going native, gaining acceptance, role disengagement, cultural shock, coding, problem selection, domain of analysis, and data gathering are no longer operative. These are modernist, positivist, and structuralist concepts. They belie a commitment to the grand narratives of the past that held that objective truths about human societies could be written.

The texts that are now brought before the reader are interpreted as accounts of experience. These personal experiences and selfstories from and of the field are considered meaningful within the narratives that contain them. Field research becomes a gendered experience overflowing with the emotions, subjectivities, and experiences of the ethnographer and of those studied. As such, the research process, and the writing of *The Alcoholic Self* (and the *Recovering Alcoholic*) were set in stark opposition to the dominant scientific theories of alcoholism. I attempted to deconstruct the traditional hierarchies and empirical preconceptions that organized this body of discourse. I turn now to the arguments in the AA literature.

AA's theory of alcoholism

As I began to research AA, it was apparent that their theory of alcoholism does not inquire into the scientific causes of alcoholism. However, I found that AA does adhere to the assumptions that alcoholism is (a) a disease, involving moral, psychological, physical, and emotional dimensions; (b) an obsession to drink involving some sort of metabolism-like allergy that (c) makes it certain that the drinker will drink against his will, and will (d) "finally deteriorate, go insane, or die" (AA 1963). The alcoholic is a person who drinks when he doesn't want to and who does "tragic things while drinking" (AA 1976: 24). He is the kind of person who has been repeatedly institutionalized for alcoholism, yet this person will drink immediately upon release from treatment. He will almost always get insanely drunk, become antisocial, go on drinking sprees, get drunk at the wrong times, go to bed intoxicated and reach for a drink the first thing in the morning, and hide alcohol from others (AA 1976: 21–22). This person will be "unable to stop drinking on the basis of self-knowledge" (AA 1976: 39).

AA suggests that the alcoholic do the following things if he wants to recover from alcoholism: (1) become abstinent, (2) admit powerlessness over alcohol, (3) turn his life over to a power greater than himself, (4) clear away the wreckage of his past, (5) make amends for past wrongdoings, (6) develop a spiritual program, and (7) carry the AA message of recovery to others.

AA and science

At the time of this study, AA was being challenged by various segments of the scientific community in that it made numerous assumptions alleged to be anti-scientific: (1) it uses the allergy-disease concept of alcoholism, (2) it does not keep records of its members, and (3) it conducts its primary work inside "closed" meetings that are not open to scientific observers (Maiste and McCollam 1980: 18–19). It has also been called a religious cult and some charge that it has closed its doors to science (Sagarin 1969). AA's alliance with the abstinence-side of the recovery controversy opens it up to challenge from those researchers who call for controlled drinking. AA's path for recovery is thus countered by those scientists who desire to control the effects of alcohol on the problem drinker. Bateson (1972), Jellinek (1960), Kurtz (1979), Maxwell (1984), and Pittman (1988), have noted that AA's emphasis on spirituality and a power greater than the person, challenges the dualistic rationality of modern science that in most cases is atheistic if not agnostic. AA's spirituality situates the alcoholic in a system that is larger than the self. By making the person "not god" (Kurtz 1979), AA locates the individual in a noncompetitive, collective whole, which is greater than the sum of its parts. This Durkheimian collective (Bateson 1972) is greater than the person, and is presented as a loving, caring entity.

AA's practical ethic of action ("Carry the message to others") directs the alcoholic to form a service relationship with the world. This is a noncompetitive relationship of love and recovery (Bateson 1972: 335). It involves a pragmatic, spiritual program. It combines the existential themes of religion, psychology, and psychiatry in a practical, secular, spiritual ethic. It blends science, religion, and common sense. It speaks to the alcoholic's problems in ways that apparently no behavioral science can (Denzin 1987b: 66).

In these ways AA's ethical, spiritual, and philosophical stance, which is anti-Cartesian, challenges much of modern science as it approaches the alcoholism problem in late postmodern society. It is fundamentally at odds with the regimes of truth and the microstructures of power that modern science has created. I turn now to the AA group as an interactional site where AA's theory of recovery is put into place.

AA and the AA group as interactional sites

In 1988 Alcoholics Anonymous counted a worldwide membership of over 1.3 million persons. Over 600,000 of these persons live in the United States.

They belong to, or participate in, one or more of the over 60,000 AA groups that AA lists in its directory of groups. An AA group is defined as follows: "Two or more alcoholics meeting together for the purpose of sobriety may consider themselves an AA group." The work of AA occurs in these groups.

An AA group is an unique historical social structure of two-, three-, and multi-person relationships. It exists within a shared universe of discourse that is unified in terms of common understandings concerning five forces: alcohol, alcoholics, recovery, AA history, and AA's conception of a "higher power." Shared understandings of each of these forces give the AA group its reason for being.

As just indicated, AA defines the alcoholic as a sick person. Alcohol is seen as a force that is to be avoided at all cost. Abstinence is the alcoholic's goal. Every AA member is encouraged, as noted earlier, to find a higher power and to turn his life over to this power. Every AA group is structured by the same sense of history, as given in the key texts, *Alcoholics Anonymous* and *Twelve Steps and Twelve Traditions*. Every meeting is organized in terms of the same key readings: "The Serenity Prayer," "The Twelve Steps," "The Twelve Traditions," and "The Lord's Prayer" (see Denzin 1987b: 102–5). Thus, any given alcoholic will find in any given AA meeting the same rituals, traditions, and shared assumptions concerning drinking, alcohol, and alcoholism. This is how AA as a self-help group works. Key to this functioning is AA's unique mode of emotional understanding.

AA's mode of understanding

The sciences of alcoholism aim for cognitive, rational explanations, predictions, and understandings of this phenomenon. They seek to reduce alcoholism to single and multifactored causal explanations. They attempt to build models of understanding that are understandable to other scientists. My observation found that AA, in contrast, and as noted here, approaches alcoholism from the standpoint of the recovering alcoholic who has been through the same processes as the alcoholic who comes to AA asking for help. AA offers emotional understandings of alcoholism, while science rejects emotion and offers rational, cognitive, non-emotional explanations of the alcoholic's situation.

AA's mode of understanding is premised on the following assumption: experience precedes emotional understanding. Every recovering alcoholic has experienced alcoholically induced despair, anguish, fear, guilt, remorse, hangovers, hidden drinking, loss of lovers and family, difficulties at work and home, financial problems, health disorders created by excessive drinking, and unsuccessful attempts at quitting drinking. Out of this experience emerges an understanding of the alcoholic situation that no non-alcoholic can emotionally understand.

Listen to the following words. The speaker has been married to the same woman for 46 years:

I've lived with that woman for 46 years. For 30 of those years I was an alcoholic, drunk every day. And after those 46 years she'll never come within a hair on a gnat's ass in understanding me. She can't. She's not an alcoholic.

Here is an alcoholic seeking help. He is talking to a recovering alcoholic who has been in AA for three years:

You know, you're the first person I've talked to who understands what in the hell I've been through. The doctor told me that I had to get out of town for treatment if I couldn't stop by myself. Christ, I can't stop by myself. My family doesn't understand. I want to stop, but I can't. I keep going back to it, even when I don't want to.

These two speakers reference the concept of alcoholic understanding. The alcoholic who comes to an AA meeting finds this understanding in the talk that goes on around the AA tables. Listen to this speaker. He is at his first AA meeting:

I couldn't find the place. Walked by four times before I saw the AA sign ... 'Fraid to come in. Guess that's why I'm here. My name's G. Guess I'm an alcoholic. Can't stop by myself. God it's good to be here. You make me feel good ... Can you people help me? Please.

Now, listen to the same man. It is two years after his first meeting, and he has just received an AA medallion for two years of sobriety.

You know when I first came here I was scared. Could hardly talk. You folks made me feel at home. You listened, you shared, and told me your stories. I felt like you understood me. You do understand me. I don't ever want to go back to being who I was before. I was a scared, lonely man who sat by himself on a bar stool, drank beer, and cried when I got home. I'm not like that today. Thanks to you people. Thank you.

At AA, this man found emotional understanding. He found a group of speakers who told stories that he could relate to. He learned how to stay sober by coming back to this group.

The self-help group

The term self-help group refers to a group of persons having the same problem helping one another resolve the problematic situation they share in common; AA is a self-help group. Its members, in groups, help one another stay sober, one day at a time. Individually and collectively, AA members recover from alcoholism.

AA began as a small social group. It then turned into a social movement that was institutionalized as it routinized charisma. It developed a body of customs, a social organization, a set of traditions, an established leadership, and a division of labor with social rules (Denzin 1987b: 95). It became "in short a culture, a social organization and a new scheme of life" (Blumer 1946: 199). Two contradictory traditions were entrenched within this culture. On the one hand, it aligned itself with science, medicine, and psychiatry. On the other hand, it attempted to maintain its focus on the alcoholic and his recovery. This tension is reflected in the stances of AA's co-founders.

Like any social group, self-help, or otherwise, AA attempts to impose its culture on its members. It does this through its literature, through the readings of its *Steps and Traditions* at meetings, and through its advocacy of sponsorship (Denzin 1987a: 181–82; 1987b: 91–92). In these ways the AA group passes on to its members a way of life, and a new set of values.

AA has many slogans: "One Day at a Time," "But for the Grace of God," "Don't Drink and Go to Meetings." One slogan deals with the word "I," which is turned into the word "EYE," and then into a slogan: "I means Eat Your Ego." In this transformation of the pronoun "I," AA expresses its attitude toward self and its romanticization. The self is to be given up, to be turned over to a higher power. In this slogan, and others like it, AA attempts to demolish the Cartesian ego and the subject/object dualism that characterizes Western culture (Bateson 1972).

Elsewhere (Denzin 1987a: 199–200; 1987b: 203–6), I have shown how the AA member moves through several stages of selfhood and self-awareness. These stages and forms of self include self as loss, self as false subjectivity, and self as transcendent. The member who remains with AA will move initially from a sense of self as loss, to an attempt to anchor self in material objects. Finally, he or she will move to a sense of self-transcendence in which the meaning of the self is given in the AA rituals, and in the AA group experience. AA urges a submergence of the self in a power greater than the person, including the AA group. In this way, AA creates the conditions for the emergence of a collective, ritual self that is outside the competitive structures of everyday life. The collective whole of AA joins the member to a transcendent group structure that is larger than the person.

Conclusions

By privileging AA's discourse structures over the discourses of rational, objective, analytic, ethnographic science, I pitted their models of truth and authenticity against the cannons of positive science. I deconstructed the behavioral views of alcoholism. This involved an emphasis on emotionality and on the forms of emotional understanding that AA values. I attempted to show, however, how science enters into the experiences AA members have with their "alcoholism." By creating spaces for AA members to speak, I attempted to produce a multivoiced text.

I created a set of oppositions in my text: science and religion, science and the alcoholic experience, AA and science, and objectivity and biography and personal experience. I began with scientific discourses, and then turned to AA. I could have started with AA, but I wanted to subvert the control of science. I did this by bringing in AA's theory of alcoholism, recovery, and the emotions and emotional understanding. And even before I did this, I told the reader that the experience of alcoholism in my family was biographically meaningful to me. I thus began with the personal, moved to the scientific, and then turned to AA. My text has been framed, from the outset, in terms of the position I value.

My version of the postmodern ethnographic project has emphasized how local, narrative knowledge, like AA's theory of alcoholism, becomes the raw material for renewed social bonds in the late modern period. By privileging these narratives, I want to show, after Sartre (1976), how persons in groups can change the course of their own collective history. I have attempted to show how the alcoholic's experiences in American society are shaped by science, religion, common sense and the cultural values of AA. Self-help groups like AA have inserted themselves into the discourse structures created by modern medicine, science and treatment centers.

References

AA (1963) "The Bill–Carl Jung Letters," *Grapevine* (January): 26–31.
—— (1976) *Alcoholics Anonymous*, New York: Alcoholics Anonymous World Services, Inc.
Bateson, G. (1972) "'The Cybernetics of Self': a theory of alcoholism," in *Steps to an Ecology of Mind* (pp. 309–77), New York: Ballantine.
Becker, H. S. (1967) "Whose Side Are We On?," *Social Problems*, 14: 239–48.
Berryman, J. (1973) *Recovery*, New York: Farrar.
Blumer, H. (1946) "Collective Behavior," in A. M. Lee (ed.) *New Outline of the Principles of Sociology* (pp. 166–222), New York: Barnes & Noble.
Cahalan, D. (1987) *Understanding America's Drinking Problem: how to combat the hazards of alcohol*, San Francisco, CA: Jossey-Bass.
Clifford, J. (1986) "On Ethnographic Allegory," in J. Clifford and Marcus, G. E. (eds.) *Writing Culture: the poetics and politics of ethnography* (pp. 98–121), Berkeley, CA: University of California Press.
Clifford, J., and Marcus, G. E. (eds) (1986) *Writing Culture: the poetics and politics of ethnography*, Berkeley, CA: University of California Press.
Denzin, N. K. (1984) *On Understanding Emotion*, San Francisco: Jossey-Bass.
——(1986) "Postmodern Social Theory," *Sociological Theory*, 4: 194–204.
——(1987a) *The Alcoholic Self*, Newbury Park, CA: Sage.
——(1987b) *The Recovering Alcoholic*, Newbury Park, CA: Sage.
——(1987c) *Treating Alcoholism*, Newbury Park, CA: Sage.

——(1988a) *Interpretive Interactionism*, Newbury Park, CA: Sage.

——(1988b) "Postmodern Ethnography," *Journal of Contemporary Ethnography*, 17: 89–100.

——(1993) *The Alcoholic Society: addiction and recovery of self*, New Brunswick, NJ: Transaction Publishers.

——(1997) *Interpretive Ethnography*, Thousand Oaks, CA: Sage.

——(2001) *Interpretive Interactionism*, 2nd ed., Thousand Oaks, CA: Sage.

——(2003) *Performance Ethnography*,Thousand Oaks, CA: Sage

Derrida, J. (1976) *Of Grammatology*, Baltimore, MD: Johns Hopkins University Press.

Foucault, M. ([1961] 1973) *Madness and Civilization*, New York: Vintage Books.

——([1963] 1975) *The Birth of the Clinic: an archaeology of medical perception*, trans. A. M. Sheridan Smith, New York: Vintage Books.

Frank, A. W. (1987) "Out of Ethnomethodology," in J. Helle and Eisenstadt, S. N. (eds.) *Micro-Sociological Theory: perspectives in sociological theory*, vol. 2 (pp. 101–16), Newbury Park, CA: Sage.

Geertz, C. (1983) *Local Knowledge: further essays in interpretive anthropology*, New York: Basic Books.

——(1988) *Works and Lives: the anthropologist as author*, Stanford, CA: Stanford University Press.

Jellinek, E. M. (1960) *The Disease Concept of Alcoholism*, New Haven, CT: Hillhouse Press.

Kurtz, E. (1979) *Not-God: a history of Alcoholics Anonymous*, Center City, MN: Hazelden Educational Materials.

Maiste, S. A. and McCollam, J. B. (1980) "The Use of Multiple Measures of Life Health to Assess Alcohol Treatment Outcome: a review and critique," in L. Sobell, Sobell, M. and Ward, E. (eds.) *Evaluating Alcohol and Drug Abuse Treatment Effectiveness* (pp. 15–76), New York: Pergamon.

Maxwell, M. A. (1984) *The Alcoholics Anonymous Experience*, New York: McGraw-Hill.

McClelland, D. C., Davis, W. N., Kalin, R., and Wanner, E. (1972) *The Drinking Man*, New York: Free Press.

Mello, N. (1972) "Behavioral Studies of Alcoholism," in B. Kissin and Begleiter, H. (eds.) *The Biology of Alcoholism* (pp. 219–92), vol. 2, New York: Plenum.

Mills, C. W. (1959) *The Sociological Imagination*, New York: Oxford.

Pendery, M. L., Maltzman, I. M., and West, L. J. (1982) "Controlled Drinking by Alcoholics: new findings and a re-evaluation of a major affirmative study," *Science*, 217: 169–75.

Pittman, B. (1988) *AA: the way it began*, Seattle, WA: Glen Abbey Books.

Sagarin, E. (1969) *Odd Man In: societies of deviants in America*, Chicago: Quadrangle.

Sartre, J-P. (1976) *Critique of Dialectical Reason*, London: NLP.

Schutz, A. and Luckmann, T. (1973) *The Structures of the Life World*, Evanston, IL: Northwestern University Press.

Sobell, M. B. and Sobell, L. C. (1978) *Behavioral Treatment of Alcohol Problems: individualized therapy and controlled drinking*, New York: Plenum.

Stockwell, T. and Clement, S. (eds.) (1987) *Helping the Problem Drinker: new initiates for community care*, London: Croom Helm.

Turner, V. (1986) "Dewey, Dilthey, and Drama: an essay in the anthropology of experience," in V. Turner and Bruner, E. (eds.) *The Anthropology of Experience* (pp. 33–44), Urbana: University of Illinois Press.

Turner, V. and Bruner, E. (eds.) (1986) *The Anthropology of Experience*, Urbana: University of Illinois Press.

Tyler, S. A. (1986) "Post-Modern Ethnography: from document of the occult to occult development," in J. Clifford and Marcus, G. E. (eds.) *Writing Culture: the poetics and politics of ethnography* (pp. 122–40), Berkeley, CA: University of California Press.

Williams, A. F. (1976) "The Alcoholic Personality," in B. Kissin and Beglieter, H. (eds.) *The Biology of Alcoholism, vol. 4* (pp. 243–75), New York: Plenum.

10

THE DEVELOPMENT OF LEISURE THEORY IN THREE NATURE-CHALLENGE HOBBIES

Robert A. Stebbins

Between May 2000 and April 2002 an assistant and I collected qualitative-exploratory data through direct interviews with and observations on a sample of kayakers, snow boarders, and mountain climbers who, in the main, pursued their leisure in the Canadian Rockies. My interest lay in a particular group of hobbies whose core activities center on meeting each in its own way a particular natural challenge. That is *nature-challenge hobbies* are a distinctive category of activities undertaken to surmount a natural challenge such as descending a roaring river or steep snow slope, climbing a rock face, negotiating a rugged trail, surfing a wave, parachuting to earth, and the like. The study of the three mountain-based nature-challenge hobbies discussed in the present chapter is reported more fully in Stebbins (2005a).

In this chapter we look first at the theoretical background of this study. Next the reasons for undertaking it are examined. Then we consider the idea of risk, regarded by many people as an unavoidable concomitant of these hobbies. Finally I discuss the principal contributions to the serious leisure perspective to issue from this research. As will become apparent, this study exemplifies use of two important types of sensitizing concepts (van den Hoonaard 1997), referred to here in Barney Glaser's (2005: ch. 2) language as "established theoretic codes" and "emergent theoretic codes."

Theoretical background

In this study I drew on several established theoretic codes that help comprise the framework known as the serious leisure perspective. Generally speaking, established codes are used in exploratory research as sensitizing concepts. They have either been validated in earlier exploratory inquiry or have gained a place in general social scientific theory. The serious leisure perspective, which since the mid-1970s, has been evolving inductively through a series of exploratory studies, had come to include by the time I undertook the mountain hobbyist study a number of well validated established concepts. These could now serve as guides for further data collection in this new area of research.

The serious leisure perspective is a theoretic framework that synthesizes three main forms of leisure, showing, at once, their distinctive features, similarities, and interrelationships (Stebbins 2007). The forms are serious, casual, and project-based leisure. They may be briefly defined as follows:

- *Serious leisure*: systematic pursuit of an amateur, hobbyist, or volunteer activity sufficiently substantial, interesting, and fulfilling for the participant to find a (leisure) career there acquiring and expressing a combination of its special skills, knowledge, and experience.
- *Casual leisure*: immediately, intrinsically rewarding, relatively short-lived pleasurable activity, requiring little or no special training to enjoy it.
- *Project-based leisure*: short-term, reasonably complicated, one-shot or occasional, though infrequent, creative undertaking carried out in free time, or time free of disagreeable obligation.

A hobby is a systematic, enduring pursuit of a reasonably evolved and specialized free-time activity having no professional counterpart. Such leisure leads to acquisition of substantial skill, knowledge, or experience, or a combination of these. Although hobbyists differ from amateurs in that they lack a professional reference point, they do at times have commercial equivalents and often have small publics who take an interest in what they do.

To arrive at a detailed understanding of the ways people experience their leisure—which was a primary goal of the present study of the three mountain hobbies—researchers must also be familiar with the idea of activity. An *activity* is a type of pursuit, wherein participants in it mentally or physically (often both) think or do something, motivated by the hope of achieving a desired end. In leisure, activities are undertaken with the aim of having an experience that is pleasant, fulfilling, rewarding, or in other ways so inviting that the participant would return for more should resources and circumstances permit. This definition of activity gets further refined in the concept of *core activity*: a distinctive set of interrelated actions or steps that must be followed to achieve the central outcome or product that the participant seeks. In sum, to gain the richest understanding of the typical leisure experiences found in a given general activity, we must first identify that activity—e.g. kayaking, snowboarding, mountain climbing—and then describe its core activity or activities—e.g. descending a mountain river or snow slope or ascending a mountain rock face.

Psychological flow

Some core activities in serious leisure are attractive in part because they generate a feeling of psychological flow. Although the idea of flow originated with the work of Mihalyi Csikszentmihalyi (e.g. 1990) and has therefore an intellectual history quite separate from that of the serious, casual, and project-based leisure, it does nevertheless happen on occasion that it is a key motivational force in the first. Indeed, flow was highly prized in the three types of hobbies examined in this chapter. It is felt there as its participants carry out their core activities.

What then is flow? Flow, a form of optimal experience, is possibly the most widely discussed and studied generic intrinsic reward in the psychology of work and leisure. Although many types of work and leisure generate little or no flow for their participants, those that do are found primarily in the "devotee occupations" (Stebbins 2004) and in serious leisure. Still, it will be evident that each work and leisure activity capable of producing flow does so in terms unique to it. And it follows that each of these activities must be carefully examined to discover the properties contributing to its distinctive feeling of flow.

In his theory of optimal experience, Csikszentmihalyi (1990: 3–5, 54) describes and explains the psychological foundation of the many flow activities in work and leisure, as exemplified in chess, dancing, surgery, and rock climbing. Flow is "autotelic" experience, or the sensation that comes with the actual enacting of intrinsically rewarding activity. Over the years Csikszentmihalyi (1990: 49–67) has identified and explored eight components of this experience. It is easy to see how these eight, when present, are sufficiently rewarding and, it follows, highly valued to endow certain kinds of work and leisure with an attractiveness that renders the two inseparable in several ways. And this even though most people tend to think of work and leisure as vastly different. The eight components are:

1   sense of competence in executing the activity;
2   requirement of concentration;
3   clarity of goals of the activity;
4   immediate feedback from the activity;
5   sense of deep, focused involvement in the activity;
6   sense of control in completing the activity;
7   loss of self-consciousness during the activity;
8   sense of time is truncated during the activity.

These components are self-evident, except possibly for the first and the sixth. With reference to the first, flow fails to develop when the activity is either too easy or too difficult; to experience flow the participant must feel capable of performing a moderately challenging activity. The sixth component refers to the perceived degree of control the participant has over execution of the activity. This is not a matter of personal competence. Rather it is one of degree of influence of uncontrollable external forces, a condition well illustrated in situations faced by the hobbyists in this study, such as when the water level suddenly rises on the river or an unpredicted snowstorm produces a whiteout on a mountain snowboard slope.

Risk

Risk was also an established sensitizing concept used in the mountain study, although it failed to be validated there. That is its popular, and to some extent even its scientific understanding, spurred me on in the study of the three hobbies. The commonsense notion that the three hobbies are highly risky and that only "crazy" people do such things had been around for some time before I decided to study them. Nevertheless, my own experience in the mountain nature activities in which I was involved in, as well as informal discussions with and informal observations of serious leisure participants in other nature-challenge activities, suggested that, in fact, only a small proportion of all participants in them are, by their own definition, risk takers there. This discrepancy begged closer scrutiny. People want to pursue leisure, including hobbies, while they seem to prefer to avoid risk.

I reviewed some of the relevant popular and scientific literature on risk (Stebbins 2005a: ch. 1). It was clear that, in this literature, the pursuit of leisure and the serious leisure perspective explaining it were being ignored (e.g. Campbell et al. 1993; Lyng 1990; for a summary see Slanger and Rudestam 1997). Here the concept of leisure, if mentioned at all, was treated of in highly general and simplified terms. My decades of experience studying leisure suggested that there was far more to understanding why people routinely undertake so-called risky activities in their free time than was being recognized in the popular and scientific literature.

Entering the field

In one way the study of the three hobbyist sports of kayaking, snowboarding, and mountain climbing, was but another step in my longitudinal research program of continued concatenation of studies related to the serious leisure perspective. Since 1973, when the first work on amateurs got under way, I have been gaining over the years, through direct exploration, an ever deeper understanding of the three forms of the perspective. Around 2003 it was clear that more exploration was needed on hobbies, particularly on those classified as activity participation. I had completed one study of this type—the barbershop singers (Stebbins 1996)—which, however, was hardly representative of the considerable range of the many subtypes in this category.

Concatenation is central in building a grounded theory (Stebbins 2006). This longitudinal process recognizes that it takes not one but many individual exploratory research projects to amass an amount of open-ended data sufficient for a reasonably complete theory. Each project, intensely focused as it must be, only generates *some* grounded theory, whereas many projects conducted and concatenated on many different samples are needed for *a* grounded theory. Emergent theoretic codes generated in earlier projects are brought forward as sensitizing concepts (established codes) to guide data collection and receive further validation (if empirically justified) in later projects. As noted, the serious leisure perspective and the concept of risk served as sensitizing concepts in the study of mountain hobbies.

Activity participation is one of five types of hobbies. It refers to the serious leisure found in noncompetitive, rule-based pursuits in such diverse fields as fishing, horseback riding, snowshoeing, scuba diving, bird-watching, and of course, the pursuits mentioned in the preceding paragraph. Each has its own rules, often cultural, about how it should be pursued. Each can be pursued without formally competing with someone else, as is done in sport and games (both being hobbies when without professional counterparts). For example, participants may compete in a context in river kayaking or snowboarding or they may simply kayak or snowboard for the pleasure of mastering the challenge presented to them by a river or snow slope.

Unlike barbershop singing, many of the hobbies considered here are based on some sort of physical activity. Thus, from the standpoint of representativeness a study of the three treated of here made sense. They were also hobbies with which I was familiar. I was at the time engaged in mountain scrambling (Class 2 to Class 3 mountaineering accomplished by hiking and climbing steep slopes to summits without equipment). Though I was never a kayaker, I had in earlier days been a whitewater canoeist. It was likewise with snowboarding: I have never snowboarded, but was at the time an experienced cross-country skier. In the interest of representativeness, I decided to look at one hobby in each of three natural elements: water, snow, and earth/rock. Furthermore, these three had never been studied as serious leisure activities; no one had collected data using as sensitizing concepts those available in the serious leisure perspective. Finally, the three were routinely practiced near my home in Calgary. Finding sites of the activities to observe and participants to interview would be easy.

To facilitate comparison, I included low-, medium- and high-challenge participants in the study, with the range of level of challenge being sampled approximately equally. Twenty-three climbers (ice and mountain), 16 snowboarders, and 24 kayakers were interviewed (N = 63), samples that included the vast majority of all possible interviewees available at the time of data collection. The data were collected between May 2000 and April 2002. Interviews were, for the most part, conducted following the sessions of observation. All three samples included both organized and unorganized participants, the latter being recruited for interviewing through the procedure of snowball sampling. Observations were made in the Rocky Mountain area west of Calgary, and interviewees resided in the Calgary-Canmore-Banff corridor, with most living just outside Banff National Park in the town of

Canmore where they have the most convenient access possible to the local sites where they pursue their hobbies. (Living in Banff, which in many ways is even more centrally located, is prohibited, unless employed in the National Park.)

Emergent concepts of risk

To guide exploratory study of the three mountain sports and give me a reasonable idea of where to look for risk as it bears on them, I developed a small set of preliminary definitions of this concept, which were effectively emergent theoretic codes. The ideas sprang from my own experience in nature-challenge hobbies and from discussion with a small circle of students, friends, and colleagues of similar leisure interest. The definitions had to admit the leisure qualities of the three hobbies as well as their participant's view of what is risky. Moreover I was concerned with "high risk" in the area of nature-challenge hobbies, since this has been the level of risk uppermost in the minds of the authors of the aforementioned literature.

I was able to conceive of four types, as seen through the eyes of hobbyists. *Unmanaged high risk*, or risk that emerges only when individuals lose concentration, get fatigued, or otherwise suddenly become unable to draw on their acquired skills, knowledge, and experience that keep them in leisure and, at its peak, in flow. The second is *fortuitous high risk*, which is greatly improbable risk from uncontrollable sources such as snow avalanches, falling rock, sudden elevations of water level (as caused by heavy rain), and ice slicks (on cross-country ski trails). These are what mountaineers call "objective hazards," hazards created by nature.

Social high risk, the third type, was considered earlier as pressure from peers to engage in the activity at a level regarded by the pressured participant as risky. In other words, it is regarded by that person as going significantly beyond his or her acquired skills, knowledge, and experience. But social risk can also include intentionally taking great risks for the fame and perhaps even the fortune that it brings. And sometimes nature-challenge hobbyists take social risks because others in their team want to press on (e.g. up the mountain face, down the river rapids). An important point to be made about their activities is that the first two types of risk can, with careful preparation and advance information, usually be avoided and, in fact, generally are. They are avoided because, in significant part, even moderate risk seriously dilutes the senses of flow and leisure. It is questionable whether either is felt at all in social risk, though that may not matter in any case, since the object here is to establish an identity as "gutsy," as a devil-may-care individual.

Finally, included in this list is what I labeled *humanitarian high risk*. For example, Jennifer Lois (2003) studied "peak volunteers"—viewed in the present book according to the serious leisure perspective as leisure participants—

who sometimes must challenge nature while carrying out search and rescue missions. They seek high risk not for its own sake, but rather confront it (presumably reluctantly) in their efforts to save lives or recover bodies. Peak volunteers are not hobbyists, of course.

In short, while the public, in general, and the press and some scientific writers, in particular, are fond of describing mountaineering, kayaking, and snowboarding in such dramatic, universalistic terms as "high-risk" and "extreme sport," this is not how the vast majority of the interviewees portrayed their routine involvement in them. Most of the time their talk about risk is focused on social risk as intentionally pursued for fame and sometimes even fortune (e.g. sponsored risk), far more often than not by people not personally known to the conversationalists. For them such activity is not leisure; it is too frightening to be attractive. Even the scientific literature in this field, with some exceptions (see Stebbins 2005a: 21), has ignored the place of leisure and flow as motivators.

Findings and other emergent concepts

The four types of risk and the idea of nature challenge, just set out, are among the several concepts to emerge from this study, and as is evident, they had to be defined tentatively before entering the field to collect data. The data collected did, however, lead to considerable further refinement of our understanding of what these two mean to the people whose nature-challenge hobbies are potentially risky.

Thus we have known for many years that participants in serious leisure find a leisure career there acquiring and expressing a combination of its special skills, knowledge, and experience. Indeed this feature is now an essential component of the definition of this form. Nevertheless the nature-challenge project specifically revealed that participants' interpretations of risk change as their careers in the hobby unfold. In other words, with more skill, knowledge, and experience, they learn to avoid unmanaged high risk as well as certain kinds of fortuitous high risk (e.g. avalanches, ice slicks, rising water levels). Moreover, to the extent that they know their hobby better than most participants in their circles, they become less susceptible to some of the pressures spawning social high risk.

The study also shed new light on the process of self-fulfillment. Mannell (1989: 286) observed that psychological research, while confirming the general existence of leisure satisfaction, had so far failed to identify "the most meaningful and appropriate factors that might affect the quality of ... [that] satisfaction." In other words, the psychologists of the day were assuming rather than empirically studying the link between leisure fulfillment, on the one hand, and the everyday life components of motivation in particular leisure activities and their settings, on the other. At the same time, they had nevertheless learned that people do see their leisure, in general, as intrinsically

rewarding, as relatively uncoerced activity they initiate for their own fulfillment. Today, we know considerably more about this link between leisure
fulfillment (discussed in the earlier literature as "satisfaction") and the
motivational components of particular leisure activities. Mannell and Kleiber (1997: 208–9) provide a review of some of the research in this area, most
of which, however, bears on casual leisure.

Three "meaningful and appropriate factors" were identified in the nature-
challenge study: the rewards of personal enrichment, self-fulfillment, and
self-gratification. All three subsamples experienced these with greater intensity than the other rewards found over the years to motivate people in serious
leisure (Stebbins 2007: 13–14). Personal enrichment refers to the cherished
experiences in the hobby. Self-fulfillment is development to the fullest of a
person's gifts and character, development of that person's full potential. Self-
gratification is a combination of superficial enjoyment ("fun"), as experienced
in casual leisure, and deep personal fulfillment.

Epics

New to the literature on serious leisure is the idea of "epic." In mountaineering (where this usage appears to have originated), as well as in the other
two hobbies, some physically dangerous, risky situations get retrospectively
defined simultaneously as both a thrill and an epic. *Epics* are harrowing
experiences of heroic proportions that the hobbyist nonetheless manages to
survive, albeit sometimes with injury. At the time they are happening, however, these situations are unpleasant. In fact the objective in question is not
successfully negotiated, but a sense of thrill is still preserved after the fact by
coming away from the failed attempt relatively unscathed. In the course of it
all, a kayaker, for example, had to "swim," fractured a limb on the rocks, or
broke up the nose of the boat. But it could have been worse, perhaps culmi-
nating in more broken bones, even death. In some epics kayakers are forced
to leave the river in inaccessible places, with the result that colleagues must
rescue them, or if the situation is perilous, as in a canyon, this task is left to
professional search and rescue.

In short, the thrill of the epic, when described as such, comes in surviving
it, an experience that all three types of hobbyists usually had no interest in
repeating, however thrilling in retrospect. The experience was, after all, a
harrowing brush with fortuitous risk. Be that as it may, recounting particular
epics makes for some fine shoptalk at social gatherings of these hobbyists. In
such sessions there are lessons to be learned, heroes to be identified, dangerous aspects of the hobby to be underscored, and so on. Epics are noteworthy, in part, because in leisure activities characterized by manageable risk
rather than high risk, they are both rare and unfamiliar. Tales of epics, no
doubt embellished as they pass from mouth to mouth in these gatherings,
come to form a significant part of the activity's local subculture.

Core activity

It was in the study of mountain hobbies that the previously mentioned idea of core activity was first formally introduced and explored. Since this idea was discussed earlier as part of the theoretic framework, suffice it to say here that the appeal of such activity was, for me, especially evident and dramatic in these three vis-à-vis some of the other serious leisure fields I had studied, among them, career volunteering, amateur archaeology, and amateur astronomy.

In fact the mountain hobbies project showed clearly how particular core activities can lead to flow and to its powerful motivation to pursue mountaineering, kayaking, and snowboarding. Yet flow is only an occasional state of mind there. That is, during any given outing in one of these hobbies, participants only experience flow some of the time. Meanwhile it is not even this central, or even present at all, in some other outdoor hobbies. For instance, it does not seem to characterize much of mountain scrambling, backpacking, or horseback riding. By contrast, it is certainly a motivational feature of mountain biking as well as of cross-country and downhill skiing.

Accordingly this study resulted in a formal definition of the idea, which it became clear in retrospect is applicable to all leisure activities, whatever their form. That is casual leisure interests have their core activities, too, often described in the name of the general activity—watching television, window shopping, taking a nap, going for a walk. It is likewise with project-based leisure, where core activities are manifested in what volunteers do at an arts festival or during a program effecting disaster relief.

Casual leisure

Finally, for all the theoretical discussion of casual leisure down through the years since its formal introduction (Stebbins 1982), only in the nature-challenge study did I get around to asking my respondents about how they use free time in this way. Two of the most common casual leisure activities for the climbers were watching videos or films in a cinema and socializing with friends, as in, for example, having a coffee, going to dinner, going out for drinks, chatting on the telephone, or taking in a party. These two were joined by a third equally common activity, namely reading. This consisted of reading books, magazines, and more rarely, the newspaper, and included material both related and unrelated to climbing and other outdoor pursuits. Surfing the Internet and watching television were by and large scorned, although some spent small amounts of time in e-mail correspondence with friends and relatives.

The most common casual leisure interests among the kayakers were reading books and magazines, socializing and, unlike the climbers, watching television and walking their dog. In this regard and giving substance to the proposition that one person's leisure is another's obligation, some other kayakers said that walking their dog was *not* something they did for fun. A second group of somewhat less common casual leisure interests was composed of reading and sending e-mail messages, watching films and videos, listening to music, surfing the Internet, and cycling around town for relaxation. On average the sample spent slightly over an hour and a half each day at these activities, somewhat less than the average for the climbers. Note that, with all three samples, such averages hide the fact that, given the tendency to pursue these hobbies on weekends, there is rather less free time for casual leisure then than during the weekdays after meeting work and non-work obligations.

The principal casual leisure of the snowboarders is reading, socializing, watching films and videos, and watching television. Here, too, socializing, in its many different expressions, reigns supreme. By contrast tending to the e-mail and walking a dog were, for this sample, the least popular. Furthermore, of the three groups, the snowboarders reported by far the largest average amount of daily time devoted to casual leisure: 3.5 hours. In good part this exceptional figure can be explained by the fact that, compared with the kayakers and climbers, many of them held part-time jobs or were unemployed, leaving thereby significantly more time for leisure of both kinds.

As for the meaning of casual leisure, the snowboarders were much in tune with the other two groups. The majority of them commented on its capacity to provide mental and physical rest in addition to relaxation.

Conclusion

The study of kayakers, snowboarders, and mountain climbers is a latecomer to the list of investigations on serious and casual leisure that began in the 1970s. That a substantial framework of established theoretic codes now exists with which to guide contemporary exploration in the serious leisure perspective is to be expected. Such is a mark of the theoretical and empirical sophistication of this part of the interdisciplinary field of leisure studies. Nevertheless, even at this later stage of concatenation of research in this area, it is still possible to discover new ideas, emergent theoretic codes exemplified here in the new meanings of risk and the nature and role of epics.

The mountain hobbies also offered an opportunity to explore the place of casual and project-based leisure in the lives of the interviewees (they reported having little time to give to the latter). The results showed how many of them fashioned in their free time optimal leisure lifestyles, ways of living peculiar to their chosen serious leisure blended with the appealing casual leisure options available to them in the Canadian Rockies and nearby Calgary. As for project-based leisure, this was the first examination of it as such, its appearance in the perspective having been very recent (Stebbins 2005b).

References

Campbell, J. B., Tyrell, D. J., and Zingaro, M. (1993) "Sensation Seeking Among Whitewater Canoe and Kayak Paddlers," *Personality and Individual Differences,* 14: 489–91.

Csikszentmihalyi, M. (1990) *Flow: the psychology of optimal experience,* New York: Harper & Row.

Glaser, B. G. (2005) *The Grounded Theory Perspective III: theoretical coding,* Mill Valley, CA: Sociology Press.

Lois, J. (2003) *Heroic Efforts: the emotional culture of search and rescue volunteers,* New York: New York University Press.

Lyng, S. (1990) "Edgework: a social psychological analysis of voluntary risk-taking," *American Journal of Sociology,* 95: 851–86.

Mannell, R. C. (1989) "Leisure satisfaction," in E. L. Jackson and Burton, T. L. (eds.) *Understanding Leisure and Recreation: mapping the past, charting the future,* State College, PA: Venture.

Mannell, R. C. and Kleiber, D. A. (1997) *A Social Psychology of Leisure,* State College, PA: Venture.

Slanger, E. and Rudestam, K. E. (1997) "Motivation and Disinhibition in High-risk Sports: sensation seeking and self-efficacy," *Journal of Research in Personality,* 31: 355–74.

Stebbins, R. A. (1982) "Serious Leisure: a conceptual statement," *Pacific Sociological Review,* 25: 251–72.

——(1996) *The Barbershop Singer: inside the social world of a musical hobby,* Toronto, ON: University of Toronto Press.

——(2004) *Between Work and Leisure: the common ground of two separate worlds,* New Brunswick, NJ: Transaction Publishers.

——(2005a) *Challenging Mountain Nature: risk, motive, and lifestyle in three hobbyist sports,* Calgary, AB: Detselig.

——(2005b) "Project-based Leisure: theoretical neglect of a common use of free time," *Leisure Studies,* 24: 1–11.

——(2006) "Concatenated Exploration: aiding theoretic memory by planning well for the future," *Journal of Contemporary Ethnography,* 35: 483–94.

——(2007) *Serious Leisure: a perspective for our time,* New Brunswick, NJ: Transaction.

van den Hoonaard, W. C. (1997) *Working with Sensitizing Concepts: analytical field research,* Thousand Oaks, CA: Sage.

11

TELLING TALES ABOUT HOW CONCEPTS DEVELOP

Stories from ethnographic encounters with the Moog synthesizer

Trevor Pinch

Introduction

Can we ever escape narrative? I doubt it. The more my career unfolds as a qualitative researcher the more convinced I am of the disjunction between the formal representation of what it is we as social scientists do and our owntales from the field. The formal representation is often couched in epistemologically loaded terms, such as "theories," "concepts," "data," "methods," "schools," (e.g. ethnomethodologist, interactionist, interpretive sociologist, constructivist, etc.) and concomitant issues of veracity such as "the adequacy of the data," the "representativeness of the sample," the "match between theory and data," the "novelty of the theoretical contribution," and so on. The ethnographic field tale, however, is more likely to be couched in terms of authentically describing what the people we talked and interacted with said and did; how they experienced their world, what it was like to be there, do that, feel that, and so on.[1] It is widely recognized that these latter sorts of experience, grounded in the contingency of everyday language and practice, can often be better narrated with the tools and skills of the journalist or the novelist. That is why a journalist writing about football hooliganism can produce an account which is as interesting, rings as true, and is as insightful as one couched in the formal language of the social sciences.[2]

A new genre of "method talk" (akin to this volume's call for a new form of "theory talk"), focused upon the realities and practicalities of doing sociological research, emerged amongst British sociologists in the mid-1970s. Colin Bell and Howard Newby's influential book, *Doing Sociological Research* (Bell and Newby 1977) seemed to offer a way of escaping the dichotomy between formal accounts of research and its practical contingencies. By asking for an account of "the realities" of social research, a counter-narrative to the officially sanctioned method talk was invited: what "really" went on as opposed to that which was officially published; the "back-stage" story versus the "front-stage" account; the dirt, the "inside story," the methods account "warts and all." But this new account had its own narrative structure of revealing, confessing, problematizing, grounding in contingency, and so on and was, needless to say, guided by ideas and concepts as to what was germane and interesting in these confessional tales. Such accounts also faced the delicate issue of credibility—especially if they departed too much from the officially enshrined version of the "method" used. Such accounts threatened to damage the credibility of the original study by revealing some of the contingencies which generated it. As with debunking strategies in science (Collins and Pinch 1979), drawing attention to the humans involved can serve to undermine research. Being aware of this, the sociologist will be circumspect, choosing what to reveal and what to hide.

My claim in this chapter is that the narratives we produce and the social science concepts and theories we work with are invariably entwined. Rather than "talk the talk" and "walk the walk," social scientists in practice "talk the walk." Two of the questions the editors of this volume asked us to address, hint at the link between the walk (theories) and the talk (narrative):

- How did your initial concepts change over time into the finished story?
- How were the key ideas settled upon in the end, refined, and presented?

For "concepts" to change and segue into a "finished story" implies that the concepts themselves are bound up with the narrative that produces the "story." That "key ideas" have to be "presented" implies that such ideas are not self-revelatory but also depend to some extent upon a discursive context. To talk about how the concepts and theories used in ethnography were actually developed is to invite yet another story—a story about where the ideas came from, what was done with them, how they gained or lost traction and so on.

In this chapter I will tell the story of the origin and development of some of the ideas used in the seven-year study which led to my co-authored book, *Analog Days: The Invention and Impact of the Moog Synthesizer* (Pinch and Trocco 2002). But in telling this story, I do not want to lose sight of the bigger issue of how social science concepts themselves figure in ethnographies and whether they need to be explicitly referenced as "ideas" and "theories" at all, and by doing so what they add to or detract from the ethnographic enterprise.

Origin stories in science

Scientists sometimes create "origin stories" of how their disciplines or schools of research started—origin stories and events associated with them (often celebrated in ritualistic ways) can be important in establishing the identity of a new field (Abir-Am and Elliot 1999). The provenance of such origin stories in science garners suspicion for the skeptical sociologist and historian of science because of the work which such origin accounts do. Also counter-narratives and contestation of particular events can be found. Scientific discoveries themselves are embedded in accounts where emphasis is placed upon where, when, and under what exact circumstances the discovery was made. Contestation can be found over exactly *what* was discovered, *when* it was discovered, and by *whom* (Brannigan 1981; Kuhn 1970; Woolgar 1976). Even dating the exact moment of a discovery in science (important in establishing priority) can be difficult, as Woolgar has shown for the case of pulsars (a Nobel Prize winning astrophysical discovery made during the 1960s). Is the date of the discovery when the first piece of repeatable scruff was found on a graph by a female graduate student (Jocelyn Bell, who interestingly did not share in the Nobel Prize), or when the later evidentiary arguments identified the scruff to be a major astrophysical anomaly, or even later still when that anomaly was taken to be a new phenomenon in the physical world (Woolgar 1976)?

If the argument can be made for the natural sciences the same is surely true for accounts of the origins of ethnographic projects. Accounts are embedded in stories which often take on a life of their own and which may serve ritualistic purposes or can be used to legitimate a particular researcher's claim that they did in fact carry out the first of a particular sort of ethnography. With this caution in mind, I will turn to my own origin story of the ethnography of the Moog synthesizer.

Origin stories of the Moog project

I first got the idea for a study of the Moog synthesizer—the first commercially available electronic music synthesizer—when I found out that it had been invented in a small rural town, Trumansburg, near Cornell University where I happened to teach. Because I had had an earlier abortive career as a musician, even having built my own synthesizer, I knew of the salience of this invention and its importance for popular music.

In early presentations describing the origins of my Moog study, I often chose to embroider the account of "how I got into this research" with a little story. The story was set in a bar in Trumansburg, the Rongovian Embassy. I described this bar as an old hippy hangout; its ambience a "cross between Lord of The Rings and Hard Rock Café" (Pinch 1998). In the story I am drinking with a colleague who happens to mention that the Moog synthesizer was invented in this little township. Then having learnt this "outstanding fact about upstate life" I decide to embark upon my research on the synthesizer. The story is of a serendipitous discovery—contingency is emphasized over all else.[3]

Three themes are important to the telling of the story which set the scene for the bigger story of the research. (1) The hippy theme—the Rongovian Embassy is an old hippy haunt, I am myself an old hippy who used to be into electronic music and build and play such instruments, and the synthesizer itself is a product of the 1960s psychedelic movement. (2) The remoteness theme—to bring home the remoteness I tell the standard joke about Cornell University being "centrally isolated—five hours from anywhere you would want to be," and go on to remark in a deadpan voice (during talks) that "this small township, Trumansburg, is *just* isolated" (Pinch 1998). Moog's rural isolation is what gave character to his factory (where he employed local women quilters), and accounts for his own ambivalent relationship to the burgeoning 1960s psychedelic movement. Remoteness also adds dramatic tension to the story, by contrasting the importance of the invention with the unimportance of the place where it occurred. (3) The personal theme—my own presence in the story was important in terms of spelling out my methodology in this ethnography. Having built synthesizers and played them, albeit a long time ago, did not only give me a useful entrée into the field (for instance it gave me some credibility with Moog himself, who was not enamored with academic types), but more importantly it offered an interesting methodological vantage point. I was carrying out a study of a cultural experience that I had myself participated in years before but now seemed remote to me. In a sense as I got more and more immersed in the field I was learning about myself, who I had been as a participant in this story, as well as learning about the social world of synthesizers. This attempt to recover a previous, now temporally and culturally remote, immersion experience was, I felt, methodologically interesting. The same sort of issue would crop up in other field studies, say an East German today studying the former East Germany. A cultural change has happened such that the form of life being investigated which was once inhabited by the researcher is now remote.

The story I told of the origins of my research could fairly easily be questioned as to its veracity. In earlier papers I refer to other key events which are effaced from this account or given less prominence. The story of the Rongo also sounds too good to be true. I have a hazy recollection of talking with my Cornell historian of technology colleague, Ron Kline, about Moog but I cannot now verify that the actual discovery took place in the famed Trumansburg bar. It could have been there; we certainly drank there on more than one occasion, but I'm no longer sure.

Theoretical fictions

In re-reading my own earlier papers about the roots of my study I find that I used a convenient historical fiction to describe how the research project developed. This is a typical formulation:

Once I learnt that the synthesizer came from Trumansburg, I did a little bit of background research and found that no-one had studied this topic seriously. Even more importantly, I quickly found out that there were all sorts of people still around dating back to the Moog … A Ph.D. student, Frank Trocco, joined me and we have tracked down and interviewed most of the relevant engineers, musicians, people who worked at the factory, sales people, PR people and so on. We also quickly found the West Coast synthesizer engineer Don Buchla—who at the same time as Moog developed a very similar technology but with a very different vision of the instrument. By and large Buchla's vision and synthesizer have been forgotten— part of our task has been to try and understand why Moog's way of doing things triumphed.

(Pinch 1998)

This sort of account renders the process of launching into research as a linear sequential process with "background research," followed by a co-researcher joining the project, and us "finding" the relevant actors. It is as if the relevant literature, the necessary funding and personnel, and the respondents are all passively waiting out there to be discovered or marshaled in a straightforward manner. What is effaced from this sort of account of course are all the contingencies of getting the necessary resources (how was the funding raised, what arguments were made to get it, etc.?), the actual setting up of the fieldwork, and the often circuitous route whereby a co-author joins a project and the subsequent negotiation over credit (did he really "join" or rather help constitute the goals of the project, what exactly was his contribution, and so on?).

Perhaps of most interest to this volume is the effacement and fictionalization of the theoretical and conceptual underpinnings of the research. The project is presented as an overly empirical endeavor whereby a "little bit of background research" is carried out and we find that "no-one had studied this topic seriously." This matter-of-fact style also uncovers the relevant people, as in "we quickly found Buchla" as if we stumbled upon him with no a priori interest. In fact, reading about the history of electronic music in preparation for the project had already led me to Buchla.

Furthermore and crucially, there is no doubt that the research was informed by a set of theoretical concerns even if these were not always mentioned explicitly. My choice of this project was shaped by my own background in sociology of technology. I saw the potential of writing about musical instrument design and use from a new perspective. My key insight was to realize that musical instruments are in fact technologies and that ideas developed in the sociology of technology might apply to musical instruments. The theoretical strategy here can be seen to be to apply ideas that work in one familiar area—technology—to a new area—musical instruments.

184

This is a strategy I have used before in my career. The well known approach, the Social Construction of Technology (SCOT) (Bijker et al. 1987; Pinch and Bijker 1984), came from applying ideas in the sociology of science to a new object of study, technology. In other words if one could talk about the *social construction of scientific facts*, as was common in the late 1970s and early 1980s, it was also possible to talk about the *social construction of technological artifacts*.

This theoretical strategy has to navigate between the poles of similarity and difference. If the new object is too *similar* to the object previously studied the new application will appear trivial—merely an application of what is already known rather than a new theoretical development. If the object is too *different*, then the theoretical approach will appear strained and unconvincing—an example of pushing a theoretical approach too far. If the approach is so easy to do it will probably have already been done and should show up in your literature survey. The hardest thing to judge is whether such a theoretical approach is going to pay dividends in the field. This is, in my experience, where the ethnographic or historical case study plays a crucial role. It is not enough to show in principle that the new area can plausibly benefit from importing theoretical ideas from another area, one needs to cash out the new ideas with a compelling case study—one that really shows how the new ideas can bring about new insights. In the case of SCOT, I doubt if the new approach would have taken off without the case study of the development of the bicycle carried out by my co-author, Wiebe Bijker. The bicycle was not only a great choice of technology because everyone is familiar with it, but also because following the different paths taken in the transition from the penny farthing bicycle (known in the 1890s as the "ordinary") to the safety bicycle (with two wheels of the same size) enabled us to show how key SCOT concepts such as "interpretative flexibility" and "closure"—ideas previously used in the sociology of science—could be applied to technology.

The "interpretative flexibility" notion came from Harry Collins' seminal ideas in studying scientific controversies. Experimental controversies were not easily resolved by more experimentation; experimental results were contested in a continued war between two interpretative camps (Collins 1985; Pinch 1986). There was interpretative flexibility over experimental results in that scientists had different meanings and explanations for the same data. But this interpretative war did not last for ever. Eventually a consensus would emerge; one camp would depart the scene with its tail between its legs and in the process a new experimental fact of the natural world would have been established. The losers might sometimes fight on, but a consensus amongst the key scientific community involved had developed. The consensus could be understood as a matter of closure, with particular "closure mechanisms" being identified. For instance a particular rhetorical display at a scientific meeting ("rhetorical closure") by an eminent scientist could help bring about consensus.

In the case of the bicycle the trick was to recast it as a case of interpretative flexibility. A key juncture in the history of the bicycle occurred when the penny farthing bike coexisted with the newly developed safety bicycle. We argued this was an example of interpretative flexibility over a technological artifact. The interpretative flexibility was linked to different meanings of the bicycle for two different social groups—those men of "means and nerve" who wanted to use the bicycle for sport and those groups, such as elderly people, women (who were prevented by Victorian fashion and etiquette from riding bicycles for sport), and other men, who wanted to use the bicycle for transport. In short there were two meanings of the bicycle and two bicycles—the "macho bicycle" and the "unsafe bicycle." Closure over meanings via a series of new artifacts (too complex to detail here (Bijker 1995)) led to the safety bicycle. In this way it could be shown how *society got embedded* within technological artifacts—a very different approach to showing the *impact* of technology on society which was standard within the sociology of technology of the day.

In embarking upon the Moog project I was thus sensitized to the idea that technologies could have contested meanings. Moog's synthesizers used a standard keyboard design as one of the ways of controlling sound. Buchla's synthesizers, on the other hand, although developed at the same time as Moog's, rejected this standard keyboard interface. Buchla reasoned that with a new source of sound, electronics, why control it in a conventional way taken over from older instruments such as organs and harpsichords? Instead he designed special arrays of pressure touch plates whereby musicians could interact with the instrument. Buchla, who had also invented a device which enabled patterns of sound to be endlessly repeated (known as a sequencer), advocated an alternative musical aesthetic for the synthesizer; a music of repetition, randomness and sweeps of sound and one not stymied by conventional melodic music played on the twelve-note chromatic scale. There were different meanings of the synthesizer to be found—in short, interpretative flexibility! Since Buchla's keyboards had not in the end become the dominant design, it would be a question of tracing the relevant closure mechanisms that led to Moog's vision winning out. Since keyboards were a familiar interface to many musicians it seemed likely that the take-up of the Moog in popular music to play conventional melodies (albeit with new timbres and added special effects) would in part explain the closure around the Moog way of doing things.

The actual explanation turned out to be a little more complicated, as part of the story also lay in the standardization of the technology. Standardization was a theme which historians of science such as Simon Schaffer (Schaffer 1992) and Ken Alder (Alder 1997) had increasingly emphasized. It turns out that Moog had designed his synthesizer around a standard known as the "volt-per-octave" standard. This means that a change of voltage of one volt input into an oscillator (oscillators produce electronic pitches and form the guts of any analog synthesizer) produces a change in pitch of the output of the oscillator by one octave. Such a standard only makes sense with conventional keyboards which play in octaves. Since Buchla did not use conventional keyboards he did not use this standard. All the main synthesizer manufacturers from this period, apart from Buchla, used some version of the volt-per-octave standard. Thus the marginalization of Buchla's approach was reinforced by the growing adaptation of this standard. The volt-per-octave standard provides a powerful exemplar of a moment in the story when culture gets embedded in technology. The sort of music we choose to play and listen to—say, conventional music based upon octaves—is part of our culture and thus this is how culture can become embedded or hardwired into technology.

Note that in this version of events the study is chosen in such a way that it is likely to be theoretically interesting. Also, because the period was the 1960s and the synthesizer was used in making the popular music of the day—psychedelic music—I knew my research might have interesting things to say about a long-standing theme in the sociology and history of technology—how culture shapes technology.

Sources of theoretical refinement

In the process of carrying out empirical work it is almost certainly the case that new ideas emerge and old ideas have to be reworked. This is the essential dialectic between data and preconceptions. Perhaps of most interest to this volume is that the process of theoretical refinement of ideas does not stop once one enters the field.

One often encounters the notion of the lone field worker immersed in the field for years, perhaps in danger of going native. This image is increasingly a myth. Certainly in the case of my own research on the synthesizer, which extended over a seven-year period, my fieldwork was punctuated by written drafts in various stages and frequent talks I was invited to give about the study. Such talks and the interaction it provided with a variety of audiences turns out to be an important source of development and refinement of the theoretical ideas.

I remember in one case giving a lecture at the University of Linkoping, Sweden, where I was a visiting professor for a couple of weeks in 1996. At that point I presented the synthesizer study as a traditional social constructivist study in terms of interpretative flexibility and closure. Part of the data I presented was a clip from a cult 1960s movie, *Performance*, starring Mick Jagger, who plays Turner, a faded rock star. Turner is at the controls of a Moog synthesizer, and in the key scene in the movie he transmutates (transmogifies) into his nemesis, Chas, a London gangster who is on the run and hiding out in Turner's house. A Linkoping-based Science and Technology Studies (S&TS) scholar, Marc Elam, pointed out to me that my study showed how the synthesizer might be used for a process of transgression, transcendence, and transformation. In short the synthesizer could be used to transgress a series of boundaries: between classical and popular music, between "straights" and "freaks," between science and art, between engineers and musicians, between salesmen and engineers, and between males and females. The goal appeared to be the classic 1960s one of transcending these boundaries to try and bring about a transformation in personal identities and in music. As a result of this conversation I started to emphasize more how the synthesizer was used to "perform" and transform identities (including gender identities). The people who played the new instrument were neither conventional engineers nor musicians—record sleeves at the time indicated that no one knew yet what to call these new synthesizer operators.

Also of significance are related theoretical developments in the field. No field is static and certain issues and problems in S&TS attracted my attention over the period of fieldwork. During the time of my study (1995–2002) there was increasing focus upon the role of users in technology. SCOT had been criticized for presenting a design-centric version of technology and neglecting the power of users to appropriate technologies or repurpose technologies for new uses. I myself had been working on this issue with a study of the use of the automobile in rural America (Kline and Pinch 1996). We had found cases where farmers first used the Model T as a source of stationary power (for farm implements and even for a washing machine). Understanding these users as potential "agents of technological change" led to more and more studies of users (Oudshoorn and Pinch 2003). This new theoretical interest led me to realize that the synthesizer story was also a story about users and in particular how Moog himself learnt from his users. He constantly tweaked his early synthesizer designs according to the needs of users. He discovered the need to make the technology more robust when he realized how some performers abused it; he also refined his keyboard designs when prominent musicians such as Wendy Carlos pointed out that portamento (the ability to glide between notes) would be a useful musical addition. In contrast to Buchla, Moog devised new ways of learning from and cultivating his users, whether it simply be by hanging out with customers after he had installed a synthesizer in their studio (as he did with Wendy Carlos), holding a workshop in his factory for users so he could learn what they wanted, or building his own factory studio which customers could use and where he employed a studio musician.

For Moog, learning from his users was not so much a formal business strategy as what he liked to do anyway. He often befriended and hung out with his customers, such as his second-ever customer, Eric Siday, who wanted to use the synthesizer to make "sound signatures"—the few seconds of sound that sell a product on TV or in radio advertising. Moog had no idea that his synthesizer would be used in this new area. He said of Siday, for whom he built a special tunable keyboard:

All the people I did business with in the early days have remained collaborators and friends and customers throughout the years ... They've been very valuable to me both as personal friendships and as guidance in refining synthesizer components.

(Interview with Robert Moog, 6/5/96)

Before I started the study I had no idea it would become a story about users. Intellectual development in the wider S&TS field at the time helped shape the theoretical interpretation in an ongoing way.

If you are an ethnographer it is hard to stop doing fieldwork. For me it is the fieldwork I carry out which most animates my career. It is where you learn new things and is the most fun part of research. Most ethnographers who leave the field, slowly (and ethnography by definition is a slow process) build up a corpus of studies they have carried out. Earlier studies form an invaluable reservoir of ideas, concepts, and experience to be used in later studies. The experienced fieldworker is always on the look out for similarities with earlier studies. In my case I had spent many years in the U.K. working on a major project studying salespeople through video and ethnographic research (e.g. Clark and Pinch 1995; Pinch and Clark 1986). When I discovered that part of the Moog story involved selling synthesizers in a new way (Pinch 2003)—they were sold for the first time ever in retail music stores—my interest was piqued. I had a framework for studying selling and seeing its relevance. I treated selling and salesmanship as key rhetorical activities where customers were persuaded of the merits of a product. My background in science studies was also important. I had been influenced by some of the ideas of Bruno Latour (e.g. Latour 1983; 1987). One of Latour's (1983) most interesting early articles was entitled "Give Me a Laboratory and I Will Raise the World." Latour argues that to understand the success of Pasteur in developing the anthrax vaccine one needs to follow Pasteur as he moves back and forth between his laboratory and the field. He goes to the field to find out what French farmers are facing with the anthrax epidemic; he moves back to the circumscribed world of the laboratory to refine his understanding of the bacteria; he develops a vaccine and then goes back to the field to enroll French farmers in tests of the vaccine. In the synthesizer study I encountered a legendary salesman who is reputed to have built the sales network in retail stores for synthesizers. Following the career of this salesman, I discovered he had taken early Moogs on the road as part of a novelty show, had built a partnership with Glen Bell (the founder of Taco Bell) to play Moogs in Taco Bell restaurants in Florida, before building his own venue where he could watch and learn how young musicians used the Moogs. Finally he moved back to the field again, successfully setting up synthesizer networks in retail stores and in the process enrolling new users. I was struck by the resonance with Latour's ideas (see Pinch 2003). Thus the applicability of earlier ideas and earlier studies from often quite unrelated contexts can be important for developing concepts in a new study.

One last important source of ideas is collaborators. The ethnographer is often presented as a solitary figure. Throughout my career I have made a habit of working closely with one or more collaborators with whom I conduct field-work. There are distinct advantages in combining different sorts of interviewing skills and it makes long fieldwork trips much more enjoyable if you can share the experience. Collaborators also always bring in new perspectives and ideas. Two examples from the Moog project come to mind. Frank Trocco, my main collaborator on the Moog project, was deeply involved in another project studying Navajo healing practices. When we were looking for a term to describe Moog's ability to move between the worlds of engineering and music and bring about a transformation, it was Frank who suggested the term "boundary shifter" with its resonances with the shaman term "shape shifter." We preferred this term to the usual economics of innovation term "boundary spanner" because we wanted to emphasize the material transformation which the boundary crossing brought about. The term boundary spanner as conventionally used implies an entrepreneurial actor who can cross boundaries between more than one social world—the boundary spanning helps stimulate entrepreneurial activity by spotting market openings in other areas and moving ideas from one area to another: in our case we wanted to stress the material transformation which boundary shifters bring about. In short the boundaries crossed are material as well as social boundaries, and boundary shifters can shift boundaries by bringing about material realignments as well as social realignments.

Collaborators from other projects can also play a part. One of my colla-borators on another project which took place during the genesis of the syn-thesizer book, Richard Rottenburg, an anthropologist, pointed out to me that a better term for the science studies notion of a "boundary object" was the anthropological term "liminal entity." A boundary object in the classic study of Star and Griesemer (1989) is an object that crosses social worlds or communities of practice and which can serve as a useful object in both worlds although it may have a different meaning in each world. The original example used by Star and Griesemer was a museum, which took on different meanings for scientists, patrons, visitors, and so on. A boundary object can be a source of tension and also a negotiating point amongst different com-munities who share it. Through Rottenburg's influence, I started to read the anthropologist Victor Turner and eventually used Turner's term "liminal entity" to describe the "betwixt and between" nature of the early synthesi-zers. Turner had described important rites of passage in tribes, where for example adolescent boys become men, as liminal events. Again I wanted a less static notion of the object—one that not only shared different meanings in social worlds but also was capable of realigning and transforming social worlds. By describing the synthesizer as a liminal entity I wanted to get at the idea that music and listeners were transformed by this device. Women synthesizer players in the early days could use the synthesizer to evolve new gender identities—the synthesizer was a source of transformation.

Lastly, I greatly value my own graduate students as a source of ideas and collaboration. It was one of my graduate students, Pablo Boczkowski who first pointed out to me that there was a gap in the science studies literature whereby there was no person with agency corresponding to the boundary object idea. In short it seemed as if boundary objects just appeared almost by magic without having humans struggling to bring them into being. It was partly to fill that gap that we came to the boundary shifter idea. In my book I described Moog as a "boundary shifter" who morphed back and forth between the worlds of engineering and music to produce a transformation. If I had not had these conversations with Pablo I might never have seen the theoretical need for this term.

In short, my advice for qualitative researchers looking for new concepts or refinement and development of concepts is to share your works and interests with as many other scholars, fellow students, and collaborators as you can find. They will not only provide helpful critique of your own work but also will be a good source of ideas and help to renew and refresh your own thinking. Take any opportunity you get to present your work and learn from these interactions. Again, this is no different from what Robert Moog learnt in developing a successful musical technology—learn from your users! And that is the last piece of advice—whoever or whatever you are studying, there are reflexive links between the projects of the respondents and your own projects.

Conclusion

In conclusion I want to return to the issue of the relationship between "theory" and "narrative." There is no doubt, as I have spelt out above, that theories and concepts guided my research on the synthesizer. They helped me understand what I was doing, where to look, and how to frame what I was finding. But the presentation of these concepts and interleafing them with the stories from the field in a manuscript is a difficult and delicate issue. In writing our book on the synthesizer, Frank Trocco and I decided on an unusual strategy, which was to minimize explicit references to theory. We had an introductory chapter where we talked about overarching themes like technology and music coming together and musical instrument design being an interesting case for S&TS. But explicit theoretical notions like "liminal entities" and "boundary shifters" were not introduced until the last chapter. This has the beauty that ordinary readers can pick up the book and read it without having to encounter too much sociological jargon; if they stay with the story, in the concluding chapter they can find explicit reference to the sociological and S&TS notions and ideas that have been implicit all along. For the ordinary reader this can be hugely advantageous, as one reviewer on Amazon.com commented:

191

Totally recommended. Apart from a little slide into sociological theory towards the end, this is a thoroughly entertaining, enthralling and authoritative look at the world of early synthesizers.

(Anonymous 2003)

We (and our publisher) wanted to write a cross-over trade/academic book and this meant that we were trying to have it both ways: make the theory and concepts explicit but not put them upfront. I am convinced that if we had put terms such as "liminal entity" in the first chapter we would have reached a much smaller readership. The paradox is that I suspect that readers who are not interested in sociological theory or S&TS probably took away as much by not reading that last chapter. But on the other hand the book would not have been possible to write at all without the guiding principles of theory. That in a nutshell is the dilemma I suspect we all face. There is no escape from narrative, or theory, but somehow the trick we have to pull off is to keep both in creative play and try and keep the readers involved. There are no easy solutions.

Notes

1 Another repertoire is that of the *bureaucratic* accounting of research in terms of the hours spent in the field, the amount of data transcribed, notebooks kept, photos taken, the ethical practices followed, the budgets spent, and so on.
2 Compare for instance journalist Bill Buford's *Among the Thugs* (2001) with the academic account provided by Peter Marsh, in *The Rules of Disorder* (Marsh et al. 1978).
3 The classic sociology study of serendipitous discovery is Bernard Barber and R. C. Fox (1958), "The Case of the Floppy-Eared Rabbits: an instance of serendipity gained and serendipity lost."

References

Abir-Am, P. G. and Elliot, C. A. (eds.) (1999) *Commemorative Practices in Science, Osiris*, 14, Chicago: University of Chicago Press.

Alder, K. (1997) *Engineering the Revolution: arms and enlightenment in France, 1763–1815*, Princeton, NJ: Princeton University Press.

Anonymous (2003) "Amazon.com Book Review of 'Analog Days: the invention and impact of the Moog synthesizer'," Online. Available at www.amazon.com/review/product/0674016173/ref=cm_cr_dp_synop?%5Fencoding=UTF8&sortBy=bySubmissionDateDescending#R2LSJ36FBUK16B (accessed 9 February 2008).

Barber, B. and Fox, R. C. (1958) "The Case of the Floppy-Eared Rabbits: an instance of serendipity gained and serendipity lost," *American Journal of Sociology*, 64: 128–36.

Bell, C. and Newby, H. (1977) *Doing Sociological Research*, New York: Free Press.

Bijker, W. (1995) *Of Bicycles, Bakelites, and Bulbs: toward a theory of sociotechnical change*, Cambridge, MA: MIT Press.

Bijker, W., Hughes, T. P., and Pinch, T. (1987) *The Social Construction of Technological Systems: new directions in the sociology and history of technology*, Cambridge, MA: MIT Press.

Brannigan, A. (1981) *Social Basis of Scientific Discoveries*, Cambridge, MA: Cambridge University Press.

Buford, B. (2001) *Among the Thugs*, London: Arrow.

Clark, C. and Pinch, T. (1995) *The Hard Sell: the language and lessons of street-wise marketing*, London: HarperCollins.

Collins, H. M. (1985) *Changing Order: replication and induction in scientific practice*, London: Sage.

Collins, H. and Pinch, T. (1979) "The Construction of the Paranormal: nothing unscientific is happening," *Sociological Review Monographs*, no. 27, R. Wallis (ed.) *On the Margins of Science: the social construction of rejected knowledge*, Keele: University of Keele, 237–70.

Kline, R. and Pinch, T. (1996) "Users as Agents of Technological Change: the social construction of the automobile in the rural United States," *Technology and Culture*, 37: 763–95.

Kuhn, T. S. (1970) *The Structure of Scientific Revolutions*, Chicago: University of Chicago Press.

Latour, B. (1983) "Give me a Laboratory and I will Raise the World," in K. Knorr-Cetina and Mulkay, M. (eds.) *Science Observed* (pp. 141–70), Beverly Hills, CA: Sage.

——(1987) *Science in Action*, Milton Keynes, U.K.: Open University Press.

Marsh, P., Rosse, E., and Harre, R. (1978) *The Rules of Disorder*, London: Routledge.

Oudshoorn, N. and Pinch, T. (2003) *How Users Matter: the co-construction of users and technologies*, Cambridge, MA: MIT Press.

Pinch, T. (1986) *Confronting Nature: the sociology of solar neutrino detection*, Dordrecht, the Netherlands: Kluwer.

——(1995)"Towards a Sociology of the Electronic Music Synthesizer: Some Ideas," paper presented at the Centre for Research into Innovation Culture and Technology, Brunel University, U.K., February 8.

——(1998) "The Social Construction of the Electronic Music Synthesizer," paper presented at the American Sociology Association Meetings, San Francisco, August 22.

——(2003) "Giving Birth to New Users: how the Minimoog was sold to rock & roll," in N. Oudshoorn and Pinch, T. (eds.) *How Users Matter: the co-construction of users and technology* (pp. 247–70), Cambridge, MA: MIT Press.

Pinch, T. and Bijker, W. (1984) "The Social Construction of Facts and Artifacts: or how the sociology of science and the sociology of technology might benefit each other," *Social Studies of Science*, 14: 399–441.

Pinch, T. and Clark, C. (1986) "The Hard Sell: 'patter merchanting' and the strategic (re)production and local management of economic reasoning in the sales routines of market pitchers," *Sociology*, 20: 169–91.

Pinch, T. and Trocco, F. (2002) *Analog Days: the invention and impact of the Moog synthesizer*, Cambridge, MA: Harvard University Press.

Schaffer, S. (1992) "Late Victorian Metrology and its Instrumentation: a manufacture of ohms," in R. Bud and Cozzens, S. (eds.) *Invisible Connections: instruments, institutions and science* (pp. 23–56), Bellingham, WA: SPIE Optical Engineering Press.

Star, S. L. and Griesemer, J. R. (1989) "Institutional Ecology, 'Translations,' and Boundary Objects: amateurs and professionals in Berkeley's museum of vertebrate zoology, 1907–39," *Social Studies of Science*, 19: 387–420.

Woolgar, S. (1976) "Writing an Intellectual History of Scientific Development: the use of discovery accounts," *Social Studies of Science*, 6: 395–422.

Part IV

CONCEPTUALIZING COMMUNITY
AND SOCIAL ORGANIZATION

12

THE ETHNOGRAPHY BEHIND
DEFENDERS OF THE FAITH

Samuel Heilman

Compelling curiosity

How shall I begin to tell the story of what went into my study of life among ultra-Orthodox Jews in and around Jerusalem? Perhaps the place to begin is with the curiosity that propelled me on what would turn out to be a quest for a world that looked quite different at first from what it turned out to be in the end. Curiosity was what compelled me to go into this world that in many ways saw itself in opposition to the one from which I, social anthropologist, academic and modern Orthodox Jew, came. But why begin with curiosity?

One of the first pieces of advice that I always give those who come to me for counsel before embarking upon some field research with the goal of completing an ethnography is that what they are about to do is not going to be easy. The tasks of carrying out observations and interviews in the real world are enormously demanding and onerous, filled with frustrations and difficulties. I warn them that the process is time-consuming in the extreme, with long periods of waiting for just the right detail to emerge that will help one figure out what is actually going on. And the chances are that after all the waiting one might not even recognize or appreciate the detail when it does emerge. I tell them that good informants, those who know what insiders need to know, are hard to find and that many, if not most, people one encounters in the places one wants to learn about are exasperatingly inarticulate and frequently do not know the answers to the questions researchers ask or the full significance of what they do—Durkheim was absolutely correct when he wrote, "Which of us knows all the words of the language he speaks and the entire signification of each?" (1912: 486). Finally, I remind them that taking field notes and packing them with the experiences and knowledge in some kind of syntactic way, transforming these notes into an account or narrative that allows others to share one's understanding (when and if it does come) as well as to appreciate its significance is astonishingly difficult, particularly when part of what one wants to share are sentiments, atmosphere, or the sheer physical experience of being somewhere. In fact, as Mitchell Duneier has correctly noted, "in real life, even the most straightforward 'facts' like age or family status can be difficult to record in a straightforward way" (Duneier 2006: 684). Add to that the often infuriating demands of IRB committees and those demanding safeguards on all research dealing with human subjects, and the prospect of doing ethnography is overwhelming.

Accordingly, because of all this difficulty and based on my own experience, I suggest to all who come for advice that it is essential that they begin with a *powerful, compelling curiosity* about the particular field setting, group, or subject they want to research. Without that compulsion, that insatiable desire to discover and uncover, followed by an equally strong need to share the discoveries with others, they ought not to embark on the project. The compulsion and curiosity, of course, are not by themselves sufficient, but in their absence much that remains is daunting in the extreme. And I have found few who have succeeded without it. The curiosity need not be purely academic or scientific. Indeed, something personal and subjective might even be better. The drive and passion that a personal quest contains can often times be more potent and sustaining than any other desire to know—and in the face of having to spend hours writing and coding notes, days waiting for something revealing to happen, endless encounters during which one is forced to show interest in dull or inane conversations and trying to make sense out of obfuscating comments or contradictory insights from interviewees who seem to have nothing of value to impart, the personal curiosity can be the extra impetus that keeps one at it long after the simple academic motive has been sapped.

It was just this sort of curiosity with which I began the research that culminated in the publication of my book, *Defenders of the Faith: Inside Ultra-Orthodox Jewry* (1992). As I wrote in the prologue of that book, the world of Jews whose Orthodoxy kept them living in enclaves in which they sought to create a life apart, insulated from what they considered to be the defiling influences of contemporary civilization and modern society, seemed to me at first to be the incarnation of a Jewish past that I felt a compulsion to visit and in which I then believed I might discover something about my own religious roots and heritage. My maternal grandparents, whom I had never met, had come, my mother assured me, from just such a world, which she too had once inhabited. In this respect, I was not, I suspect, too different from those who imagine that in the faces of the bearded men in black and the bewigged women in long skirts, the dozens of earlocked little boys and pigtailed little girls, often arrayed in schools around long rows of desks and loudly reviewing ancient texts or hearing timeless tales, they are looking at the reincarnation of those ghettoes of a pre-Holocaust Eastern Europe, a world somehow caught in time and for some bathed in nostalgia. I too thought at the outset, these were people and places that time forgot and that learning about them would enable me to turn back the clock and see a world that had seemed to be part of my Holocaust-survivors-family's past. To be sure this is a nostalgia that does not necessarily signify a desire to live like that but simply to glimpse what is sometimes viewed (falsely, I should add, in light of what I learned) as a more primitive and hence authentic version of Judaism that has somehow insulated itself against the ravages of time and change—and given the Holocaust—even death and destruction.

Without a doubt, there are those partisan boosters of this way of life who argue just that: that these sorts of Jews, *haredim*, as the fervently religious call themselves, are the real thing, the true defenders of the faith and keepers of the immutable tradition against all of modernity that tries to erode it. They feed this nostalgia and often feed off it, drawing financial and political support for their institutions and ways of life from those who do not live like them but have become convinced that without them Judaism would ultimately wither. But all that I would learn later. At the outset, my curiosity, powerfully subjective and not all that well informed—in spite of my previous research on Orthodox Jews and my own personal background in a corner of the modernist, acculturated wing of that Judaism—was enough to get me going and past many of the early obstacles.

The questions I was trying to answer

At the heart of my study were a series of questions I sought to answer. These I listed in the prologue to the book: "In a world rushing headlong into tomorrow, why are there people who appear to cling tenaciously to yesterday? Is it really yesterday in which they live? Can a fortress of timeless tradition stand inviolate and unimpaired through the barrage of today's demands? Or is it an illusion to believe in today's shrinking world that one culture can remain untouched by another on its doorstep?" By the end of the book, I had discovered as I watched the extent to which these people set the agenda of their lives *in opposition* to the demands of the contemporary society and culture that had reached to that doorstep, that the process of opposing had in effect forced many of these people to shape themselves to every element of that which they opposed and create a counter-form of it. They were not untouched by the modern world outside their own. On the contrary, they were never very far from it because they were always trying to counter it, and they often did that by taking elements of it and either camouflaging what they had taken or reshaping it to their needs. Thus, for example, they learned the rhythms of the music of the modern world but then adapted them to fit to the tunes and words of the songs they sang that celebrated tradition, as if those tunes and musical arrangements were their own. What seemed to be indigenous dances at the Hasidic gatherings were, as I discovered when I listened carefully, but a version of the rocking rhythms

I would hear elsewhere in town. Indeed, in one infamous case, a tune by a German heavy metal group, Genghis Khan, which had been an entry in the Eurovision contest that much of Israel had been watching on television, was adopted as a popular dance in haredi circles, but now the lyrics were Yiddish and the themes messianic. Or similarly in their zeal for technology, the haredim sought to be no less expert (and in some cases more so) than their contemporaries in mainstream society. When I interviewed a Belzer Hasid about the world he inhabited, he insisted on also talking to me about the word processing program I was using on my computer.

Perhaps the moment that crystallized my understanding that even what seemed at first look to be steeped in tradition was not so but reconstituted in modern terms, came in a moment I describe in the book. It occurred when I visited a scribe whose work with tefillin and life seemed, as I put it, "a tableau of the past nearly perfectly preserved, everything done as it always had been, no changes, no disturbances, no contaminations." The closer I looked and the more I learned from him, the more I discovered that even here in the hole-in-the-wall workshop, as the scribe happily explained, the "new was improved," and "today only looked like yesterday," but was not the same. The quill he used was only a small part of the past; the phone he used and the manufacturing method he embraced were far more important to him. And I found that "where others are absorbed by and celebrate the present, haredim may have found a way to absorb the present while celebrating the past."

In the culture war that seemed to be the essence of the way haredi Jews looked at the modern world from which they claimed to distance themselves, I discovered a curious reality. Combatants must enter the mind and share the reality of those whom they oppose if they are to successfully oppose them. But in so doing, they end up having to acquire two kinds of consciousness, two minds, two faces. One was the one they used to be an insider, the face of faith. But the other was the one they used when they tried to close out the cultural other. Both had become part of who they are. And when they could find an opportunity to harmonize the two, as in their interest in and competence with technology or music, one could see both faces and consciousnesses at once. It was at these moments that one could not help but realize that these were people who only appeared to be untouched by today and in some timeless yesterday.

The insider advantage and cultural competence

These insights that came from spending much time moving between the two worlds—haredi and contemporary mainstream culture—were aided by my personal and professional experience as well as my training as a social anthropologist. At the outset, I still clung to the fantasy that in the ghettoes of late-twentieth-century ultra-Orthodoxy I would be going back in time.

Indeed without it, I might not have had the necessarily compelling curiosity that would sustain through all of the difficulties I would subsequently encounter in my research. But the curiosity and the fantasy were insufficient. I drew as well on my cultural competence, which provided me with a good understanding of where to look to find the people about whom I wanted to learn and whose precincts I wished to penetrate. Moreover, my subjective feelings tinged with nostalgia provided the basis for the empathy that is a necessary starting point for anyone engaging in the methodology of participant observation, the approach I chose for my research.

In theory, of course, anyone can research anything. The literature is replete with studies carried out by people who approached their field from an altogether foreign position. And Jews studying a world very distant from their own are so common as to be a cliché: from Franz Boas, the German-born Jew with a Ph.D. in physics who studied the Kwakiutl of the Pacific Northwest, Elliot Liebow, the Jewish man documenting black street-corner men's society and later the lives of homeless women, and of course Claude Lévi-Strauss, the cosmopolitan Parisian Jew who explored the natives in the heart of the jungle along the Amazon river. Indeed, it was Lévi-Strauss' *Tristes Tropiques* (1974) that served as a template for my own study. As he had navigated into the darkness of the Amazon in a kind of anthropologist-as-seeker journey in search of the true primitive who had somehow held off time and change (and found instead that there were no true primitives left), I too wended my way into the darkest of Jewish ghettoes in Jerusalem in search for the "utopia of the past," as Stanley Diamond (1974: 208) has called the seeking after primitives.

Yet unlike these others who began largely as complete strangers to the worlds about which they were curious and that they wanted to discover, I began as at the very least a kind of native and insider. I was an Orthodox Jew, albeit university-trained in social science and one who valued modern secular society, investigating other Orthodox Jews who did not share fully in this same background. Elsewhere I have written about the relative benefits of beginning research as at least a partial native rather than a complete stranger, my argument being that the taken-for-granted understandings about a population that an insider has, the knowledge of where best to look and what to look for—as shaped by the disciplinary techniques of social science and ethnographic training—provides natives with advantages that complete outsiders lack. In the case of the ultra-Orthodox, the fact that I knew about the Jewish observances, the way the day and the calendar are organized, that I had some idea when and where spiritual experiences might occur, that I had requisite linguistic skills (a fluency in Hebrew and Yiddish) as well as liturgical competence, that I knew much about the basic rules of order, that I possessed much of the ritual gear and knew how to use it—all this and more that comprises what may be summed up as *cultural competence*—made it possible for these people who were still quite distant from me to sense that they could share with me aspects of their existence that would simply be too hard to explain to someone who was from elsewhere in the human universe. As such, I was, I believe, well situated to explore their world: close enough to be able to understand what I saw but distant enough to not take it for granted and to remain sufficiently curious about it.

These advantages were captured perfectly one evening when, by now comfortable in the field and well along in my research, I had occasion to take a colleague, a photo-anthropologist, son of a Protestant minister, who knew absolutely nothing about Orthodox Jews but was on a field trip to document their lives photographically, on a tour of one of the more obscure corners in the world of Jerusalem's ultra-Orthodoxy. As I guided him around some of the more insulated corners of the precincts of Jerusalem's ultra-Orthodox quarters in the cold twilight of a December evening, we were beckoned by an old bearded and black-frocked man to follow him into a tiny one-room synagogue to help complete a *minyan*, a prayer quorum that was short by one of the minimum 10 males needed. I explained to our summoner in Yiddish that my friend was not a Jew and could not be counted, but this did not bother the old man; he already had eight in the room and with him, I would be enough. We all went inside, and my guest alternately sat and stood in the pews watching in fascination while the rest of us completed the prayer service. Afterwards, as we walked out the door and back into the night, I asked for his reactions. He had seen the way everyone turned in the same direction and prayed. But he missed the significance of many of the displays of piety that were part of the activity. Not only did he fail to understand the meaning of the outcries during several prayers (a common show of piety and devotion), the significance of the timing (how knowing who was the last to complete the *Shema* prayer or the silent *Amida* before the prayer leader's closing was an indication of who had the highest status in the room), but he completely misunderstood the meaning of the swaying and gesticulation (traditional displays of spiritual intensity) that one familiar with the nature of Orthodox Jewish prayer could not have missed. My guest took these bodily movements for "aerobic exercises," and told me how he tried to figure out their connection to the prayers, asking if what he had seen was a way to keep the body fit while the spirit was engaged.[1] This was an interesting theory around which one could build a creative thesis, but it was completely mistaken in part because it was not supported by cultural competence and insider's knowledge.

Being there: feeling native

Thus, the need to prepare oneself before engaging in ethnography with a kind of basic cultural competence cannot be gainsaid. This of course is a dilemma, for the very process of acquiring that competence is one of the goals of the ethnographic enterprise. Perhaps the key to solving this conundrum is that the observer must become immersed in another culture before things begin to make sense and come into focus. Echoing this notion, anthropologist Ruth Behar, in a work subtitled *Returning to Jewish Cuba* and stimulated by the improbable desire similar to mine to somehow uncover a community and place that time forgot where a personal past might be recovered, writes, "When I finally returned again to Cuba in the 1990s, my aim wasn't to study the Jews. I wanted simply to be a Jew in Cuba" (2007: 15). She wanted to be absorbed in the atmosphere of the place. Elsewhere she calls this "the longing for memory, the desire to enter into the world around you and having no idea how to do it, the fear of observing too coldly or too distractedly or too raggedly ... " (Behar 1997: 3). This is not "going native," that taboo of field research when the observer loses all pretense of objectivity. Rather, it is what we might call "feeling native," where one shares in the sentiments of being an insider, what Clifford Geertz (1973) has called "sentimental education."

Had my guest spent enough time among these Jews he wanted to document, had he acquired some basic experience in what Jewish communal prayer entails—spirituality, devotion, a way of gauging the level of involvement of one's co-worshippers, and so on—gained by sufficient exposure before focusing his observations, he might have been able to integrate his experience more meaningfully and understand that he had not been watching aerobic but rather spiritual exercises. Hence much of the first stage of ethnography may simply be spending time with the people in the field and gaining some of the taken-for-granted knowledge that is the essence of cultural competence. One might call this simply "being there." This of course is where one who begins even as a partial insider has an advantage over the complete outsider.

So how did I proceed? At one level the approach was deceptively simple. I began to frequent synagogues, spend time in yeshivas, wander along the streets of haredi neighborhoods; I even dipped myself in mikvahs. I began my account with a chapter called "Taking the Plunge," an account of my immersion in a *mikveh* (ritual bath) on Yom Kippur eve. This "plunge" was both a metaphor for and a symbolic illustration of my desire simply to be an insider, to be immersed in the world about which I was so curious. At the same time, I understood that if I allowed myself to become too much the insider, to drown in it, I would lose the capacity to provide a conceptual view that helped me see these people's otherness. Hence, the very cultural competence that allowed me inside might prevent me from retaining the distance that would permit me to see the patterns, sociological implications, and conceptual elements that would make what I experienced and witnessed meaningful ethnographically.

Wherever I went, I struck up conversations, often beginning with small talk (in which my quasi-insider status helped) but in time developing into questions that required explanations and insights from those who talked with me. I spent hours talking to them—not simply trying to plumb them for information. I haunted a variety of neighborhood shops, made my way to all sorts of gathering places, both informal and formal, from workshops to bus stops to *shtibblach*, one-room chapels. I was present at the sermons and public discourses of countless rabbis and religious lecturers and went to a number of places of pilgrimage—most commonly graves of holy men. I rushed to various Hasidic rabbis' *tisches*, the ceremonial meals at which the faithful gathered to share food and camaraderie with one another and their "rebbe." Some of these venues were places with which I was already familiar; others were new. Gradually I arrived at sites and established relationships with people that I found accessible. By that I mean I went to places where my presence was tolerated, where people would answer my questions, where at the same time I could gradually become unobtrusive. I spent hours, days, weeks, and months in the precincts of haredi Jewry *just trying to feel at home* there, until my presence was taken for granted. I had of course learned to do this in my earlier fieldwork, as when I joined Talmud study circles in all sorts of places and with all sorts of people, an experience described in *The People of the Book* as well as *The Gate behind the Wall*.

Some places were sites where I already had contacts from previous fieldwork. Thus, for example, I returned to the workshop of a wood turner, described in an earlier book, *A Walker in Jerusalem*. This man made the decorative dowels on which Torah scrolls were mounted, and his place of business, which was a kind of hitching post or hang-out where many people from the haredi world found their ways, turned out to be a good place to meet some of the people whose way of life I would end up documenting in *Defenders of the Faith*. Whereas my earlier observations here had focused on the manifest functions of the shop and the personality of the craftsman and shopkeeper, now I focused upon the people who passed through the place.

Each venue brought its own rewards and difficulties. For example, I spent four intensive months sitting in at haredi schools, particularly in several all-boys kindergartens and first grade classes. The teachers in these places (all of whom were males), I discovered, actually appreciated having another adult around—particularly a "professor"—before whom they could show off their considerable skills that remained largely invisible in their community, where scholars, rabbis, and yeshiva heads were far more respected than the "*melamed* in the *cheder*," the teacher in the primary school. At the same time, it was more difficult becoming an unobtrusive presence in such small spaces (though in fact I did in time).

Some places were difficult to bear, and I abandoned them. A visit to the *chevra kaddisha*, the volunteer burial society, and the body preparation rooms where they worked, proved personally troubling. I left, convincing myself that I would meet the people who worked here in other venues and did not need to spend time watching them handle corpses. In fact, this place haunted me, and I would return there years later, a field trip that would expand dramatically and bear fruit nine years later in my ethnography on Jewish death, bereavement and mourning, *When a Jew Dies* (2001).

The role of theory versus intellectual bricolage

There are those who argue that having a theory, a thesis that puts facts into some order, can compensate for the absence of cultural competence or can abbreviate the time one needs to be there. My documentary photographer's theory and the erroneous conclusions to which it led neatly suggest the problems with this argument. Indeed we learn that even E. E. Evans-Pritchard, among the more important practitioners of the ethnography craft, found that while he spent a great deal of time trying to frame what he witnessed in terms of a theory that would allow him to make sense of it, only in the final few months of his stay among the Nuer could he converse at all effectively with informants, begin to get at what it meant to be Nuer (see Evans-Pritchard 1969: 261).

This is not to deny the value of having a conceptual framework that can structure one's observations and interviews. But by itself it is not enough. Perhaps James Clifford got it right when he suggested that one must instead engage in "a continuous tacking between the 'inside' and 'outside' of events," in order to make sense of otherness (Clifford 1988: 34). One moves between immersion in a culture along with the competence this yields and a theoretical framework, participation and observation, rapport and analysis, entering and leaving the world being studied, being and watching while we are doing. Put differently, there is both an inchoate and amorphous element to the ethnographic enterprise as well as a developed and syntactic one.

In a sense, finding a way to tack between the two, between hypotheses or theories and being there and drawing on my insider's knowledge and feelings, became for me the first great challenge of my work. The world I was examining sought in some way to assimilate me, mistaking my desire to feel like a native for one of going native. The approach that I used for my tacking I have called "intellectual bricolage," a process in which one makes "sense of reality—which is often inconsistent and constantly changing, and not nearly as ordered as sociologists and anthropologists would have us believe—by improvising ideas, making 'do with whatever is at hand,' moving freely from one insight to another as the need arises," (Heilman 1992: xviii) while also drawing upon one's participation and observation, self-consciousness and the awareness of otherness. This bricolage, aided by keeping elaborate notes that combine observations as well as working hypotheses with feelings and personal narrative, allows the observer to transcend the looking from the outside and to avoid being carried away by acting like a native on the inside. There is a polyphonic and contrapuntal quality to this sort of improvisational effort. The ethnographer must engage in multiple discourses, a creative dialogue between an insider's participation and empathy and an outsider's observation and scrutiny. This requires constant reframing, resulting in the ethnographer's seeing a vision that is in many ways different, perhaps even deeper than what the pure participant does.

These multiple discourses, which were implicit in my work on the *Defenders of the Faith* but muted in the narrative account, become far more explicit in a subsequent book, *When a Jew Dies: The Ethnography of a Bereaved Son* (2001). Here the different perspectives or discourses are identified by different voices that are reflected in distinctive orthography in the text, allowing the readers to see the different sides of the ethnographer. One denotes and reveals my insider's voice as a bereaved son, and the other signals my outsider's one as an analyst and decoder of what is involved in Jewish bereavement. In *Defenders of the Faith*, these two voices are combined as one, the more common ethnographic method.

Let me offer an example. In a chapter entitled "Rosh Yeshiva," I provide the head of an advanced Talmudic academy an opportunity to express his ideological beliefs, much of which seek to draw a sharp line between the world he inhabits and the world that he understood me, university professor and social anthropologist as well as a Jew who has chosen not to live as he does, to represent. It is one of several such dialogues—which I understood from my life experience as a non-haredi yet Orthodox Jew—was part of the ongoing culture war over what constitutes the proper and ideal way of being a Jew. Some of the continuing battles in that war can be perceived in the chapter, even though they are muted in the desire to allow the Rosh Yeshiva to present his perspective. Thus, for example, the haredi contention that the ritual review of sacred texts that does not have as its goal some degree or end-point but has ontological meaning as a way of life is asserted as inherently superior to the way of life that my person and profession represent. It was here that I realized, as I reviewed my notes of the interview, that as much as my questions elicited his answers, my position, the ongoing debate that we represented within contemporary Jewry, and the desire to draw clear lines of distinction and demarcation informed and shaped what I learned and what he had to say. Without it, the elements of haredi culture that were built into his thinking would have remained unexpressed. On the other hand, had I allowed myself to be drawn into active debate about those judgments and perspectives, as I might have had I not been disciplined by my social anthropological training, I would have not allowed his worldview to emerge as clearly as it did. The ability to stand in two places at once was an expression of what I am calling my intellectual bricolage. It can be seen at work in similar chapters, which document my conversations with a variety of other characters who populate the pages of my book. It is the way I was able to empathize even with positions and people who at their core sought to negate the legitimacy of what I did and who I was. But at the same time, it enabled me to elicit from them powerful expressions of who they were and what they believed. It was not a theory that made this possible but rather the ability to draw on who I was, what I represented and believed, disciplinary training, and the ongoing cultural dynamic my encounters played out that made so much of this book possible.

Bricolage and the imperative of inscription

I did not realize at first that I was a bricoleur. I only discovered this as I re-read my notes, the actual tools of intellectual bricolage. Putting time in at particular sites or events or establishing relationships with a broad array of people, like cultural competence and curiosity, while necessary prerequisites for this book, were far from enough. What transformed all of them into something more than life experiences and the raw material of ethnography was their inscription, the writing down of my experiences and reflections into field notes that were both a means for recalling what I had witnessed or heard and even more so a mechanism for making those experiences coherent. Here Vincent Crapanzano's (1986) reading of Goethe, as articulated in his seminal essay "Hermes' Dilemma," is crucial for understanding what I did. He argues that "for an experience to be more than ephemeral it must be described—given coherence and order" (1986: 67). Writing these extensive notes, critical, albeit often exhausting to compose, particularly at the end of a full day of activities, served as the mechanism for integrating the contrapuntal views, framing and re-framing the complex discourses, and the various perspectives I had into some coherent whole. They enabled my intellectual bricolage precisely because they offered me a chance to explore and reflect upon my relationships and the nature of my encounters with the people whom I was studying. Residues of these notes and the feelings they describe linger in the background and the careful reader will find them, both in the selection of things described and even in the descriptions themselves. For example, in choosing to point out the failure of the haredi youngsters to have even a rudimentary knowledge of geography, one can sense the ethnographer's and modern Jew's astonishment (and perhaps even something of my exasperation, albeit shared by some, for example the teacher described in the scene) that these primary school pupils could not figure out where Israel was in part because of the enforced insularity of haredi culture, or that they could not get beyond their ideological beliefs to figure out the time it would take in their day to travel the distance between the cities of Jerusalem and Beersheba because to do so would, they believed, force them to conclude that today's Jews could improve on the patriarch Abraham's ability to traverse this distance in three days. Similarly, in a quoted interchange between the author and a Rosh (head of a) Yeshiva about the relative religious outlooks of the modern Orthodox and haredi Jews, the perceptive reader will discern the undercurrents of a debate about values that went beyond the accepted limits of ethnography.

In time these notes and their thick descriptions evolved into a kind of first draft of my final account. In a sense, these running written records were the key elements of my field enterprise, proving for me the truth of Stephen A. Tyler's insight in his own work that, "experience became experience only in the writing" (1986: 138). Of course, as is now freely admitted, ethnography, in which the instrument of observation is a person with a set of values, feelings, personal history, prejudices and the like, can never be completely freed from all those elements. As Gelya Frank (1979) has put it, the ethnographer's biography is always in the shadows.

To be sure, I share with many of the new ethnographers the conviction that we must take that biography out of the shadows to let readers know about the instrument through which they are observing. Now, and properly so, we expect ethnographers to reveal far more about themselves because the perspective of the researchers can not ever be completely separated from who they are. That is why as part of my ethnographic work I have increasingly also written about myself, my background, and the aspects of my biography that are in play in my role of participant observer and writer. In some ways this reached its logical conclusion in the aforementioned *When a Jew Dies: The Ethnography of Bereaved Son*, in which both voices, the personal and subjective as well as the professional and objective, share in the analytic task and thick description but with separate orthographic identities.

At the same time, such biographic revelations and their associated subjectivity are now and then subject to severe criticism as "embarrassing or distracting," and one critic of such an approach has even gone so far as to assert that "the lives of anthropologists are rarely as rich and as fascinating as that of their subjects" (see Frank 1979: 85; 1995: 357). This is the dilemma of a postmodern ethnography, and while it played a part in my work on *Defenders of the Faith* it remained unspoken.

Influences on my work

As should be clear by now, Lévi-Strauss' *Tristes Tropiques* served as a kind of model for my book. As he went upriver to find the past and also to some extent to test his own capacity to understand it, I went into the alleyways and streets of the ghettoes of ultra-Orthodoxy, the courts of the Hasidim, the yeshivas of the haredim and the like also to find a past. As Lévi-Strauss discovered—that the past he sought was in his imagination and no longer there even in the Amazonian jungle, that the "primitives" he encountered were very much touched by contemporary Western civilization—so too I discovered that what appeared to be a reiteration of a vanished world of Eastern European Jewry was in fact a contemporary reaction to modernity and the civilization and societies to which the lives I examined had become simply a counter-culture.

The approach that I used to reach these conclusions, the work of the new ethnographers, and in particular those collected in the volume *Writing Culture* (from which I have already quoted a number of times) profoundly affected my way of thinking as I was in the throes of the fieldwork and even more so the writing. They persuaded me both that who I was affected how I saw things and that the way I wrote about them was inseparable from the way others would understand and see them. The impact of these readings built upon perhaps the single most influential text in both this book and several that preceded and followed it. I refer to the series of essays by the late Clifford Geertz collected in his *The Interpretation of Cultures* (1973). It was Geertz who, first in his essay on the Balinese cockfight and later almost all he wrote, allowed me to think about behavior as constituting a text subject to interpretation and reinterpretation. His notion of thick interpretation, in which the process of ethnography becomes a task of sorting out "structures of signification" in which the ethnographer's construction of other people's social constructions is as much a revelation of who the ethnographer is as it is of what is described and explained, awakened in me the idea that I need not be omniscient nor did I have to be invisible when I presented my understandings. This allowed me to build on my cultural competence and the strengths of my taken-for-granted understandings.

The work of Erving Goffman, who served as my dissertation supervisor when I was working on what would become my first book, *Synagogue Life* (1976) and who showed me what ethnography first was and persuaded me that I could indeed turn my eye on a world in which I had been an insider, was another important influence. In particular his later insights about how much of what people do and say is really a reply and response to some earlier event or statement, as well as his notion of frame analysis that sees the real world as made up of a series of primary frameworks of meaning that are then re-framed in their reiterations, would serve to show me how interpretation was where participation and observation intersected. That is to say, both require one to make coherent sense out of what is happening, the former in order to act and the latter in order to comprehend.

Of course, beyond all of them Emile Durkheim and his students Robert Hertz and Marcel Mauss tower over my writing. Their ideas about collective representation, the relation between religion and society, the role that collective effervescence has in the emergence of collective consciousness—these ideas and others too numerous to mention played so large a role in my ability to look upon everything from the place that children play in haredi culture to the conditions under which religious sensibilities and devotions get expressed and how these can be understood through the perspectives of sociology, made most of what I have done in this book and perhaps all the others I have written conceivable to me. While it may not always be fashionable to refer to these founders of the canon today, I have no doubt that their work and thinking continues to shape the character of much that defines the field.

One is tempted to try to find some pithy line with which to conclude such an essay as this; something that will epigrammatically capture the essence of

SAMUEL HEILMAN

the lessons I would impart. Ethnography as I have practiced it, built upon the foundation of participant observation, is an endeavor in which one is somehow torn between the gnawing desire to observe life in order to learn about it from others and the equally compelling desire to live it. One must somehow learn to discipline the two and navigate between them. One can perhaps find help in learning from the experiences of others, but in the end there can be no substitute for learning by oneself while on the job.

Note

1 A similar misreading of the events in the synagogue by an observer who lacked basic cultural competence is to be found in Samuel Pepys' (1663) entry in his famous diary for October 14, 1663. Witnessing the dancing and merriment in a synagogue when people put on their prayer shawls and take turns dancing with the Torah scrolls on the holiday of Simchat Torah, a day of barely controlled chaos which is uncommon the rest of the year but common on this occasion, Pepys erroneously concluded that what he saw was

> the men and boys in their vayles, and the women behind a lattice out of sight; and some things stand up, which I believe is their Law, in a press to which all coming in do bow; and at the putting on their vayles do say something, to which others that hear him do cry Amen, and the party do kiss his vayle. Their service all in a singing way, and in Hebrew. And anon their Laws that they take out of the press are carried by several men, four or five several burthens in all, and they do relieve one another; and whether it is that every one desires to have the carrying of it, I cannot tell, thus they carried it round about the room while such a service is singing. And in the end they had a prayer for the King, which they pronounced his name in Portugall; but the prayer, like the rest, in Hebrew. But, Lord! to see the disorder, laughing, sporting, and no attention, but confusion in all their service, more like brutes than people knowing the true God, would make a man forswear ever seeing them more and indeed I never did see so much, or could have imagined there had been any religion in the whole world so absurdly performed as this.

References

Behar, R. (1997) *The Vulnerable Observer: anthropology that breaks your heart*, Boston, MA: Beacon Press.
——(2007) *An Island Called Home*, New Brunswick, NJ: Rutgers University Press.
Clifford, J. (1988) *The Predicament of Culture*, Cambridge, MA: Harvard University Press.
Crapanzano, V. (1986) "Hermes' Dilemma," in J. Clifford and Marcus, G. E. (eds.) *Writing Culture: the poetics and politics of ethnography* (pp. 51–76), Berkeley: University of California Press.
Diamond, S. (1974) *In Search of the Primitive: a critique of civilization*, New Brunswick, NJ: Transaction.
Duneier, M. (2006) "Ethnography, the Ecological Fallacy, and the 1995 Chicago Heat Wave," *American Sociological Review*, 71, 2006, pp. 679–88.

Durkheim, E. (1912) *The Elementary Forms of Religious Life*, trans. J. Swain (1915), London: Allen and Unwin.

Evans-Pritchard, E. E. (1969) *The Nuer*, Oxford: Oxford University Press.

Frank, G. (1979) "Finding the Common Denominator: a phenomenological critique of life history method," *Ethos*, 7: 68–94.

——(1995) "Ruth Behar's Biography in the Shadow: a review of reviews," *American Anthropologist*, New Series, 97: 357–59.

Geertz, C. (1973) *The Interpretation of Cultures*, New York: Basic Books.

Heilman, S. (1976) *Synagogue Life: a study in symbolic interaction*, Chicago: University of Chicago Press.

——(1992) *Defenders of the Faith*, New York: Schocken Books.

——(2001) *When a Jew Dies: the ethnography of a bereaved son*, Berkeley: University of California Press.

Lévi-Strauss, C. (1974) *Tristes Tropiques*, New York: Atheneum.

Pepys, S. (1663) *Pepys' Diary*, Online Available at www.pepysdiary.com/archive/1663/10/14/index.php (accessed October 22, 2007).

Tyler, S. A. (1986) "Post-Modern Ethnography: from document of the occult to occult document," in J. Clifford and Marcus, G. E. (eds.) *Writing Culture: the poetics and politics of ethnography* (pp. 122–40), Berkeley: University of California Press.

13

ON PIECING THE PUZZLE
Researching Hassidic Jews

William Shaffir

The circumstances surrounding my decision to study Hassidic Jews[1] are mostly clear. While the decision was mine, the idea wasn't. Malcolm Spector, who would later serve as my advisor both for the master's thesis and doctoral dissertation, suggested it. To the best of my recollection, over dinner at his rented flat that bordered the Hassidic neighborhood, his wife innocently asked if I knew anything about the Jews that were dressed in black. I believe Malcolm then said: "It would be interesting to study them." The Spectors knew that these were strictly observant Jews, but not much more. I certainly didn't know much more than they did about the Hassidim's lifestyle or community organization. However, I could recall their distinctive presence along the Park Avenue area of the Mile End district of Montreal in the late 1950s when I was growing up nearby. Identified facetiously by many of my peers as the Park Avenue White Sox after the famous Chicago White Sox baseball team—many of the married men wear breeches tied below the knee so that their white stockinged calves were visible below their long black coats and slipper-like shoes—the Hassidim not only appeared out of place but, to my surprise, seemed impervious to the secular influences of modern society.

My study of the Hassidim replaced another project I had begun of a pool hall in downtown Montreal when I learned that I had been accepted into the master's program at McGill University. I had begun hanging around the Windsor pool hall that attracted, among others, business people who came to hustle over the lunch hour, seniors who mainly sat and watched the action, and the unemployed who also hustled but for much smaller stakes. It certainly wasn't unusual to see money change hands. I guess I had become a somewhat familiar face because, on occasion, I would be asked to keep score of some matches. Ned Polsky's (1967) *Hustlers, Beats and Others* sparked and maintained my interest in this project. However, try as hard as I might, I could not convince my father that a study of a pool hall constituted reputable research. When this project was later abandoned, he confided that he was thoroughly relieved that I had chosen to write about the Hassidim. For reasons I could understand, he held a low opinion of pool halls and this colored his assessment of my proposed study. At any rate, though I mistakenly believed that the Hassidim spoke only Yiddish, I believed that I could qualify to study them as I wrote, read, and spoke Yiddish fluently.

Once my new research plan became more widely known, the general advice offered by those claiming to be familiar with the Hassidic community, though well intended, was of little value. The generalizations were profuse. Hassidim, I was informed, are extremists in their religious practices, and wouldn't take kindly to an outsider entering their synagogue. It was hardly conceivable, I was told, that I'd be able to penetrate their cloistered settings. On the other hand, however, I suppose it was good to know that this research wouldn't be a cakewalk. However, no amount of advice and warning ever offers a suitable substitute for entering the field and experiencing the response to one's presence first-hand.

First forays, two initial themes, and one false start

My first contact with the Hassidim was in July, 1968. At the time, I was employed at a Jewish summer camp in the Laurentian Mountains, 60 miles north of Montreal, and accidentally discovered that a group of Hassidic families had formed a colony nearby—a distance of some 15 minutes by foot from the camp. I concluded that the Hassidic presence in the immediate area was nothing short of prophetic—this study was surely meant to be. Moreover, why wait until September to begin? I visualized the following: I would, nonchalantly, walk past the Hassidic colony, located at the very end of a long, winding road, some Hassidim would approach me, we'd exchange some pleasantries, and I'd be invited to join them at my leisure. Nothing of the kind occurred—even remotely.

Though I walked confidently down that winding road, nearly reaching the study hall (*bays medresh*) that virtually abutted it, I panicked. As soon as I spotted young Hassidic boys playing near a bridge facing one of the synagogues, I convinced myself that the research was best inaugurated another day and returned to the summer camp. As I recall, I failed to handle this situation much differently the following morning when I heard voices chanting loudly from the synagogue where males had gathered for *shachris*, the morning's prayer service. On this occasion, however, I invented a different excuse: I concluded that I had dressed inappropriately. Whereas the Hassidim wore long black coats, white shirts, and black hats, I arrived in white jeans, a white skull-cap, and a multi-colored sports jacket that I had borrowed from the camp director. Only on my third attempt did I summon the courage to enter the synagogue to participate in a prayer service.

My initial impression was that I had entered a totally foreign space. I had never stood next to Hassidic Jews, and I felt totally out of place among them. Most of all, I found it uncomfortable to endure their stares. The younger boys, it seemed, inched their way close to where I stood to observe whether I had donned my *tefillin*[2] (phylacteries, in English) correctly or whether I was even familiar with the organization of the prayer book. Even more frustrating, as I remember only too well, was that my presence during these initial visits hardly elicited any formal response, or even the faintest welcome.

Though discouraging, in one sense, these initial visits to the Hassidic colony were exciting and challenging. Though I knew not a soul, I sensed that I might be able to penetrate this setting for purposes of research. Indeed, by the summer's end, I had befriended a couple of the yeshiva students of one of the Hassidic sects living in the summer colony. These young males, about 17–18 years old, I recall, never declined the cigarettes I offered, as they escorted me along to the winding road leading back to the main highway where we'd part company. As we talked, I was offered a glimpse into their world. They were Kausenburger Hassidim, they offered and, they added, not to be confused with the Satmar Hassidim who formed the majority in the colony. They emphasized that the Satmar sect was more extreme than most others—not in matters of halakhic observance but in stringent measures employed to guarantee insulation from mainstream culture. I discovered, for example, that their homes did not include television sets or secular newspapers, and that the extent of their secular education was severely limited. This, I realized, was a hermetically sealed social world, aimed at offsetting intrusive secular influences. When I asked about their daily routine in the colony, I was surprised to learn that it was totally organized around intensive religious studies. Sports or any other leisure activities, with which I was so familiar, were simply not included. Here was where I also discovered that the sexes were strictly segregated, and this accounted for why I rarely, if ever, observed young girls in the vicinity of the synagogues. While strange to me, it seemed so obviously natural to them. As interested as I was about them, they were intensely inquisitive about my daily practices. These exchanges made me wonder whether this summer colony was actually a microcosm of the Hassidic community I'd encounter in Montreal.

I don't recall being asked what brought me to the colony, or what prompted me to attend the religious services. In the event that I was asked, I had rehearsed something very general. I would focus the spotlight on myself, that as a Jew I wished to learn more about Hassidim, as I had read a little about them. I certainly wasn't about to introduce any of them to my soon-to-be graduate student status. Indeed, based on the few Hassidim I did meet, and snippets of conversation I had with them, they seemed as unlikely to understand an account of a graduate program in sociology as I was about the intricacies of a tractate of the Talmud they studied; in other words, as their world was foreign to me, so was mine to them.

A good reason I was fortunate not to have been asked specifics about my research—I did mention, in the most general of terms, that I was going to university and might want to, perhaps, write something about Hassidim in the future—is that my thinking about the study was considerably more amorphous than anyone might have imagined. Quite frankly, I don't recall any sharp, or even general, formulation that guided the research in the earliest months or even for some period during my first year in the graduate program. Nor do I recall any specific advice along these lines from my supervisor. I was encouraged to explore facets of community life that seemed important to the preservation of the Hassidic lifestyle. And how was I to go about doing this? By hanging around and by meeting people, and striking up conversations with them. While field research was the modus operandi by which information was to be gathered, I was left to my own devices as to how this was best accomplished. The invaluable help that my supervisor did extend, however, was to listen patiently as I recounted my experiences in the field, to read and comment on my field notes, and to offer encouragement that the study was progressing well. (Based on this experience, I have counseled graduate students that the choice of a supervisor is, likely, the most important decision that will affect their progress in graduate school and in the completion of their dissertation.)

In fairness, there was one conceptual strand that, in my earliest days in the field, seemed relevant—*stigma management*. However, equally important is that its relevance was abandoned almost immediately as I carefully examined my data. As I observed the Hassidim in their distinctive garb, I somehow convinced myself that I should pay particular attention to their highly unusual appearance. It seemed reasonable, I thought, to rely on Erving Goffman's (1963) *Stigma* that I had recently read, and to conceptualize the Hassidim's appearance as a spoiled identity. What possessed me to think along this line isn't clear but, somehow, it made sense. After all, surely everyone noticed how differently they were dressed and didn't it follow, then, that they would be self-conscious about their appearance and attempt to deflect the attention it garnered? In short, I would investigate the strategies they employed to disavow their deviance. The problem with this conceptualization, I discovered, was simple: I soon discovered it made no sense. Whereas I expected their appearance to generate unease, the Hassidim thought nothing of the kind. An additional feature of this discovery was that the Hassidim, more generally, were unconcerned about what their neighbors thought of them. Indeed, their distinctive garb, I'd eventually realize, served as the single most central feature for establishing a boundary separating insiders from outsiders, a task so vital for creating a distinctive identity.

Boundary maintenance, as an underlying theme connecting to the twin challenges of insulation and identity preservation, seemed like a reasonable way of conceptualizing the research. My master's thesis included a chapter titled "Withdrawal and Isolation," in which I raised the following: "In which specific areas have the Chassidim [my earliest choice of spelling] sought to avoid contact with the larger pervasive non-Chassidic culture? Given that some contact is unavoidable, how have the Chassidim transformed these

215

contact experiences so as to fit with their own cultural perspectives" (Shaffir 1969)? This theme proved to be a winner. From the outset, the importance of dress, language, and secular studies were increasingly evident.

While my speculation that Hassidim felt stigmatized by their appearance had to be rejected, the centrality of an informally enforced dress code was not. Their clothes were dark-colored or muted: The men, having grown ear-locks and a beard, dressed in white shirts, black coats and hats, while the women's dresses were high-necked and long sleeved and, despite dark-colored stockings, came to well below the knees, while a wig or kerchief covered their hair. Such a distinctive appearance, varying only slightly among the Hassidic sects, could not be mistaken and set the Hassidim apart from their neighbors. And whereas the majority of Hassidim could express themselves in English (I had no need to speak to them only in Yiddish), they, generally, did so haltingly and in an accented manner, indicating that English was not their mother tongue. Indeed, Yiddish served as the language they used to communicate with one another, and it served to intensify identification with others that were like-minded.

The most strictly enforced insulating mechanism was undoubtedly the careful supervision accorded secular studies in their Hassidic schools. When I realized that teachers were carefully selected and scrupulously coached on subject matters deemed appropriate for presentation and discussion in the classroom, and that all English books were heavily censored to insure that inappropriate words and pictures were excised, I appreciated that here was an excellent example of how the Hassidim were determined to control the intrusion of unwanted influences. In fact, for most Hassidic sects, secular studies, particularly for the boys, were deliberately organized to be ineffective: they were offered very late in the afternoon for no more than an hour or so with little attention paid to the teachers' pedagogical qualifications.

As much of the data I collected reflected on how the Hassidim strove to create a cocoon surrounding their institutions to shield themselves from mainstream culture, boundary maintenance became an overriding theme. What struck me from the outset as well, however, was that while the followers of the Lubavitch sect were also as concerned about matters of acculturation as any of their more seemingly committed Hassidic counterparts, their approach for sustaining and reinforcing a distinctive identity included a twist that seemed so contrary to reason. I return to this point below.

My first days, and even first months, in the field were trying. I managed to read a couple of studies about Hassidic Jews that were available, but my real challenge was to meet Hassidim and these accounts weren't very helpful along this line. For example, Solomon Poll, who had studied the Hassidim in Williamsburg, Brooklyn, had attended a Hassidic yeshiva and that experience clearly helped him negotiate his presence in the Hassidic community. I enjoyed no such advantage. The single best place to meet people, I reasoned, was where they met to pray—the synagogue. It was easy enough to find out when services were scheduled; moreover, as I soon realized, this institution also served as the central meeting place for males. As I familiarized myself with the geography of Montreal's Hassidic community, I discovered that each of the sects provided for a central meeting place for prayer. In the process, I learned to adjust my daily schedule to coincide with prayer services, and I began visiting Hassidic synagogues and *shteeblech* (small prayer and study halls) with regularity. Interestingly, such visits among the Hassidim failed to modify my religious convictions in any noticeable manner. For reasons that may be even more complex than I can imagine, I believe I didn't allow myself to be convinced to become more observant. At the same time, though, while my prolonged experiences among the Lubavitcher Hassidim attracted me to some of the ideals for which they stood, I never came to practice Judaism as they expected or hoped I might.

As it happens, the insulation theme was also introduced through my contacts with the Tasher Hassidim—another Hassidic sect—when I became an employee in their yeshiva in May 1969. Though Hassidim were, generally, urbanites, the Tasher exemplified the exception and, by so doing, conveyed the importance of achieving insularity into much bolder relief. In the early 1960s, the Tasher rebbe, the sect's charismatic leader, moved with many of his followers from Montreal to a rural area, some 20 miles north of the city. This isolated environment, claimed the rebbe, was more spiritually conducive to Torah study and would, perforce, eliminate unnecessary distractions. This new location would enable the sect to achieve optimum insulation. I note that securing this position in Tash demonstrated that gaining access to a setting might occasionally turn on chance and good fortune—qualities that are hardly subject to meticulous planning. Though I seemingly digress from the main story line, my experiences there underscored the Hassidic community's insularity.

Situated, as it was, outside of Montreal, I could hardly appear at this enclave claiming that I just so happened to be in the neighborhood and decided to drop in for prayer services. This spiel worked reasonably well in Montreal, but was an impossible stretch in this case. And yet, it seemed clear to me that any comprehensive analysis of the Hassidic community would necessarily have to include the Tasher in their secluded enclave. Responding to a Tasher advertisement in a Jewish newspaper to teach secular subjects, most notably English reading and writing, to young Tasher boys, proved unsuccessful. Though I knew that I was the most qualified candidate to be interviewed, I was offered the rather lame excuse that my physical appearance would be upsetting to the boys; actually my unobservant Jewish lifestyle was the real reason for their rejection.

Enter good fortune. While interviewing a former employee of the Tash community, a non-hassid, I mentioned my interest in spending some time there to study these Hassidim. The solution was obvious, he said. "Work there." When I recounted my recent experience as a potential teacher, he promptly proceeded to telephone someone in Tash, explained, in Yiddish, that he had found a "suitable person," and then said to me: "You have an interview on Sunday morning at 10 to work in the office." The interview, it turned out, was to the point, and conducted entirely in Yiddish. To prove myself worthy of the position, I was asked to demonstrate that I could compose a convincing letter to a particular Canadian politician explaining that the Tasher yeshiva was in financial straits and required immediate assistance. I proved myself worthy and for the next eight weeks was responsible for composing letters to various ranking political figures, public officials, and Jewish business people either requesting financial support or thanking them for it.

To be sure, my employment in Tash enabled me to conduct field research up-close, but it also introduced me to the pitfalls of covert research. As to the former, the office where I worked was a hub of activity in the community. Yeshiva students and adults came by to make inquiries of the two Tasher Hassidim that worked there or to seek specific advice. I was often privy to telephone conversations that related to financial challenges the enclave was facing but, most of all, I became aware of the Tasher rebbe's pivotal role in the community, and the unusual relationships that the Hassidim cultivated with him. Observing this relationship, first-hand, was entirely different from reading about it, as I had done. As importantly, my daily presence in the community magnified the degree to which it was insulated from its general surroundings. The enclave, I felt, was suspended in a time warp that sought to control pernicious secular influences. The element of control, I realized, was most immediately reflected in my relationships—actually the lack thereof—with the yeshiva students. The dynamic was fascinating. Seeing me as a curiosity, yeshiva students typically tried engaging me in conversation; for example, where did I learn to speak Yiddish, my thoughts about the enclave, and so forth. Their efforts were immediately resisted by the Tasher with whom I worked; I was far too busy to chat, they informed these students, advising them to leave me alone. I, in turn, was repeatedly reminded that I wasn't to distract students from their studies, a kind way of requesting that I keep my distance from them.

Although I readily shared my status as a graduate student, I didn't reveal my interest in writing about the Hassidim that served as the raison d'être for becoming an employee in the community. When I finally did mention the requirement to write a master's thesis, the Tasher that hired me strongly suggested that I write about Tash. (He changed his mind three days later. There's a fascinating story, here, that I hope to write about some day.) Effectively, then, the field research in Tash was conducted covertly.

The greatest challenge to gathering data by such deception was the constraints it imposed. Present in the community as an office employee, my curiosity in matters such as family socialization, coordination of secular studies, connections between Hassidim and their rebbe, was not meant to be sustained for any length of time. The typical questions posed by the interested outsider were reasonable but, for obvious reasons, could not be pursued at

218

RESEARCHING HASSIDIC JEWS

length. On the other hand, the data I did gather during this period pertaining to how matters of finance were organized and negotiated offered a slice of community organization that, I believe, couldn't be obtained otherwise. Along this line, over the years, I have increasingly appreciated the wisdom offered by Julius Roth (1962), emphasizing the largely fictitious line separating overt from covert research.

I completed the master's thesis in late summer, 1969, some twelve months after beginning the study. It offered an overview of Montreal's Hassidic community, featuring the mechanisms in place for sustaining a distinctive identity, chief of which was insulation. The work focused on how Hassidim remained separated from the mainstream despite their presence in the urban setting. The Hassidim in Tash were outliers in this regard but, as mentioned, their decision to organize in a rural setting actually placed the insulation theme into sharper relief. The piece of the puzzle most difficult to fit centered on the seemingly inexplicable activities of the Lubavitcher Hassidim. To shed light on this aspect, I must backtrack.

Encountering a new twist—the proselytizing of Lubavitcher

When I began studying Hassidic Jews, I had no reason to suspect there were significant distinctions among the various sects. My brief experience with them over that initial summer convinced me that they all shared a deep distrust of outsiders, and did what they had to in order to minimize contact with them. As mentioned, the summer colony was very uninviting and I always felt that my occasional presence was, at best, only tolerated. However, by complete chance, a brief conversation with one of the colony's religious teachers, who was a Lubavitcher Hassid, helped me realize that I might feel more welcomed among the Lubavitch sect, and he informed me where they were situated in Montreal. Upon my return to Montreal in late August, 1968, I headed there. He was absolutely right: Lubavitch's reception was totally different. Herein, also lay the puzzling question: Why?

The entrance to the Lubavitcher yeshiva, in the Snowdon district of the city, was adorned by a large sign that read: 'Join Millions of Jews the World Over that Have Begun to Put on Tefillin.' That so many Jews were donning tefillin came as a surprise. What was the occasion? I found out in no time. Upon entering the yeshiva, I was immediately asked: "Did you put on tefillin today?" My hesitation said it all: a Hassid urged me to follow him to a table and he promptly proceeded to help me fulfill the commandment. Along the way, I learned that the Lubavitcher rebbe, the sect's charismatic religious leader, had initiated a Tefillin Campaign. This campaign had begun shortly before the outbreak of the Six Day War in the Middle East in 1967 when the rebbe urged his followers throughout the world to ensure that as many Jews as possible observed this commandment. According to the rebbe, fulfilling this commandment would aid Jews in Israel, especially those in the army, in their war with the enemy. To the uninitiated outsider, which I was, the degree to which Lubavitcher invoked their rebbe—including his personal background and accomplishments, his stature in the Jewish world and beyond, and the indispensable advice and blessings that his followers, and Jews more generally, sought and received from him—was both impressive and startling. Prior to the research, I hadn't heard of the Lubavitcher rebbe, but discovered immediately that his Hassidim spoke about him incessantly, particularly when attempting to persuade unobservant Jews to fulfill halakhic commandments of Judaism.

What I found to be truly impressive about the Lubavitcher went beyond the Tefillin Campaign. By and large, these Hassidim were genuinely friendly and welcoming. As eager as I was to initiate contact with them, they seemed as interested in extending invitations for me to join them for sabbath services and other community celebrations; moreover, they offered to arrange for me to spend an entire sabbath with a Lubavitch family, and at my convenience. This was a researcher's paradise, I concluded. People were not only superfriendly but the more senior rabbinical students, slightly younger than me, regularly invited me to hang out with them. (To my amazement, I discovered that far more than a handful of these students were from unobservant families.) These Hassidim were surely not like the ones I had met over the summer. And yet, strangely enough, they weren't entirely dissimilar either. Lubavitcher, too, were obsessed about the deteriorating secular climate, and determined to safeguard their Hassidic identity. But their way of doing things was different; in fact, radically different. Since the matter of access seemed so much more straightforward with the Lubavitcher, my decision to focus my doctoral dissertation on this religious community was, rather, simple.

Lubavitcher and witnessing work

As I surveyed the Hassidic scene, it became increasingly clear that Lubavitcher were set apart—and even set themselves apart—from the other sects by their outreach practices among Jews of all stripes of religious observance. Whereas the other sects uniformly discouraged unnecessary contacts with outsiders, I was puzzled by Lubavitch's extensive proselytizing among Jews, an activity, I was repeatedly reminded, that was spearheaded by the Lubavitcher rebbe but which, Lubavitcher emphasized, was actually the hallmark of this Hassidic sect from its inception. So here were Lubavitcher aiming to achieve and protect a distinctive identity, on one hand, but involved in the kinds of activities that could potentially offset their successes along this line, on the other. After all, couldn't contacts with outsiders result in situations where the group's tenets and practices were challenged and even attacked?

Anyone visiting the Lubavitcher yeshiva at this time could not help but be impressed by the publicity accorded the Tefillin Campaign. It included pamphlets as well as advertisements in the Yiddish and English press extending invitations to Jews to visit the Lubavitch yeshiva where they could learn to observe this religious commandment. I soon discovered that the Lubavitcher orchestrated a witnessing drive to help in the campaign's success. In fact, "tefillin booths" were established at favored locations, such as shopping and commercial centers, known to attract a Jewish clientele. The campaign also featured "tefillinmobiles"—suitably decorated camper trailers—that were parked along selected streets in Jewish areas of the city. Such activities, it seemed so obvious, I thought, diluted the boundaries separating insiders from outsiders. Why couldn't Lubavitcher make this obvious connection?

Equally surprising was that Lubavitcher readily admitted that while initiating and maintaining these booths, mobiles, and routes—the latter typically encompassed particular streets in a neighborhood for which one or two Lubavitch students assumed responsibility for meeting the Jews living and/or working there—it wasn't unusual to be rebuffed, or even confronted by claims that Lubavitchers' proselytizing was disgraceful. But such reactions failed to diminish the campaign's intensity and Lubavitchers' fervor. On the contrary: the unfavorable reactions signaled all the more clearly that more concerted efforts should be devoted to raising the levels of Orthodox Jewish consciousness among Jews in the larger community. In this, Lubavitcher Hassidim were sustained by their rebbe's assurances that their proselytizing was meaningful, necessary, and in keeping with the sect's philosophy.

Most puzzling, perhaps, were the central participants involved in the proselytizing activities. Logically, it seemed, that the Lubavitch community would be most concerned about their adolescents' undue exposure to secular influences. As younger persons are believed to be highly impressionable and susceptible to outsiders' influences, it seemed reasonable that adolescents—those least likely to be committed to the Lubavitch lifestyle because of their age—would be excluded from the proselytizing efforts or, at best, would be offered a minimal role, while adults—more firmly entrenched in the community—would be engaged in the bulk of the witnessing. In fact, I found the opposite to be the case.

While the Lubavitcher didn't officially delegate the proselytizing to any specific age group, practically speaking, the more senior rabbinical students, ranging in age from 17–20, organized and administered the bulk of it. They coordinated the tefillin routes, staffed the tefillin booths, and visited college and university campuses. What was the logic in immersing younger people in the very kinds of encounters that would seemingly most threaten their developing identity as Lubavitcher? After all, based on my readings about Amish, Hutterites, and most certainly the Hassidim in Williamsburg, Brooklyn, the presence of outsiders inside the community, or even contacts with them, would only obscure the distinctions between insiders and outsiders, a distinction so crucial to the very existence of the religious community.

To briefly summarize, then, it appeared that Lubavitchers' witnessing in the larger Jewish community would threaten the preservation of their distinctive identity by blurring the group's boundaries. This threat did not, however, decrease these Hassidim's witnessing zeal nor, in fact, did it weaken the community boundaries. In fact, far from threatening the group's efforts to maintain and consolidate its identity by blurring and eroding boundaries, witnessing, I discovered, accomplished the opposite: It reinforced a distinctive identity both for the individual and the community.

Witnessing as identity consolidation

Part of this puzzle began falling into place upon reading Festinger et al.'s (1956) study of a religious cult. In it, they maintain that if a group's central beliefs are questioned or challenged by others, proselytizing serves as an effective means of reaffirming the members' identity with the group. In their words: "If more and more people can be persuaded that the system of belief is correct, then it clearly must, after all, be correct" (Festinger et al. 1956: 28). Readily conceding that most Jews they encountered neither practiced the Torah's commandments, nor even heard of the accomplishments of the Lubavitcher rebbe, stories abounded, nonetheless, of countless men and women that had, for the first time, donned phylacteries, lit sabbath candles, or koshered their homes.

As I reviewed the data I had collected, the picture gradually clarified. As the pieces were fitted into place, and as the puzzle took shape, I began to see a connection between proselytizing activities and boundary maintenance. My chief discovery, as far as I could tell, was that those engaging in prose- lytizing *were expected to control the contexts in which the interaction unfol- ded.* Encounters with outsiders were bounded by the specific expectations that they would quickly assume a religious base, making religion the explicit focus of attention. Indeed, as the data revealed, the contact situations that were most threatening both to the individual and the group were those that failed to be directed to matters of Jewish religious observance. So, while Lubavitcher would rely upon whatever hook they considered appropriate to entice the individual to further discussion—for example, matters relating to health, university education, music, life's meanings—the objective, as the yeshiva students understood only too well, was to quickly turn the exchange to the importance and meaningfulness of religious observance and the cen- trality of the Lubavitcher rebbe's teachings along this line. Once this was accomplished, yeshiva students would find themselves on firmer terrain. After all, these students were armed with a plethora of tales about people that had been miraculously helped as a result of donning tefillin, or fulfilling some other essential commandments to which they had been introduced by Lubavitcher, such as lighting sabbath candles (for women) or koshering their dishes. As well, stories about the Lubavitcher rebbe—his selfless commitments to all Jews, and his seemingly superhuman qualities and powers—were more than plentiful and Lubavitch students could recount them at will. Armed with such an arsenal, as well as the rebbe's repeated assurances that encounters with outsiders would fail to steer Lubavitcher from their rightful course, the rabbinic students, with encouragement of adult teachers and mentors, felt that they could confidently withstand questions and even attacks mounted by critics and skeptics.

The involvement of the rabbinic students in witnessing was now understandable. These young men were the very members of the community whose beliefs and commitments required strengthening. Their commitment to the Lubavitch lifestyle was less intense than that of adults who had raised families and whose daily life was organized around the Lubavitch community. Involving these students in witnessing was no doubt an important way of building their belief system. By teaching and becoming witness to their beliefs, and by urging them on others, they learned to think of themselves as Lubavitcher Hassidim and intensified their commitment to their rebbe's teachings.

Conclusion

When my book on the Lubavitch community was published (Shaffir 1974), I expected that it would circulate in the community and become a topic of conversation. It didn't. I handed copies to a few Lubavitcher, either because they were most helpful during the research, or because I was eager to learn their reaction. I eventually heard back that one individual was slightly embarrassed because she was most readily identified despite my efforts to disguise her identity. Another Lubavitcher thought my material was "interesting," but couldn't offer much more than this, while a third was surprised that, despite my familiarity with the community, I failed to understand the obvious: It wasn't, as I claimed, that the rebbe's advice to his followers could not be disconfirmed owing to the reverence accorded him, but that his advice was infallible by virtue of his special personal qualities. By and large, the volume's publication made no impression and was seemingly ignored. In a way, this was fitting as Lubavitcher always insisted that they were less interested in my sociological work than in my progress toward becoming a more observant and committed Jew.

In retrospect, I can't recall any particular "eureka-type" moment when the pieces of the research puzzle magically fit together to provide a total understanding of how the larger Hassidic community, but more particularly the Lubavitcher, were organized and carried on. If anything, I had to be convinced that I understood more than I thought I did. My advisor served well in this capacity. We were both right. As I was so deeply immersed in the project, I failed to appreciate the wealth of data I had actually gathered. On the other hand, I think we generally know less about the research topic we've completed than we let on. For reasons that are easily understood, we find it difficult to fess up that our data about specific aspects of community life are incomplete; for example, I never learned much about the financial side of things, and how the Lubavitcher supported the various institutions in their community. In part, this was due to my lack of interest in this dimension of community life. While I initially believed that the absence of such data rendered the research incomplete, I now better appreciate that there are always gaps in our knowledge, that this is unavoidable, but not necessarily indicative of shortcomings in our work.

Notes

1 Over the years, I have continued to study Hassidic Jews (see, for example, Shaffir 1978; 1987; 1995; 1999; 2004; 2007). While my initial interests focused on the Lubavitch sect, I have, more recently, written about the Tasher Hassidim, a relatively small sect centered in Boisbriand, Quebec. For a more complete list of my publications on the Hassidim, the reader is invited to visit my website on the Tasher sect, www.kiryastash.ca

2 The observance of tefillin—phylacteries in English—is incumbent on all Jewish males that have reached the age of thirteen. The tefillin consist of two small leather cubes with straps, each containing a piece of parchment inscribed with specific biblical verses. Men fulfill the commandment of tefillin during the morning religious service except for the sabbath and Jewish holidays, one cube strapped around the left arm (or right) and the other on the forehead.

References

Festinger, L., Riecken, H. W., and Schachter, S. (1956) *When Prophecy Fails*, Minneapolis: University of Minnesota Press.

Goffman, E. (1963) *Stigma: notes on the management of spoiled identity*, Englewood Cliffs, NJ: Prentice-Hall.

Polsky, N. (1967) *Hustlers, Beats, and Others*, Chicago: Aldine.

Roth, J. (1962) "Comments on Secret Observation," *Social Problems*, 9: 283–84.

Shaffir, W. (1969) "The Montreal Chassidic Community: community boundaries and the maintenance of ethnic identity," unpublished master's thesis, McGill University, Montreal.

——(1974) *Life in a Religious Community: the Lubavitcher Chassidim in Montreal*, Toronto: Holt, Rinehart and Winston of Canada.

——(1978) "Becoming an Orthodox Jew: the socialization of newcomers in a Chassidic community," in L. Driedger (ed.) *The Canadian Ethnic Mosaic: a quest for identity* (pp. 295–309), Toronto: McClelland and Stewart.

——(1987) "Separated from the Mainstream: the Hassidic community of Tash," *The Jewish Journal of Sociology*, 29: 19–35.

——(1995) "Boundaries and Self-presentation among Hasidim: a study in identity maintenance," in J. Belcove-Shalin (ed.) *New World Hasidim: ethnographic studies of Hasidic Jews in America* (pp. 31–68), New York: SUNY Press.

——(1999) "Doing Ethnography: reflections on finding your way," *Journal of Contemporary Ethnography*, 28: 676–86.

——(2004) "Secular Studies in a Hassidic Enclave: 'what do we need it for?'," *The Jewish Journal of Sociology*, 46: 59–77.

——(2007) "Hassidim Confronting Modernity," *The Jewish Journal of Sociology*, 49: 5–35.

14

USING A GESTALT PERSPECTIVE TO ANALYZE CHILDREN'S WORLDS

Patricia A. Adler and Peter Adler

The work of ethnographers is not always easy, but it's never dull. Although people may pick their research topics on the basis of theoretical interests or voids in the literature, most qualitative researchers choose their settings out of some personal interest. In fact, it's not uncommon for people to study things that are near and/or dear, a tendency we noted in *Membership Roles in Field Research* (Adler and Adler 1987), where we discussed some of the ways that people studied settings in which they had either a peripheral, active, or complete membership role.

In this chapter we pause to reflect on one of our major research projects that culminated with the publication of our book, *Peer Power: Preadolescent Culture and Identity* (1998). We begin with a discussion of how the choice of the setting occurred, and then examine two important foci of this research, paying particular attention to the way we developed our conceptualization of the data and more abstract theoretical analyses.

Entering the setting

In 1987 we moved to Boulder, Colorado, the data already gathered for our book on college athletes (see Adler and Adler 1991), and scoped our new geographical location for a new field setting, while we spent the first few years in Colorado completing the basketball project. We have always over-lapped the end of one study with the start of another by several years in order to get a few years of participant observation under our belts before we started mining the new topic for papers, so that our field relations and understanding of the new scene would be adequately deep and rich for the type of analysis we prefer.

Our style has involved "researching in our backyards" to gain the advan-tages of regular and intimate insight into our subjects' lives. For this we created an overlap between our research and personal lives, so that our everyday paths intertwined with the people we were studying. We preferred to have access to setting members on the weekends as well as the weekdays, the evenings as well as the daytimes, during periods of crisis and conflict as well as quiescence. We value the depth of hearing what people have to say, but we try to cross-check this by observing their behavior first-hand to see if their actions support their assertions. Direct personal observation enables us to sometimes challenge assertions people make about their lives and behavior with empirical examples that contradict these. This helps us and them to probe deeper into the causes and consequences of their actions than most people customarily do while naturally engaging in life.

At the time we arrived in Boulder our two children were nine and five, and fascinated us with the richness of their daily experiences. We thought about famous scholars such as Charles H. Cooley, Erik Erikson, and Jean Piaget, who studied their own children, seeing in them the laboratories of human nature. Our children's social worlds enticed us as an object of study, not only because they were fresh, challenging, important, and unbelievably complex, but because studying them offered us the ancillary benefit of spending more time with our children during their important and formative years.

We entered the social world of preadolescent children with empirical and methodological interest only; we had no driving research questions. The mark of good sociologists, we believed, lay in their ability to wield what Mills called the "sociological imagination": the insight to discover the connections between the personal and the public, the situational and the social, the generic social processes contained in everyday life interactions. Like other qualitative scholars, then, we pursued an emergent analytic strategy, first familiarizing ourselves with the scene and all the while looking for things that would be sociologically interesting.

Entering into children's worlds is not always easy for adults, as children spend some time in the private company of their peers and other time in institutional settings to which access is restricted. By using the role of the "parent-as-researcher" (see Adler and Adler 1996), we capitalized on a naturally occurring role where our presence was less artificial and unwieldy, where we already had role immersion, and where the need for role pretense was diminished.

Gestalt abduction

Taking a setting where we already were members and converting it into a research site necessitated a very different process from initially entering a scene as researchers. First, a lot of contemplation went into assessing this as a potential topic before we made the decision to study it, to see if it would be a good focus for sociological analysis. This is when our initial efforts to *shift the frame* begin. Erving Goffman (1974) suggested that we "frame" the world with our sociological concepts when we analyze it. Beyond our natural stance as everyday life actors, we had to sharpen and apply our theoretical stance. Instead of just thinking about the arena for the purpose of living in it, which involved asking a lot of "what" questions, we had to start thinking about the "why" and "how" issues that lay below the surface. What drew us to studying our children and their social worlds was the range of fascinating activities occurring there. From even a surface examination, it was clear that elementary and middle school kids were engaged in tumultuous social negotiations as they learned how to forge friendships, create alliances, figure out how to fit into their shifting (and occasionally roiling) social worlds, and decide who they were. Progressing through different grades each year, moving from homeroom to homeroom, being thrust into the company of different peers as kids appeared and disappeared from their zones of relevance was extremely challenging. So as we watched and observed them, we began formulating sociological concepts of their worlds.

Second, once we started thinking about this scene sociologically, we had so much taken-for-granted knowledge about it that we had to cull the relevant from the irrelevant. Gathering data in a membership role was easier for us because we were already entrenched in the setting, but it typically makes analysis more challenging. We could not recapture the Martian perspective of the newcomer where everything looks strange. We had to add a sociological lens to the way we viewed the world, opening our minds to more basic questions we had skipped over as members about how the scene operated. This required thinking analytically about the world.

As we cast around for sociologically interesting themes to address, we considered, discarded, and reformulated many ideas. This is when we started writing things down. We have always divided our field notes into the three categories typically described by ethnographers (cf. Charmaz 2006; Lofland et al. 2006). We used one file for empirical notes, writing down the facts of what was happening. A second file contained our analytical notes, where we tried concepts out for size, thought about the trends and patterns by which conceptual elements fit together, and pondered their relation to more abstract theory. In the third file we made methodological notes elaborating on our fieldwork, field relations, methodological decisions, their implications, and our barriers and breakthroughs.

As established setting members, our initial writings fell in the analytical category. We pressed ourselves to go beyond our previous ways of understanding children's worlds to more conceptually framed ones. Although we were constantly watching, thinking, and talking about the kids, our analytical field note writing involved organizing and coding their behavior into concepts, developing these concepts, and thinking about the interrelation between concepts. We then made notes about empirical developments that pertained to the concepts that were emerging.

As a creative research process in the context of discovery, one of the hardest and most important, yet most intellectually rewarding aspects of ethnography is *framing analytical questions*. We develop a polemical nexus that will organize and guide our conceptualization. We always start by trying to think of one sociological question at a time. A sociological question defines a theme, and that guides us to our sociological answers. So coming up with the question is the key to our creative spark.

In framing and answering our questions, as ethnographers we used a *gestalt* approach to understanding the complexity of social life. In contrast to experimental design with its isolation of dependent and independent variables or survey research's hypotheses and correlations, observing people in their naturalistic settings lets field researchers take a holistic perspective, studying the social world as an overarching configuration, pattern, or organized field having specific properties that cannot be derived from the simple summation of its component parts.

Using a gestalt approach, we saw no need for the kind of formal line-by-line methods of coding and analysis Glaser and Strauss (1967) long ago proposed in grounded theory. Our interest did not lie in isolating pieces of data and coding them into quantifiable instances to see how they added together. These strictly bottom-up approaches may be useful for people new to their settings, in research projects where the data are gathered by a host of different people, or where ethnographers want to produce work that can appear "scientistic," but for us they failed to capture the holistic nature of the setting. Embedded within our sociological perspective lay a larger array of concepts that could be used juxtaposed against the trends and patterns we observed in the field. We wanted to bring ideas to the table from both the members' activities and the realm of ideas.

In our analytical thinking we continually moved back and forth between our observations, interactions, and thoughts about the empirical world and the concepts we were developing. New developments led us to ponder and extend our conceptualizations, and new conceptualizations led us to re-examine the empirical world to see how they fit. This process of creative foment between the empirical world and conceptualization is called abduction.

The power of the group

Using this abductive or gestalt approach, we first became fascinated by the power of children's peer groups. How, we wondered, did kids make choices in their worlds, develop patterns and styles of behavior? As the children around us aged we could see them evolve from relatively undifferentiated beings who played with any child who was near (propinquity), to become more discerning creatures in both their self-presentations and choice of playmates. We began to wonder what kinds of forces shaped them into people who exhibited different styles, and how they clumped together into groups.

We could see the rise of two or three distinctly different kinds of kids, starting in first grade, but really forming in earnest by third grade: the popular kids, the average (or unpopular) kids, and the ones who stuck out at the other end as loners. What, we wondered, stratified these kids so that some were popular and accepted while others were rejected and lonely? We focused on these issues as a result of our direct observations of our children and their friends, as we asked ourselves both personal and sociological questions about why some children were so easily able to wield power and others were powerless. We used these questions to guide our analytical thinking and further conceptualization.

We noticed that as they moved through early elementary school they separated into gendered groups, yet their stratification and positioning remained parallel. Lever (1976; 1978), Thorne (1986), and Eder et al. (1995) had written about gender segregation by this time, but their discussions were focused on different aspects of kids' lives or on older kids than ours. Their interests served more as a foil to complement our own rather than as an impetus or guide to our developing analysis.

We could clearly see that popularity was a paramount concern for kids, and that the popular kids dominated the less fortunate ones. What features, we wondered, pushed some to the top of the social hierarchy and others to the middle or bottom? Popularity seemed of preeminent importance. We observed kids, we talked to them, talked to their friends, and talked to their parents, coming up with analytic ideas about what makes kids popular, rejecting them, and modifying them. Different qualities seemed to make girls popular than boys. Studying these variations in the popularity variables of boys and girls, we noticed that these coalesced into different models of enacting gender. Boys gained status by being athletic, tough, cool, defiant, socially sophisticated and, especially by the end of elementary school, being successful with girls. Girls' popularity rested on their family backgrounds (socio-economic status), their looks, their social precocity, and conforming to social norms by doing well in school. We noted, with dismay, how achieved the features were that elevated boys' status compared to the girls' ascribed ones.

This led us to think about the gender models that boys and girls were absorbing from the larger culture. Why were girls internalizing such passive gender images compared to the active boys, we wondered, especially after the women of our generation had fought so hard to expand their opportunities? What happened to the women's liberation movement and its efforts to free both girls and boys from the confines of their traditional gender roles? Although we felt sure that gender traditionalism was still widespread, we thought that if any group of youngsters had the potential to exhibit less stereotypical gender roles, it might be this one from an affluent university town. As we were working on an article from these data, we discussed our thoughts with a colleague, Margaret Eisenhart, who was writing with a friend, Dorothy Holland, about the gendered culture of romance (Holland and Eisenhart 1990). We were struck by how apparent the roots of the patterns they saw in college appeared to be among our preadolescents.

In analyzing our data, we drew out the implications of these boys' and girls' subcultures. Their idealized gender images embodied differential polarities in several cultural attributes. Elementary school boys' culture emphasized a "cult of masculinity" through which they could demonstrate their growth, maturity, and distance from the femininity characterizing their early family-oriented lives. They adopted elements of the machismo posture through their competition, bragging and boasting about their exploits and distancing themselves from academics. It embodied an "expression of physicality" in its central focus on active participation and prowess in sport. Their exploits on the playground and in afterschool activities involved dominance and hierarchy, physical displays, and aggression. Boys' lives were tied to their "orientation of autonomy," preparing them to grow up as independent and self-reliant men. They cut themselves and each other off from the "cult of coddling" with sharp remarks and derogations against baby-like behavior, toughening themselves for their adult role. Finally, they entered into the "culture of coolness," assuming suitably unemotional and detached postures that, again, replaced the weakness and dependence of femininity with the instrumentality and strength of masculinity.

Focal concerns of the girls' peer culture and gender roles revolved around an entirely different set of skills and values. In contrast to the boys' defiance, girls became absorbed into the "culture of compliance and conformity." They practiced and perfected established rules, adhering to the normative order. From an earlier age, girls were attracted to the "culture of romance," relating to boys through traditional roles that fostered passivity and dependence by waiting for boys to select them. They carved out inner space in which to enact the "ideology of domesticity," playing house, nurturing each other, smoothing over problems or inequalities, and doing emotion work. Hovering over all this was an "orientation of ascription" that incorporated an understanding of the female role as based on attracting a man who will give them status. They therefore looked to see what was attached to other girls in their material possessions, houses, and appearances. As part of this reflected role, girls also displayed their perception that women often got what they wanted through indirection and manipulation.

In the end, we concluded that the expansion of gender roles in society had little if any effect on girls' (and even less on boys') behavior and measures of popularity. Traditional gender roles prevailed, and although the women's movement of the 1970s had proclaimed social change, we found that girls, in their parlance, "had *not* come a long way, baby."

Our analysis then led us to ask the larger question of how kids formed these gendered cultures. From where did they derive? Messner's (1990) cogent analyses of the socializing impact of such institutions as sport, which we read with interest, offered one explanation for how kids were held into gender stasis. But a lot of the behavior we saw grew out of the general peer subculture and not in subfields such as sport. What mediated between individuals and society, so that these kids extracted their particular versions of femininity and masculinity? With a range of gender models from which to choose, how did they all coalesce around these shared understandings?

From the literature we had read, we learned that sociologists considered families the dominant group influencing children of this age. Yet these children seemed to look more to their peer group. They were not making individualized choices for themselves about how to resolve the conflicting demands placed on them and the choices offered to them, but were, instead, looking around to see what their peers were doing. They were learning from their peers the socially acceptable modes of patterned adaptation and imitating these; they were learning kids' peer culture and peer norms. Particularly in determining how they would enact gendered behavior, they were selecting, not as individuals, but as a subculture, what features of gender roles they would value and which they would ignore.

It was at this time that we became particularly impressed by the power of the peer group as a mediator between the individual and society. Children derived their identities, their social-relational position in the hierarchy of status groups, and their identities and feelings of self worth as individuals by their ranking in the social ladder of the group. We were further struck by the critical role of peer status in vesting these children in this social system. Not only was the peer group the key variable mediating between the individual and society, but peer status struck us as the most important determinant of how individuals behaved, rewarding or punishing them with positive or negative assessment.

We had always avidly discussed, as graduate students, our interest in the level at which the various great theorists we studied fixed their gaze. To us, this was an indication not only of the location at which they preferred to lodge their analysis, but we read it as a sign of where they located the key factor intermediating between individual and society. For Durkheim it was his social facts, those obdurate and objective social institutions and forces that existed sui generis, outside of individuals, shaping their tabulae rasae into group conformity. Weber focused on the level of social organizations with his interest in class, status, and party, looking at the way these formed the most compelling affiliations for people and shaped their social location and outlook on the world. Simmel directed his analysis toward the crystallized interactions that formed the patterns of social interaction, bonding people into micro-structured relations with each other and society. This research convinced us that the most critical level of analysis was the peer group and the guiding determinant of people's behavior was peer status. People's actions, we became convinced, were overridingly influenced by their drive to attain status among their peers and the feelings of identity and self-esteem that this bestowed on them. Ironically, then, peer groups represented a coalition of all three theorists' concerns: Durkheimian social facts, Weberian sources of group status and honor, and Simmelian crystallized interactions.

PATRICIA A. ADLER AND PETER ADLER

Clique dynamics

Once we had thought, analyzed, and written about popularity, we cast about for our next topic. Naturally, we had been making observations and writing empirical and analytic field notes about a host of themes. We chose to turn our attention next to the social dynamics of these peer groups. We had watched our two children, an older girl and a younger boy, navigate the vicissitudes of these groups, trying to fit in and be popular, being accepted or rejected (sometimes daily) by the choices they made. We had been studying not only them, but those around them, to see which kids were making the choices that led to acceptance, success, and happiness, and which were making choices that led to derision and rejection.

Our daughter had arrived in Boulder in the fourth grade and experienced what we thought was a successful social year, filled with friends, dates, and activities. Pretty and smart, she quickly developed a best friend and a busy social life, emerging as one of the most popular girls. We were stunned at the end-of-year picnic, when a mother approached us and told us that she'd like to scratch our daughter's eyes out for what she had done to her child. Shortly thereafter, on the advice of the teacher, our daughter's best friend was banned by her mother from playing with her. Roiling underneath the apparently smooth waters of our daughter's social life were clearly serious waves. Fifth grade saw her separated from her former friend and placed in a classroom with a clique leader whose social manipulations far eclipsed hers. We suffered with her in misery as she was first wooed into the popular clique and then made insecure and miserable by this demanding and capricious classmate. She spent that year and the next working continuously to retain her standing among the popular elite. Long before the term "alpha girls" emerged in the popular lexicon, we encountered the dilemma faced by many parents as their children were buffeted by the capriciousness of clique dynamics.

Following behind her, our son, initially accepted for his athletic prowess, progressively failed in fourth and fifth grades to develop the social skills and masculine toughness necessary to keep him in the graces of his popular former friends. He had been a member of what we now recognized as a clique, but after being cast out, had difficulty making and holding any new friends. Rather than being accepted into a circle of lower-status unpopular kids, he sunk to the bottom of the hierarchy and became a pariah. Old friends who tried to play with him were taken aside and told that they faced expulsion if they didn't jettison him. In a parent–teacher conference we learned that his life was "hell" every day. Kids derided him on the school bus and beat him up at recess to curry favor with the clique leader and his current lieutenants.

Driven by the pain of our son and the apparent pain caused by our daughter, we found our second research focus: how did this whole clique thing work and how did these clique leaders get and hold so much power? What made them so popular, how did they rise to and keep their positions, and how did they get other kids to do their bidding? We became convinced at this point that a critical part of the sociological imagination in inductive field research lay in developing the important analytical questions to be asking. Finding the answers would follow; finding the right questions to ask took great creativity. We then set out to study third through sixth graders, attempting to sociologically investigate what gave these kids so much power.

We watched the subtle and overt machinations underlying the behavior of the powerful kids and their interactions within and outside of their groups. We studied the sociological attributes of these groups to understand what differentiated the popular cliques from the smaller friendship circles formed by the unpopular kids. We became convinced that the most critical defining feature of the popular clique was its exclusivity; not everyone who wanted to join was accepted. In fact, membership was a prize. Another important element that we found in cliques involved the dynamics of their membership: kids were continually drawn into or pushed out of the group. Being in the group one day offered no guarantee of acceptance the following day. Moreover, in contrast to the undifferentiated leveling of the unpopular kids' small friendship circles, cliques were hierarchically ordered. Clique leaders, atop the groups, had best friends, next favorite henchpersons, lesser-regarded but still accepted friends, clear followers, and (at the periphery) a coterie of wannabes. Individuals moved up and down the status ladder, depending on the dictates of the leaders. When leaders favored them, followers did as well, and people found themselves relatively secure and happy. When leaders turned against them, they had few, if any, friends. Kids learned to bend with the leaders' changing attitudes toward their friends like "links in a chain," reading the way the wind was blowing and shifting with it so that they could go along. Socially aligning themselves with the leaders advanced their social position; challenging it invited their own expulsion. Clique members, we saw, were working hard, daily, to read social situations, to assess social groups, and to discern subtle shifts in hierarchy, favor, and power, in order to protect themselves from isolation and ridicule.

Extended conversations with people in the field, focused interviews, pondering, and talk between ourselves finally yielded the analytical model that we felt best explained the dynamics of how cliques operated. Everything hinged, we decided, on the dynamics of inclusion and exclusion, the double helix of the dynamic power processes occurring daily.

Techniques of inclusion began with desirable individuals' recruitment into or application to join the group. New members led to friendship realignments within the clique, as these people were elevated to highly favored status, displacing others (who despite their resentment, had to fawn on them). Throughout, members of all sorts had to work at ingratiating themselves, practicing either supplication toward those above them or manipulation of those below them to maintain their own power and position.

Although inclusionary techniques reinforced individuals' popularity and prestige while maintaining the group's exclusivity and stratification, they failed to contribute to other, essential clique features such as cohesion and integration, the management of in-group and out-group relationships, and submission to clique leadership. These features were rooted, along with further sources of domination and power, in cliques' exclusionary dynamics.

Techniques of exclusion began with out-group subjugation, where leaders (when they were not being nice to keep outsiders from straying too far from their realm of influence) picked on lower-status individuals. Turning people against outsiders solidified the group and asserted the power of the strong over the weak. Subjugation was directed at in-groups members as well, however, with followers and wannabes taking the greatest brunt. Occasionally, however, ridicule and rejection was directed at individuals whom the leaders decided could become a potential threat to their power, undercutting their position and support. Members complied with these shifts of favor, going along either passively or actively taunting targeted others to improve their standing. Although excluded individuals usually regained their membership after a while, others endured the brunt of ridicule, taunting, and derision for months at a time, becoming stigmatized. The worst form of exclusion was permanent expulsion from the group. Members so cast out often sunk far in the social hierarchy, since the unpopular kids who they had taunted sometimes declined to accept them, despite their aura of former popularity.

Our general abductive approach in gathering data, analyzing it as we went along by looking for empirical trends and patterns and forging and modifying concepts, was to avoid overly immersing ourselves in the extant literature, either empirical or theoretical. We had been warned in graduate school that if we read relevant literature too early in the research process we ran the risk of unduly influencing our own interpretations with others' analyses. For the most part we held to this ideal, going to the literature only once we had our own ideas firmly in place. We often organized and wrote the data sections of the articles we were producing as we went along, in fact, before we had a clear idea of where we were going in our conclusions. Searching the literature afterwards, we were struck by two theoretical models that resonated with ours, in their similarities and differences. Eder's (1985) work on the cycle of popularity added a linear dimension to our analysis, as she discussed the tendency for girls to invite newcomers into their cliques, favoring them initially, only to replace them in favor with more recent arrivals. Blau's (1964) work incorporated a cybernetic feedback model that we incorporated to show the continuing reciprocal and reinforcing influence of these dynamics. We often then returned to the field to ask kids if they thought these models (presented in simplified form) resonated with their experiences.

Some of the analyses we developed were aided by the peer reviews we received along the way as we submitted articles for publication to journals.

Anonymous referees offered suggestions for literature that we had over-looked, particularly in the areas of mainstream social psychology including such concepts as in-group and out-group dynamics, the role of groupthink, and the ultimate attribution error. Whenever we found a new work that looked relevant we snowballed from its references to further literature. This reinforced our feeling that we need not restrict our research interests to only those areas with whose literature we were familiar, as we could find what we needed as we refined our data-gathering and analyses. Engaging in the peer review process while we were still doing research thus helped us to clarify the relation of our findings to existing scholarly knowledge, and helped us to anticipate potential reactions or critiques of our work before we completed the final book version of our study.

From gestalt analysis to theoretical reach

Theoretically, we believed that this model held great explanatory potential. We then turned to the extant theoretical literature to see how the con-ceptualization of our empirical data contributed to more generic ideas of group inclusion and exclusion. Several ideas that we found appeared to have critical roots in the behavior of the children we observed.

While social conformity has many prosocial functions, ensuring the survi-val of the group, it represents an opposing force to self-awareness and, in its extreme, can lead to "groupthink," the reduced capacity for critical reflec-tion. Sociologists have long sought to understand the basis for the kind of excessive social conformity that can foster adherence to totalitarian regimes (partly through the now infamous Asch, Milgram, and Stanford experi-ments). The depth and severity of this early socialization in peer group sub-servience helps explain the foundations of conforming behavior and the reward and punishment system through which it is learned.

These clique dynamics also teach preadolescents to reproduce society's strong feelings of differentiation between in-groups and out-groups. They learn in-group favoritism and intolerance toward out-group members leading to the "ultimate attribution error," where they overvalue the abilities of in-group members and devalue the contributions of out-group members. These dynamics teach young people the fundamental values of conflict and prejudice, forming the basis for racism, anti-Semitism, sexism, and other forms of bigotry and discrimination.

Finally, these clique dynamics teach preadolescents the subtleties of intra-group jockeying for position based on power, popularity, and interpersonal social status. Kids learn that stratification is not fixed but fluid, a feature of all social settings. To thrive, they learn *that* they should and *how* they should compete with both adversaries and friends, disadvantaging others and advantaging themselves through skillful combinations of leadership and strategic following. These dynamics constitute the politics of human group life, from the micro world of everyday interaction, to the meso world of social and work organizations, to the macro world of governmental politics.

Generalizations from qualitative research are often more applicable to theoretical models than to patterns of empirical behavior. Of all the research we have ever conducted, these clique dynamics represent the most generic and widely applicable analysis we have ever formulated. Their existence in every organization, office, political party, and social scene is nearly universal.

Summary

In the course of nearly a decade of research, thus, we learned a great deal about our own children, their friends, and the driving motivations that kept them together and split them apart. Ironically, 20 years later, some of their most ardent enemies as children have now turned into lifelong friends, and some of the influential leaders who guided their behavior have long been lost. More important, this research taught us about the issues of inclusion and exclusion, popularity and derision, and self-identity as grounded in peer relations. Sociologically, each of these observations was then taken back to the academic literature, compared and contrasted with previous studies of children, and fit into more macro theoretical models of human behavior. The resulting conclusions, we feel, take us beyond the particularistic features of just "kid-culture" to more universalistic extrapolations about the relations between individual and society and the root nature of such dynamics as sexism, racism, and bigotry. As in all inductive research, then, we started with just a general idea of the scene and, only later, teased out the grander theories represented there.

References

Adler, P. A. and Adler, P. (1987) *Membership Roles in Field Research*, Newbury Park, CA: Sage.
——(1991) *Backboards and Blackboards: college athletes and role engulfment*, New York: Columbia University Press.
——(1996) "Parent-as-Researcher: the politics of researching in the personal life," *Qualitative Sociology*, 19: 35–58.
——(1998) *Peer Power: preadolescent culture and identity*, New Brunswick, NJ: Rutgers University Press.
Blau, P. M. (1964) *Exchange and Power in Social Life*, New York: Wiley.
Charmaz, K. (2006) *Constructing Grounded Theory*, Thousand Oaks, CA: Sage.
Eder, D. (1985) "The Cycle of Popularity: interpersonal relations among female adolescents," *Sociology of Education*, 58: 154–65.
Eder, D., with C. C. Evans and Parker, S. (1995) *School Talk: gender and adolescent school culture*, New Brunswick, NJ: Rutgers University Press.
Glaser, B. and Strauss, A. (1967) *The Discovery of Grounded Theory*, Chicago: Aldine.
Goffman, E. (1974) *Frame Analysis*, Cambridge, MA: Harvard University Press.

Holland, D. and Eisenhart, M. (1990) *Educated in Romance*, Chicago: University of Chicago Press.

Lever, J. (1976) "Sex Differences in the Games Children Play," *Social Problems*, 23: 478–87.

——(1978) "Sex Differences in the Complexity of Children's Play and Games," *American Sociological Review*, 43: 471–83.

Lofland, J., Snow, D., Anderson, L., and Lofland, L. H. (2006) *Analyzing Social Settings*, 4th ed., Belmont, CA: Wadsworth Thomson.

Messner, M. (1990) "Boyhood, Organized Sports, and the Construction of Masculinities," *Journal of Contemporary Ethnography*, 18: 416–44.

Thorne, B. (1986) "Girls and Boys Together … But Mostly Apart: gender arrangements in elementary schools," in W. Hartup and Rubin, Z. (eds.) *Relationships and Development* (pp. 167–84), Hillsdale, NJ: Lawrence Erlbaum.

15

HOOKERS, ROUNDERS, AND DESK CLERKS

Encountering the reality of the hotel community[1]

Robert Prus

Hookers, Rounders, and Desk Clerks (*HR&DC*) (Prus and Irini 1980) is a study of the social organization of the hotel community that I developed with Styllianoss Irini. It is a study of hookers, strippers, and other entertainers, of bartenders, waiters, waitresses, desk clerks, and other hotel staff, and a variety of hustlers and thieves as well as an extended assortment of patrons. It is these people who collectively constitute the hotel community through their involvements, activities, interchanges, identities, and relationships with one another and others whose lives intersect there.

Attending to the "what and how" of ongoing community life, this study was organized around activities, the things these people do on the day-to-day, moment-to-moment basis. Focusing on people's activities as meaningful, purposive instances of human endeavor and interchange, we attempted to provide a thorough, highly detailed account of people's lived experiences from the viewpoint of the participants and the ways that they entered into the flows of human group life as agents. Given the elements of disrespectability and illegality that permeated much of this life-world, we also were determined to do this in ways that were void of sensationalism, moralism, and remedialism.

First published in 1980, this study began in 1976, following an unexpected meeting between Styllianoss Irini and myself. Styllianoss was in the process of completing an undergraduate degree in sociology and had visited the University of Waterloo as one of the schools he was considering for graduate studies. Waterloo had only a few openings that year and Styllianoss was not admitted to our program. However, during this preliminary contact we had a chance to talk and, as things worked out, Styllianoss would contribute notably to the broader sociological venture. I could not possibly have anticipated it at the time, but this chance encounter also represented the beginning of another major education for me as a social scientist. Indeed, the study of the hotel community would become an exceptionally enabling reference point and provide a set of resources that would help inform virtually all of the work I subsequently have developed as an academic (see Kleinknecht 2007).

At the time Styllianoss and I met, I was completing an ethnographic study of card and dice hustling (*Road Hustler,* Prus and Sharper 1977) and, as we talked, I learned that Styllianoss was working as a desk clerk in a hotel that served as a "home base" for people involved in a considerable variety of disreputable and illegal activities (e.g. prostitution, exotic dancing, and theft).

Having been focused on the thief subculture and people's involvements, activities, and relationships therein through the work I had been doing with C. R. D. Sharper, I quickly became attentive to the social world that Styllianoss was describing. He said that for his undergraduate thesis he was trying to answer the question of whether there was a community in the hotel setting. "Of course there's a community there," I said, "but the more important question is, how does it work? How do all of these people fit their lives and activities together?"

Looking back, I am a little surprised at the direct nature of my comment. Still, from the work I had been doing with C. R. D. Sharper, I learned about the card and dice hustlers' connections with the broader thief subculture and that bars and hotels represented an important set of contact points for many of these people. I also knew that deviance was to be understood as a social process rather than the product of people's individual qualities or vague sociological notions of social structure. Still, the setting that Styllianoss was describing was much more than a single subculture of the type that characterizes most ethnographic research in sociology. The life-world that Styllianoss was discussing consisted of a set of subcultures embedded within a more extended community. It was a community within the community. Although I couldn't fathom the fuller scope or the intricacies of people's involvements therein at the time, it was in many respects a microcosm of the larger society.

Our first contact lasted about an hour and, while I found Styllianoss' situation and his experiences therein very interesting, I had no expectation of anything particularly consequential materializing. Nevertheless, Styllianoss seemed authentic in the things he had talked about and I suggested that he keep notes on the things he was observing. The idea was that he would keep a journal of the things he had observed and experienced while working as a desk clerk in the hotel setting, entering these each day on a tape recorder after he finished work.

As I listened to the tapes and discussed these and related matters with Styllianoss, I became more intrigued with the interconnections of the people in the hotel setting in which he worked and their interlinkages with other hotels, bars, and places that he had mentioned. What struck me were the instances and details—the references to the arrangements people had been working out with one another and the overall fluidity of the hotel community—amidst a wide mix of people and the various relationships and interchanges that these people had with one another.

Most research on crime and deviance focuses on one occupational category or one subcultural realm of activity, almost as if these categories or fields of endeavor existed unto themselves. As well, most research on crime and deviance focuses on some set of factors, variables, structures or forces that are presumed somehow to cause or produce certain outcomes (crime and deviance as dependent variables). Most of this research neglects people's activities and fails to establish the linkages between these antecedent conditions and actual instances of crime and deviance (see Grills and Prus 2008). *Road Hustler* had taken me well beyond this, but as I reflected on the materials that Styllianoss had provided the importance of the community as an extended set of realms of activity was beginning to crystallize much more explicitly in my mind.

Much like C. R. D. Sharper in *Road Hustler*, Styllianoss was both my primary contact and research associate in the hotel setting. Styllianoss was a much less accomplished operator than was Sharper in their respective settings but the people in the hotel community generally liked Styllianoss and many of those he introduced to me seemed sufficiently comfortable with me that they quickly opened up more of their life-worlds to us.

For my part, I tried to fit in as best I could and used all occasions to learn as much as possible about the situations at hand. I was not there to judge these people, educate them, reform them, or anything of that sort. Just to learn and understand. I kept notes on my experiences and the interchanges I had with these people. Initially, this was not intended as systematic research but instead was approached as part of my own education as a sociologist.

Because university-related research has to be approved by an ethics committee, I approached ethics with a proposal to study the hotel community. Whereas much research is processed in more stereotypic terms, this proposal resulted in a hearing before the fuller committee. As I saw it, it was to be a study of activities and relationships but I didn't know how the study would work out. The people assembled brought a variety of other standpoints to the hearing. Amongst other things, this was a study that not only might be defined as disreputable and dangerous, but also as unscientific and even entertaining.

In addition to comments pertaining to the disrespectability (i.e. immorality) generally associated with a "deviant" subject matter as well as those who study deviance, especially in more sustained, close-up ways, there were questions of these sorts. "Do you carry a gun?" "What would you do if you found yourself in a violent confrontation?" "Why can't you get these people to sign letters of permission (prior to being interviewed)?" "Couldn't you just get a random sample of prostitutes to come to your office for interviews?" And, more humorously, "I was wondering if I might come along?" I tried to deal with people's comments and answer their questions as patiently, openly and reasonably as I could and we did receive approval for the research project.

We had been in the field for about six months before I began to see how we might achieve a more substantial, focused sense of direction for the project. It had been necessary to learn much more about the "what and how" of hotel life—the things these people did, their involvements and experiences, and other more immediate interchanges as well as the interconnections that they developed with one another. I also realized that the study had to assume a tentative, open, emergent, adjustive quality.

Even so, I still had questions and reservations. Is it even possible to do this study? How might it work out? What would it look like? Building on *Road Hustler* and the interactionist literature (what I knew of it at the time) associated with Herbert Blumer, Erving Goffman, Howard Becker, John Lofland, and others, there would be a focus on activities, relationships, identities, careers of involvements and related sets of processes. Nevertheless, we would be venturing into new territory and any major concepts that we used would have to be assessed and adjusted relative to the instances we encountered in the field.

Methodologically, we would be employing the same basic procedures in developing an ethnographic account of hotel community as Sharper and I had used in *Road Hustler*. The hotel study would be informed by observations pertaining to the things that others were doing, but participant observation and extended open-ended interviews would be the primary resources for learning about people's lived experiences. This might seem simple enough. However, I found that it had been a genuine challenge to develop a large ethnography of the sort that *Road Hustler* had entailed. There had been so many matters to deal with in developing that study. The hotel project seemed much more daunting. Not only were there so many more things going on at once in the hotel community, but we also would have to deal with an exceptional level of complexity and ambiguity. It would be extremely challenging to collect, organize, and analyze all of the material that would be required and I had no idea how we might actually produce a viable, coherent account of the broader hotel community. I didn't realize it at the time, but it later became apparent that the hotel study was somewhat like putting four or five studies like *Road Hustler* together into one volume.

Moreover, even though there was so much to be learned in the setting, there also were many misconceptions of crime and deviance in sociology, psychology, and criminology that we would need to overcome. Thus, although some ethnographic studies such as Edwin Sutherland's (1937) *The Professional Thief*, Clifford Shaw's (1930) *The Jack-Roller*, Paul Cressey's (1932) *The Taxi-Dance Hall*, Erving Goffman's (1961) *Asylums*, and Jacqueline Wiseman's (1970) *Stations of the Lost* were extremely helpful, most of the literature (especially positivist and Marxist) on crime and deviance was of little value for comprehending the things we encountered in the hotel community.

Although patience, perseverance, and an intense desire to learn were essential aspects of the research process, it needs to be emphasized that this study was something that we could not have done on our own. *HR&DC* required extended levels of assistance from a great many people. Moreover, it was necessary that they take us into their life-worlds—their home territories and back regions—and share so many things with us in open, extensively detailed ways.

Still, because of the ambiguous, uneven, and emergent nature of community life, the hotel study required extensive openness, flexibility, and ongoing adjustments. It required balancing intimacy and distancing amidst the relentless pursuit of information. Involving considerable emotional control and impression management, this project also took as much courage and resourcefulness as we could manage in what was a risky, potentially threatening, and sometimes highly volatile setting.

Hookers, Rounders, and Desk Clerks—an overview

Having presented some background material on the development of *Hookers, Rounders, and Desk Clerks*, I next provide a very brief, conceptual and methodological chapter-by-chapter synopsis of this text. This is extremely important for comprehending the overall study and the ways it took shape as an emergent social process. Whereas many readers may be intrigued with the substantive materials to be found in this text, the primary intellectual payoff is a conceptual one; that is, "what can we learn about human group life in more direct, sustained, and precise conceptual terms from examining the things that people do in this or that particular setting?"

Following an introduction (chapter 1) to the concept of deviance as a community phenomenon, chapter 2 ("Hooking in the Lounge") examines the life-worlds of women involved in prostitution in the bar setting. Beyond an account of their involvements, situations, activities, careers, and the relationships that the bar hookers develop among themselves and their clients, consideration also is given to the interchanges that "the working girls" (as they often like to call themselves) develop with bar staff, exotic dancers, pimps, boyfriends, and families.

Still, because people's involvements as bar hookers are not as singular or exclusive as these might seem, we also inquired into the experiences of women working on the streets, in massage parlors, escort services, and operating as call girls. These additional realms of material proved to be invaluable, not only for indicating the interconnections of the women working in these different settings and their affiliations with other participants of the hotel community, but this broader aspect of the study also generated a highly instructive set of comparison points for comprehending the nature of people's involvements in prostitution more generally.

Whereas chapter 3, "Working the Desk," might seem more marginal in some ways, it provides some extremely valuable insight into the matter of keeping order (and regulating deviance) in the hotel setting. In addition to denoting back regions of considerable importance to a wide array of women working as prostitutes, this chapter also depicts the relationships that desk clerks in "hotels catering to the working girls" have with hookers, their tricks, and other patrons as well as desk clerks' relationships with the strippers, other entertainers, other hotel staff, management, and the police. Thus, while attending to the symbiotic relationship of hookers and desk clerks, chapter 3 also considers a variety of other hustles, realms of activity and modes of people's involvements and interchanges in the hotel setting.

Chapter 4, "Providing Entertainment," primarily deals with women working as strippers or exotic dancers, but parallels the materials on the hookers (chapter 2) in many respects. There are differences to be sure, but much can be learned by attending to the similarities as well as the ways that these two sets of performers come to terms with their respective and sometimes overlapping involvements in the hotel community.

Whereas attention is given to people's involvements, identities, and performances as exotic dancers, consideration also was directed to the relations that the strippers develop with one another, their audiences, the hookers, the hotel staff, and various other associates. As with our earlier mentioned attempts to learn about the working girls beyond the bar setting, we utilized opportunities to learn more about those performing as exotic dancers in other settings. As well, we also inquired into the experiences of those assuming roles as other entertainers (mostly musicians) in the bar. These additional realms of information and the comparisons they fostered were very important for achieving fuller understandings of the processes, allures, and problematics of those involved in generating entertainment.

In addition to shedding light on a wide range of other activities taking place in the hotel community, chapter 5, "Working the Bar," provides another close-up account of the broader "service" or "hospitality" industry. Although we set up each of the chapters in somewhat different ways (in part to provide some diversity for ourselves as authors), we again focused on people's activities, identities, and relations with one another as well as their involvements and their interconnections with the other people involved in the hotel community. As with the hookers, strippers, and desk clerks, we extended the comparative base of people working in bars as much as we could. Thus, while we gathered a good deal of information from those working at Main and Central, the two "action bars" around which most of our study revolved, we also ventured into a much wider assortment of bars in order to examine more fully the activities and interchanges of those working as bartenders, waitresses, waiters, and managers

Notably, once one looks past the decor and general ambiance associated with any particular bar, the activities, relationships, and interchanges among bar staff, managers, patrons, and entertainers are remarkably parallel. Still, I might note that this last observation was something that we realized most explicitly after writing out two separate accounts of "action bars" (catering to hookers, strippers, and their clientele) and other "more conventional" drinking establishments. After recognizing the redundancy of these two statements, we decided to merge these into one chapter while indicating qualifications along these lines wherever these seemed appropriate. Notably, this experience provided a very instructive case of "overcoming the deviant mystique" (Prus and Grills 2003) for ourselves as analysts.

Focusing on the ways that people may fit into bar life as customers, chapter 6, "Being Patrons" represents another vital component of the hotel community. Although the individuals patronizing particular bars or taverns may believe that they are the most important participants in the hotel community (and they clearly are essential for "paying the bills"), it is strikingly apparent from the preceding chapters that those working in this setting as hookers, strippers, or hotel staff do not share this view. Indeed, these people typically consider the bars in which they work to be "their place" and envision the patrons of these establishments as essential but generally more transitory and relatively inconsequential individuals in the setting.

Still, there are great variations among those who may be considered patrons. Hence, in addition to the, often considerable, drinking involvements of hookers, strippers, other entertainers, and bar staff, people defining themselves as "regulars," "hustlers," and "heavies" also tend to envision particular bars as their own territories. As with the people whose activities are considered in the preceding chapters, we attended to the fuller sets of involvements and activities of those assuming roles as "customers" in the bar setting.[2] Thus, we were mindful of the interchanges that those spending time in bar settings might develop with one another as well as the bar staff, the hookers, the strippers, the hustlers, and others.

In addition to the shifting, uneven, and multiplistic nature of people's involvements in bar life, we also recognized that people's involvements in bars frequently spill over into other arenas. Thus, we considered it necessary to examine the associations and interchanges that people from the hotel community might develop in area restaurants and "after-hours" places that catered to this broader clientele.

Although we addressed many role-related comparisons and cross-role interconnections in the course of developing the preceding chapters, we used chapter 7 ("In Perspective") to more explicitly address the theoretical and methodological implications of this study. In addition to discussing the processes and problematics of developing this project, we focused more directly and explicitly on deviance as a set of social processes.

We had been learning a great deal about the hotel community by taking it apart piece-by-piece, asking what was going on, trying to see how things were taking shape, and attending to whatever variants and linkages we encountered. However, we also found that developing this study was like trying to assemble an evershifting, multilayered jigsaw puzzle. Not only did we not know what the eventual picture might look like, but the pieces also kept changing shape—although not completely, evenly, or consistently. As a result, we became highly mindful of the fluid, resilient, adjustive, and extensively interlinked nature of people's activities, interchanges, and relationships.

Focusing on the ways that people, as agents and interactants, entered into the ongoing flows of community life, we became increasingly attentive to the arrangements, shifting characters, and the continuities and transformations that we encountered in the hotel setting. Whether these involved longer-term participants or people who were comparatively new to the setting, each person, group, and interactional context represented objects to be noted, examined, sorted out, and comprehended—not only relative to these people's more immediate circumstances, activities, and interchanges but also mindfully of the histories and longer-term relationships that particular people might develop with others in this broader setting.

While acknowledging people's definitions and concerns with activities and associations that might be considered disrespectable and/or illegitimate within as well as beyond the hotel community, this focus on process was extremely important. Not only did this emphasis on process enable us to achieve extended insights into the hotel community with respect to the activities that were taking place in that setting, but it also enabled us to better comprehend people's capacities as agents, the emergent nature of human interchange and influence work, and the relevance of people's identities, reputations and interconnectedness for ongoing community life. This emphasis on process also fostered comparative analysis of a more generic or transcontextual sort.

Those who examine chapter 7 will see that we talk about deviance as a central feature of the hotel community. However, in contrast to those adopting positivist or Marxist (and postmodernist) approaches, we emphasized the relativistic, humanly defined, actively engaged, and interactively achieved nature of deviance. From an interactionist viewpoint, nothing is inherently deviant and deviance is a matter of audience definitions. Still, despite the relativist nature of audience definitions, deviance is far from being an arbitrary matter. People's conceptions of deviance, as with their notions of that which is acceptable or desirable, reflect the moral orders of the communities or subcommunities in which they participate.

It is the shared or intersubjective, group-based understandings that people develop as they collectively make sense of their situations, organize their life-worlds, and go about their activities that give "reality" to the particular notions of deviance with which people in specific communities, or subcultures within them, work.

Insofar as people organize their life-worlds around particular sets of activities, the people involved in each realm of activity will develop a moral order around each of those sets of activities. The people engaged in each of these "theaters of operations," thus, develop more particular variants of their own moral orders. Still, the people involved in each of these specific realms of activity typically also share and participate in other sets of life-worlds within the larger community (see Prus 1997). Indeed, almost everyone will be involved in multiple subcultures on a more or less simultaneous basis. Sorting out these fields of activity and people's practices and emphases within them, as well as the overlapping moral orders that may be associated with particular realms of activity, was an especially challenging aspect of the hotel study. However, an attentiveness to the moral orders associated with these multiple realms of activity generated a great deal of insight into the nature of community life.

As well, because we took the viewpoint (also see Prus and Sharper 1977) that "one does not need one theory for the deviants and one for the so-called normals," we approached the study of deviance in the hotel setting in much the same way that we might examine people's involvements in any other life-worlds, subcultures or realms of community life. Relatedly, although the hotel community may be characterized by considerably more pervasive and higher levels of drinking, hustling activity, and violence, the normative, often taken-for-granted features of these matters have important implications for comprehending community life more generally.

Building on some materials developed in *Road Hustler*, we also used chapter 7 to elaborate on the concept of "career contingencies" or people's "careers of participation" in various realms of community life. Accordingly, we addressed people's initial involvements, continuities, disinvolvements, and reinvolvements in their roles, activities, and relationships in the hotel community, along with some more specific, processually integrated features of these involvements.

Thus, in discussing people's continued involvements in the hotel community, more explicit attention was given to the processes of people's conversion to particular perspectives or world views, people's interconnected realms of activity and relations with others, and the relevance of people's identities and reputations for their longer-term participation within the hotel community.

More focused attention also was given to "deviance as activity." Because it is people's activities that represent the most basic features of community life, and activities are to be understood in process terms, any social science that does not centrally focus on activity as a fundamental, emergent feature of the human condition will be woefully inadequate.

The theoretical material in chapter 7 concludes with a discussion of "deviance as community." Here, we stress the point that deviance, as with crime or any other realm of meaningful endeavor, cannot possibly be understood on the basis of individual qualities or by relying on research that decontextualizes outcomes (dependent variables) from the instances of the actual interactional contexts in which these arise (also see Grills and Prus 2008). Crime and deviance, thus, are best understood within the context of community life as "something that is more or less continuously in the making."

Conceptuality in the making

Despite the considerable amount of conceptual material that one finds in *Hookers, Rounders, and Desk Clerks*, there were few if any "eureka" moments or particular instances of dramatic conceptual realization in this study. As a participant-observer, Styllianoss had been witnessing a wide array of front and back region activities of the people in this setting as well as their interchanges and interconnections. For my part, I had become highly attentive to the relevance of activities, contacts, and teamwork as well as the processes and problematics of impression management and deception in *Road Hustler*. As a result, even though there was still so much to be learned about people's activities and relationships within the hotel community, most of our time was spent attending to people's activities and interchanges as these took place, and most of the concepts emerged through ongoing inquiry, sustained comparative analysis of the instances we encountered, and dialogue with the existing interactionist literature.

Thus, rather than encountering "intense flashes of insight," Styllianoss and I were embarked on a sustained research process that was characterized by continual exploration and inquiry. This involved observation, participant observation, and especially extended open-ended interviewing that was focused on people's activities and interchanges. As much as possible, we also kept detailed records on the various people we met, the things they did, those with whom they interacted, and the ways they related to these other people. We also used the things we encountered in the field, through observation and earlier interviews, as points of departure for further investigation and extended inquiry, striving to be more thorough, more comprehensive in subsequent inquiries.

Although we found the things that people did and told us to be highly informative as well as interesting in many ways, if not also somewhat puzzling and perhaps downright disconcerting at times, we tried to be patient, thorough, and emotionally composed throughout the study. We particularly attempted to avoid jumping to conclusions or making presumptions. Instead, we let our materials accumulate as much as we could, pursuing information on all aspects of the hotel community and investigating the things we were learning about in as much detail as possible.

Later, we sorted our materials out into categories. We organized our notes and interview materials around the roles that people assumed and their activities and interchanges therein. Subsequently, we sorted things out further, attending more precisely to whatever similarities and differences we encountered in the ways that people did things and how they related to others. When we ran into uncertainties or found that we had missed following up on something, we made more concerted efforts to learn about these things through subsequent observations and interviews with people in the field. Still, as we attempted to prepare our materials for analysis, or our analysis for conference papers or other statements about people's involvements in the hotel community, we kept finding that there were more matters to pursue in depth, and we were sometimes surprised to realize particular things (at that point seemingly very obvious) we had missed. I don't recall specific instances, but I know that this was not an infrequent experience. Additional areas of inquiry as well as omissions became more evident as we tried to provide more adequate accounts of the various things we encountered in the field. This, I might observe, has been a fairly common experience in all of the ethnographies I have done and attests to the value of continuing to conduct field research even as one develops the analysis.

Clearly, we were learning more about the hotel community as we sorted through these materials and tried to make sense of the things we had encountered. Still, we did not have to develop all of these conceptual themes on our own. Thus, we not only continued to read other ethnographies as we sorted through the materials on the hotel community, but also examined, reexamined, and reflected on the texts that Herbert Blumer, Erving Goffman, John Lofland, Howard Becker, and others in the interactionist tradition have developed. Our intention was not to prove or verify what these others had found or said but rather to assess the things we encountered in this literature relative to our own materials by engaging in yet other instances of comparative analysis and trying to articulate our findings and the conceptual inferences thereof in more informed and precise ways.

I also might note that our conceptualizations of the various features of the hotel community did not develop as more singular or isolated sets of analyses but rather became more thorough, precise, authentic (i.e. representative, accurate, informed) and integrated as we reworked our statements amidst reexaminations and reflective considerations of the fuller sets of instances we encountered in the field.

Relatedly, we took the viewpoint that the data had to assume priority over any conceptual materials we might invoke and, thus, approached our own formulations as well as the materials that we had located in the literature as tentative. Whereas the conceptual and substantive ethnographic materials in the literature represented important reference points for contemplating the things we had encountered in the field, we were determined that our analyses not be unduly shaped or limited by these other materials.

As well, because the hotel community was enshrouded by disrespectability and deception as well as more clear matters of illegality, we tried to be mindful of potential discrepancies between front and back region activities (Goffman 1959) and the ways that people associated with one another in this setting. Further, although this was something that characterized the study from the outset, we also made notes of things that didn't fit together as they more typically might and tried to follow up on these instances (people, activities, relationships). Still, we were concerned that we not dwell on the more idiosyncratic features of the setting to the relative neglect of more fundamental or prototypic matters. Consequently, anything that might seem more sensational in some way would be contextualized relative to the more common occurrences, practices, and associated variants thereof.

Some might be disappointed that we did not have more intense, "defining moments of insight," but for us conceptualization was very much embedded within and emerged from the research process. It reflected our preliminary concerns (following Blumer) not only of developing intimate familiarity with one's subject matter but also on focusing on people's activities and interchanges as these took place in instances and then subjecting these materials to sustained, comparative analysis, in the quest to develop transsituationally informed conceptualizations of human group life.[3] We tried to provide the most authentic, thorough, and detailed account and analysis of the hotel community that we could. We leave it to the reader to judge the adequacy of this endeavor.

Notes

1 I would like to thank Mary Suljak, along with the editors (Bill Shaffir, Steve Kleinknecht, and Tony Puddephatt) for their thoughtful comments on earlier drafts of this paper.

2 Interestingly, one of the areas to which we did not give sustained attention in *HR&DC* was the matter of "drinking as activity." Thus, although we provided considerable material pertinent to people's drinking practices in the text, readers will find a more extended consideration of "drinking as activity" in Prus (1983). Although this may seem embarrassing in some ways, I might observe that we not only had wanted to focus on the social organization of the hotel community but also had realized fairly early in the project that alcohol was *not* an essential element of the hotel community.

Whereas the sales of alcohol enabled these particular businesses to survive, the bar (like the hotel more generally) was a setting in which people could meet, pursue a variety of interests, and work out various facets of their lives in conjunction with an assortment of other people. Thus, although less complex in various ways (especially matters pertaining to disrespectability and illegality), somewhat parallel communities may develop around restaurants, hospitals, churches, and other settings in which people assemble. As a case in point, a coffee shop (no alcohol was available) several blocks away from Main and Central in Eastville served as a regular meeting place for some hookers and their clients. Likewise, we encountered two theaters featuring exotic dancers that did not serve alcohol.

3 Although it is difficult to find ethnographic materials of historical and cross-cultural sorts that focus on people's activities in more detailed and sustained terms, these materials are of great importance for generating comparisons and assessing existing conceptual understandings of our human subject matter. Comparisons of these sorts would, of course, add another valuable dimension to the study of the hotel community as well as a fuller appreciation of human group life more generally. See Blumer 1969; Strauss 1993; Prus 1996; 1997; 2007a; 2007b; 2007c; Prus and Grills 2003.

References

Blumer, H. (1969) *Symbolic Interactionism*, Englewood Cliffs, NJ: Prentice-Hall.

Cressey, P. (1932) *The Taxi Dance Hall*, Chicago: University of Chicago Press.

Goffman, E. (1959) *The Presentation of Self in Everyday Life*, New York: Anchor.

——(1961) *Asylums: essays on the social situation of mental patients and other inmates*, New York: Doubleday.

Grills, S. and Prus, R. (2008) "The Myth of the Independent Variable: reconceptualizing class, gender, race, and age as subcultural processes," *The American Sociologist*, 39: 19–37.

Kleinknecht, S. (2007) "An Interview with Robert Prus: his career, contributions, and legacy as an interactionist ethnographer and social theorist," *Qualitative Sociology Review*, 3: 221–88.

Prus, R. (1983) "Drinking as Activity: an interactionist analysis," *Journal of Studies on Alcohol*, 44: 460–75.

——(1996) *Symbolic Interaction and Ethnographic Research*, Albany, NY: State University of New York Press.

——(1997) *Subcultural Mosaics and Intersubjective Realities*, Albany, NY: State University of New York Press.

——(2007a) "Human Memory, Social Process, and the Pragmatist Metamorphosis: ethnological foundations, ethnographic contributions and conceptual challenges," *Journal of Contemporary Ethnography*, 36: 378–437.

——(2007b) "The Intellectual Canons of a Public Sociology: pragmatist foundations, historical extensions, and humanly engaged realities," in L. T. Nichols (ed.) *Public Sociology: the contemporary debate* (pp. 195–235), New Brunswick, NJ: Transaction.

——(2007c) "On Studying Ethnologs (Not Just People, 'Societies in Miniature'): on the necessities of ethnography, history, and comparative analysis," *Journal of Contemporary Ethnography*, 36: 669–703.

Prus, R. and Grills, S. (2003) *The Deviant Mystique: involvements, realities, and regulation*, Westport, CT: Praeger.

Prus, R. and Irini, S. (1980) *Hookers, Rounders, and Desk Clerks: the social organization of the hotel community*, Toronto, ON: Gage.

Prus, R. and Sharper, C. R. D. (1977) *Road Hustler: the career contingencies of professional card and dice hustlers*, Lexington, MA: Lexington.

Shaw, C. (1930) *The Jack Roller: a delinquent boy's own story*, Chicago: University of Chicago Press.

Strauss, A. (1993) *Continual Permutations of Action*, Hawthorne, NY: Aldine de Gruyter.

Sutherland, E. H. (1937) *The Professional Thief*, Chicago: University of Chicago Press.

Wiseman, J. (1970) *Stations of the Lost*, Englewood Cliffs, NJ: Prentice-Hall.

Part V

CHALLENGING ESTABLISHED WISDOM

16

MAKING THEORIES FROM WATER
Or, finding stratification in competitive swimming

Daniel F. Chambliss

"Insight such as this falls to one's lot but once in a lifetime," wrote Sigmund Freud, famously, in his *The Interpretation of Dreams* (Freud 1932: 9).[1] Freud was referring to his discovery of the unconscious, the insight that makes his book arguably the twentieth century's single most influential work of social science. Freud's work stands alone. But his experience of "this is my single great idea," the pinnacle of one's intellectual life, can be shared by many of us. Luckily for me, I have once enjoyed such a feeling.

My moment came in 1984, at the age of 31, while conducting ethnographic research on world-class competitive swimmers. Sitting on a concrete pool deck in Mission Viejo (Orange County), California, leaning against a chain link fence, watching scores of teenagers swim back and forth for hours on end, I had grown bored—nothing much was happening. True, some of them were world record holders, graceful and strong in the water; but each day, basically, they just swam back and forth. And on many days, coaches would come from all over the world just to see them swim, to listen to their coaches (such as Mark Schubert, one of the best in the world), to discover their secrets. And within a few short hours, those visitors, like me, would grow bored. Recognizing that fact—"I'm bored! Sometimes *they're* bored!"—eventually led me to broader conclusions: there's nothing special or magical about excellence; normal people can achieve extraordinary things; our understanding of excellence is obscured by mystified notions of talent or genius. For those who actually achieve it, excellence is created by characteristically rather mundane actions. It arises from a normal daily pattern of routine, doable activities. For me, that was a profound realization, my own Freud moment of "once in a lifetime." The curtain had been pulled back; I had seen the wizard. I knew, at the time, that this was at least a good idea, and probably for me a great one; I knew it was probably the best idea I would ever have as a sociologist. It eventually led to a book, *Champions* (Chambliss: 1988) and an article called "The Mundanity of Excellence" (Chambliss: 1989) that won the American Sociological Association's Theory

Section Prize. The article has enjoyed a good run in reprints and readers, and lots of undergraduate students still read it 20 years after its publication. It grew out of that "Freud moment."

The swimming research emerged when professional necessity joined hands with personal passion. The necessity was to find a new research project. I'd just completed a doctoral dissertation on moral problems in hospital nursing, and was emotionally exhausted from long months of observation in newborn intensive care units, cancer wards, operating rooms and emergency rooms, watching a big slice of the world's misery. Personal tragedy was routine to the people working in hospitals ("How was your day?" I once asked a nurse I was taking out to dinner. "Some guy fell dead in front of me," she replied), but the nurses' world was not mine, and I was looking for something a little more fun. Besides, as an untenured college professor, keeping my job required doing more research. That was the driving necessity.

The passion was for competitive swimming, which since my early teens offered everything I desired: excitement, sun, water, bodily and aesthetic beauty, girls, speed, raucous socializing, the thrill of victory, and—for a 120-pound kid with no muscle but lots of self-discipline—the prospect of justice achieved. After all, nothing satisfies an undersized teenaged boy quite so much as defeating 6ft 2in, 200-lb jocks in something athletic. Through competitive swimming, I became a skinny 15-year-old strolling around my high school wrapped in a big leather letter jacket. Pretty nice; lots of benefits. Swimming was physically challenging and sensually pleasurable; it was intensely competitive but not dangerous, either physically or socially; and it demanded, if one really took it seriously (which I did), a greater commitment of all one's resources—physical, emotional, moral and intellectual—than anything I'd ever seen before or since. By my senior year in 1970, I made it to the finals of the Tennessee State Championships: not great, considering the work I put in, but quite satisfying overall. I loved the sport. So in 1983, looking around for a new sociological topic to study, and seeing that the 1984 Olympic Games were to be held here in the United States, in Los Angeles, my decision was really pretty easy. I'd study swimmers training for the Olympics, and find out what made them so good.

Initially I had no "theory" or hypotheses, only an inchoate, almost unconscious collection of assumptions—lots of them, as it happens—about elite swimmers, gathered from seeing them on television and in magazines. I imagined them, for instance, to be personally attractive yet modest; full of interesting ideas about swimming; and the center of attention wherever they went. I thought they'd be cool. I also expected them to be celebrities, which I discovered they weren't, except for during one Olympic week out of every four years. (It turns out most of them were ordinary teenagers, although exceptionally athletic ones.) My sociological footing was a thick mixture of symbolic interactionism, Randall Collins' version of Durkheim's ritual solidarity theory, and the basics of organizational social psychology. The sociology of sport literature I rejected as too thin and politically tendentious, but I voraciously read what was called "New Journalism," practiced by writers such as David Halberstam, Tom Wolfe, and Gay Talese. These journalists did what I wanted to do: they wrote true stories as if they were fiction, from a third-person omniscient point of view. I wanted to see, and know, and describe, the swimming world from the inside, as the swimmers lived it.

The basic research method was total immersion (an apt metaphor!) in Southern California swimming. I spent many months, over a four-year period, with a group of Olympic-class swimmers, living with their coaches for part of that span. During the same period, I took up coaching myself, beginning rather badly (bottom of the local league for two years) and ending four years later rather well, with several swimmers in the "Top 20 in the U.S." in their age groups, and one national collegiate champion. Once in a while, I even got back in the water myself, to remember what it was like; it's much harder than it looks. Mainly, though, I watched swimmers swim and talked with them and their coaches about swimming, or anything else. And all those implicit beliefs I had held about great swimmers proved, mostly, to have been wrong. One day in at the pool I literally sat down with a lined pad of paper and wrote, one item per line, all of the things I felt I'd learned in the research, with no self-censorship: "They're kids." "Everyone calls them kids, too." "The coaches never yell." "They laugh a lot." "Some of these people have nothing to say." "I'm frequently bored." "Turns and pushoffs matter a lot." "The divers on this team are narcissists." "Coaches make sure the deck area is clean." "Everyone works very hard, but some swimmers are called lazy by the others." "Coaches exist to eliminate excuses." The list ran to several pages. Reviewing the list later, I realized that my childhood images of great swimmers had been fantasies, and my adult notions had been myths, variations on what I had heard through magazines and television. About almost all of it, I had been wrong.

Each little surprise—each thing I learned—emerged from some characteristic of the research. Some insights came from doing *observation*—actually watching my subjects live their lives. Others came from observing over several years, doing *longitudinal research*. And a third group of ideas emerged as I actually tried to use what I had learned, testing the developing theory with practical *application*, as a coach, to my own swimmers and their careers.

Observation: go and look

At the outset, I put down my books and went to see for myself. I flew to California, got access to a team (the best one in the country, in fact), then sat down and watched, trying simply to see what was in front of my face. What I saw was that these swimmers were, more or less, ordinary teenagers: laughing, horsing around, talking a lot, flirting, and gossiping. They were kids, and they were having fun, together. Very friendly, not oddballs at all, far from isolated individuals grinding away in solitary discipline, the way the dramatic stories sometimes tell it. They were, in a word, sociable.

This was a revelation with several implications. Among swimmers training for the highest level of competition, I found, rewards came not just once every four years (or once a year, at the National Championships), but literally every day. To swimmers in the water, the training itself was more or less enjoyable. They liked swimming—the physical activity itself; many found it quite relaxing or even meditative; almost all, I found, enjoyed the bodily sensation of being in the water, sliding along gracefully, experiencing the sensation of great speed. Just as many football players actually enjoy hitting and being hit ("I like the contact"), the best swimmers are not suffering something unpleasant in order to achieve secondary gains; the activity is in itself enjoyable. This holds distinctively for elements of swimming that other people clearly don't like—intense competition, physical effort, enforced concentration. And, as I saw every day, they certainly didn't suffer socially; indeed, they typically had lots of friends, not only across the country but around the world. Yes, some missed their senior proms in high school—perhaps to attend the National Championships; but they were also featured in the local newspapers, honored with prizes at school assemblies, and idolized by ninth-graders, and not a few other people as well.

And the daily rewards are social in nature. Even in this individual sport where performance is measured by a clock, virtually all world-class swimmers train with top-level teams. There they reinforce each other's commitment to athletic excellence; seriousness about swimming was part of being popular. It's the expectation, from the coaches, as well. When one boy came in a few minutes late to a practice, head coach Mark Schubert pulled him aside and said, pointing to the 40 or so swimmers already in the water, "You see these people here? They want to be national champions. If you want to be a national champion too, then you can swim with them. If you don't, there are lots of other teams out there that would be happy to have you." They want to be there. Allowed only one week off from practice each year (in early September) some of them showed up at the pool anyway, a few days early. I asked one fellow why he did. "Because I'm a swimmer," he replied. "This is what I do."

I, on the other hand, had grown up in a world where deep commitment to a sport was a little suspect, if not actually denigrated, perhaps like studying too hard at a typical high school. It was prestigious to be a good athlete, but less cool to be truly passionate about it. But on the best teams, passion for the sport isn't just cool; it's taken for granted.

Why had I not understood this before doing direct observation? Media portrayals of great athletes focus on the individual performer, picking out, after the competition is over, the few stars who rise above the rest. Cameras, whether still-photography or television, isolate what is in the frame, and photographers are always taught to "get in close," zeroing in on a particular person, even one face, to bring out the humanity—but ironically, the most human feature of sociability may be lost. And the stories are pointedly dramatic, even romantic (in the broad sense of the term). The athletes' sacrifices are emphasized, their family tragedies are recounted in soft-focus, their performances reshown in slow-motion. The story is often told that they "spend four years" or even "their entire lives" working toward an Olympic gold medal, and that therefore a loss, or even a second-place finish, is devastating. Perhaps; but remember the daily rewards, the races and medals won, the articles in school and local newspapers, the perhaps brief appearances on TV, or in swimming magazines. Almost anyone at the elite levels of a sport has received great adulation over many years, quite frequently. And, more importantly, swimming for these athletes is not something suffered through for gain; sacrifices aren't being made; friends are not abandoned. To the contrary. It's enjoyable. It's rewarding. It's social.

My initial perceptions, then, had been systematically distorted through a media filter. When I actually saw for myself the daily lives of elite athletes, I was surprised; my "theory" had to be modified quite a bit.

Longitudinal research: spend some time

The sociability of the swimmers was evident from the first day of observation. Other lessons, though, came only with time: the routine attention that coaches and athletes give to seemingly small details; the seemingly paradoxical connection of these tiny details with great achievement; and the normal, even boring, quality of the daily work of athletic training. Only over an extended period of time can one identify these persisting activities that in the long run lead to success in sports.

Every discipline has its necessary routines. Great pianists do their scales every day, as beginners do (or should!). Ballet dancers work at the barre, an insurance seller works through the Rolodex and makes cold calls as well. An elite swimmer does laps, completing anywhere from 400 to 1,000 lengths of a pool every day, six or seven days a week; swimming the freestyle (crawl), she might take 15,000 rotational armstrokes in a single day, day after day, from four to six hours a day, for 15 or even 20 years of a career. This level of repetition, the necessary daily grunge work of the discipline, is at or beyond the physical maximum possible for the human body. (Many, perhaps most, elite swimmers eventually suffer shoulder problems, with surgical correction.) Within that pattern of endless repetition, our swimmer concentrates on details unseen by the novice: the exact pitch of the hand entering the water; the position of the elbow over the hand underwater; the rotation of the wrist when the hand leaves the water. One day at Mission Viejo, for instance, the coaches' attention was all on "pushoffs," the skill of streamlining the body when pushing off the wall after a turn: one hand firmly pressed on top of the other, arms fully extended, ears just below and between the extended arms, body sliding out just under the resistant bow wave that has followed it into the wall. In one day, there were hundreds of pushoffs for a single swimmer; tens of thousands for a team, with coaches standing over the end of the pool moving around to check each one, correcting the details. Tomorrow the attention would be on the proper angle of entry to the water on starts (dives); or the timing of the head lift when coming up after a pushoff; or the upsweep of the feet at the end of the breaststroke kick; or an apparently limitless array of other techniques. And this is only for the swimming itself. The same attention is paid to the weightlifting programs, plans for proper diet and rest, plans for adjusting one's biological clock when meets are held in different time zones, how to warm up for competition, how to warm down after competition (to more rapidly dissipate lactic acid in the muscles), the proper use of massage, not to mention all of the psychological factors that affect one's approach to practice, competition, and the inevitable need to deal with victory and defeat. All of these are written and read and talked about at great, even endless, length; in fact, attention to detail may well be almost a defining feature of excellence in all sorts of realms. Even how one talks to outsiders can matter, and so is studied. As Kevin Costner's character Crash Davis says in the baseball movie *Bull Durham*, if you're going to be in the major leagues, "you're gonna have to learn your clichés. Write this down: 'We gotta play it one day at a time.'"

Each of these little pieces contributes, in some way, to better performance. Great performance, when studied from birth to maturity over an athlete's entire career, seems to consist of little more than the folding together of a host of such little particulars, each one contributing some added advantage, however small. For important meets in other cities, the Mission Viejo team had catered meals delivered in their hotel, so everyone got a reliably good breakfast—after their good night's sleep, enforced by Mark Schubert's lights-out policy. Busses or vans, running on a strict schedule, got everyone to the pool on time for warm-ups. And so on. There's no end to the number of such details to be managed, since each one can add, however slightly, to the chances of an excellent performance. In the 1984 Olympic finals of the men's 100-meter freestyle—the premier sprint event of the sport—Rowdy Gaines, having studied the official who was starting the race, gained a split-second advantage by nearly jumping the gun, and became the gold medalist through that advantage. The little things do add up. Little things, I argued, aren't just important; *the little things are the only things*.

But an outsider may see only the apparently endless tedium of repetition of apparently trivial actions, which is real enough. Even visiting coaches, familiar themselves with the technical intricacies of the sport, became bored watching practices—pushoffs aren't that exciting. Of them, head coach Mark Schubert would say with a smile they were "coming to Mecca to find out our secret." But, as I said in *Champions*, Schubert knew, and I was beginning then to suspect, the "big secret" that all the visitors from around the world came looking for was—that there is no "big secret." There is only the will to swim for miles and miles, all the turns done correctly, all the strokes done legally, all the practices attended, all the weights lifted, and all the sprints pushed to the point of simple exhaustion, day after day for years and years.

(Chambliss 1988: 54)

For the athletes themselves, most of their world (and it is a world, a coherent section of social humanity) really is the daily routine of training. The daily details of technique and planning are not in themselves exciting. Only at the end of years of athletic training does the spectator see a stunning performance. A researcher can see that only by extended observation, over time, even over some years.

Applied research: try it out

During the several years I spent researching the book *Champions*, I was also coaching a small swim team in central New York State, where I live. For the research I was away from home for days or weeks at a time, and occasionally for months, during which time my team either was on a break or was managed by my assistant coach Bill McCormick. I would return from California filled with ideas about raising our goals, planning incentive trips to big meets, focusing on technical details, trying new motivational strategies, or finding corporate sponsors. My developing theories about swimming and excellence, then, could be tried out on the swimmers (and coaches!) of my own team. Soon, as we completely reshaped the culture of our workouts, and saw the (phenomenal) results, my initial belief in talent—natural inborn ability as a major predictor of success—slowly but surely dwindled, and eventually vanished. "Talent" is a reification that obscures the actual work of creating elite performance. Seen up close, over time, excellence becomes far less mysterious.

Consider three steps we took with our team, trying to apply the lessons from the research:

1 Discipline: Discipline grew tighter. We announced that everyone had to be at practice on time, at 6:00 p.m., or they would not be admitted. No excuses were allowed, for swimmers or coaches. At first, parents became angry, swimmers stamped about and argued vehemently. Excuses—many of them in fact quite reasonable—blossomed like daffodils in the spring. But as we stood fast on the policy, something happened: everyone started coming on time. And it turns out that when no excuses were allowed, none developed. People found ways to get there on time, virtually always. They planned better, they built in room for error, and they became more

disciplined about when to start the trip to the pool. That planning and discipline carried over to what they did in the pool, too.

2 Details: We focused on details. For two weeks, for instance, we'd spend twenty minutes every day working on pushoffs. And in the next meet, every swimmer did better pushoffs, and so they swam faster! Then for the next two weeks, we'd spend twenty minutes every day working on finishes—touching the wall properly at the end of a race. At the next meet, all of our kids had better finishes, and again got faster. Then two weeks on starts, then two weeks on getting the hips up in the butterfly, and so on, and on. After each meet, Bill and I would talk over the races, and pick one or two details where our team was weak. Then, for the next two weeks, we could pay concentrated attention on improving that particular skill. Then the team got better. It's that simple. It was absolutely exhilarating.

3 Goals: We raised our sights, and our swimmers'. In October of our "new" year, we announced an incentive meet, scheduled to be held at the magnificent Pepsi Marlins' team facility in Cincinnati, Ohio, home to several Olympians. The meet would include many of the finest swimmers in the East; athletes needed a AAA qualifying time in the national ranking system to enter the meet. When we made the announcement in October, we had not a single swimmer with a AAA time; only one or two were even close. But Bill and I said, "We're going to the meet. We'll take anyone who gets a triple-A time." *That day*, everyone on the team swam faster—indeed, some of them began swimming ferociously, immediately. And they started paying close attention to our advice, and urging their teammates to go faster. In the vernacular, kids got incredibly pumped up. Parents, on the other hand, thought we were—well, the word "insane" cropped up a few times. The trip was too long. The goal was unrealistic. Kids would be crushed if they didn't make the cutoff times. If they did make the cutoff times, they'd be crushed in the meet. But two months later, we took eight kids to that meet, and seven of them made the finals. One girl nearly won her event, the 50-yard butterfly. The kids were ecstatic. The parents couldn't believe it.

What amazed me was how doable it all was: the discipline, the details, the goals. For years as a budding coach I'd known all the technical details of the sport, of physiology and training, of what swimmers should do to go faster. I'd read all the swimming books, and had a closet filled with boxes of notes scribbled down during clinics, while listening to some famous coach go on about stroke drills, diet plans, and the intricacies of the backstroke, which I still don't understand. But what I'd lacked was the willingness—the courage, if you will—to make people do what they needed. Once I had that willingness—partly through seeing other coaches do it, partly through the constant encouragement of my assistant Bill—the rest was easy. Just *do* it (that was our slogan for years before Nike appropriated it!).

Once again, this was a surprise. I'd always thought (my initial implicit theory about excellence) that top swimmers were "talented". They seemed to have some mysterious inner quality one is born with that separated them from the rest of us. What I discovered, instead, is that top swimmers are just people who swim fast. The best swimmers are just those who swim faster than anyone else who happens to be doing it. There's no particular mystery. Talent, then, is just the name that we give to "explain" performance when we don't understand how it actually develops. Having discovered this, our team stopped worrying about whether a kid had natural ability and started working on the hundreds of particular actions that make a swimmer a little bit faster. And we discovered that lots of people, if they want to, can learn to swim fast.

Lessons learned

Having discovered an important and surprising reality, then, I needed to capture it in a word or phrase. The basic idea, while controversial, was not particularly difficult to present: There's no magic to excellence; one just needs to do all the things that excellent performers do. It may be tremendously difficult or tedious, or require astonishing commitment, but the natural wherewithal to accomplish it is probably widely available. In a sense, excellence is ordinary. From one of my graduate teachers, a philosopher named Maurice Natanson, I had learned the word "mundanity"—referring to life's ordinariness. At the same time, somewhere in my unconscious was the title of Hannah Arendt's 1963 book, *Eichmann in Jerusalem,* in which Arendt strove to explain the shocking ordinariness of one of the most influential perpetrators of the Holocaust, Adolf Eichmann. Arendt's book was subtitled *A Report on the Banality of Evil.* Natanson's word came together with Arendt's phraseology and my own idea, and I christened my concept "The Mundanity of Excellence," giving that phrase to the article I wrote as well as the epilogue of my book. The phrase was odd, but I wanted to emphasize the paradox in a memorable way. After all, this was my Big Idea.

So where had the idea come from? I spent many months with the people I wanted to understand, and some years testing my ideas on my own team. I observed, trying to see what was right in front of me; studied for a long time, having the chance to see entire careers develop, discern broader patterns and correct my own misconceptions; and applied what I had learned, discovering along the way where I'd been right and wrong. In retrospect, maybe that last adjective is the crucial one: where I'd been *wrong.* Even with no explicit hypotheses, I had entered the research with a host of implicit, unexamined notions about the people I was going to study. In a sense, that was my working theory. And having spent time with swimmers, I then sat down and asked "What was surprising? What do I know now that I didn't know before? What is obviously true—even if silly, startling, paradoxical, or apparently trivial? What, in short, have I learned?" The answers, first scribbled on a legal pad while I leaned against the chain link fence, provided the raw material for a theory. Going over that list, I saw some patterns; certain ideas kept coming up, for instance: *This is boring. Nothing special is going on. It's the same stuff every day.* How was that possible? And yet it was. The Big Idea—the ordinariness—was right in front of my face. When I set off to study the kind of people I had worshipped throughout my own swimming career, I never expected to find that watching them was boring. Yet it was, and therein I found the kernel of an important idea. If there's any lesson I can pass on to others, especially novice social scientists, it might then be this: Learn to accept, and even welcome, the startling experience of having been wrong.

Note

1 The comment, often quoted, comes from the foreword (not the preface, as many Internet citations have it) of the third English edition; there are other preliminary sections, a translator's introduction, an introductory note, etc. The foreword is signed "Freud, Vienna, March 15, 1931," although the publication date is 1932. I am indebted to reference librarians Kristin Strohmeyer and Paula Skreslet for their finding of these references.

References

Arendt, H. (1963) *Eichmann in Jerusalem: a report on the banality of evil*, New York: Viking.
Chambliss, D. F. (1988) *Champions: the making of Olympic swimmers*, New York: Wm. Morrow and Company.
——(1989) "The Mundanity of Excellence: an ethnographic report on stratification and Olympic athletes," *Sociological Theory*, 7: 70–86.
Freud, S. (1932) *The Interpretation of Dreams*, 3rd ed. (revised), London: George Allen & Unwin; New York: Macmillan.

17

SOLVING THE MYSTERIES OF SHELTER WORK FOR THE BATTERED WOMAN

Donileen R. Loseke

My task is to write the story behind the conceptual development in my 1992 ethnography, *The Battered Woman and Shelters*. The story genre will be a mystery because ethnography is detective work, the process of piecing together clues about the underlying meaning of the buzzing confusion of practical experience. This makes my character a sociological detective attempting to solve the mystery of how workers at the "South Coast" shelter understood the characteristics, problems, and needs of women residing there. I will attempt to show how the mysteries of shelter work presented themselves to me, and how clues solving one mystery did nothing to solve others. I will continue with how my findings from this research have led me to explore several more general questions about social life, and I will close with some reflections on doing this research. Because both ethnographers and mystery writers know that story plots and characters make sense only within context, that is where my story begins.

Contexts: setting the scene

My story starts in the late 1970s when I had finished my third year in a Ph.D. program and was offered a job on a grant to evaluate the newly formed Family Violence Program (FVP). As one of the first publicly supported programs in the United States to respond to the perplexing problems of wife abuse, the primary goal of the FVP was to develop models for changing criminal justice procedures for this newly defined crime. A minor element in the FVP was the South Coast shelter, which, on-the-record, was merely a resource for police: the police would arrest abusive men, the shelter would take care of the women. Although my formal job as program evaluator most often took me to the district attorney's office, the courts, and police station, I went to the shelter to interview workers about their activities and to tally statistics from the forms women completed when they entered as new residents.

By choice and by chance I was pulled further into life at South Coast. There never were enough workers; workers learned I would cheerfully stop my tallying of records in order to help, and, as a self-proclaimed feminist, I quickly became a strong supporter of the work done there. To add complexity, while my evaluator job had fairly little to do with the shelter, given my emotional commitments it only made sense that this would be the site of my dissertation research. This is the personal context of my story.

Because I have been asked to focus on conceptual development, the academic context of the late 1970s and early 1980s is critical in understanding the source of the mysteries posed by South Coast. Two primary literatures informed my initial research plans, the first of which was associated with the anti-battery social movement (for examples see Dobash and Dobash 1979; Martin 1976). At the time this was such a small body of work that I remember when I could say with all honesty that I had read *everything* written about wife abuse and the battered woman. This was a distinctly politicized literature conceptualizing wife abuse as a feminist social problem symbolizing all that was wrong with the patriarchal social order. The battered woman was a pure victim of brutal male violence who desperately wanted to free herself, but was trapped by an unresponsive social service system and by the multiple economic and psychological problems linked to the consequences of patriarchal society in general, victimization in particular. Such a woman wants, needs, and deserves help and the anti-battery movement literature promoted a new type of organization, shelters, as the type of help a battered woman needed. Shelters were to be distinctly client-centered and allow women to do what they wanted to do: leave their abusers and become independent and strong women. Shelters would be places where women would live together in self-managed, semi-communal environments; they would be places where women would help themselves and help one another shake off the bondages created by victimization. The anti-battery movement literature was a perfect frame for my research because South Coast explicitly identified itself as a feminist alternative organization. The formal manual of shelter operations began:

> The shelter operates from the philosophical base that women are strong within themselves. The staff lends its strength to women in crisis to help them help themselves become independent and responsible ... The residents assist each other in building self-esteem which results in women learning to take control over their own lives.

Because the anti-battery movement literature conceptualized shelters as feminist alternative organizations, it also made sense for me to draw insights from sociological writings on alternative organizations in general. While not of major interest to academics in the current era, organizations seeking new and more humane ways to live and offer social services were a hot topic in the late 1970s (for an example see Case and Taylor 1979). The alternative organization and anti-battery movement literatures came together nicely in that writings on alternative organizations focused on the problems of achieving radical ideals of non-hierarchical, non-professional, distinctly client-centered service provision, and allegations were beginning to appear in anti-battery movement writings that shelters likewise were failing to meet these ideals. These two literatures therefore were the core of my dissertation project, which would explore relationships between anti-battery social movement ideals and practices at South Coast.

This takes me to the political context of this research. Remaining to this day are beliefs that battered women probably "deserve" to be hit, that violence against women is not all that serious, that shelters are "homes for runaway wives" that brainwash women into believing they should leave their partners. In the late 1970s these ideas were even more prevalent because the perplexing problems of wife abuse were just coming to public attention and had not yet been accepted as a social problem. In my first public relations try I confirmed what I had been reading about how publics were slow to accept wife abuse as a social problem and quick to blame women for the victimization they experienced.

A scene: Very soon after I started working for the FVP, administrators asked me to give a presentation to the local Kiwanis Club. This was logical because, after all, I was the person who proudly claimed that I had read everything. They hoped my presentation featuring indisputable academic logic would lead to a major contribution to South Coast, which always was desperately short of funds. The meeting was at 7:00 a.m. on a Monday morning and I came dressed in my finest professional attire. I gave my short and very scripted talk and then asked for questions, the first of which was: "Aren't women violent, too?" I started my reply, "Yes, women can be violent, but ... " I never finished that sentence which would have placed women's violence into context because the calm was shattered by a roar of men's voices: "You gotta keep the little woman in line!" "Yeah! The bitches dish it out!" "A slap or two upside her head shows her a thing or two!" For them, it was laughter and raucous conversation, for me it was trauma. Although I remained trapped at the podium, I never regained control of the conversation and, needless to say, I left without securing the donation I had been sent to obtain. With some embarrassment, I reported my Kiwanis Club experience at the next FVP staff meeting. I was not held responsible. Rather, my story was taken as a moral tale: any talk in public *must* conform to the public image of the battered woman as a pure victim of brutal male violence.

This is the personal, academic, and political context of my mystery. My ethnographic detective wears many hats and has divided loyalties. I am a Ph.D.

student collecting dissertation data while serving as an external evaluator at the FVP and volunteer at the shelter. The FVP and South Coast are located within the social and political environments of the late 1970s and early 1980s where funding is insufficient and community support tenuous. With a conceptual framework informed by the anti-battery movement and alternative organization literatures, I set out to compare the workings of the South Coast shelter with ideal images of what shelter work should be.

The mysteries of shelter work for the battered woman

To be perfectly clear, the concept of "ideal images of shelter work" was *my* concept. Neither FVP administrators nor shelter workers ever spoke of an "ideal" model of this work. Shelter work for them was not an abstraction, it was a reality and, from the first FVP meeting onward, it was clear there were numerous *practical* problems at South Coast. Some were so obviously structural that they needed little pondering. For example, the shelter was too small to honor all requests for services, it was old and dingy but there was no money to fix it up, workers desperately needed a car so that they could take women to their appointments, and on and on. These were understood in the FVP as sad but irresolvable problems of the lack of funding; to me they were instances of what the existing literature loudly proclaimed: The problems of women in general, battered women in particular, are not evaluated as important enough to warrant adequate funding.

There were myriad other events at South Coast discussed in FVP meetings that were taken as signs of problems with *workers*. Although not explicitly framed as such, I eventually saw how events were problems when they challenged the characterization of South Coast as a feminist alternative organization. For example, the shelter had only the most basic rules for residents (maintain the secrecy of the shelter location, no violence, no alcohol or drugs), but workers routinely made up new rules (such as detailing hours within which women had to do their chores to keep the common living space habitable, curfews, expectations for participation in support group meetings). Workers could become quite rigid in their rule enforcement (at one time the shelter coordinator complained in a FVP meeting that her workers were acting like "prison guards"), yet new rules could be quickly forgotten. In addition, workers sometimes decided to not admit more women although there were available rooms; at other times they admitted so many women that the South Coast environment was simply unlivable. The most perplexing problem was that workers did not treat residents equally. They rigidly enforced rules for some women and suspended rules for others; they spent much time helping some women while all but ignoring the needs of others.

What was the source of such perceived problems with workers? On one hand, workers did meet the ideals of workers in alternative organizations in that they were not professionals criticized in the literature for lording their "credential" power over residents. However, workers were paid with CETA (Comprehensive Employment and Training Act) funds, which required new hires to be unemployed and without marketable skills. According to a shelter coordinator, this was very problematic because few women qualified for it so "it's not like I have seven candidates for one job opening. I have maybe one candidate if I can scrape her up somewhere and one job opening." This meant there could be no hiring criteria mandating that new workers shared anything near the feminist understandings underlying the model of service provision at South Coast. My detective character saw such problems as verification of a staple argument in the literature on alternative organizations: workers without the appropriate belief systems can undermine the radical potentials of such places.

So far in this story, I am an excellent detective. I had gone out into the world and found empirical evidence of how structural constraints and uncommitted workers can interfere with achieving service ideals in alternative organizations. I might have closed the mystery there. I had sufficient data to frame it as a case study of how a new type of alternative organization, shelters for battered women, faced the same problems as those confronting alternative organizations in general. This would have been a neat and tidy study because the findings would have confirmed what was already known.

Yet two other mysteries that proved far more challenging remained lurking in the background. The first surrounded the ways in which workers divided the world into two categories of women, the "battered woman" and the "not battered woman." Workers in interviews talked about how South Coast was for "the battered woman," and how "our services are best for the battered woman." This was not mere rhetoric because workers routinely used these categorizations to account for the sensible nature of their activities toward particular women. For example, the ongoing record of communication among workers was the "shelter logbook." Written by workers and available only to workers, the log was a running commentary on life inside South Coast. Workers used the log to inform those on upcoming shifts what had happened and what might happen; they used it to account for the sensible nature of their decisions and actions. For example, the battered/not battered categorizations often accompanied workers' notes about their intake decisions. One such note read simply, "call on crisis line from Dora, battered woman. Brought her in." Another note read: "Woman called on crisis line, landlord threw her out ... We should not let her in since she is not battered."

On the surface, this makes sense for, after all, South Coast was for the battered woman. But the more I listened to workers, the more I read the shelter log, the more obvious it was that there was no straight line between experiencing violence and being accorded the status of a battered woman. So, for example, one note in the log illustrates how workers could categorize a woman as a battered woman even though the woman herself might disagree:

After meeting Elisa I realized that she was quite a classical battered woman, although she puts it that her husband is just ill. He actually is a severely deteriorating alcoholic who is unmotivated to get treatment.

Yet as illustrated by another log note, a woman might talk of violence yet not achieve the categorization of battered woman which justified shelter entry:

Crisis call from Amy—she was talking so fast that I could barely understand. She said she needed shelter because someone she knows is beating her. She sounded real spacey. I suggested friends, relatives. She said everybody hates her. I followed my instincts and said we were full.

This, then, was the first challenging mystery: What were the criteria for inclusion or exclusion in the category of "battered woman?"

The second mystery had been apparent from the beginning because it was a recurring topic in FVP meetings: workers did not treat all residents equally. This was troublesome on two counts. First, South Coast proudly characterized itself as a feminist alternative organization and the most central value in such organizations is that of equality. Second, South Coast was for the battered woman, a type of woman who is victimized through no fault of her own, a type of person deserving sympathy and its behavioral expression of help (Clark 1987). Such an image certainly cannot justify unequal treatment. Yet it remains that residents were not treated equally. As an example, consider the following log entries, both reporting incidents where residents broke two rules: Each woman had come back to the shelter after curfew and each had been drinking. Yet these two women seemingly encountered much different worker reactions:

She came back late, smelling of booze. I asked her if she'd been drinking and she said she'd had a beer ... She was sobbing hysterically—it was good to see her let out her feelings. She saw her husband and he said to her he didn't want to make their marriage work ... She is beginning to realize that she can only count on herself and she is best to go ahead and make plans and take responsibility for her own life.

We asked her to leave. She would take no responsibility for her behavior—coming in late and drinking. She rationalized her behavior and criticized staff as a means to divert us off her case.

How can unequal treatment of residents be understood? When I directly asked workers they either flatly denied they treated women unequally, or they cited idiosyncratic characteristics of residents' "personalities." So I spent innumerable hours trying to "code" log entries in order to categorize the types of *events* seemingly associated with unequal treatment of residents. It was an incredible waste of time because my only "finding" was that there was no obvious categorization system. That is, there was no rule or set of rules that somewhat automatically led workers to withdraw their support or to evict women. I turned to examining the relationships between women's characteristics and workers' decisions. I explored the possibilities that workers withdrew support from women who failed to follow workers' advice, that workers were prone to be unsympathetic toward women with many problems who therefore created much work, and that differential orientations were a reflection of underlying racism. True, I did find concrete incidents that could indicate each of these possibilities. Yet I found just as many—and sometimes even more—counter-examples. I only had to recall Eugenia, who was perhaps the most beloved South Coast resident of all time. An African-American woman, she entered the shelter penniless with six small and unhealthy children and with very complicated legal problems. With workers' blessings, she and her children stayed far longer than the 30-day maximum and workers remained tireless in their efforts to help her.

These, then were the two mysteries: How to make sense of worker categorizations and their differential treatment of residents? These mysteries were very slow to unravel because to solve them I needed to change my thinking in two ways. First, I had explicitly designed my research to compare the workings of South Coast with an ideal model of shelters as feminist alternative organizations. In other words, I had been using images in this ideal model I pieced together from the literature as a yardstick by which to measure the workings of South Coast. I needed rather to question the model: What is it about the ideal model of shelter work that makes it so difficult to put into practice?

I also needed to bring women residents into a quite different focus from what I had originally planned. Because part of my job as evaluator was to use the information on the shelter intake forms to construct a composite portrait of the women using South Coast services, it seemed a good use of time to transport this into my own research. So, I had the expectable demographic data associated with the battered woman (years of violence, types of violence, types of injuries, years of marriage, number of children, types of economic support and so on). Likewise, my fieldnotes on individual women focused on the stories they told about the violence they had experienced. But just as my attempts to code the log yielded nothing, I could see little in the way of relationships between women's demographic characteristics or the details of their victimization and the mysteries of shelter work. I began to wonder: What characteristics of women lie behind easily measureable demographics and details of victimization that might explain workers' categorizations and differential treatment?

DONILEEN R. LOSEKE

Mysteries solved

I can summarize *The Battered Woman and Shelters* in one sentence: In theory and in practice, South Coast was organized for the battered woman. It was as simple as that. Yet this is incredibly complex because the cultural image of a battered woman is far more than simply a "woman who has been hit." The "battered woman" rather is a gestalt image of a *particular* type of woman who has experienced a *particular* type of violence, who has a *particular* type of biography, subjectivity, and motivations. This is the type of person, who, in *theory* and in *practice*, would want and need what South Coast had to offer, the type of person who would be a good, responsible member of the semi-communal environment, the type of person who would benefit from shelter services. Worker categorizations and their differential treatment of women therefore were not two mysteries. They rather were two consequences of designing an organization to meet the needs of a particular type of person known as a "battered woman."

The practical reality of shelter work is that real women are remarkably heterogeneous in their characteristics, decisions, wants, needs, and behaviors and can seem far different from those of the cultural image of the battered woman. To be absolutely clear, the majority of residents and potential residents acted in ways and told stories that were more or less understandable as those of the battered woman. But more than a few women at South Coast did not. So, for example, the cultural image of the battered woman as passive, shy, and riddled with fears and anxieties makes it difficult to understand a woman who verbally and physically lashes out at those around her, or a woman who simply refuses to do her share of the communal work. The cultural image of the battered woman as utterly devastated by her victimization makes it difficult to understand the several shelter residents who once decided they would leave their children with workers in order to do a "night on the town to find new men." The cultural image of the battered woman as immensely grateful because the shelter offers her a chance to escape her victimization makes it difficult to understand a woman who would enter South Coast only if guaranteed her own bedroom, or a woman who left because the meager shelter food supplies included only off-brand coffee and not the Folgers coffee she demanded. Here is what I never have said in print before but which pretty much summarizes consequences of disjunctures between cultural images of the battered woman and the characteristics of real women: If each resident at South Coast had acted as an exemplar of the cultural image of the battered woman there would be no need for workers to do the most hated task of deciding whether or not to admit a woman because they could admit *anyone* and *everyone*. Women would get along with one another and not mind sleeping on the floor or sharing a bathroom with countless others; women would appreciate living with many others who shared only the characteristic that each was a battered woman; women would engage in

270

self-help and require little of workers. And clearly, there would be no need for rules, much less rule enforcement, because women's behaviors would be exemplary.

Part and parcel of work at South Coast was making sense of residents who sometimes more, sometimes less, and sometimes not at all conformed to expectations about the battered woman. The cultural image of the battered woman was a part of the cultural "tool kit" (Swidler 1986) workers used to make sense of their experiences and justify their decisions and actions toward particular women. The more a woman's stories, characteristics and/or behaviors could be understood as those of a "battered woman," the more workers reacted kindly and offered much help. The more difficult it was to understand a particular woman as an individual instance of a battered woman, the more workers could distance themselves from her and withdraw their support.

> A scene: Gail was a quiet young mother of two small children who had arrived at South Coast absolutely penniless; the three had only the clothes they wore. Without money, Gail and her two children had been forced to eat only the food in the pantry which held donated items including such taste treats as stale bread, fruits and vegetables long past their prime, and miscellaneous cans of spinach, soup, and tuna. Workers had been heroic in their efforts to arrange for Gail to receive some emergency money from welfare. She had taken the bus downtown that morning to pick up and cash the check. She returned with a large "boom box," two party dresses and what remained of the emergency funds. I was livid. Yes, I knew that Gail's husband was incredibly controlling and it was very likely that this was the first money that was under her control so it was good that she had made her own decisions about how to spend it. Yes, I knew that battered women are known for putting the needs of others first so I should applaud her for doing something for herself. Yet try as I might, I could not neutralize my anger. I found myself boiling in rage when one of her children tugged on Gail's pants and said "What can we have for dinner, mommy?" and she answered "We'll check in the food pantry." Because I was a volunteer, I had the privilege of simply leaving the office when I found it impossible to even look at her. Hence, I understood how workers could withdraw their support from some residents.

Understanding that South Coast was organized for the particular type of woman called the battered woman solves many small mysteries of apparent inequalities inside South Coast. For example, workers sometimes admitted far too many women; at other times they denied entry to a woman although there was available space. This makes sense: regardless of space availability, workers would not deny the request for shelter entry from a woman deemed to be a battered woman, and, because they could not predict when the phone would ring bringing such a request, they often tried to protect space availability by denying entry to women deemed not battered.

Understanding that South Coast was for the battered woman also might resolve the mystery of why workers did not feel more anger toward residents who took considerable worker time yet decided not to enter South Coast or decided to leave South Coast to return to their former partners. Common sense would lead to a prediction that such events would lead workers to experience anger because their time had been wasted. But they did not.

A scene: For several months, any calls to the shelter from midnight and 8:00 a.m. were automatically routed to my home phone. My phone rang one night at almost 2:00 a.m. It was Sharon, and, because she had a car, we arranged to meet at a local all night restaurant. Over the next two hours Sharon and I drank innumerable cups of coffee and smoked countless cigarettes as she told me her story that centered on two major themes. One focused on the great wealth of her husband. Sharon, her husband, and their two teen-aged children lived in a lavish home and she drove a new Porsche. Because Sharon had only a high school education and no work experience she knew that her economic circumstances without him would be far different. The second theme was her wretched life within this luxury. She talked about his sexual demands which she experienced as humiliating and dangerous, she told me of continuing and demeaning emotional abuse, as well as physical violence that seemed to be escalating in its severity. Earlier that evening when her husband had demanded a type of sex that she refused, he threw a lamp at her. When she threatened to call the police he took the credit cards from her purse before throwing the purse at her. He had pushed her out of the house telling her to not return and to not expect to see her children again because, of course, they would prefer living a life of luxury with him rather than the life of poverty Sharon most certainly would be living without him. By 4:30 a.m. I convinced her to go to the shelter because it seemed the only alternative given that she had told me she had no friends, no family, and no money. It would give her a place to stay and time to consider her options—which she evaluated as bleak. She followed me in her car to the shelter, I fixed a room for her and gave her a packet with a toothbrush, toothpaste, and other personal items. I said I needed to leave but a regular worker would be there at 8:00 a.m. and they could begin to sort things out. I went home and, fully clothed, fell into bed. My alarm rang an hour later because I had a 10:00 a.m. class to teach at the university. At 9:00 a.m. my office phone rang. It was the on-duty worker saying that Sharon had left sometime before

8:00 a.m. when the worker arrived. She had left a note thanking me but saying she had phoned her husband and he would "allow" her to return home. So—I had spent all night listening to a woman who believed she was in danger, who I believed was in danger. I was bone tired but not angry. I felt disappointment, frustration, and above all, concern for her. She had gone back to her husband which he could take as a mandate: he could treat her any way he chose and she would not leave. How could I feel anger? Such is the plight of a battered woman.

In brief, the interactional system inside South Coast privileged what is associated with the battered woman. This makes perfect sense because, after all, South Coast was a shelter for the battered woman. Once I figured this out, it was so very simple and I chided my detective character for taking so long to piece together what now seemed patently obvious clues.

This is a story about social structure, about workers, and about cultural images of types of people. If South Coast had experienced more structural support then workers and—residents'—lives would have been much easier. If workers had been drawn to shelter work as a moral commitment rather than as a job, my hunch is that they would have neutralized more of women's unexpected characteristics and behaviors as those of the battered woman. Yet while problems likely would have been reduced with different structure and different workers, they would not have disappeared because the underlying tension is *irresolvable*: Not all individual women drawn to shelters have the *particular* types of wants, needs, and personal characteristics associated with the battered woman type of person. It is so very logical: The shelter was organized to assist one type of woman and, in consequence, it was not organized to assist others. Mysteries solved, case closed.

Conclusions and new mysteries

Ethnography is detective work where a solved mystery often leads to further questions about the buzzing confusion of social life. For example, is the image of wife abuse/battered woman underlying shelters peculiar to shelters because they are alternative organizations? No. I examined how the cultural image of wife abuse as extreme, repeated, unstoppable violence by an unrepentant man on a pure victim woman also underlies criminal justice system responses to wife abuse (Loseke 1991). Is it peculiar to shelters that cultural images of types of people, such as the battered woman, inform organizational form? No. There now is a substantial literature demonstrating how culture, social policy, and organizational form are reflexively related (see Loseke 2007 for references; also, Asen 2003; Emerson 1997). Is it peculiar to shelters that workers attempt to modify women's personal understandings to more-or-less conform to images of clients as types of people? No. There now

273

is a huge literature documenting this process in a range of organizations from prisons to informal support groups (see Loseke 2003 for a review). While here I have referenced my own work in order to demonstrate how academic careers can follow logical trajectories of questions, the simple fact is that my works now are a mere part of long lines of other research demonstrating that the workings at South Coast were anything but unique.

Retrospective reflections

My dissertation was theoretically vacuous and conceptually garbled and it seemed to take me forever to write the first journal articles describing aspects of this research. While I could offer a variety of excuses and justifications (there are stories behind the one I tell here), I want to reflect on how I became immobilized after doing this research. It seemed my detective character had been somewhat successful in finding the clues that unraveled the mysteries of the South Coast shelter, but my academic character was not very quick to organize these clues into a coherent story.

In remarkable hindsight, I see how I overcame my immobilization in three ways. First, a significant part of my problem was that every time I started to write I would become paralyzed as I recalled that horrible morning talking to the men in the Kiwanis Club. I was immobilized by fear that someone, somewhere, would pull out a sentence—or sentence fragment—and use it to discredit social activism on behalf of the battered woman, or to argue that such women do not deserve sympathy or help because they can be less than "perfect" people in one way or another. I at least partially overcame this fear by establishing rules for myself about how I would present these data. My first rule was that I would not offer interviews about this research to anyone in the media. Although this has prevented me from doing public sociology, I know that interviews lead to sound bites, that sound bites necessarily take statements out of context, and that taking statements out of context is a recipe for political misuse. Hence, I write only for academic audiences where I have another rule to include repeated and strong statements about the importance of continued effort to resolve the myriad problems associated with violence, continued and strong statements about the perplexing problems of women needing assistance. Strung throughout my writings also are my anticipations of readings I do *not* want and strong declarations such as "I am definitely *not* saying that … ," or "this can *not* be taken to mean … " In brief, I became less immobilized when I realized that while authors do not have control of how their work will be read and used, I could at least refuse to take my work into the world of strident public debate where it most likely would be misinterpreted, and I could make it difficult for others to take my comments out of context. So far, so good. While I have seen some interpretations of my work that seem somewhat odd, I have not seen it used to discredit the social movement on behalf of women victims.

Second, I gradually came to the conclusion that while the anti-battery movement and alternative organization literatures had been an adequate frame for encountering the mysteries of shelter work, they were the wrong frame for conceptualizing the meaning of data. I increasingly experienced these literatures as a cage keeping me focused on the politics of wife abuse and shelter work, while not offering the conceptual tools necessary to explore the micro-interactional questions that comprised the most challenging mysteries. My immobilization was lessened as I discovered the newly emerging perspective of the social construction of social problems (Spector and Kitsuse 1987), as I applied the concept of "social problems work" (Miller and Holstein 1989), as I started thinking more systematically about relationships between cultural images and practical understandings (Swidler 1986), and as I brought emotions more into the forefront of analysis (Clark 1987).

Finally, while finding and developing conceptual frames helped me to construct the theoretical meaning of the mysteries at South Coast, my desire to write had—and has—a very practical motivation. Over time, I have become increasingly concerned about the unintended consequences of the cultural images of wife abuse and the battered woman. To be absolutely clear, the cultural images of "wife abuse" and the "battered woman" have been effective in encouraging the public to take this victimization of women seriously. The evidence is indisputable that the anti-battery movement has resulted in very real and very positive social change for women victims who, in the past, all but invariably encountered a hostile public and no social services organized to assist them. Social change has literally saved the lives of countless women. That can neither be denied nor discounted. My concern is that, for all the good accomplished by these cultural images, there have been negative consequences in that these images have become yardsticks used to evaluate real women. What this means in practice is that to receive sympathy and support, a woman must be accorded the status of a "battered woman," and to do this she must display her bruises and broken bones, she must be evaluated as a pure victim who is an exemplary person in every way (see Bible et al. 2002 and Picart 2003 for elaborations). Given such a yardstick, there are countless women denied assistance. These women are my concern.

The mysteries of South Coast are one reflection of a culture where we are prone to be unconcerned with anything but the most devastating of human trouble, where we are prone to withhold sympathy and assistance from any but the most pure of victims. How can that be changed? This is the mystery that needs to be solved.

References

Asen, R. (2003) "Women, Work, Welfare: a rhetorical history of images of poor women in welfare policy debates," *Rhetoric and Public Affairs*, 6: 285–312.

Bible, A., Dasgupta, S., and Osthoff, S. (2002) "Guest Editors' Introduction," *Violence Against Women*, 8: 1267–70.

Case, J. and Taylor, R. C. R. (1979) *Co-ops, Communes, and Collectives: experiments in social change in the 1960s and 1970s*, New York: Pantheon.

Clark, C. (1987) "Sympathy Biography and Sympathy Margin," *American Journal of Sociology*, 93: 291–321.

Dobash, R. E. and Dobash, R. (1979) *Violence Against Wives: a case against the patriarchy*, New York: Free Press.

Emerson, R. M. (1997) "Constructing Serious Violence and Its Victims: processing a domestic violence restraining order," in G. Miller and Holstein, J. A. (eds.) *Social Problems in Everyday Life: studies of social problems work* (pp. 191–218), Greenwich, CT: JAI Press.

Loseke, D. R. (1991) "Changing the Boundaries of Crime: the battered women's social movement and the definition of wife abuse as criminal activity," *Criminal Justice Review*, 16: 249–62.

——(2003) *Thinking about Social Problems*, 2nd ed., New Brunswick, NJ: Transaction Books.

——(2007) "The Study of Identity as Cultural, Institutional, Organizational, and Personal Narratives: theoretical and empirical integrations," *The Sociological Quarterly*, 48: 661–88.

Martin, D. (1976) *Battered Wives*, San Francisco: Glide Publications.

Miller, G. and Holstein, J. A. (1989) "On the Sociology of Social Problems" in J. A. Holstein and Miller, G. (eds.) *Perspectives on Social Problems*, vol. 1 (pp. 1–18), Greenwich, CT: JAI.

Picart, C. J. S. (2003) "Rhetorically Reconfiguring Victimhood and Agency: the violence against women act's civil rights clause," *Rhetoric and Public Affairs*, 6: 97–126.

Spector, M. and Kitsuse, J. I. ([1977] 1987) *Constructing Social Problems*, Hawthorne, NY: Aldine de Gruyter.

Swidler, A. (1986) "Culture in Action: symbols and strategies," *American Sociological Review*, 51: 273–96.

18

THE PATH TAKEN

Opportunity, flexibility, and reflexivity in the field

Jennifer L. Dunn

This is a story about how "starting where you are" (Lofland and Lofland 1995: 11) turned into "starting over where you end up." It began with a chance encounter with media that resonated with my own problematic personal experience. This linkage shaped my initial theoretical orientation, set of research questions, and methodological approach. But, when I set out to study intimate stalking, fortuitous opportunities in the setting, an equally fortuitous training in reflexivity under the tutelage of my mentors, and the nature of the data itself led me in a direction very different from what I had planned and envisioned.

When I began the study, I had just identified myself as a stalking victim and I was a naïve feminist intent on revealing the workings of a patriarchal culture condoning "sexual terrorism" (Sheffield 1987). Because I was also a budding symbolic interactionist (Blumer 1969), I hoped that my research would reveal the situated "vocabularies of motive" (Mills 1940) that oppressed victims used to account for the instrumental and violent actions of men seeking to control them and to prevent them from leaving violent relationships. I would find, I thought, that victims would draw on their culturally dictated notions of emotions such as jealousy and love and psychological constructs such as an obsession to explain behavior, that I had found in my own experience and in a survey of sorority women (Dunn 1999) to be frightening but also confusing. I expected that stalkers, like the convicted rapists whom Scully and Marolla had earlier described (1984), would use the language that popular media, social science, the criminal justice system, and their own victims provided for them as "accounts" (Scott and Lyman 1968). I was thus going to explain stalking and illuminate victims' gender-socialized complicity in their own victimization. My data would be the stories victims and law enforcement actors told about stalking, in interviews and "victim narratives" in police reports. Although I was interested in the meanings people conferred upon stalking, my perspective was nonetheless objectivist—stalking was a serious social problem—and my goal was to situate it (Mills 1940), that is, to show its roots in social structure.

This essay describes how all of that changed. We often tell our students that there are important and necessary relationships between our theoretical perspectives and the methods we choose. We tell them that ontology, what we believe to be real, is inextricable from epistemology, what we think it is possible to know about reality. My own research experience confirms this. In the course of my study of intimate stalking, I was given the opportunity to gather different stories than the ones I had initially set out to, and to collect entirely different data through different methods than I had planned. I started as an "outside researcher" (Lofland and Lofland 1995). In the end, I also became a participating observer of victims as *witnesses* and of their advocates in the criminal justice system. My data now included interactions between victims and the law enforcement actors they encountered as they happened, and I was privy to the stories advocates told each other about victims.

Moreover, the new and different accounts that I heard revealed more of the deviance of victims than that of stalkers. Ambiguous emotions remained important, but the work of managing them (Hochschild 1979) took theoretical precedence over their use as explanation. My focus shifted from the objective condition of stalking victimization in a patriarchal social structure to the process of claiming the identity (Holstein and Miller 1990) of stalking victim in a hierarchically arranged organization. Advocates' attributions of complicity were more consequential for victims than the latter's actual compliance with their former partners' demands, and judgments of their resistance were also problematic. My perspective became social constructionist—"stalking victim" was a label people could attach to women—and my goal was not only to situate it, but more importantly, to articulate this experience as a complex and consequential definitional process. And my predominantly structural feminist stance became more nuanced as I recognized victims' agency and resistance as well as their constraints. As my mentor Lyn Lofland would put it, my "passivist" orientation became "activist" (Lofland and Lofland 1995).

Where I was

In 1995, in the summer between my second and third years of graduate school, I sat by a swimming pool indulging myself in an old issue of *Cosmopolitan*. I happened upon an article (Sherman 1994) about an emerging social problem called "stalking," and I was struck by how the symbolic messages left by stalkers in the article resonated with me. I had been briefly and violently pursued by a former partner who did not want me to end our relationship, and I shivered at the recollections that descriptions of black roses and teddy bears with knives in them triggered in me. The surveillance, following, and threats to which I had been subjected were terrifying and baffling, but until then, an experience I had thought uniquely my own and due to the psychopathology of my pursuer. As a young sociologist, I had been studying various forms of violence against women from my first opportunity to conduct my own research, but I had not linked this substantive interest to my personal biography.

Because I was a novice symbolic interactionist I was attuned to the significance of symbols and speculated that stalking was a culturally derived and learned phenomenon. And as a person who had been a young and radical woman during the second wave of feminism, as I thought about the phenomenon of stalking, it was easy to appropriate the feminist ideology of "sexual terrorism" (Sheffield 1987) and to conceive of all gendered violence as a means of controlling women within a patriarchal culture. I was steadfast in my understanding of women as victims; I had yet to consider the ways in which we are agents. Agency, in fact, was not yet part of my conceptual repertoire, and when it emerged, it did so in unexpected ways.

Courting Disaster did not start out as an ethnography; my original plan was to interview stalking victims. This was the methodology with which I had the most experience, having learned about and conducted intensive interviews as a research assistant for Kathy Charmaz during my undergraduate study at Sonoma State. I continued this kind of data collection and symbolic interactionist analysis for my field methods seminar in graduate school at the University of California at Davis, in which we read *Analyzing Social Settings* (Lofland and Lofland 1995) and where I began taking seminars with Lyn Lofland. I started to tell faculty and peers about my interest in stalking, and a friend put an issue of a local magazine on my desk when she saw that there was an article in it about stalking prosecution efforts in a nearby city. I contacted a victim advocate quoted in the article, and when I learned that she had begun a survey of stalking victims, I offered to help her collect data for her purposes and asked if she would recruit potential in-depth interview participants for my own study. As I look back over my earliest jottings, over a decade ago, I see that I entered the large, urban, busy, Domestic Violence Unit in the district attorney's office with the goal of

> getting at the relationship between culture and action by looking at how various actors in the stalking dynamic account for this behavior [and examining] how the cultural "toolkit" (the vocabulary of motive) informs behavior in specific interactions.
>
> (These are my early notes to myself:
I was referring to Mills 1940 and Swidler 1986.)

I wanted to explain stalking as a form of "strategic interaction" (Goffman 1967) and a culturally situated phenomenon made possible by people's explanations for it, by the emotional "motive talk" I believed I had discerned in a survey of sorority women's responses to a hypothetical stalking scenario. Essentially, I was approaching stalking as a form of socially constructed deviance, and drawing on the literature in symbolic interactionism on "aligning activities" (e.g. Stokes and Hewitt 1976). This body of work suggests that when people engage in activities that violate norms, they seek to account to others and themselves for their deviance, and others may similarly account for the deviance of the violator. These accounts or "vocabularies of motive" reveal larger cultural understandings, because people draw upon the latter for their efficacy. Mills had said "the differing reasons men give for their actions are not themselves without reasons" (1940: 904) and I expected that the reasons people gave for stalking would show that we live in a "stalking culture" condoning and fostering the controlling actions of men and passive responses of women to them.

When I learned that I would have access to prosecutors' case files as well as to victims whose cases had been referred for prosecution, I was delighted— I would learn what stalkers had done, hear their voices in their communications with victims on answering machine tapes and endless "love" letters, see the evidence of their use of shared understandings of what was frightening, and I would hear (albeit secondhand) how they explained themselves. And I would read about these events from victims' perspectives, and about their responses to them. My focus was interactions between stalkers and their victims, as narrated by victims. Ironically, even though I was headed into the bowels of the criminal justice system, the "lion's den" as I later described it, I did not yet think seriously about the importance of interactions between victims and their *audiences*. I was especially interested in how victims' interpretations of stalking behaviors shaped their own actions and thus continuing interaction, when they might, like the sorority women and myself, have mixed or ambiguous feelings about their former partners and what they were doing. I had not considered the relevance of advocates' interpretations of victims' actions, and the consequences of those interpretations for how advocates responded to victims, for my conceptualization of the stalking process.

What happened

It was only after I entered what I did not then think of as the "field" that I realized that I was perfectly situated to include participant observation as a method, that is, that "everything is data," and, more importantly, that it would only be through this incorporation that I would gain true insight into the "*situation* being dealt with" and the "strategies being employed in dealing with that *situation*" (Lofland and Lofland 1995: 146, emphases in original).

Fortunately, I had been inspired by Lyn Lofland's description of how she had studied grief in part by "greedily" collecting any and all materials she thought relevant. I thus had an orientation toward treating every interaction related to my research as potentially fruitful and worth recording, beginning with my first meeting with Eliza Nash,[1] the supervising Victim Advocate in the Domestic Violence Unit, and Donna D'Amato, the victim advocate newly hired to work specifically with stalking victims. At our first encounter and in many that followed, I took notes, I made analytical comments as I transcribed my notes, and later, when I realized what I had, I coded them. This shift, toward the inclusion of the advocates and their social worlds in a study of victims' lived experience, was inspired by what I early on and then throughout the study recorded in those notes.

This is so because the idea of victim "credibility" came up immediately, when I observed and recorded in my notes an exchange of glances when the advocates discussed a particular victim as an example of a woman who had "truly made the break." Later I was to learn that this particular victim (Nadine Peterson), violated some of the advocates' normative expectations for typical victims, and realizing this, I would refine my conceptualization of the stalking process and link it to Holstein and Miller's (1990) formulation of "victim accomplishment." At the time, I simply noticed that advocates were evaluating the presentations of self (Goffman 1959) of victims, that they were conferring meaning on the actions of victims, and that they were defining some victims differently than other victims.

My observations from my second meeting with Eliza and Donna are more telling; the longest section is devoted to Eliza's discussion of "victim presentation and credibility," particularly their affect, followed by her description of problematic victims who were overly "dramatic" and became demanding. I concluded my notes with this comment:

> So it is interesting that the victim hierarchy obtains even among the advocates, but this has obvious practical reasons as they must make decisions about allocating resources and a "bad" victim doesn't just make them look bad, but is a waste of time and energy that could be better spent on someone more likely to convince a judge or jury.

Herein, in retrospect, lay the seeds of the contribution my work makes to the study of social problems in everyday life, what Holstein and Miller have called "social problems work," and to the sociology of emotions. I was beginning to get the first glimmer of understanding of the ways in which victims who were trying to manage their stalkers' emotions sometimes stumbled when managing their own, and of the consequences for this within the organizational constraints of the Domestic Violence Unit.

In my next meeting with Eliza and Donna, I learned why Nadine Peterson, whom I had by then interviewed, was held in some suspicion by the advocates—she was enjoying her celebrity and really "likes the limelight," they said. I began to see and to think about how even initially well-thought-of victims might not be able to maintain victim identities because of how they interacted with the people trying to help them, and that staying in advocates' good graces was a process that took place over time. But perhaps more significant at the time was Donna's first mention of the "grassroots" group then being formed by the "grounded" victims I would later come to know quite well as the founders of the River City Survivors of Stalking. I asked Donna if I could interview them, and she said "I was thinking the same thing; I'll get back to you on that."

This was the start of a period in which I had to work hard to get interviews. Initially, the plan was for me to have the advocates administer a survey they had written and that I modified for them, and to interview survey respondents who wanted to talk more about their experiences. Because the first couple of "extremely grounded" victims Donna and another advocate gave the survey to were a bit shaken by reliving their experiences, Donna was hesitant to steer victims my way. Early in the study, after parking myself in the lobby across from her door where she could not miss that I was waiting for her, I wrote this:

> Donna expresses strong desire to help but equally strongly the need to "protect" her clients so she will be extremely selective about who she interviews [and] who she refers to me—have decided the best strategy is to keep regular hours at the [District Attorney's office], inform them (the [victim advocates]) and try and get them to send people in to talk about the study with me.

This was a wise and consequential move on my part. I had been given an office; I started to occupy it. I started talking to people when I bumped into them in the hallways and I went out with Donna on her "smoke breaks," where I quickly became a person with whom she could vent her many job-related frustrations.

In a few short weeks I had been invited to give a talk on stalking to the River City Survivors of Stalking. Here I made another methodological decision with fruitful theoretical ramifications. Reluctantly, I chose to introduce myself to the women in the group as a victim of stalking, and in doing so, became a participant as well as an observer. Not long after, I realized that I could also participate in the life of the Domestic Violence Unit—indeed, it seemed difficult not to, the longer I was there. I informed the advocates of this shift in my methodological approach ("everything is data," I asserted), and began taking many more notes while attending staff meetings and TRO (temporary restraining order) workshops, accompanying victims to court, and going to lunch with victims and their advocates, among other activities.

Immersed simultaneously in the Unit and in the group as I was, it is probably not surprising that my interest in vocabularies of motive for stalking began to shift toward a different kind of "aligning activity" (Stokes and Hewitt 1976), that of explaining victims' actions that caused *them* to be defined as deviant by various audiences. Victims' credibility was a constant source of concern and this permeated innumerable conversations, in which it became very clear that how victims responded to their stalkers influenced how they were perceived in the Unit.

Here are early notes I made to myself as I waited for Nadine to come for an interview, based on the first conversation I had with her on the telephone, in which she told me about her experiences as a public speaker on stalking victimization:

> So clearly she is presenting an "expert" self, on more than one level— she has the experience which qualifies her to talk about stalking, but she has also read everything she can find, learned the "lingo"—perhaps to increase her credibility?

I also make reference to the "public performance of stalking victim" and I can see that later, I came back to these notes and coded them "victim identity." At that time, I hadn't figured out that she was not the "ideal victim" the advocates wanted to represent stalking in their claims-making efforts, but said "[Nadine] speaks forcefully, is very direct, and is the person the [district attorney's] office holds in high regard ... for her perseverance and ability to follow through with the prosecutor." I had not yet figured out that it was her very pursuit of publicity that had soured the advocates on her, but these notes reflect an abiding interest in presentation of self (Goffman 1959) and hint at what would become an overarching emphasis on the social construction of identity in the study as it progressed.

It became increasingly apparent as I gained the advocates' trust that how victims responded to the criminal justice system actors with whom they were working, as well as to their stalkers, was a consequential definitional process. I learned that stalking victims who complied too easily with the demands of their former partners were seen as complicit, and that women who made too many demands on the Unit were seen as histrionic or worse. As an observer of the advocates doing their jobs, I began to think more about how they evaluated the women seeking their help. Even more importantly, I was a participant in their advocacy who had been taught to self-consciously and rigorously "record whatever aspects in your emotional life are involved in the setting" because these records "may lead to important analytic trails" (Lofland and Lofland 1995: 94–95).

Thus, the following, as I learned that stalking victims often comply with stalkers' demands and that this shapes how they are viewed by advocates. I thought about a recent interview I had conducted with a woman who had been repeatedly victimized and who asked me if she had a sign, like a psychiatrist had told her, on her forehead saying "vulnerable." I wrote:

> When I told a friend about the victim who goes somewhere with the guy, her first response is "why did she go somewhere with him?" So even though compliance is so common, it seems that women have little sympathy for other women who comply. As the [victim] is telling me her story, I find myself wondering the same thing.

283

So as much as I think I know, I find that my response is just as non-critically critical.

In this excerpt from my notes, I realized *and recorded* that I was still as judgmental about victims' claims to victimization as any non-sociological audience. This gave me cause to think more about the significance of people's responses to victims' efforts, especially when those people determined eligibility for help, as the advocates did.

Eventually, I came to think and feel as advocates thought, but because of my training to be reflexive, could "bracket" (Husserl [1913] 1982) my own cognitions and emotions. Below, I describe meeting with Eliza after interviewing Caity Ingalls, a victim who had both supporters and detractors in the Domestic Violence Unit. Eliza and I talked about this, leading to our first discussion of "borderline personalities":

And I thought out loud with her about how these traits might be constructed or instilled, rather than inherent in victims prior to the relationship.

Here I was still thinking along naïve feminist lines, where the psychopathology attributed to victims obscures the fact that they are subsequent to domestic violence (Walker 1979). Then I wrote:

And borderlines are "histrionic" another term Eliza uses, but something that is evident even to a casual observer (like in the TRO workshop this morning) ... Certainly it is easy to quickly develop a degree of skepticism about victims and their credibility, something I discussed at length with Eliza. In the TRO workshop, it was very hard not to categorize the women almost immediately into sympathetic characters, and, conversely, women about whom you found yourself asking the question: "what is HER part in this?"

I believe these adjacent but very different pieces of the conversation I was holding with myself represent a fundamental change occurring in how I thought about stalking victimization, *from the perspective of advocates.* I was coming to understand that advocates' feminist ideals notwithstanding, they felt sympathy for some victims and not for others, and that this was linked to victims' emotional presentation of self. And it was from this new "insider" perspective (Lofland and Lofland 1995) that I wrote about Melinda Sanchez, a woman who had thoroughly alienated the law enforcement actors with whom she'd interacted and could not get the district attorney's office to take an interest in her case.

First, I noted that Melinda "has had no luck getting anyone to take her seriously, and it mainly seems to be because of her emotional display, that it is anger rather than fear or tears that she is showing." And I reflected on this emotional deviance in conjunction with the issue of compliance, which I had come to see by that time as pervading every case. My notes read:

> She said she told [the police] she was angry and she had no more tears to cry ... but it's real clear that this woman has a huge credibility problem, and that this is why she is getting nowhere.

Then I recorded that she was so anxious to tell her story that she told it to me on the phone before I could formally interview her.

> There's that "borderline" thing again, creeping into my thoughts, about how some people just can't stop talking, they are so desperate for someone to talk to ... this woman is like Lemert's paranoids, cast into roles created for them by the stalker and supported by everyone they come in contact with, who raises the skeptical eyebrow at this hysterical woman, who is so buffeted by her experience and inability to convey it that she cannot act strategically, it seems, she just seems to do the wrong display no matter which she chooses.
> (I was referring to Lemert 1962.)

Finally, I commented to myself: "And this is a phenomenon where display is everything, from the perspective of someone trying to get help. If she only knew the importance of demeanor ... " and, wishing I could say something to her directly about this, added "I can write about it, and maybe she and other women will get to read about it some day, and learn how to act in ways that get them the help they need—if this is even possible." These notes began to capture the ideas that would become the core of *Courting Disaster*, that emotional and other deviance (e.g. compliance with the stalker's demands) limits women's ability to create credible victim identities for themselves.

    The final piece of the puzzle was to emerge through my position as an "honorary" member of the River City Survivors of Stalking, a place I had initially earned through my disclosure of the lived experience I shared with the group. Because I was attending their meetings, interviewing members of the group, chatting with them regularly, and on occasion joining them for social events, I was also privy to victims' increasing understanding of the importance of their presentation of self. Through this I came to believe that the strategic interaction of the stalker mattered less in the totality of victims' experience of stalking in some ways, than victims' own ability to successfully claim victim identities over time. Just as the importance of victims' credibility from advocates' perspective became salient as I became a pseudo-advocate, the work that victims did to establish this legitimacy came to the fore as I identified with the latter. And as I came to know them better,

I learned that it was their fear that led them to the very actions that, I now was aware, belied this emotion in the eyes of those assessing them.

Where I ended up

It is not a little ironic that my own hyper-awareness of the risks and benefits of claiming a victim identity in order to establish my own credibility heightened the salience of victims' efforts to do the same. As I reflected on my initial unwillingness to call myself a victim, I realized that there were negative connotations to the label I was strategically applying to myself. This examination of my own motives and feelings sensitized me to what I came to see as the first of a series of interrelated "identity dilemmas," situations in which actors are forced to construct themselves in ways that do not always benefit them. Indeed, the significance of the concepts of identity and of the active practices of people seeking to establish, maintain, and transform or repair the meanings others attach to them, became a core component of the theoretical framework I was developing.

As these realizations dawned on me, I discovered Holstein and Miller's (1990) "rethinking" of victimization, in which I was introduced to two ideas that cogently captured the ideas swirling around in my notes and late-night reliving of my daily experiences with victims and their advocates. The first was the idea of "social problems work," the work that victims (aided by advocates) do when constructing stalking as a social problem and themselves as exemplars. When I listened to stalking victims discussing how to be taken seriously and their stories of repeated efforts to get law enforcement to respond to their cries for help, it struck me that this was an enormous effort and often intensely discouraging or futile. When Holstein and Miller went on to describe successful endeavors as the "accomplishment" of victimization, and I thought about the ways in which advocates characterized the victims whom they liked and those whom they did not, it seemed as if my data made empirically visible what the authors described in mostly abstract terms.

Because I did not know that I was going to do ethnography as well as formally interviewing people and analyzing documents, I did not realize in the beginning that I would write more about stalking victims' lived experience of the criminal justice system than about their lived experience of stalking. A consequence of my methodological opportunism and greed was that I did both. The theoretical implications of this were realized in showing how one construction of reality influenced the other, a revelation that finally crystallized when I was putting the book together, and determined that a chapter showing what it was like to be stalked would precede a chapter showing what it was like to be a victim-witness in the criminal justice system. Because I had and took the chance to participate in the emotion work and identity work of victims *and* the social problems work of advocates, I began to see how the three were related, and furthermore, to link these processes back to how women interpreted and responded to the stalking behaviors that initiated their involvement with the criminal justice system.

Ultimately, this put me in a position where I could tell a more nuanced and complex sociological story about victims' situations and some of the multiple, interrelated constructions of victimization effected by and affecting them. I was able to talk about being stalked, about how the meanings women conferred on stalking shaped their responses to it, and about how as a result they were subsequently judged as agents or as victims, but not both. In the end, I had something to say about the condition of stalking, but more about accounts of stalking victimization, and of the latter's perhaps greater import. I took advantage of the opportunities presented me, followed where they led me, and revised my thinking accordingly. I thought about my *thinking* too, as victim, as advocate, and as observer all in one. I still wrote about the influence of patriarchy and culture. In the end, however, my account was grounded in the multiple stories of the people acting within these social structures, and so, I hope, "makes the social realm human again by focusing on human intention and authorship" (Lofland and Lofland 1995: 148).

Note

1 I am using the same pseudonyms here that I used in *Courting Disaster.*

References

Blumer, H. (1969) *Symbolic Interactionism: perspective and method,* New Jersey: Prentice-Hall.
Dunn, J. L. (1999) "What Love Has to Do With It: the cultural construction of emotion and sorority women's responses to forcible interaction," *Social Problems,* 46: 440–59.
Goffman, E. (1959) *The Presentation of Self in Everyday Life,* New York: Anchor Books.
——(1967) *Interaction Ritual: essays on face to face behavior,* New York: Anchor Books.
Hochschild, A. (1979) "Emotion Work, Feeling Rules, and Social Structure," *American Journal of Sociology,* 85: 551–75.
Holstein, J. and Miller, G. (1990) "Rethinking Victimization: an interactionist approach to victimology," *Symbolic Interaction,* 13: 103–22.
Husserl, E. ([1913] 1982) *Ideas Pertaining to a Pure Phenomenology and to a Phenomenological Philosophy,* The Hague: Nijhoff.
Lemert, E. (1962) "Paranoia and the Dynamics of Exclusion," *Sociometry,* 25: 2–20.
Lofland, J. and Lofland, L. (1995) *Analyzing Social Settings: a guide to qualitative observation and analysis,* 3rd edn, Belmont, CA: Wadsworth.
Mills, C.W. (1940) "Situated Actions and Vocabularies of Motive," *American Sociological Review,* 5: 904–13.
Scott, M. and Lyman, S. (1968) "Accounts," *American Sociological Review,* 33: 46–62.
Scully, D. and Marolla, J. (1984) "Convicted Rapists Vocabularies of Motive: excuses and justifications," *Social Problems,* 31: 530–44.

Sheffield, C. (1987) "Sexual Terrorism: the social control of women," in B. Hess and Ferree, M. (eds) *Analyzing Gender: a handbook of social science research*, Newbury Park: Sage.

Sherman, W. (1994) "Stalking: the nightmare that never ends," *Cosmopolitan*, 216: 197–201.

Stokes, R. and Hewitt, J. (1976) "Aligning Actions," *American Sociological Review*, 41: 838–49.

Swidler, A. (1986) "Culture in Action: symbols and strategies," *American Sociological Review*, 51: 273–86.

Walker, L. (1979) *The Battered Woman*, New York: Harper and Row.

19

WALKING THE TALK

Doing *Gravity's Shadow*[1]

Harry Collins

Preamble

I have never thought of myself as an ethnographer but as a sociologist who bases his analysis in the world of the actors. Thus, though this volume is about ethnography, I am going to discuss the development of new concepts in participatory, or quasi-participatory, fieldwork. Ethnographers sometimes seem wary of new concepts invented by analysts—as though these can only distort the description of actors' worlds. I think this is ethnography's loss. But I do take the world of the actors very seriously. Indeed I take it so seriously that I have even exposed myself to a test of whether I achieved a degree of understanding that allowed me to pass as a genuine native—something that, so far as I know, no one else has tried. My longest fieldwork immersion has been in a scientific specialty—the detection of gravitational waves. In 2005 I asked gravitational wave physicists to ask technical questions over e-mail of myself and another gravitational wave physicist without knowing who was giving the answers. The questions and answers were then given to other gravitational wave physicists to guess who was who (they knew that I was one of the participants). I passed the test with flying colors, showing that I possessed a reassuring level of what I call "interactional expertise" (see below).[2]

Having said I am going to talk about developing new concepts, let me also say that I think that the way I do things has more in common with the natural sciences than the humanities and social sciences. Though all my degrees are in social science, I suspect the influence of the science I studied in (high) school still dominates, reinforced by long fieldwork among scientists. Very roughly, my first instinct is always to try to work something out for myself rather than go to the literature. I'd say that concepts develop through the interaction of three things: conceptual heritage—what one has been taught, or read or learned through academic socialization; what one learns from the field—at least when one is being an empirical sociologist; and the page—the process of organizing, talking about and writing down the argument. In my case the second two take precedence over wide reading. Of course, without an initial academic socialization one would be lost, but academic socialization is not the same as assiduous scholarship. For me the page is particularly important: I find I have to do about 25 revisions of nearly everything I write if the process is to do its work of sorting out the other elements. The different weighting given to these elements may account for the ways concepts develop in different disciplines and different individuals—there's a whole research project there for someone—but there is no doubt that my particular emphases account for some of the strange goings-on described below.

Gravity's Shadow and before

I'll lead up to talking about *Gravity's Shadow* (Collins 2004a), my 870-page book on the sociological study of the search for gravitational waves, published in 2004. For me, the study of gravitational wave detection science has been a 35-year project so far, broken into two phases, the first ending around 1980. The project is still going on and I hope that there'll be another book when gravitational waves are finally detected. The first phase of the project was marked by the publication of a paper in 1975, which was the second paper I published in my research career; it was called "The Seven Sexes" (Collins 1975). This paper was crucial for what was to follow. But the origin of the "The Seven Sexes" can't be understood without knowing about the paper that preceded it, which was on laser building (Collins 1974). I'll get back to *Gravity's Shadow* later but I'll start with those two papers.[3]

In the case of neither paper did I know what I would produce when I set out to do the fieldwork. In the case of the first paper I had no "hypothesis" and no idea of doing a "test." I was just finding out about something that looked interesting. It did turn out to be interesting but in a way which I did not predict at the outset. In the second case I began with something much closer to an "experimental design," but the design was faulty. Luckily, I did not notice the mistake until most of the fieldwork was finished. The result was that I was forced to do something with the data which would not have occurred to me otherwise. This, I think, turned out to be a lot more interesting than the original idea.

Paper 1: TEA-lasers

The first paper grew out of my M.A. dissertation—a short piece of work tacked on to the end of nine months of courses and essay writing. When I began the research all I knew was that I wanted to do fieldwork in science laboratories and a university was a good location to begin.

After a few false starts I wandered into a laboratory where they were trying to make models of a specially powerful laser that had been discovered a couple of years before in a Canadian laboratory. Powerful lasers, with their death-ray connotations, seemed interesting; the devices were two or three feet long and the crucial parts were mounted inside transparent tubes of glass or Perspex with the electronics outside, so you could see the whole thing and you could see quite a lot of the ways in which one of them differed from another. Better still, it was very hard to make them work, and this made the science seem less forbidding. What I decided to do was study the British "knowledge diffusion network" for this kind of laser.

I did bring a conceptual legacy to the field. I had in my head the Kuhnian idea of "paradigm" which I believed was, in essence, the Wittgensteinian idea of "form-of-life" applied to science. Thus, I knew I wanted to look at "knowledge diffusion" as though it was the spreading out of a new language rather than as the mechanical passing out of discrete "bits of information." One typical knowledge diffusion study that I knew was about the spread of knowledge about new drugs among doctors (see Coleman et al. 1966). It took the "discrete bits of information" approach and I knew I wanted do something different to that.

The theoretical framework I took to the field made me attend to certain features of my diffusion network more carefully than others might have done. First I was interested not so much in those to whom knowledge of the new kind of laser had spread, but in those who had learned what we might call "the language of laser-building." Thus in the drug diffusion study the data comprised which doctors knew of the drug and how they had learned of its existence. The rather nice "two-step theory of communication" was central to these studies. This theory said that there were often knowledge "gatekeepers" in an organization, whose role was mainly to read all the literature and keep their ears open to all the networks and inform their colleagues of what was going on in the world around them. But I wasn't interested in information transmission, I was interested in language-learning. This meant that I was specially alert to the difference between those scientists who had successfully built models of the laser and had them working on their bench and those who knew of the laser's existence and principles—who had all the information and had even put a device together—but had not succeeded in making a device that worked; this difference is invisible in the two-step theory. Incidentally, though I didn't realize its importance at the time, it was easy to know whether a laser of this kind was working because the beam was so powerful that if you put a lump of concrete in the way of it the concrete would start to smoke.

The second thing that the language-learning metaphor caused me to look at closely was aspects of interpersonal interaction that one would associate with learning a language. Immersion in the culture of the language is about personal contact rather than the exchange of documents. Thus, fluency in French is not learned from dictionaries and grammar manuals, it is learned by talking to French people. Incidentally, the new kind of laser was the Transversely Excited, Atmospheric pressure, carbon dioxide laser, or "TEA-laser" for short. My question was "Who has learned to build a TEA-laser and how did they learn to do it?"

What I actually did was drive around the country interviewing scientists who had built TEA-lasers and recording their words on tape. Inter alia, I seemed to have invented a new fieldwork approach to science since nearly all previous work on contemporary scientists involved visits to single laboratories, or to a few organizations, or doing some kind of representative survey, or studying the science citation index. My population was neither scientists, nor scientific organizations, nor the scientific literature, but the complete set of TEA-laser builders in the U.K. They were defined, in other words, by their interest in a specific scientific project rather than by an institutional affiliation or formal qualification, or their statistical representativeness. In retrospect there was more to this than finding a new way to draw a sample: doing the fieldwork this way emerged out of an interest in the way scientific knowledge worked rather than the way scientists worked, so it too was linked to the whole language-learning metaphor.

As can be guessed, what I was asking the scientists was whether they had a working laser, how they had reached the point at which they could make it work, what sources of information they used to get to that point, and how they dealt with enquiries about their own work. I enjoyed the whole thing enormously—getting out of the library, seeing the inside of new kinds of institution and talking to new kinds of people, visiting distant parts of the country I would not otherwise have gone to, and learning things about other people's working lives. I wasn't entirely sure what I was doing but it "felt right."

I analyzed the results primarily by drawing networks on transparent sheets which could be overlaid and, by cobbling together various of my essays on network analysis and so forth, I managed to produce something that looked like a dissertation with an argument supporting the notion that building a TEA-laser was more like learning a language than gathering discrete bits of information. In particular, it slowly dawned on me that the only people who had made the laser work (aside from the original inventor), had strong personal contacts with another laboratory which had made it work. Those who had tried to build one of the things from written sources alone had always failed until they developed personal contacts and had lots of conversations. This was a very clean finding—they always failed.

The eventual form of the paper that came out of this owed a lot to the remarks of colleagues. One of the referees (Mike Mulkay) pointed out my ignorance of a whole raft of relevant literature turning on the notion of "tacit knowledge." The physical chemist Michael Polanyi had written books on the tacit knowledge of scientists—knowledge that they possessed but could not express. Surely, said the referee, what I was revealing was more of this working out of tacit knowledge. So I re-wrote the paper using the terminology of tacit knowledge.

The change of title and the setting of the paper within the tradition of tacit knowledge was probably a good thing as it helped readers recognize what it was about and saved me from critics who would otherwise have said it had all been done before. On the other hand, Polanyi's version, which has a lot to do with preserving the autonomy of scientists in a "republic of science," includes a lot of stuff about scientists' creativity and intuition. It does not lead in the same direction as the deeper and more general Wittgensteinian notion of form-of-life. So the Polanyi connotation, though I have stuck with it, has occasionally been a nuisance and led people to misunderstand what I was trying to do in subsequent work. In retrospect, writing first and reading later was a very good thing to have done or the paper could have been "hog-tied" by Polanyi's questions rather than Wittgenstein's.[4]

Paper 2: the beginning of the gravitational wave work

For my Ph.D. in 1971 I decided I would extend the TEA-laser study and do some comparisons with other areas of science. The TEA-laser was very clearly normal science and I thought I should do some comparisons with some science that had, in Kuhn's terms, more revolutionary potential. I picked two "extraordinary" areas for comparison: parapsychology and the attempt to detect cosmic gravitational radiation. My supervisor also persuaded me to pick a theoretical area and I chose the theory of amorphous semi-conductors. The parapsychology study was good fun, went well, and led to a number of publications, but at the end of 13 hours of interviews with the semi-conductor guys I still had no idea what they were talking about. I did not even know who agreed with whom and who disagreed. This was another truly valuable experience for reasons that could not have been anticipated. The whole point was that the data were worthless—and who would ever design a study to collect worthless data? Yet, in retrospect, the experience has given me much more confidence in doing work in areas where I do know what the scientists are talking about because I now know the difference between understanding and not understanding.

To go back to the main thread, my next tranche of fieldwork, conducted in 1972, saw me buying an old car and driving 5,000 miles around and across America interviewing scientists working in the four areas of science. As can be imagined, the trip satisfied all my criteria for good research—plenty of open air and visits to new places and little time spent in libraries. I'll concentrate on the gravitational wave work which led to the publication of the 1975 paper. (I still think of it as my best ever publication—how sad!)

Joe Weber, a University of Maryland physicist, had pioneered the detection of gravitational waves. In the late 1960s he had set up bars of aluminum weighing a couple of tons inside vacuum chambers and isolated them from all known forces. He claimed that the residual vibrations in the bars were evidence for the existence of gravitational waves.

Joe Weber found a lot of gravitational waves and other scientists were either sufficiently excited by his claims to want to join in the search or sufficiently irritated by the seeming unlikelihood of the claims that they wanted to disprove them. Whatever the motivation, about half-a-dozen other groups had built Weber-type detectors but were seemingly failing to see what Weber had seen. In interviewing all these scientists I had inadvertently invented what became known as the "controversy study" and in the spring of 1981 I was able to edit a special issue of *Social Studies of Science* containing a collection of these (see Collins 1981). The controversy study is still a staple of sociology of scientific knowledge.[5]

Anyway, this is how I remember it: I had done the large majority of these interviews and was driving across Nevada in my old Ford Galaxie on my way to a last interview in Stanford, and I was thinking about how I would write up all the interesting data I had gathered. In my head I was going through the paper I would write, modeling it on the TEA-laser study of knowledge diffusion among scientists. Crucial, you will recall, was the transmission of real understanding, not just bits and pieces of information. Suddenly the hair stood up on the back of my neck. Vital to the TEA-laser study was my ability to tell whether a group had a working laser on their bench—whether they really had developed "fluency in the TEA-laser language." But, disastrously, there was no equivalent in the gravitational wave field because no one knew what a "working" gravitational wave detector was. Whereas the TEA-laser scientists knew they had to make concrete smoke no one could agree what the gravitational wave detectors ought to be doing. Should they be seeing gravitational waves or not seeing gravitational waves? How could I have made such a huge mistake in my experimental design? How could I not have spotted this elementary error until after I had driven 4,000 miles carrying out interviews? I was in a state of panic.

If I remember rightly it took me about another half-hour's driving to work out what to do and when I had worked it out I immediately knew I was "on to something." The point was this: If I didn't know when a gravitational wave detector was working, then neither did the scientists! In the case of the TEA-laser, scientists knew how long they had to go on making phone calls, visiting other's laboratories, and rebuilding their lasers in slightly different ways, because they had a clear criterion of when they had attained success—smoking concrete. Without this clear criterion some of them would have believed they had succeeded when they had not, and others would not have succeeded because they would not have known just how hard they had to try. Now, in the case of the gravitational wave detectors there were many scientists claiming they had built detectors that were failing to do the equivalent of making concrete smoke—detecting gravitational waves—but they could not be sure whether this failure was to do with there not being any gravitational waves to see or their failure to build a machine that was good enough to see them. In "normal science" I realized, this problem did not arise because there was consensus about what any device ought to see when it was working. In "extraordinary science", however, what the device should see when it was working was precisely what the scientists were building the devices to find out.

This dilemma, its working out in scientific controversies, and its meaning for the foundations of scientific knowledge became the subject of the paper. It seemed to be still more exciting than the topic of the transmission of scientific understanding that I originally thought I was investigating and that was how I wrote up the fieldwork in the 1975 paper.

In my 1985 book, *Changing Order*, I called the problem of being unable to tell whether an experiment was not finding anything because it was badly done or because there was nothing to find, "The Experimenter's Regress." This can be summed up as "to know whether experiments have been done well you have to refer to the results, but to know what the results should be you have first have to do the experiments well." The experimenter's regress is, perhaps, my best known concept and, in part, my career and much of my subsequent research was built around it.

Gravity's Shadow

Gravity's Shadow is also the result of a series of accidents though, disappointingly in terms of the thesis I am promoting here, no mistakes (*pace* those reviewers who see the whole thing as a mistake). I planned none of it from the outset. It just grew by itself when, in 1993, I paid a curiosity visit to Joe Weber in Irvine and he rekindled my enthusiasm for following up the fate of his ideas. I had no interest in the big science that gravitational wave detection had become but the encounter with Weber, who hated big science, drew me in.

There are about half-a-dozen nameable new ideas in *Gravity's Shadow* (some were first published in a series of papers that led up to the book). The best "stories" concern the genesis of the idea of evidential individualism and collectivism (first set out in a 1998 article in the *American Journal of Sociology*). I had been sitting in conferences observing the Americans criticizing an Italian group and the Italians defending themselves and criticizing back. Listening to a group of the usual antagonists yelling at each other in a corridor I said, "Come on chaps, why don't you sit down and argue this out properly over dinner so I can record it," and we all went off to the Legal Sea Foods restaurant on the MIT campus. I simply plonked the mini-disk down in the middle of the table. By this time I was well enough known and trusted to get away with that kind of thing. It sheds a new light on the notion of participatory fieldwork but it is obviously the right kind of thing to do if you can do it. No one said anything "for my benefit"—I just picked up on an already half-started conversation and made sure it continued to the end in such way that I could get it down. My *AJS* paper on the subject starts with an extract from this conversation and finishes by explaining how to understand what was going on in a sociological way (see Collins 1998).

The notion of evidential individualism and collectivism, which is the centerpiece of the sociological account of the disagreement recorded at Legal Sea Foods, "gelled" as the result of another "fieldwork experience." One day I found myself sitting in my rented car completely blocking one lane of an access to the Grande Raccordo Anulare—Rome's busy ring road. I had lost my way en route to the Italian gravitational wave lab at Frascati and was conspicuously consulting a map. What surprised me was that the traffic just maneuvered round me without so much as an angry glance whereas in Britain it would have been all honking and fist-shaking. In other words, in Italy the collectivity of drivers were taking responsibility for a mistake and making it good whereas in Britain it is always the individual's fault. The group of Italian scientists I was studying also thought it appropriate for collective responsibility to be taken for separating mistakes from genuine findings so they were ready to publish findings even when they were merely suggestive not conclusive; they treated it as the job of the wider community to take responsibility for the safety of scientific truth rather than it being the job of each individual "driver of an experiment" as it were. The American "evidential individualists," on the other hand, thought that no one should publish a result until they were certain it was right: each "driver" had to take full responsibility for scientific "accidents." The arguments between the groups were heated and sometimes bitter with accusations of bad faith being made on the one hand and accusations of censorship on the other. My argument was that both systems worked so long as everyone knew what was going on, and that both were essentially the same, with evidential individualism just keeping more of the process behind closed doors for longer—not necessarily a good thing.

Notice how far these descriptions are from just "following the scientists around," or just describing what they do. In each case the analysts' categories were imposed on top of actors' categories. Things were drawn together in a way that would be unlikely to occur to the actors: learning French and learning to build a laser were treated as like each other; testing lasers and testing gravitational wave detectors were treated as crucially different; car-driving etiquette turned out to bear on detecting gravitational waves! A source of enmity between groups was shown to be based on a false premise—that they were doing fundamentally different things whereas really it all amounted to the same thing when looked at from a distance. It is only the analysts' imposition of concepts on top of the actors' that makes sense of these things.

Is this kind of work ethnography? Many ethnographers seem to think they are finished once the "thick description" has been produced. I think that is just the start. Social analysis involves finding the patterns that link one set of actions to another and those patterns emerge from the analyst's world, not the actors' world. Sometimes this involves the analyst telling the actors that their view of the world is just plain wrong! I've done quite a lot of that. Gratifyingly, the actors have occasionally come round to seeing it my way. That's the best experience of all but it is a long way from mere description—after all, the result is that the actors' world changes!

Another example of the outsider imposing outside concepts is the idea of interactional expertise. This idea is found in *Gravity's Shadow* and grew from the field study, but is first mentioned in the paper by myself and Evans: "The Third Wave of Science Studies" (Collins and Evans 2002). This time the driving force was reflection on the nature of the fieldwork itself rather than substantive field observations. I realized that after 30 years studying gravitational waves I tended to spend a lot of my time talking physics to my respondents. This wasn't a matter of me being instructed (though one never stops learning), but of the normal to-and-fro of technical conversations not too dissimilar from those the physicists would have among themselves. Quite a few times I would say something like "in my view you should be doing this," and the "this" would refer to something like the installation of seismic isolation at the Hanford interferometer. Mostly I was wrong, of course, and the reasons would be explained, but my remarks were not stupid. That they were not stupid was indicated by the fact that the prospect had already been thought about and that was why there could be a ready response. Often it was a matter of fine judgment, and in different circumstances my idea might have been implemented. So I was not just "talking the talk" to these physicists, though I certainly was not "walking the walk"; what I was doing was what I like to call "walking the talk." As we will see, this is not something that is done just by participatory sociologists—walking the talk is everywhere.

One day I started to puzzle about this: here was I, a mere sociologist, but I was capable of taking part in the technical discourse in an engaging way and seemed to be able to make judgments that were close to the judgments of my respondents. (On one notable occasion concerning a radical design for a prototype interferometer, my judgment was better than the judgment of my respondents.)[6] The important point was that, in spite of my walking the talk, I could not "do" gravitational wave detection. I was never going to publish a paper in the field, nor invent new ways of building or testing an instrument, nor be capable of analyzing the data it produced. What I had was "interactional expertise" as opposed to the "contributory expertise" needed to do things such as experimentation or technical theorization.

It then occurred to me that the managers of the project, who had, in this case, made their main contributions to science in high-energy physics, were also not publishing papers in the field nor designing new kinds of interferometer. In a way, their contribution to the discourse, though it was much more accomplished, was not different in kind from mine. None of us had "contributory expertise" in the field of gravitational wave physics—the ability to write the theoretical papers or design and build the devices—but we had learned interactional expertise from immersion in the technical discourse

297

in the absence of the practice. I went on to publish a paper with Gary Sanders, the project manager of the Laser Interferometer Gravitational-Wave Observatory (LIGO), about the expertise he brought to management and we agreed that interactional expertise was vital. We also teased out the crucial differences that made someone like him rather than someone like me the right person for the manager's job. The paper is called "They give you the keys and say 'drive it'" (Collins and Sanders 2007). Again, that is a respondent coming to share, and even help develop, new categories belonging to the analyst. These new categories then feed back into actors' worlds.

We, analysts, also invented some experiments—mentioned in the introduction—to explore the idea of interactional expertise. This again was unforeseeable. The best known of these experiments showed that color-blind persons are fluent in the language of color perception because they have been immersed in color-talk all their lives. Again analysts' categories are here imposed on those of actors—how else would one see the connection between the discourse of the color-blind and the judgments of gravitational wave physicists? Actually some people from my own field didn't understand the concept and could not see the connection—something that still astonishes me—while physicists grasped it immediately.

Interactional expertise is acquired through embedding in the discourse of the world of one's respondents in the absence of practical engagement. What then is gained by practical engagement? Let me say straight away that I grab every chance I get for practical immersion as well as immersion in the discourse, and one would be a fool not to grab it. In the case of gravitational wave physics the option just was not available. But the crucial point is that when one has finished immersing oneself in the actors' world, whether it is through discourse or practice, one is thrown back on interactional expertise as soon as one starts to describe for one's audience. Loïc Wacquant (2004) became a boxer and learned to punch so as to study boxing but his book, *Body and Soul: Notebooks of an Apprentice Boxer* does not convince by throwing punches but by throwing words. A huge amount of the world runs on interactional expertise—management has already been mentioned but the same goes for all organized decision making processes—decisions are made by people sitting in committees and talking, or reading and talking. The same goes for most forms of communication in any setting. So even Wacquant has to ply his ethnographic trade in the world of his academic peers via his interactional expertise, not his contributory expertise. The reason it is good to practice as well as talk if the option is available is that it is a quicker route to gaining interactional expertise: for one thing being practically immersed is a way of increasing the immersion in the talk of others who are practically engaged; for another, a picture, or a bruise, is worth a thousand words. What we call in *Rethinking Expertise*, "the strong interactional hypothesis," holds that if you work at it hard and long enough those thousand words will give you the same as the picture or the bruise when it comes to producing the talk for your audience, but it is a much more difficult way to get to the end point (Collins and Evans 2007).

Some more features of the gravitational wave study

One of the oddest features of the overall gravitational wave study is that it is led by the science not by the analyst. I have to wait for gravitational waves to be discovered before I can write my second volume and complete the story and I really struggle to explain this to my funding agency: "give me some more money to watch the community for longer though I can't guarantee anything of interest will happen." The sheer duration of the extended project also has an impact on my relationship with the community. When I published my conclusions about gravitational waves in 1975 and 1981 I made no attempt to apprise the scientists of what I had said—in fact I tried to keep the stuff hidden. As far as I know no-one knew much about it until the first volume of *The Golem* series (see Collins and Pinch 1993; 1998; 2005) started to get publicity due to its involvement in the "science wars"—that bitter period when a group of scientists took it upon themselves to denounce the sociological approach to the study of their enterprise.

I remember very clearly one conversation that I had right at the beginning of the intense fieldwork period on the big interferometer science. This was in 1995, the height of the science wars. From Britain, I telephoned Rich Isaacson, who was Director of Gravitational Physics at the NSF, to ask for an interview. After a couple minutes Isaacson suddenly said something like "Hey—are you the Harry Collins who wrote that Golem book?" "Yes," I said, "I'm afraid I am," my blood running cold. "I'd be delighted to talk to you," said Isaacson, to my astonishment. And it turned out that, Joe Weber apart, all the scientists I met who had read the earlier work, loved it. I think they were impressed by its technical proficiency and analytic accuracy of the work in spite of the fact that the science warriors were saying we knew nothing; after reading lots of popularizations and lightweight attacks, I suspect they were just pleased and surprised that an outsider could get this stuff so right in terms of the science and the dynamics of the arguments. Isaacson and I remained friends for a long time after that, though he eventually took against one of my *Gravity's Shadow* chapters.

The point I am getting to is that in such a long-term project you cannot keep your work secret, and what I did for the second phase was to set up a website in which I explained everything I was doing and the way I thought, including a quite open and clear section on my relativistic approach—a main target of the science warriors. Along with the fact that I have worked conspicuously hard at attending the meetings—trying to grasp the technicalities, and never acting in a dishonest or deceitful way—my respondents valued having everything laid out for them so they knew exactly what they were dealing with. As a result, one or two misunderstandings, and one or two individuals, aside, my relations with this community have got better and better over the years. I now feel I am among friends when I am with these scientists. I like and admire them, their integrity, and their heroic and crazy project. And I learned to see the point of big science.

No, none of this means I have lost my objectivity and "gone native"; my project is not the scientists' project and both parties know it, and they realize there will always be some natural antagonism between what I have to say and what they have to do and believe. The sources of this antagonism are laid out in chapter 42 of *Gravity's Shadow* and include the fact that the sociologist of scientific knowledge is always opening up disagreements that the scientists have left behind and need to forget about if they are to get on with their scientific lives.[7]

That said, there have also been moments when the two sides have learned from each other. I remember the time when I complained to one of my respondents that he had used my ideas in a paper he presented. That was a shameful thing to do because he was a friend and a person of utmost integrity, and it was stupid thing to do because, as he pointed out to me, the ideas had grown out of conversations with him. Fortunately we have remained friends. The ideas in question were about modes of competition and collaboration. Evidential individualism and collectivism have also been cited back to me quite often and scientists have told me that this way of looking at things may have eased the tension among warring groups. As mentioned, the expertise categories are the subject of a joint paper between myself and a respondent and *Gravity's Shadow*'s analysis of the tension between big and small science (along with the expertise categories) is now a regular feature of the annual NSF sponsored "Project Science" workshop for big science managers and organizers (with me giving an invited paper at the 2007 Irvine meeting). Again, I am not sure how some social analysts of science, such as ethnomethodologists and ethnographers, would describe what is happening when analysts' categories come to contribute to the constitution of the actors' world in this way, but I am quite sure it is one of the most rewarding experiences one can have, especially when the starting perspectives of oneself and one's respondents are far apart.

The sense of community that I now have with many of the gravitational wave scientists is another thing that was not foreseeable. My best prediction in advance (witness what I said above about my "blood running cold") would have been that the immanent tensions would have over-ruled the mutual understanding. What it shows is that Max Weber's plea for "science as a vocation" can triumph over some of the more Machiavellian models of science that populate our sociological community.

Conclusion

Mostly this has been a tale of lucky accidents. The phrase "in retrospect" keeps showing up. I could build further on this theme were I to go into my other work such as that on artificial intelligence.[8] It is hard to draw any systematic conclusions from a series of lucky accidents. But there is one big conclusion: "Put yourself in the way of lucky accidents." One can be completely sure that nothing as fortunate as what happened to me will occur to you if you do not put yourself in a position to benefit from the luck. If you ever experience that mid-sentence realization that something big has gone wrong—savor it; you may just have taken the first step toward discovering something. Be confident and "stay light on your feet" during fieldwork; that first framing of the problem may not be the right one. Nowadays, if I don't get some kind of disturbing surprise during the course of fieldwork, or thinking about the fieldwork, or writing up and analyzing the fieldwork, I start to worry. Nearly all the interesting things I come up with are different in a bigger or smaller way from what I set out to find, and a good proportion of them arise as a result of talking about the ideas or interacting with the page.

A second message is that, conventionally, the novice humanities or social science researcher reads first and investigates later. For me it has always worked best if I don't read too much before I start work. Once you have your overarching approach—in my case it was the idea of form-of-life—then start in. There is a chance that you will "rediscover somebody else's wheel" but in my experience this never exactly happens. Often, what the other person has done is similar but crucially different and, if you are too assiduous in reading, the subtleties may be overlooked and the work might never get off the ground. And, by the way, I do know that this advice about not reading too much before you start has been anticipated by Auguste Comte under the heading of "mental hygiene."[9]

I am convinced that "put yourself in the way of lucky accidents and stay light on your feet" is advice that nearly every social researcher can use. The advice about not reading too much before you start is something that may not be good for everyone. It works for me but there is certainly a division of labor in the social sciences just as there is in other sciences. If everyone read as little as me we would have a poor discipline and I am always learning from people who have read more (ironically, living out the two-step model of communication). On the other hand, what I am sure of is that if the discipline as a whole is conceived of as essentially a matter of shuffling the ideas that are found in the existing literature then it is worthless as a science. Unfortunately, shuffling others' ideas is what we teach undergraduates, and the hardest thing for the novice researcher to do is break that habit. I think that rapid exposure to the world outside the library is the key.

The final moral has to do with raising the bar for ethnography. An extra inch or two could be added by thinking really hard about what it means to immerse oneself in the world of the actor; use of the imitation game could help. The bar also needs to be raised well above thick description as an end in itself—that's just too self serving. The embedding within the actors' frame of reference that makes thick description possible is the vital starting point for rich qualitative research but the "estrangement," which opens up the actor's world for reassembly, makes the whole thing worth doing. The invention of new concepts and ideas developed out of the analyst's sociological expertise is what social research is for—the new ideas are the highlights of a researcher's life. Sometimes these new ideas will feed back into the world of those who are being studied; so long as analytic integrity is never compromised so as to make it happen, this can be the most gratifying experience of all.

Notes

1 An earlier and longer version of part of what follows that describes the origin of the first two papers was first published as "Qualitative Methodology in Practice: My Experience" (Collins 2004b). I am grateful to the editors for making suggestions about how earlier drafts could be fleshed out which have had a significant impact on the direction the paper developed. All faults are my own, however.

2 I would encourage other ethnographers or participatory fieldworkers to try it. We can offer access to an Internet platform for running "imitation game" tests (e-mail CollinsHM@cf.ac.uk or EvansRJ1@cf.ac.uk). One does not have to pass such a test to find it a useful way of probing what one does and does not know about the natives' world. For description of these tests see Collins et al. 2006 and Giles 2006.

3 It is a lot of attention for two papers, but both of the papers have been cited many times and continue to be cited up to the present. The first paper was reprinted in 1982 (see Edge and Barnes 1982), again in 1999 (see Bagioli 1999) and again in 2005 (see Smith 2005). The second paper was reprinted twice in 1982 (once in English, once in French, see Edge and Barnes 1982 and Latour 1982 respectively), and twice in 1995 (once in English, once in Spanish see Nowotny and Taschwer 1995 and Iranzo et al. 1995 respectively). The two papers also form the backbone to my fairly well known 1985 book, *Changing Order*, and an edited version of the second is a chapter of *The Golem* (Collins and Pinch 1993) (which has been translated 12 times).

4 I wrote a follow up study to the 1974 (see Collins 1974) paper in 1975 (see Collins 1975). In 2001 I wrote another paper, "Tacit Knowledge, Trust, and the Q of Sapphire," that is very similar to the 1974 paper though it is about a different group of scientists.

5 Recently, in a contribution (Collins 2008) to an edited volume called *Clashes of Knowledge*, I found myself asking critical questions about the way sociologists handle controversy studies in policy areas where the imperatives are somewhat different to the sociology of scientific knowledge.

6 The scientists assured me they had changed their design, into which they had put a lot of effort, after I pointed out the flaw.

7 But see the paper (Collins 2008) in *Clashes of Knowledge* where I suggest that a similar tension applies to the study of scientific controversy in policy-urgent areas.

8 Thus, the concept of "polimorphic and mimeomorphic actions," first mentioned using different terminology in *Artificial Experts* (Collins 1990) and fully worked out in *The Shape of Actions* (Collins and Kusch 1998), arose out of a mistake which I noticed only when, in about 1987, I was lecturing to an undergraduate class on the sociological impossibility of the project of artificial intelligence.

9 For an example of how the concept of "experimenter's regress" could have been killed stone dead by scholarly critics see Godin and Gingras 2002 and Collins 2002.

References

Bagioli, M. M. (ed.) (1999) *The Science Studies Reader*, New York: Routledge.

Coleman, J. S., Katz, E., and Menzel, H. (1966) *Medical Innovation: a diffusion study*, Indianapolis: Bobbs-Merrill.

Collins, H. M. (1974) "The TEA Set: tacit knowledge and scientific networks," *Science Studies*, 4: 165–86.

——(1975) "The Seven Sexes: a study in the sociology of a phenomenon, or the replication of experiments in physics," *Sociology*, 9: 205–24.

——(ed.) (1981) "Knowledge and Controversy: studies in modern natural science," Special Issue of *Social Studies of Science*, 11(1).

——(1985) *Changing Order: replication and induction in scientific practice*, Beverly Hills, CA and London: Sage.

——(1990) *Artificial Experts: social knowledge and intelligent machines*, Cambridge, MA: MIT Press.

——(1998) "The Meaning of Data: open and closed evidential cultures in the search for gravitational waves," *American Journal of Sociology*, 104: 293–337.

——(2001) "Tacit Knowledge, Trust, and the Q of Sapphire," *Social Studies of Science*, 31: 71–85.

——(2002) "The Experimenter's Regress as Philosophical Sociology," *Studies in History and Philosophy of Science*, 33: 153–60.

——(2004a) *Gravity's Shadow: the search for gravitational waves*, Chicago: University of Chicago Press.

——(2004b) "Qualitative Methodology in Practice: my experience," in C. Humphrey and Lee, W. (eds.) *The Real Life Guide to Accounting Research* (pp. 481–90), Amsterdam, The Netherlands: Elsevier.

——(2008) "Actors' and Analysts' Categories in the Social Analysis of Science," in P. Meusburger, Welker, M., and Wunder, E. (eds.) *Clashes of Knowledge* (pp. 101–10), Dordrecht, The Netherlands: Springer.

Collins, H. M. and Evans, R. (2002) "The Third Wave of Science Studies: studies of expertise and experience," *Social Studies of Science*, 32: 235–96.

——(2007) *Rethinking Expertise*, Chicago: University of Chicago Press.

Collins, H. M., Evans, R., Ribeiro, R., and Hall, M. (2006) "Experiments with Interactional Expertise," *Studies in History and Philosophy of Science*, 37A: 656–74.

Collins, H. M. and Kusch, M. (1998) *The Shape of Actions: what humans and machines can do*, Cambridge, MA: MIT Press.

Collins, H. M. and Pinch, T. J. (1993) *The Golem: what everyone should know about science*, New York: Cambridge University Press.

——(1998) *The Golem at Large: what you should know about technology*, New York: Cambridge University Press.

——(2005) *Dr. Golem: what you should know about medicine*, Chicago: University of Chicago Press.

Collins, H. and Sanders, G. (2007) "They Give You the Keys and Say 'Drive It!' Managers, referred expertise, and other expertises" in H. Collins (ed.) *Case Studies of Expertise and Experience*, Special Issue of *Studies in History and Philosophy of Science*, 38: 621–41.

Edge, D. and Barnes, B. (eds.) (1982) *Science in Context: readings in the sociology of science*, Cambridge, MA: MIT Press.

Giles, J. (2006) "Sociologist Fools Physics Judges," *Nature*, 442: 8.

Godin, B. and Gingras, Y. (2002) "The Experimenter's Regress: from skepticism to argumentation," *Studies in History and Philosophy of Science*, 30A: 137–52.

Iranzo, J. M., Blanco, J. R., Gonzalez de la Fe, T., Torres, C., and Cotillo, A. (eds.) (1995) *Sociologia de la Ciencia y la Tecnologia*, Madrid, Spain: Consejo Superior de Investigaciones Cientificas.

Latour, B. (ed.) (1982) *La science telle qu'elle se fait*, Paris: Pandore.

Nowotny, H. and Taschwer, K. (eds.) (1995) *The Sociology of Science*, Cheltenham, U.K.: Edward Elgar.

Smith, M. (ed.) (2005) *Philosophy and Methodology of the Social Sciences*, London: Sage.

Wacquant, L. (2004) *Body and Soul: notebooks of an apprentice boxer*, New York: Oxford.

Part VI

THEORIZING FROM ALTERNATIVE DATA

Documentary, historical, and
autobiographical sources

20

WRITING THEORY IN(TO) *LAST WRITES*

Laurel Richardson

When I was in graduate school, I was totally awed by my advisor Edward Rose's ability to look at reams and reams of computer print out and figure out from that looking how next to proceed. When I was an undergraduate, I was totally taken with the challenge of figuring out the genetic make-up of the drosophila in my mating experiments. And when I was not yet a school child, I spent hours during the summer organizing and categorizing the quartz-like gravel that filled in the 238 steps leading from our summer cottage to the lake front.

I have done qualitative research following the standard logico-empirical research protocol of propositions, hypotheses, and tests (Richardson 1990), and I have taught graduate seminars in theory that favored that approach. Inductive work was viewed as relevant for "exploratory" work, when the student did not know much about the problem s/he was planning to study, but it was not considered the right approach for actually testing hypotheses. Although the logico-empirical approach to knowledge-making has satisfied my needs for direction and closure, my greatest pleasure has been in working inductively: immersing myself in the "data"—the print-outs, the matings, the gravel—trying to discover what I might. One of the major things I have discovered is that theory can be discovered.

Of course, the idea of an applied phenomenology—looking at something without a lens to look through—is an absurdity. I look at the world through my sociological lens, but that lens is more like a crystal than an eye-glass, thereby inviting refraction upon refraction.

My need for intellectual novelty is great. Sociology suits me because it allows for near endless possibilities for categorizing, conceptualizing, and revisioning. It even allows for alternative ways of doing and telling about research. Those alternative ways have deepened my understanding of my field, my research, and myself. I tell you all of this because I believe that one does one's best and most enjoyable work when one is true to one's own disposition.

For the past 20 years or so, I have favored reconceptualizing the writing of qualitative research as not simply a "mopping-up" activity at the end of one's project, but as a method for finding theoretical ideas that were not apparent before the writing process. That is, writing is itself a method of inquiry that leads to new ideas—new concepts, maybe even theories. To engage this method one need only be willing to accept uncertainty for awhile, and then take the risk of finding out things one didn't know—or even want to know.

Fortunately, I have not been alone is this reconceptualization of qualitative research (Denzin and Lincoln 2005). The world of ethnography has expanded in ways unimaginable two decades ago. One of the new approaches is autoethnography, where the researcher looks with an ethnographic eye at one's Self (Ellis 2004). These works are grounded in the lived-experiences of the researcher and linked to the sociohistorical conditions that surround the Self. Autoethnographic research fulfills C. Wright Mills' famous definition of sociology—the internexus of the biographical with the historical (Mills 1959). Conferences and journals not only accept these new ethnographies, they call for them.

Because of this broadening (and deepening) of the ethnographic, students and young professionals can report their research in both conventional and non-conventional ways, and find venues for both. And students who can become so alienated from their own work (their own strengths and Selves), that they take ungainly amounts of time to complete their work—or leave ABD ("All But Dissertation")—can now nurture themselves while in graduate school by writing in ways that honor their "voice," while also writing a standard dissertation. They are not contrary to each other.

My work is both creative and analytic. These are not contrary to each other, either. I allow myself great freedom in the collection of "data," holding off the generation of concepts until I am at the computer, writing. This practice is unlike the grounded theorist protocol where winnowing takes place during the data-collection phase. But like grounded theorists, I am more interested in generating theory than in proving facts. I have no interest in reporting frequencies or percentages of who and what. That kind of reporting maps logico-empirical protocols on to qualitative work, even though the assumptions of that protocol are not met. I am saddened when good qualitative works—deep descriptions of the social world—are destroyed by their authors/editors emulating "hard science" writing—complete with tables and graphs. It is as if a perfectly lovely and interesting tiger is passed off as a vole.

Unlike quantitative work which can carry its meaning in its tables and summaries, qualitative work carries its meaning in its entire text. Just as a piece of literature is not equivalent to its "plot summary," qualitative research is not contained in its abstract. Qualitative research has to be read, not scanned; its meaning is in the reading.

All writing is a sociohistorical invention, and therefore mutable. Foisting writing-protocols that cohere with quantitative research upon qualitative researchers created serious problems. These protocols have undercut writing as a dynamic, creative process; they have undermined the confidence of budding qualitative researchers because their experience of research is inconsistent with the writing model; and they have contributed to a flotilla of qualitative writing that is simply not interesting to read because writers write in the homogenized voice of "science" rather than honoring their own voice, vision, experience with the "data." But, now, because we work in a postmodernist climate there are a multitude of approaches—formats, theories, perspectives, and methods—that exist side-by-side.

I favor the perspective of poststructuralism. Poststructuralism suggests two important things to qualitative writers: first, it directs us to understand ourselves reflexively as persons writing from particular positions at specific times; and second, it frees us from trying to write a single text in which everything is said at once to everyone. Nurturing our own voices releases the censorious hold of "science writing" on our consciousness, as well as the arrogance it fosters in our psyche: writing is validated as a method of knowing and generating theory.

I coddle my writing-self, which has led me to experiment in different genres—not only for the pleasure of learning but because each genre provides an opportunity for knowing one's "data" differently. The concepts one might develop through poetic-representation, for example, may be quite different from those developed through science-writing. Thus in my career, I have written "findings" as poetic representation, ethnodrama, lyric poetry, personal essays, autoethnography and in standard prose. Writing in different genres does not undo writing in the social-scientific genre, any more than learning a second language undoes the first one. Elsewhere I have discussed at length the theory and rationale behind my writing practices (Richardson 2000), and provided examples of the same in my co-authored book, *Travels with Ernest: Crossing the Literary/Sociological Divide* (Richardson and Lockridge 2004), and in various articles, some collected in my book, *Fields of Play: Constructing an Academic Life* (1997a).

This multi-pronged approach to knowledge-making has led me to a different way of thinking about theory construction, as well. The logico-rational method of theory construction I learned in graduate school and taught to graduate students is not the only way to construct theory, nor necessarily the best way for qualitative researchers to theorize, particularly those who favor inductive reasoning.

A different way of thinking about theory is to consider how narratives—story telling, character development, tone, and so on—carry conceptual ideas about the "data" (cf. Bochner forthcoming; Bochner and Ellis 2002; Ellis and Bochner 1996; Richardson 1997b). In writing a narrative, one is embedding concepts, possibly building toward a larger theoretical understanding of the material, or similar materials. I have come to prefer this "embedding" because it allows me to create texts that are intellectually and emotionally evocative. Such texts encourage readers to be active readers, discovering that which is embedded, like the hidden figures we looked for in pictures when we were kids. And like the flush of excitement felt when we found those hidden figures, readers so experience the finding of "embedded" theory. Unlike the more formal "suggestions for future research" that conclude standard social scientific articles, my kind of theorizing creates reading experiences where the reader comes to their own ideas of what's next. As a sociologist who has made a career of doing the work I want to do, it is important to me to move others to do the work that matters to them, in the way that works for them. In this way, theory is turned into *practice*.

This near life-time of preparation, however, did not prepare me for how I wrote theory into *Last Writes: A Daybook for a Dying Friend* (2007). To understand how I did that, I need to begin at the beginning, before I had an inkling I was writing a qualitative research book.

The daybook phase

It is my habit to write everyday in my daybook, a writerly place where I can record as I wish the events of the day, memories, dreams, ideas and longings. It is an open format that invites reflection, and it is a place to hone my writing craft and explore my anxieties, stresses, and fears. I never know when or where something I write will be of theoretical use later on. In what follows, I will write in italics or indent material I am reproducing here from the daybook, hoping that the reader will come along with me and sense the theoretical notions that are embedded in the text. I will not review the book in its entirety for my intent here is not to provide an inventory, but to demonstrate *how* I work.

I begin with October 2nd, the first daybook entry:

> Last night I dreamt that my pearl necklace was holding on with but one thread.

The next day, a nurse phones to tell me that my best friend and sociology colleague, Betty Kirschner, is in intensive care in Robinson Hospital near Kent, Ohio. She is barely holding on to her life. Her emphysema has reached the perilous stage. On the hospital forms, she has declared me her "sister." *We are not real sisters. We are best friends. We have been best friends for thirty-five years.*

> One of the most perfect days in my life I shared with Betty ... We went to a street fair ... We went to the Heritage Rose Garden ... We feasted on Katzinger's corned beef on Jewish Rye ... We talked

without restraint ... In the evening we went to hear Vladimir Horowitz ... At the end of the concert silence prevailed ... an encore ... then more sweet silence ... Perhaps a half hour later, people began filing out in silence, the way pilgrims do when they depart a sacred space ... Betty and I have been deeply bonded ever since we shared this perfect day.

I pack my bag and drive the 100 miles to see her. The pulmonologist explains that Betty has *two paths* open to her: to be intubated, which she has refused, or to be made comfortable:

"I've been ready to pass over for the past six months," Betty says.
"But I don't go. Why is it so much work?"
I say, "Maybe because you've worked all your life." I think people do their dying the way they do their living.

Betty and I spend the next few days preparing her cremation plans, memorial service, obituary, hospice papers, and talking about games of chance. *Betty loves games of chance. I like duplicate bridge.* She says she wants me to have *her strand of double pearls.*

On October 9th, I *drive home at peace.* On October 11th, Dr. Nash phones to say Betty refuses to go into hospice. Anger overcomes me. *I have accepted her dying. Why hasn't she?*

For the next two weeks, my husband Ernest and I are in Sedona, Arizona, a place that Betty introduced me to, and one that is very *dear to both of our hearts. "Bring me back some red sand," she says.* While I'm gone, Betty is in and out and in and out of the hospital.

Up to this point in my writing, my only concern was dealing with my friend's dying by keeping a clear record of our exchanges and my feelings. I was not yet consciously doing theory—or doing "research."

On October 26th my Researcher Persona entered my daybook. Here is the last part of the entry for that day:

"Betty," I say on my Sedona phone, "We forgot to do your Ethical Will."
"I don't feel the need," she says.
"Why?" I ask.
" ... I've lived an ethical life and that's the model ... "
"So your life is the ethical will?"
"Exactly!"
To myself I say, "What am I doing? Interviewing her? Collecting Data?"

My husband and I return from Sedona and Betty asks me to *change the final papers* we had worked on earlier. I do and I mail them. Betty changes her mind again. *I feel had.*

311

On October 31st, I have this entry:

> "You sound funny," Betty says on the phone.
> "Oh, I'm just writing," I equivocate. I don't tell her that I'm writing about her dying. I move to the couch, taking my daybook with me.

I am willfully, now, taking notes about our conversations, not for emotional relief, but for some other reason that I haven't yet formulated, and it has moved me into a deceptive stance, much as happens in ethnographic research—the ethnographer deciding to withhold information so that the host will speak more freely; so the ethnographer can get a "truer" picture.

My entries now are verbatim accounts of her plans for *doctor-assisted suicide, smoking, pain, steroids, emphysema, meds, hives, cataracts, osteoporosis* and her preparations for moving to Delaware to live with her daughter. My old friend Betty is often, now, consumed by negativity. And, my entries are about my older son's *spinal surgery*, my younger son's *chronic back pain*, my *sick days, my mother's breast cancer death, my father's murder, my near death experiences in cars and planes.* Listening to Betty's suffering brings out the pains, fears and anxieties in my own life. But the entries are also about the joys of *grandsons, travel, Sedona, birds, jokes, music, fathers, retirement,* and *feminist friendships in the academy.* Her life is not all bad; my life is not all good.

Although I had never shared any part of any of my daybooks with anyone, I decide to bring entries to my Memoir Writing Group. Their discussions help me think about my own death and dying. Their conversations make their way into my daybook as do my conversations about Betty with my *sister, good friends, and children.* Many ask how come I am still friends with Betty. I don't know the answer to that, yet.

By December, Betty is getting weaker. She finally *quits smoking.* Much too late. Twelve years earlier we had almost ended our friendship over her smoking. Quitting now, I felt, only extends her time of suffering—and the suffering of those who care about her. Like me. I felt *betrayed.* That feeling led me to write about a betrayal three years earlier, about the time when Betty became seriously ill. We were having one of our routine get-togethers in the Sheraton Hotel in Cuyahoga Falls. But now our *personal sharing routine* of exchanging writing and photos was altered. Betty only wanted to watch *American Idol.* At the end of the program,

> I take a deep breath and say, "I've been thinking about my shadow side ... This might be painful ... In some ways, Betty, you are my shadow ... the person I fear I'll become ... sick ... self-centered ... slothful."
> Betty says, "I'm not surprised, because I've become my own shadow."

On January 7th Betty's going to a mother-in-law suite in Dover, Delaware; she'll have home-care assistants 16 hours a day. On February 8th Ernest and I are going to Australia for six weeks where I will hold a Distinguished Fellowship at the University of Melbourne. I'll give lectures and workshops on qualitative research; Ernest will paint. We'll live in our own "assisted living"—a Visiting Scholar Residence in University College.

Having not seen Betty since October, I determine I'll drive up to Kent on New Year's Day. *"Oh! This makes me cry,"* she says. *"No. Don't come. It'll be too much."*

She plans to invite her "suicide-assisting" doctor for tea. No, I can't come another time, either. *Does she think we'll never see each other again ... and she doesn't want that painful secret exposed? I feel rejected, relieved, angry, confused, bitter ... How can so many conflicting emotions coexist? I may never see her again. I may never see her again.*

For the next couple of days, I want to ask Betty scores of questions, but I *can't make myself do it because I am questioning my motives ... Have I become a writing vulture, picking the bones of my friend before she dies?*

At this point I am unsure what my role and relationship to my friend and to my writing is or will be. What I came to think of as the "Truman Capote" syndrome haunted me. Capote befriended the murderer, Perry Smith, because Capote saw the potential for a good narrative, a best-seller—*In Cold Blood* (1966). Each stay of execution frustrated Capote because the narrative needed the drama of Smith's death. It seemed to me that Capote's blood was also running cold.

Did I want my friend to live a long time so I'd have a long narrative—or because she was my friend? Or was I simply angry at her? For what? For dying? For not dying? Ethics and emotions rebounded. My only choice, always my choice: write through it.

The book-draft writing phase

"Take notes about everything," Betty says to me on my cell phone as my Qantas plane taxis toward the LAX runway. Betty and I used to love to travel together. We both loved it. But then she developed a fear of flying, panic attacks, and lastly serious illness. I do take notes about Australia, and about phone calls I make to America and emails I send and receive. I am accumulating a lot of material about Betty, Ernest, myself, Australia and Australians—people I came to think of as rambunctious younger siblings. Before long, Ernest has plantar fasciitis. Both of us have *breathing problems* and *exhaustion.* We're both disoriented by the sun crossing the northern sky; *shadows.*

On February 23rd I am facilitating a workshop for the Critical Discourse Group:

> "My twin desire is that my writing be both artful and true," I say to the assembled group ...

313

"What are you working on now, Laurel?" someone asks ...

What was I working on? ... I seem to be working on *not* working, but that was not the answer I could give this workshop. How embarrassing would that be! ... What was I working on?

Aha! I was diligently working on my daybook. I was writing a BOOK.

At that moment I realized that because my creative process requires an audience writing for myself and reading to my Memoir Writing Group would not suffice. *I would want my daybook published.* The daybook would become *The Daybook.*

Because I am an ethnographer-at-heart, I had recorded in my daybook, as I would in ethnographic fieldwork (1) what I saw and heard, (2) what I felt, and (3) ideas generated by the observations and self-reflections. There was no "research plan" before I began. I know students are required to present their research plans before they receive approval from their committees; I also know, after having served on dozens of these committees, that the "plans" often are shoved aside, when the actual engagement with the project leads the student to new ideas—or even to projects they had not intended to study. Serendipity can be major source of innovation and creativity in science. Isn't it a bit ironic, then, that the doing of research in an open and unprogrammed way needs to be justified to those who adhere to "science"?

Despite the materials already in my daybook, actually writing a draft of a book is different than writing in a daybook. Different issues, concerns, and approaches dominate the writing. Attentiveness to my life now became super vigilance. Not knowing what might be relevant to the book because I didn't know yet what the book was about, I erred on the side of obsessive excessiveness—just as I have in other fieldwork.

The fieldwork I was doing for *The Daybook* was both external and internal. I needed to shift my mental focus from dealing with my friend's death to writing the book.

One of the shifts was the engagement of my (learned) ability to remember verbal exchanges, nonverbal activities, and scenes. When I was a preschooler my father insisted I commit our family grocery lists to memory; as a young thespian I was required to memorize the entire play, not just my part; and as an ethnographer I learned and deployed simple techniques for remembering what I heard and saw. As a participant-observer (listener), I distance myself from the setting, the scene, the experience. Because of that distancing, I am better able to see "it" through a sociological lens, barely smudged by my fingerprints, but misted by my breath—my sense of humor.

An example of this externalization is an email I sent to Betty about my dinner with Australian royalty, university administrators, faculty and my husband following my Distinguished Miegunyah Lecture at the University of Melbourne. I experienced the event through a sociological lens that focused on two stratification systems: (1) the intersection of Australian social class hierarchies with university hierarchies and (2) the social/cultural division between the able-bodied and the physically challenged. I published the body of the letter as the free-standing article, "My Dinner with Lord Esqy" (2008). It could stand alone because stratification theory is the spine of sociology. But the letter also found its way, unaltered, into the book draft. Unintentionally, stratification theory was becoming one of the book's themes. In life, people are categorized and differentially evaluated based on various criteria—not just social class, but well/sick, able/disabled, productive/consumptive, old/young and so on—and those lived-experiences were being captured in my writing.

My writing had to be true to my feelings and attitudes, too: writing the draft required that I lock The Censor in a corner of my mind and leave her there. Write honestly, I would tell myself. Do not edit out your feelings during this "fieldwork" stage. How often I had taught that to my students not only because feelings will out anyway, undercut and unconsciously shape one's work, but because, if you feel a certain way about something most likely other people do too. Aha! Now you are on an unexpected path into thematic and conceptual frameworks. During this phase, for example, I wrote about my *fears* for my *grandson's health*, my son's *recovery* from alcoholism, and my troubled relationship with my department. These were painful to write about, not just because of the experiences, but because I was seeing my complicity, and failings. I also wrote: *I do not like Betty.* And then, *Will I let those words stand?* Betty was my best friend. What was I saying? Why is she my best friend? What is friendship, anyway? Who am I? Who is she? How is what I am writing of conceptual value?

The book-writing phase

Just as writing in a daybook is different than drafting a book, drafting a book is different than producing the final manuscript. I edit and re-edit; I take out; I put in; I take back out. I awaken The Censor, my internal critic.

One of the jobs of The Censor is to read every word as a literary and ethical critic. I attend to the sound of words strung out, one after the other, sentence by sentence. And I attend to paragraphing, tone, dialogue and the like. I do this not only for literary reasons but because literary devices carry ideas—theories, concepts, questions—much as the harmonies and dissonances of music and visual art evoke thoughts not evidenced by the sound of the oboe or the thickness of the paint stroke.

The Censor also considers ethical questions. In general, I want my writing to "do good" and do as little harm as possible, knowing, nevertheless, that the author cannot control others' responses to the text. The "do good" imperative was fulfilled rather easily with the "My Dinner with Esqy" piece, for although it was critical of the rich and powerful, they are rich and powerful, after all, and so whatever little I do to nudge at their coats is little compared to their ability to make others coatless. So, taking them on through description and irony is "doing good," in my book. And, although the stratification theory is subtexted in a light mannered way it divulges "ruling class" behaviors, therefore tying theory to ethical practice. Further, the tone I use toward the "ruling class" is the same ironic one I use toward myself and my husband when we're being "uppity." This is a writing choice—I want to stress—that sees literary decisions as ethical ones, and in this case one that speaks harshly, without using any harsh language, about arrogance and privilege.

This same relationship between theory, ethics and practical action, I felt, should pervade *Last Writes*. My vision of the value of sociological understanding requires this. So, during one of the editing stages, for example, I inserted more descriptive materials about the nature of our health care system, the aging, infirm, smoking diseases, dying. In one of those inserts, I went on a rant borrowing theoretical ideas from a paper I had published some years earlier (2001). I poked fun at myself, but not at the message: the older and the sicker, the more the cost and the greater the bureaucracy. I hasten to add, I did not know at the outset of the writing that I would be thinking at times in these standard propositional statements. How I resolved the specific ethical questions of writing a book about a friend's life and death, I leave to the reader of *Last Writes*.

What holds *Last Writes* together—and I hope keeps the reader reading—is its narrative arc: How do these two friends, who have shared so much in their early years, end up on such different paths 35 years later? How do they each work to sustain the friendship, despite their changing circumstances? What social processes—identification, female socialization, affective ties—function to reshape this friendship? How does the impending death of one change the other's relationship to death, especially her own future one?

I tell stories, describe interactions, and engage literary techniques to propel the narrative. We began our friendship similar to each other, and I use that similarity to ground the book through the literary device of *doubling*—from the concrete *double strand* of pearls to repetitious playful language, such as "lugging luggage," "Ernest earnestly," and "Shearer's sheer beauty." How are Betty and I like each other? How are we different? This technique is more than a mere device, though; it came from an unconscious (until seen) and deeply intuitive truth about our relationship. How come we stayed friends? How could we not! Then, as our later lives unfold, I am traveling about the world and she lies dying. *Two paths*. Betty becomes her *own shadow*, and "my shadow, double, sister."

The grand(er) theory phase

Writing for me is always a place for discovering that which I did not know; if I already know it, I have to force myself to write about it. As I age, I am less willing to force myself to do anything—but I also almost always fulfill commitments I have made. So, when the time came to fulfill the commitment to write this piece, I procrastinated because I thought I'd have nothing new to say (to myself). But I was wrong.

My *twin desires* to bring literary and sociological domains together have moved up a notch. Nowhere in sociological theory is there a "theory of doubling"—yet that was my experience of my friendship, and I would guess the experience of many others in their friendships as well as their personal and professional unions. I would not have thought about this without deploying literary analysis. "Doubling" is a common literary device from Poe to Plath, who wrote her honors thesis on it. Further, the devolution of the "double" into the "shadow," again a literary motif, does not exist in sociology. Yet, it might well explain how care-takers of the dying experience their changed relationship to their loved one, as well as one's sense of oneself as age tolls.

Doubling and shadow.

Maybe, just maybe, a Unified Theory of Sociology and Literature might be in the offing. Let me next write about that.

References

Bochner, A. (forthcoming) *Researchers as Storytellers: the narrative turn in the human sciences*, Walnut Grove, CA: Left Coast Press.

Bochner, A. and Ellis, C. (eds.) (2002) *Ethnographically Speaking: autoethnography, literature and aesthetics*, Walnut Creek, CA: AltaMira.

Capote, T. (1966) *In Cold Blood*, New York: Vintage.

Denzin, N. K. and Lincoln, Y. (eds.) (2005) *Handbook of Qualitative Research*, 3rd ed., Thousand Oaks, CA: Sage.

Ellis, C. (2004) *The Autoethnographic I: a methodological novel about autoethnography*, Walnut Creek, CA: AltaMira.

Ellis, C. and Bochner, A. (eds.) (1996) *Composing Ethnography: alternative forms of qualitative writing*, Walnut Creek, CA: AltaMira.

Mills, C. W. (1959) *The Sociological Imagination*, New York: Oxford University Press.

Richardson, L. (1990) *Writing Strategies: reaching diverse audiences*, Thousand Oaks, CA: Sage Qualitative Methodology Series.

——(1997a) *Fields of Play: constructing an academic life*, New Brunswick, NJ: Rutgers University Press.

——(1997b) "Narrative Knowing and Sociological Telling," in L. Richardson, *Fields of Play: constructing an academic life*, New Brunswick, NJ: Rutgers University Press.

——(2000) "Writing: a method of inquiry" in N. K. Denzin and Lincoln, Y. (eds.) *Handbook of Qualitative Research*, 2nd ed., Thousand Oaks, CA: Sage.

——(2001) "The Metaphor is the Message: commentary on Arthur Frank's 'illness and the interactionist vocation'," *Symbolic Interaction*, 23: 333–36.

——(2007) *Last Writes: a daybook for a dying friend*, Walnut Creek, CA: Left Coast Press.

——(2008) "My Dinner with Lord Esqy," *Qualitative Inquiry*, 14: 13–17.

Richardson, L. and Lockridge, E. (2004) *Travels with Ernest: crossing the literary/sociological divide*, New York: AltaMira.

21

CONCEPTUALIZING A PROFESSION IN PROCESS

The New Pediatrics revisited

Dorothy Pawluch

Beginnings

While there are probably many sociologists who end up producing studies quite different from those they envisioned when they started, mine is more a story about stubbornly resisting the kind of study I eventually produced. *The New Pediatrics: A Profession in Transition* was published in 1996. The book, an extension of my Ph.D. dissertation, presented an account of the emergence and development of pediatrics as a primary care specialty in North America. Based mostly on a review of documentary materials, especially pediatricians' own professional literature, I tracked the struggle of the first pediatricians to get children recognized as more than "miniature adults," to get children's health problems recognized as deserving of special attention, and to get those who studied and treated children recognized as legitimate specialists. I followed the development of pediatrics as it evolved into a primary care specialty—a point of first contact for children with health problems—and through a series of crises the specialty experienced during the 1960s and 1970s that led pediatricians eventually to expand their scope of practice to include not only children's physical health, but their behavioral and social problems as well. The expansion changed the practice of pediatrics, but it also changed how children's behavioral and social problems were viewed, framing them as medical issues.

Clearly, in terms of its analytical focus, the *New Pediatrics* was a study about a profession and processes of professional transformation. That is not, however, how the study began. In fact, in the initial conceptual stages of the research I deliberately tried to avoid a study of professions. I had just completed a master's thesis on a profession—chiropractors in Quebec and their quest during the 1970s for legislative recognition and legitimacy. Forcing myself perhaps a bit too soon after the fraught completion of my M.A. to

318

make a decision about the topic of my dissertation, I resolved to do anything but another study on professions. I could say the decision was driven by a high-minded desire to expand my sociological horizons and explore bodies of theoretical literature beyond the literature on professions. I may actually have uttered something to this effect on occasion as a justification for my change in direction. In truth, it was more a matter of feeling burned out and quite sick at that point of the professions literature. Sitting with Malcolm Spector, my advisor, for a "what next" kind of discussion, I can recall saying: "Nothing to do with chiropractors or professions!" I expected an argument about the wisdom of building on what I had already done. Instead, Malcolm simply said: "OK, not chiropractors or professions. So what do you think you would find interesting?"

I thought back over the courses I had taken and the readings I had done over the course of my graduate training—in medical sociology, deviance and social problems, and symbolic interactionism, labeling theory and the social constructionist perspective. The ideas in much of that work seemed to converge in exciting ways, it struck me, in the case studies that were emerging during the late 1970s and 1980s on medicalization. Sociologists working in a diverse range of areas were writing about the extent to which so many aspects of life, including behaviors and social conditions defined as deviant, objectionable or problematic, were seen as medical concerns. Many of these case studies were published in *Social Problems*. Malcolm served as editor of *Social Problems* between 1979 and 1984, and through those years generously allowed me to help out with the journal. The experience gave me the opportunity to read many of the manuscripts that came in. The growing interest in medicalization was clear.

That experience coincided with the publication in 1980 of Peter Conrad and Joseph Schneider's book *Deviance and Medicalization: From Badness to Sickness*. The book offered a collection of studies that Conrad and Schneider had conducted, some together, others individually, on the medicalization of such conditions as alcoholism, mental illness, hyperkinesis and opiate addiction. The book also presented a general framework for studying processes of medicalization. Influenced, as Conrad and Schneider themselves were, by Spector and Kitsuse's writing on social constructionism, I imagined processes of medicalization to be essentially about claims-makers framing their claims about putative conditions in medical terms. I thought it would be useful to look at the process more explicitly in these terms.

Searching for a case to examine, I was inspired by a series of papers on medicalization that I found particularly fascinating, all of them involving children. The earliest of these studies, one that has since become a classic in the medicalization literature, was Peter Conrad's account (1975; 1976) of how the hyperkinesis (hyperactivity) label was created and then promoted as a way of understanding children's misbehaviors and poor school performance. Another study that had stayed with me was Stephen Pfohl's (1977) "The

'Discovery' of Child Abuse," which shows how through the claims-making efforts of pediatric radiologists, the neglect and maltreatment of children came to be understood as a manifestation of "child abuse syndrome." A paper I worked on during my stint as editorial assistant for *Social Problems* was Johnson and Hufbauer's (1982) analysis of how a group of parents agitated to get babies dying inexplicably in their sleep researched in a way that led ultimately to the construction of the "sudden infant death syndrome" label.

Each of these papers made passing reference to the medical profession and in some cases more explicitly suggested that pediatricians were implicated in these new medical understandings of old problems, but there was not much clarity in the literature on how pediatricians were involved. I wondered what role pediatricians were playing in the medicalization of so many childhood issues. If not the primary claims-makers themselves, I assumed that pediatricians at least endorsed these new understandings. As the medical specialty most closely connected to children, was the medicalization of any condition related to childhood even possible without pediatric endorsement and if so, what did that say about processes of medicalization and the role of the medical profession in these processes? I decided I would look more closely at where pediatricians fit into the picture. While I was studying pediatricians, I did not think of my project at that stage as a study in professions. Rather, since my questions were framed in terms of debates in the literature on social constructionism and medicalization, I envisioned a project that would contribute more centrally to a better understanding of the medicalization of childhood.

I was persuaded that the questions I would be asking had the potential to make both substantive and theoretical contributions. Above all, though, I found them intrinsically interesting. When Malcolm asked if I could see myself living with the topic I had chosen for the years that it would likely take me to finish the dissertation—warning me that there would be days where my interest in the subject and that alone would carry me forward—I did not hesitate to say yes. I sometimes hear colleagues, and especially graduate students, thinking more strategically these days about "hot" areas of sociology with which to connect themselves, wondering what potential employers and other audiences would find engaging or relevant and ruminating about what kinds of intellectual alignments would be most career-enhancing. Such considerations have probably always figured in some way in the decisions that sociologists make about what to study and how to study it. Or possibly the field and the world have changed in ways that make it sensible to take a pragmatic approach to the selection of topics and approaches. However, if I might be permitted a caution it would be this: Doing ethnography, like old age, is not for sissies. The task can be challenging enough without pushing oneself to study something that one does not find personally engaging or an approach that does not resonate on some level. There is wisdom in the advice that seasoned researchers often give—"study something that grabs you." If it grabs you powerfully enough, you will figure out how to make it interesting, relevant and engaging to others.

Rethinking ethnography

Having settled on a topic, my first steps were predictable enough—to familiarize myself to at least a minimal degree with the specialty and to do some basic library work before venturing out into the field. That I ended up venturing not much beyond the library had to do in part with my location. As home of one of the oldest medical schools in North America, McGill University houses not only a well stocked medical library, but also the Osler Library of the History of Medicine, named after Sir William Osler who taught in McGill's Faculty of Medicine for a time. The McGill collection includes a rich assortment of journals, monographs, textbooks, training manuals, conference proceedings, organizational policy statements and the like. Many of the documents go back well into the 1800s, with layers of dust betraying not only their age but also how infrequently some of them are consulted.

The wealth of material I found in the library presented me with my first dilemma. Trained in interpretive perspectives and qualitative methods, I expected that my study would be done largely on the basis of intensive interviews with pediatricians both in positions of leadership as well as those working on the clinical front. I also assumed there would be some participant observation to give me an idea of how the medicalization of childhood deviance looked on the ground. As the weeks I expected I would be spending in the library turned into months I grew nervous about the delay in "getting out into the field." I began to get in touch with pediatricians. Several agreed to be interviewed; others allowed me to hang around their offices and clinics. I spent time in the two local children's hospitals and their various clinics. I also finagled an invitation to the regular meetings of a group of pediatricians, epidemiologists and social scientists interested in children's problems.

However, through these months I was continually drawn back to the library. As informative as I found my conversations with pediatricians and observations of their workplaces and interactions with patients, I found more compelling and revealing evidence of the issues preoccupying pediatricians' time in the pediatric literature. I was fascinated by the endless stream of journal articles, discussions and debates in their literature about school difficulties, attention deficits, eating and sleeping problems, over-dependent relationships with parents, oppositional behaviors and myriad concerns related to adolescents, an age-group in which pediatricians were clearly developing an interest. More through the pediatric literature than through my interviews and observations, I became aware of the fact that pediatricians themselves recognized that these concerns represented a shift in their traditional scope of practice. In fact, the pediatric literature often made reference to "the new pediatrics" or "the new morbidity" in pediatrics.

A particularly exciting discovery I made in the literature that had not come up at all in my interviews and observations was the controversy that existed among pediatricians over the new directions the specialty was taking. While some pediatricians were enthusiastic about moving into new areas of care and assuming responsibility for the psychological, social and even spiritual well-being of children and young adults, others felt the specialty was treading in areas where it did not belong and where pediatricians, as physicians, had no expertise. Pediatricians were clearly not of one view when it came to their role in children's lives.

I had a system for highlighting observations or finds I thought were going to be significant. The system, crude but effective, involved a series of margin notations (mostly stars and exclamation points) in the handwritten notes I made on each document I read. Where I was able to articulate why I thought the observation was significant or how it fit into the account I saw emerging, the notation would be accompanied by a conceptual note that I would attach to the summary. In writing these conceptual notes I would try to "translate" the substance of what I had found into more analytical language. I have not kept these notes, but I have a vague memory of a red, rather than my usual blue, pen being involved in this particular find. The note was probably attached to a letter that a pediatrician had written in to *Pediatrics*, the official journal of the American Academy of Pediatrics, complaining about the valuable journal space devoted in a previous issue to a discussion of some subject (sibling rivalry or possibly the teaching of religion or moral values in schools perhaps) about which the letter writer did not think pediatricians ought to be concerned. The conceptual note would probably have included a more preliminary version of how I eventually wrote about the conflicting views on the proper boundaries of pediatric care.

As the process of reading through documents continued, I became more engrossed in what I was finding. At first tentatively, and then with growing conviction I began to feel that I would find the story behind pediatricians' involvement with the medicalization of childhood in these documents. There was no "eureka moment," only a growing sense that "the field," as it were, lay in the pages of the materials I was reading. Questions arose then and have arisen since about whether a study based on documents rather than on intensive and in-depth interviewing of social actors or a more or less total immersion in their social worlds can be described as true ethnography. On this question I can only say that although I worked mostly in solitude in far flung corners of the library where I would go for hours without sighting a soul and where I would often be reading about events long past, after a certain point there was no doubt in my mind that I was doing an ethnography. Writing about the value of documentary materials in the generation of grounded theory, Barney Glaser and Anselm Strauss (1967) capture better than I could the experience of working with such materials. They write:

When someone stands in the library stacks, he is, metaphorically, surrounded by voices begging to be heard. Every book, every magazine article, represents at least one person who is equivalent to the anthropologist's informant, or the sociologist's interviewee. In those publications, people converse, announce positions, argue with a range of eloquence, and describe events or scenes in ways entirely comparable to what is seen and heard during field work. The researcher needs only to discover the *voices in the library* to release them for his analytical use.

(1967: 163, emphasis added)

The longer I listened to *the voices in the library*, the more intimately familiar I became with the communities of pediatricians I was studying, generations of them. The richness and range of materials I found, including photographs, biographies, autobiographies, festschrifts, tributes, letters to the editor, opinion pieces, commentaries and presidential addresses, allowed me to acquaint myself with pediatricians of different eras, on different sides of assorted issues and in different positions within the specialty—some academicians, some editors of journals or executives in their professional associations, some working in hospitals, some in private practices. They spoke in such remarkably detailed and personal ways about their careers, work experiences and specialty, I felt I knew them. I often wondered whether my experience working with these documents resembled what it must have been like for W. I. Thomas and Florian Znaniecki (1918–20) going through the letters, diaries and life histories of Polish immigrants to produce their classic five-volume ethnography *The Polish Peasant in Europe and America*. When *The New Pediatrics* was eventually published and Malcolm graciously offered to write a foreword, what flattered me most were his comments about the study's ethnographic qualities. At the risk of appearing immodest, I will quote him directly:

> Professor Pawluch recalls the finest period of the "old" University of Chicago tradition of Hughes, Blumer, Becker and Strauss, in which the researcher plunged into a social world, learned its language and history, its secrets, its hopes and fears, and then produced an ethnographic and interpretive account that made contributions to a whole range of specialties within sociology.

Lost in data

One of the more unfortunate ways in which producing an ethnography based on documents can be analogous to producing one on the basis of interviews and interactions with social actors, is in the volume of data generated and the possibilities of getting lost in the data. The next and longest phase of the study I recall as one where the data appeared to take over and where my sense, looking back, was that I did not have total control over where things were going. Novelists often describe how characters in the books they are writing seem to take on lives of their own, steering the course of the narrative in unanticipated directions. Though not a writer of novels I can understand how this happens. In debating whether the specialty should be redefining its mission to incorporate the treatment of children's behavioral and social problems, references were often made by those on both sides of the debate to "solving the specialty's problems." What problems? To answer that question I was led back to developments during the 1950s and 1960s, namely the state of disaffection among so many pediatricians bored with looking after essentially healthy children; the perceived need for new professional challenges; the competition that pediatricians faced from newly emerging groups (like family practitioners and pediatric nurse practitioners) ready to take over tasks pediatricians were not sure they wanted to perform; and pediatricians' desire to find a unique niche in child health care. But what accounted for these developments? Every answer generated a new list of questions, pulling me further and further back into the specialty's history to the point where I found myself researching the earliest efforts of a small group of doctors in the late 1800s with a particular interest in children to figure out how to get their colleagues to see them as different and what to call themselves. (They rejected their first choice—pediatrists—because it was too easy to confuse with podiatrists, doctors of the foot.)

Without understanding quite how I had ended up in such a bind, I found myself with a massive amount of detailed information about pediatrics and pediatricians dating back into the late 1800s, only a small proportion of which seemed to relate in any obvious way to the medicalization of childhood deviance I had wanted to explore. Prioritizing the theoretical questions and re-focusing on the most recent years in the development of pediatrics—those years after the 1950s during which the new pediatrics had started to emerge—was one option I considered. I thought I had sufficient data to take this route and if not, I could get more.

However, I was loath to set aside the thousands of pages of notes on the earlier years in the specialty's history. It had taken entirely too long for me, a non-historian, to gather and learn how to sort out all that history. More than this, I was persuaded that there were sociological insights to be gleaned from the history. But what insights? I struggled for much longer than I care to admit with the problem of what to do with my data, how to present it as more than a straight history and especially how to connect it all, not simply the most recent decades, to the medicalization literature I still hoped I could use as a theoretical frame for the study. In wedding myself too rigidly to that frame, I could not see the obvious. I ignored that most basic of lessons— listen to the data.

Moving forward

In situations where our own imaginations fail us or where we may not have the necessary openness and/or distance to see for ourselves what our data is insistently trying to tell us, mentors, teachers and colleagues can be god-sends. One day, after a brief presentation I made on my work-in-progress, Joan Stelling, a member of my supervisory committee commented tentatively as we walked along: "Very interesting. But you know, I'm not so much hearing a story about medicalization as I am a story about the ups and downs of a profession." I do not recall whether I stopped dead in my tracks, literally, but the impact of Joan's observation was immediate and dramatic. I had my hook.

I went back to the professions literature, a literature I knew relatively well but had not thought to relate to what I was currently doing. I pulled out Rue Bucher and Anselm Strauss' (1961) paper on "Professions in Process," a paper that had proven useful in my study of chiropractors. Bucher and Strauss took issue with the structural view of professions that prevailed at the time as relatively stable, homogeneous and cohesive groups with objective qualities that set them apart from other occupations. They proposed instead a processual or emergent view of loose clusters of occupational segments constantly in a state of flux, forming, developing, modifying themselves, and sometimes disappearing. They suggested that it would be useful for sociologists to treat the movement of these segments, some of which might have won for themselves the privilege of being called professions, as analogous to social movements—collective attempts to promote, maintain or resist changes affecting the segment and its work. Viewed through a *professions in process* lens, more of the data on pediatrics began to make sociological sense. More than a background history of pediatrics, I had a story of a professional segment from its inchoate beginnings through its various permutations to the group as it currently defined itself.

After my analysis took a professions turn, Joan provided me with another paper that Bucher (1980) had written, a paper that Bucher was not able to publish before she died, but which was published posthumously (Bucher 1988) by the time I completed my study. The paper, following up on the idea of professions as social movements, laid out a natural history model with three stages to it—emergence, consolidation, and transformation. In relation to my data, I began to think about how and why professional segments move through these stages. What did my data show about the contexts under which professional segments emerge, consolidate, and then transform themselves? What did it have to say about how they negotiate their passage through these stages?

Another key conceptual turning point occurred when I realized that in incorporating a "professions in process" frame I did not have to abandon the questions I had started out with about medical and social problems claims-making. On the contrary, the two sets of questions were complementary and could be integrated in ways that would enrich the analysis. It was yet another Bucher paper (1962) that prompted me to consider the points of connection and possibilities for integration. In a paper the purpose of which was largely to demonstrate the value of a professions in process approach, Bucher applied the approach to an analysis of pathology. While the particulars as they relate to pathology are not important, Bucher introduced in that paper the notion of a threatened segment, hypothesizing that any segment facing extinction as the result of the development of new technologies, changing relationships with other segments, or other changes in its context of work, must find a revitalization formula if it is to survive. I began to think of the new pediatrics and pediatricians' involvement in the medicalization of children's lives as a revitalization formula, a strategy that pediatricians had adopted—though not without controversy—as a way of salvaging a role for themselves in primary child health care at a time where their relevance in that area was being questioned.

Carrying that thought, I began to appreciate that pediatricians had always engaged in social problems claims-making and that this claims-making had always been inextricably linked to the specialty's development. I went back through my data and notes, looking at the various forms that this claims-making took and at how precisely it connected to the debates, dilemmas, crises, and challenges the specialty faced. It struck me as nothing short of remarkable how easily the dots connected and the pieces fell into place. Just as remarkable—and I often share this with students who appear to be close to a state of despair, wondering whether they will ever be able to see order in the chaos of their data—was the abruptness of the transition from feeling that I was mired in data I did not know how to handle to finding myself with a clear story to tell.

The professions in process framework, as it happened, also suggested an obvious sequence for the story. Arguing that in order to understand current developments in pediatrics, it was important to have a more general sense of the specialty and to understand how decisions about its course made in the past contributed to the issues it has been facing more recently, I followed a chronological line. Starting at the beginning I explained how pediatrics had first emerged as a specialty on the strength of the successful claims made about the terrible toll that infectious diseases were taking on children's lives and the need for a medical specialty devoted to studying and treating children. I went on to describe how pediatric involvement in the claims-making campaigns of the 1920s and 1930s, championing the benefits of well-baby care, allowed the specialty to continue to thrive after the threat of infectious childhood diseases largely disappeared.

Similar processes playing themselves out in other occupational segments, I pointed out, created new crises for pediatricians, crises that forced them to again re-assess their purpose. General practitioners, who at one time seemed doomed to disappear, found their revitalization formula in making claims about the value of their traditional mission, resurrecting themselves as family practitioners and insisting that they were in a better position than pediatricians to monitor the growth and development of basically healthy children. Pediatric nurse practitioners, on a quest for greater status linked to nursing's troubled occupational history, also had ambitions to take over the provision of primary health care to children. Pediatric sub-specialists (cardiologists, neurologists, nephrologists, neonatologists, etc.), themselves emerging occupational segments intent on clarifying the boundaries of their terrain, had shut general pediatricians out of curative pediatrics. While I had to restrict myself to analyzing all of these developments only insofar as they affected pediatricians, it was all I could do to resist the temptation to do side studies on each of these groups whose histories, it seemed to me, could also be mined for theoretical insights into occupational adaptive strategies.

The final part of the analysis focused on the new pediatrics as a revitalization formula. I looked at pediatricians' efforts to implement the new pediatrics, changing training programs and producing research to guide pediatricians in their treatment of the developmental and behavioral problems of children. I pointed as well to a number of factors that raised questions about whether the new pediatrics would indeed secure the future existence of primary care pediatrics, including continuing dissent with pediatric ranks and the persistence of competition from other groups of child health care providers. I ended by suggesting that more change might yet be in store for the specialty.

Over the past year I have had occasion to go back into the pediatric literature to see where things stand (Pawluch 2008). The talk now is not of *new* morbidity but *millennial* morbidity. Millennial morbidity takes in such threats as violence, obesity, family distress, environmental degradation, and poverty. According to some pediatricians (Palfry et al. 2005), the millennial morbidity calls on pediatricians to achieve the optimal physical, mental and social health and well-being for children by changing the social and physical environments in which children live rather than simply delivering traditional health care services. To the extent that pediatricians heed the call, they will become involved in even more obvious ways in social problems work, making pediatrics a specialty from which we can continue to learn about how professionalizing processes overlap with social problems processes.

Ontological gerrymandering

It is perhaps worth reflecting finally on something that could have, but did not, throw me off track. In the middle of my study of pediatricians I wrote, with Steve Woolgar (Woolgar and Pawluch 1985), a paper about how social constructionist arguments work. That paper discussed the selective relativism that characterizes constructionist analyses where definitional histories and the socially contingent understanding of assorted phenomena are explained without drawing attention to the socially contingent nature of the "phenomena" themselves. Put differently, while how we view things is a matter of definition, "things" themselves are constituted by our definitions of them. In arguing, for example, that childhood deviance has been variously defined by social actors as either willful misbehavior or symptomatic of an underlying medical disorder, attention is drawn away from the fact that what constitutes childhood deviance or even childhood for that matter is itself a question of definition.

Read as a call for a more consistent relativism or a caution to avoid any objectivist assumptions about the nature of reality, the ontological gerrymandering critique could have paralyzed me in connection with my study of pediatrics. After all, the entire study rested on the idea of a distinct (objective) group redefining itself in response to changes in its (objective) situation. I did emphasize a fluid view of professions (as professions in process) and tried to underline that the changes pediatricians were responding to were changes *they* defined and understood through the prism of their professional experiences and interests. But there were certainly places where my account hinged on readers accepting certain "facts" about what was "really" going on. Joseph Gusfield (1985), in a commentary on the critique, was right in his observation that, taken as a call for theoretical purity—the unattainable "Holy Grail" of sociologists, the "hobgoblin of the theoretical mind"—the ontological gerrymandering critique undermines the very possibility of explanation in sociology. To explain is to assume that there is something to be explained.

From the start, however, I understood the ontological gerrymandering critique in terms of two alternative readings we offered in our paper. We suggested that the critique could be viewed as a description of how definitional accounts are put together and could, in fact, be used as a kind of recipe for producing such accounts. We stressed as well that, rather than treating constructionists' selective relativism as a problem or as slippages into objectivism, the explanatory strategies used by constructionists could be viewed instead as artful accomplishments. How is it that an analysis based on the fundamental premise that all meanings are socially constructed can focus on the meaning-making of the social actors being studied while successfully bracketing its own meaning-making and indeed, its very status as a meaning-making exercise? We suggested more thinking about how theoretical inconsistencies are negotiated in the course of explanation.

My involvement in formulating the ontological gerrymandering critique, then, an exercise which could have gotten in the way of my empirical study of pediatricians or even rendered it undoable, instead made me more reflexive about the conceptual argument I was pulling together. There was a moment of musing out loud before the book was published about how to handle whatever expectations there might be with respect to the kind of analysis an author of the ontological gerrymandering critique would produce. Malcolm's advice was to tackle the issue head-on and to write about how I saw my study of pediatricians in relation to the ontological gerry-mandering critique. This I did in the book's appendix, ending with the comment that while the theoretical debate over social constructionism, its assumptions and implications continues, constructionists routinely use the perspective to research a broad range of issues and empirical questions. I offered the book as a demonstration of how ontological questions that are in principle irresolvable, are somehow managed by constructionists as they (we) get on with the task at hand—trying to understand some slice of social life.

Concluding thoughts

George Herbert Mead (1932: 95) wrote that "we speak of the past as final and irrevocable," adding: "There is nothing that is less so." Our memories of the past are built in the present. The contours of those memories change. It is also no doubt true that in constructing those memories we introduce an order and coherence to events that we may not have experienced as we lived through them. The chronologies we recall are relatively smooth and, in hindsight, the paths we have followed appear almost fated. Though I have made an effort in these reflections to be forthright about my experience writing *The New Pediatrics* and to recall some of the false starts, forks in the road, dilemmas, hesitations, detours and moments of simply feeling totally lost—and there were certainly enough of those—I am not sure that my account captures the true messiness of the process of making one's analytical way through a study while one is in the midst of it. While there may be a variety of useful strategies for getting there, strategies that this collection probably captures, the only real course is to persist and to work through the messiness, confident that a story worth telling will emerge in the end.

References

Bucher, R. (1962) "Pathology: a study of social movements in a profession," *Social Problems*, 10: 40–51.

——(1980) "On the Natural History of Occupations," paper presented at the Health Care Issues of the Eighties Conference, University of Illinois, Chicago.

——(1988) "On the Natural History of Health Care Occupations," *Work and Occupations*, 15: 131–47.

Bucher, R. and Strauss, A. L. (1961) "Professions in Process," *American Journal of Sociology*, 66: 325–34.

Conrad, P. (1975) "The Discovery of Hyperkinesis: notes on the medicalization of deviant behavior," *Social Problems*, 23: 12–21.

——(1976) *Identifying Hyperactive Children: the medicalization of deviant behavior*, Lexington, MA: D. C. Heath.

Conrad, P. and Schneider, J. W. (1980) *Deviance and Medicalization: from badness to sickness*, St. Louis, MO: C. V. Mosby.

Glaser, B. and Strauss, A. (1967) *The Discovery of Grounded Theory: strategies for qualitative research*, Chicago: Aldine.

Gusfield, J. (1985) "Theories and Hobgoblins," *Society for the Study of Social Problems Newsletter*, 17: 16–18.

Johnson, M. P. and Hufbauer, K. (1982) "Sudden Infant Death Syndrome as a Medical and Research Problem Since 1945," *Social Problems*, 30: 65–81.

Mead, G. H. (1932) *The Philosophy of the Present*, LaSalle, IL: Open Court.

Palfry, J., Tonniges, T. F., Green, G., and Richmond, J. (2005) "Addressing the Millennial Morbidity: the context of community pediatrics," *Pediatrics* 115: 1121–23.

Pawluch, D. (1996) *The New Pediatrics: a profession in transition*, Hawthorne, NY: Aldine de Gruyter.

——(2008) "Millennial Morbidity in Pediatrics: professions and social problems work," paper presented at the International Sociological Association Research committee on the Sociology of Health and the Canadian Medical Sociology Association Inaugural Meeting, Montreal, Canada.

Pfohl, S. (1977) "The 'Discovery' of Child Abuse," *Social Problems*, 24: 310–24.

Thomas, W. I. and Znaniecki, F. (1918–20) *The Polish Peasant in Europe and America*, Boston, MA: Gorham Press.

Woolgar, S. and Pawluch, D. (1985) "Ontological Gerrymandering: the anatomy of social problems explanations," *Social Problems*, 32: 214–27.

22

THE HISTORY, MYTH, AND SCIENCE OF MASADA

The making of an historical ethnography

Nachman Ben-Yehuda

Introduction

One Friday I was reading, with increased interest, an intriguing paper by David Rapoport (1984) in which he compared three groups of assassins: the Thugs in India, the Islamic Assassins and the Jewish Zealots-Sicarii. The Sicarii was a group of Jews which flourished during the time of the Jewish "Great Revolt" against the Romans (66–73 A.D.). They advocated the use of assassinations and terror, and put these tactics into practice. It is probably the only known Jewish group up until 1940, which had such an explicit ideological commitment, resulting in a corresponding practice. It does not take much to consider the Sicarii a "bunch of assassins."

One can imagine my amazement, indeed indignation, at reading Rapoport's statement that this "bunch of assassins" perished on top of Masada. I still vividly remember reading this and skeptically thinking: "here is another American who wants to tell me, the Israeli, what happened on Masada." After all, I "knew" what happened on Masada. I learned it in school, in the army— I climbed to the top of Masada. I knew that there was a group of Jewish freedom fighters who fled Jerusalem, after its destruction by the Roman Imperial Army in 70 A.D., to Masada. There, they—the few—staged a last-stand battle against the mighty Roman army. When the Romans were about to conquer the fortress, all these heroic Jewish freedom fighters chose to commit collective suicide rather than surrender to Rome and become slaves or die in some strange and painful ways (e.g. in the arena). However, to think that these Jewish freedom fighters were in fact a group of detested assassins? "Ah," I thought, "this is a bunch of bull." However, trained as a social scientist, I became very curious as to how Rapoport could possibly have made such an obvious mistake? Checking his references, I realized that his major source was Josephus Flavius, who is considered the main historical source concerning the period.

It being a Friday, a very short workday in Israel, made me hurry and rush into the library just before it was to close for the weekend. I managed to grab from the shelves the English and Hebrew versions of Josephus Flavius. I was quite sure that reading them would help me to find out how and why Rapoport made such a mistake. I returned to my office already formulating in my head the letter I would have to write Rapoport, protesting his mistake. As Hebrew University was shutting down at around noon (Friday, Friday ...) I went home with the two books and spent that weekend frantically reading the relevant parts from Josephus. To make a long story and a painful weekend short, let me state that on Saturday night I knew that Rapoport was right and I was wrong.

Emotionally, this was not an easy conclusion to reach. To put it mildly, I felt cheated and manipulated. I tried to reconstruct in my own mind how—during my formative years, going through the Israeli socialization process—I acquired "knowledge" about Masada that was not only wrong, but also very biased. Moreover, mind you, Masada is not just an innocent story. Masada provided, certainly for my generation of Jewish Israelis, a major and important ingredient in the very definition of our Jewish and Israeli identity. Now, what was I supposed to do when it turned out that such a major element of my identity was based on falsehood, on a deviant belief?

The professional angle

Once the anger and resentment of having been manipulated subsided, I decided to research the Masada mythical narrative. This inquiry most certainly had a strong personal element in it, but it also had a very strong professional element. Studying the Masada mythical narrative could easily give us a clue as to how a myth (which could be conceptualized as a deviant belief system) is created; why it is created; by who; under what circumstances; how it is diffused into the population; how the suspension of natural disbelief in such a fantastic story is created; how it is maintained; etc. In addition, studying the Masada myth could give us a clue as to how other mythologies work in other cultures. My own personal reaction really puzzled me. Why was I so angry? As I would witness in later interviews, this type of anger could be observed again and again when I confronted fellow Israelis with the historical, that is Josephus', Masada narrative. This anger has an important pedagogic and educational lesson hidden in it. The emotional angry response indicates that some raw and very sensitive nerve is stimulated by the confrontation of Jewish Israelis with the conflict between the Masada mythical narrative and the original, historical narrative. That nerve touches a major ingredient of the Jewish Israeli identity and world view. This anger indicates just how important the mythical view is and how disturbing the original narrative is. The emotion of anger, therefore, provides a good indication of a strong socialization-generational effect about an emotional attitude toward a symbol. Thus, this particular emotion was not only used as a propelling motivation, but as an important indicator for social relations.

Studying the Masada myth was a natural extension of my professional interests. This study fitted well in my interest of studying unconventional behavior in the context of cultural change and stability (Ben-Yehuda 2006). Moreover, as my professional interests crystallized, I found myself being drawn more and more to—and involved in—natural histories and much more so in the theoretical perspective of constructionism. There are a few reasons for that. While I found the Marxist conflict approach appealing and persuasive, I found the contextualization of that conflict in a deterministic historical process unpersuasive. Manheim's point about ideology and its influence was influential, but I was unpersuaded by his idea of relationism. Yet, I was concerned, as he was, by the issue of relativism. Foucault's idea that knowledge is based on the rhetorical devices used in interactions was almost the last punch in these deliberations. When construction theory began to surface powerfully and strongly, I realized that it offers an excellent solution to the problem.

There are two variants of the constructionist perspective: strict constructionism, and contextual constructionism. The first variant argues that the expert, or scientific evaluation, of deviance, social problems, as such simply represents one "claim making" activity out of many such activities. This view—very Foucauldian—argues that scientific claims are also socially constructed, as are other claims, and can be studied as such. The second variant argues that while deviance and social problems are the results of "claim making" activities, the so-called "objective" dimension can be assessed and evaluated by an expert, on the basis of agreed upon scientific evidence. Sociologists working from this theoretical perspective typically tend to contrast the "objective" and the "constructed" versions of reality. Contextual constructionism focuses on the nature of reality as it is agreed upon by experts. It outlines the defining parameters of reality at a particular point and hence provides the researcher with a powerful analytical docking anchor. In fact, contextual constructionism allows using positivistic elements (if one so wishes) but emphasizes that accepted knowledge is the result of a temporary consensus. "Scientific truth" in this perspective is anchored in contextual interactions among scientists and is not eternal. In fact, this observation is valid for any social construction of reality. Furthermore, this perspective resonates very well with important developments in the sociology of science such as those made by Kuhn, and the social construction of scientific knowledge. A consensus among relevant scientists is a direct result of interactions among them that, by definition, will involve ideology, power, interests, conflicts, agreements, and the like (e.g. see Latour and Woolgar 1979). All in all, when I became acquainted with contextual constructionism, I realized that this is the way to go, for me. In addition, the methodologies allowed and requested by this perspective demand studies that are based on: observing symbolic interactions (e.g. joining tour guides), interviews, examining written texts, listening to electronic media. Such ethnographic components were essential to understanding the significance of the Masada myth and how the history is contested. This historical ethnography thus had one foot in the past and the other in the present.

I found that the development of the Masada mythical narrative is a superb illustration of contextual constructionism. Using this perspective meant that contrasting the two narratives was the focal point. Thus I began a long and fantastic voyage into the past and the present, a study in the "archaeology of knowledge," to use Foucault's terminology, and of an historical ethnography.

This research illustrated for me, again, that the main intellectual, cultural and political debate in Israel is not so much about the country's future or present per se, but rather concerns the interpretation and social construction of what is considered to be its past roots, and the impact of particular constructions on the present and future. During my quest, I also discovered a few fascinating facts. Among them, that voices against turning Masada into a myth were raised, sometimes very loudly, to no avail. Also, I could observe how Masada was turning from a central national ideological myth into, how shall one put it, a tourist attraction which uses the myth for some very down-to-earth economic purposes. Moreover, this transformation of Masada clearly indicates a major and basic change in Israeli society and culture. In the end, studying the Masada myth yielded two books (Ben-Yehuda 1995; 2002), some papers (e.g. 1998) and many talks in academic and public arenas, including the media in and outside of Israel.

Logic of study

This study was planned as a historical ethnography of ideological belief to support Jewish identity, which examined how different groups' and moral and political entrepreneurs attempted to reconstruct history toward their own interests. Because there were so many people and groups involved in different ways in the crystallization of the mythical tale (religious leaders, historians, tour guides, archeologists), the ways in which they constructed Masada, and offered different angles as a result of their own particular interest in the issue, were of utmost importance. Covering these angles demanded a logic of research that—deliberately—drew on a large variety of maximum sources: observations, interviews, and document analysis.

The research project

The research question branched out into two directions. One was establishing the differentiation of (and contrast between) the historical narrative from the mythical narrative. To accomplish this, all that was required was to read carefully Josephus Flavius' first-century A.D. account and contrast it with accounts that were manufactured almost 1,900 years later. Second, once we[1] had established this first-century historical baseline, we could find out how twentieth-century entrepreneurs (e.g. intellectuals, tour guides, youth movements, school textbooks) supported the mythical narratives in different social arenas, and pinpoint how actually far from Josephus' baseline these various modern narratives have gone, when, by whom, and why. Doing this required that we chart all the different relevant aspects of Israeli culture and inspect the Masada narrative in each one of them in an historical perspective. Later on, I became particularly interested in how and why archaeological scientists were willing to support the mythical narrative. Specifically, the major archaeological excavations of Masada took place in the early 1960s. These excavations, headed by the late Professor Yigael Yadin, provided solid support for the mythical narrative. How and why was that done was the main research question discussed in the second book. From the above points of view, my Masada project fully reflected contextual constructionism: theory and methodology.

In addition, and as I became more exposed to emerging issues of collective memory, I contacted Barry Schwartz (see, for example, Schwartz 1991), who is one of the main figures in this area, and visited him. My discussions with him affected me in a profound way and helped, in a later stage, to frame the study within contemporary formulations in collective memory. "Collective memory" has become one of the hottest issues in social sciences. The general meaning of the concept refers to what, how, and why cultures and societies remember, and forget. Collective memory scholarship suggests that there are two basic ways to answer the question of whether there was a "past." One assumes that there was such a past and we need to contrast that past with its present constructions. That is, the assumption is that some events, processes, did indeed take place and the interesting and valid research pattern to follow is to examine how this past is interpreted, molded and presented in the present, and why. The other assumes that there was no "past" and that the "past" is a construction of manipulative and interested agents who create pasts that fit various interests (e.g. political, ideological) of the present. Clearly, formulations in collective memory implicitly include debates and solutions to many of the issues raised originally by Manheim. The first approach—the one which I took—fits almost perfectly with contextual constructionism. But, as Schwartz (1991) suggested, and later on Jeffrey Olick (2005)—whose work also influenced me in a profound way—elaborated, the two need not contradict. Olick makes two important points. One, memory is not a "thing" but an interactive process—much like a conversation or a dialogue in which meaning is not "there" but emerges interactively. This process requires that we examine combined and integrated cross-fields. Two, from a sociology of memory perspective—the relation between real and constructed pasts is not one of restoration or revolution, but rather of reconstruction (2005: 332)—that is, a critical mixing of the old with the new. Using the collective memory analytical contextualization helped put together the issues of how and why ideology intervenes in shaping world views, including scientific archaeology. Historical ethnography can help contextualize historical projects by investigating how present-day ideology helps shape those histories and sciences of the past.

Historical vs. mythical Masada

Put shortly and concisely, in 66 A.D. the Jews in the Roman province Judea revolted against the Roman empire. The Roman imperial army crushed that revolt with an iron fist, and in 70 A.D. destroyed Jerusalem and burnt the second Jewish temple. Masada was the last remnant of that revolt. On top of Masada remained a group of Jewish assassins Josephus refers to as the Sicarii. They fled Jerusalem a long time before the Roman siege on the city, refused to take part in the defense of the city, raided, looted, and murdered hundreds of Jews in nearby Masada (e.g. Ein Gedi). In 73, the Roman army constructed a siege system around Masada and in probably a few weeks of a standard siege campaign, breached the walls of the fortress. Josephus does not report of any battles during the siege, but when the Sicarii realized that the Roman breach was imminent they decided to kill themselves and die free. Only seven of the besieged hid themselves and survived the self-inflicted bloodbath. Josephus' historical narrative is thus of a doomed and failed revolt, of mass killings of Jews by the Romans, of razing Jerusalem and burning the temple, and of a mass suicide as a final act of defiance. Not a very heroic narrative.

Contrary to this dreary, sad and tragic narrative, the mythical narrative used some elements of the historical narrative, ignored and invented others, and wove a heroic tale. In essence, the Masada mythical narrative may be sketched briefly as follows. The leaders of the popular Great Revolt were Zealots. The Zealots who survived the siege and destruction of Jerusalem escaped to Masada. From there, they harassed the Romans and created such a threat that the Romans decided to make a tremendous military effort and destroy Masada. Consequently, the Romans gathered their army, surrounded the fortress and put it under siege. After three years of heroic fights, the Zealots on Masada realized that their situation was hopeless. They faced a grim future: either be killed by the Romans, or become slaves. They decided to kill themselves, a heroic and liberating death, rather than become wretched slaves. When the Roman soldiers entered Masada, they found only silence and dead bodies. This mythical narrative constructs Masada as a symbol for an heroic "last stand." In the words of the famous Israeli chief-of-staff and politician Moshe Dayan (1983: 21):

Today, we can point only to the fact that Masada has become a symbol of heroism and of liberty for the Jewish people to whom it says:

336

Fight to death rather than surrender;
Prefer death to bondage and loss of freedom.

Clearly, the popular, widespread Masada mythical narrative has some elements of historical truth in it, but in the main, it is significantly different from what Josephus tells us. It takes a long, complex and at some points unclear historical sequence and reduces it to a simple and straightforward heroic narrative, characterized by a few lucid themes of heroism. The Masada mythical narrative is a reconstruction of a tragic historical event into a heroic fable. The hapless revolt is transformed into a heroic war. The questionable collective suicide on Masada is transformed into a brave last stand of the few against the many.

Does Josephus tell the "truth"?

Why should we not view Josephus' historical narrative just as another mythical version? We can, of course. But that does not make much sense. If Josephus had not written a history, there would "be" no Masada, Sicarii, revolt, and so forth. In fact, without Josephus "the history of the last two centuries of the Second Commonwealth could be reduced to a few pages—and a good part of that would be legendary" (Aberbach 1985: 25). Yadin stated in a radio interview that in Josephus' statements "there is a genuine accuracy that stuns us today, at least in terms of the facts" (September 13, 1966) and added that "the only source for the history of Masada is the writings of Joseph Ben-Matityahu" (Yadin 1970: 374). Indeed, the interpretations of the archaeological findings in Masada "make sense" only if one knows Josephus' account.

However, the accuracy and validity of Josephus were not a focus of my study. I simply had to take Josephus' version as our fundamental historical baseline. The analytical puzzle of my work is how and why some modern Israeli moral entrepreneurs, interpreters and scientists, constructed their versions of Masada, how much these deviated from the baseline, and in what direction. Moreover, the likelihood that Josephus lied and cheated his own contemporary Roman masters as well as those who were actually involved in the events, and fabricated—on a mass scale—a siege that never was, people who never existed, an event that never took place, and the like, does not seem very high. And, why should he have done that in the first place? Josephus' account was written very close to the events, he was part of, and witness to, the Great Revolt, and all later interpreters, myth makers and other well-meaning researchers, took Josephus' version as their departing point.

Moreover, I must admit that I find incredible the claim that Josephus' narrative, written only a few years after the events by an important, involved, knowledgeable contemporary figure, is somehow "equal" to an imaginary mythical and fabricated narrative concocted by a variety of creative moral entrepreneurs some 1,800 years later. It must be stated that no shred of evidence exists supporting the claim that—as some would have us believe—Josephus did create a myth, and that all of his account is false.

Examining cultures

In order to examine how the Masada myth was created and projected, we delved into the main sections of Israeli culture going from the early decades of the twentieth century to the 1980s. We examined: youth movements, the pre-state Jewish underground groups, the Israeli army, history textbooks for elementary and high schools, children's books, fiction books, movies, music, theater, tourist guides. The examination was carried out by reviewing hundreds of texts, carrying out dozens of interactive interviews, and observing tours on Masada. These observations allowed us deep historical and contemporary perspectives on the crystallization and development of the myth. I found the combination of examining texts, interactive interviewing, and participant observations extremely useful and powerful.

The mythical narrative began its existence when the renewed Jewish immigration to then British occupied Palestine and Trans Jordan began and the secular Zionist movement was searching for heroic narratives it could use as identification models for the new type of Jewish identity that this movement tried to mold. A Jew whose identity was grounded in a glorious history, in ancient warriors' pride, who saw him or herself connected to the land and to the legacy of ancient heroic figures that—like him or her—were willing to live and die for the land, and were willing to be involved in agriculture. The fear of a possible invasion by Nazi Rommel's Afrika Korps in the early 1940s boosted this motivation and helped crystallize the myth. The decline of the myth took place in the mid-1960s when the June 1967 war opened such new sites of heroism and remembrance for Jews as the Wailing Wall, Rachel's tomb, the Tomb of the Fathers in Hebron, and more.

Dozens of interviews were carried out. One glaring illustration of an interview is the one I had with Shmaria Guttman (January 1987), who was the most powerful figure behind the mythical tale until the early 1960s, when Professor Yadin took that role. I had two lengthy interviews with Shmaria in his Kibbutz home—Na'an. When I first interviewed Shmaria, he was in his very late 70s, still energetic, persuasive, firm, charismatic and exceptionally charming. Shmaria was very convincing in explaining to us his perception regarding Masada. As the interview proceeded, I asked him specifically about the massacre that this sect of assassins—the Sicarii on Masada—committed in Ein Gedi. This was his response:

I am not sure that his [Josephus'] statement about what exactly they [the Masada people] did in Ein Gedi is the most accurate. However, what is entirely clear to me is that they came to Ein Gedi and took food by force, this I am sure about. So, on top of Masada sits a group of people that is isolated from the world, does not suspect that the war with the Romans is finished, and believes that there still may be a chance to beat them, the empire ... They are lucky, they have water, but additional food is needed too ... and they come to Ein Gedi and tell the people there: "we ask you to give." And then they [the people of Ein Gedi] showed them their finger, so they took it by force. Look, guys, this is not a nice thing to do. Nevertheless, in order to live people do things that are not nice. However, the people of Ein Gedi could show more courtesy and give them something of their own. Therefore, they took it by force. So he [Josephus Flavius] turns it into "butchered and burnt" etc. etc. I do not have to take it as an absolute truth ... it is possible that they did a few things that ... were not moral ... I want ... to build a picture of the people who were in Ein Gedi ... They were land tenants of the Roman regime ... So, they [the people of Masada] had the feeling that they were taking something that the Roman empire was robbing from them, and they wanted to take that back. So, there was an act in Ein Gedi. Do we have to build on this act mountains of arguments about types of people?

What does Shmaria say here? First, that we do not have to trust Josephus Flavius too much about the Ein Gedi massacre. Second, he implies that the people of Ein Gedi almost "deserved" their victimization by "refusing" to provide the Sicarii from Masada with food. Third, where he gets his information about the Sicarii "request" and the people of Ein Gedi's "refusal" is very unclear.

Just to remind ourselves what Josephus actually says about the massacre in Ein Gedi, and how far off it is from Shmaria's "interpretation," let me quote directly from Josephus Flavius:

> There was a fortress ... called Masada. Those that were called Sicarii had taken possession of it ... when once they were informed that the Roman army lay still ... at the feast of unleavened bread, which the Jews celebrate in memory of their deliverance from their Egyptian bondage ... they came down by night, without being discovered ... and overran a ... small city called Engaddi ... they prevented those citizens that could have stopped them, before they could arm themselves and fight ... They also dispersed them, and cast them out of the city. As for such as could not run away, being women and children, they slew of them about seven hundred. Afterward, they had carried everything out of their houses, and had seized upon all the fruits that were in a flourishing condition, they brought them into Masada. And indeed these men laid all the villages that were about the fortress waste, and made the whole country desolate ...
>
> (*Wars of the Jews*, book IV, chapter VII, p. 537)

To my first interview with Shmaria Guttman, Ms. Vered Vinitzky and Ms. Einat Usant, my two research assistants at that time accompanied me. We all drove to Na'an in my then old, beat-up VW "Bug," looking forward to an interesting interview. What we got instead were about four hours of socialization. Shmaria, clearly, made an effort not only to be nice, but spent the entire time trying to persuade us of the validity of his views. He knew very well why we had come as I had explained the purpose of the visit and interview. As we left his home, in the early afternoon hours, he accompanied us to my car, put his arm around my shoulder and asked: "You are not going to do bad, Dr. Ben-Yehuda, are you?" "No" I answered, "that is not my intention." As we got into my car, there was silence. We dropped Vered off at the central bus station in Ramla and Einat and I continued on to Jerusalem. Along the way, we came to a railroad crossing just as a train was roaring by. I stopped the car and we waited in silence for the train to go by. As the roar of the passing train was receding, Einat suggested: "Why don't we drop the whole research?" meaning that annulling a formative national myth may not be such a great idea. I told her that I did not think we should end the project. However, I returned home in a very thoughtful and reflexive frame of mind. Whether directly linked to the interview or not, I did put the study on the lower side of my priorities for almost a year and a half. In the end, the study was completed long after both Einat and Vered had left Hebrew University. I think, and hope, that in publishing the book on the Masada myth I was not doing something "bad." As I was beginning to work on the excavations of Masada, I had a second interview with Shmaria. This time with another RA—Iris Wolf. At that point in time he was not in good shape, tired and sad. He mentioned, sadly, that he would probably never again set his foot on Masada. When I returned to Jerusalem, I contacted one of my graduate students who had excellent connections in the Israeli army. The result of that contact was that the Israeli air force allowed one of its helicopters to fly Shmaria to Masada. I was not there, but the reports that came in described a very excited Shmaria on top of Masada making a speech against those that try to destroy the myth ...

Joining tour guides with their groups on Masada was important and instructive because it provided contemporary observations of the "here and now" on the way tour guides presented Masada. I made a number of trips to Masada, some with students, some without and observed tour guides "explain" Masada. I attached myself to groups of tourists and listened to the explanations guides gave to the tourists who they were accompanying. Generally, the guides spent a great deal of time describing the site itself (architecture, excavations, etc.), devoting very little time to the most fascinating "thing" about Masada, that is, the narrative. When the narrative was related, invariably the Masada mythical narrative unfolded, the emphasis being placed on the suicide. The method by which these guides attempted to grapple with this issue is fascinating. The best "undoing" of the suicide I heard was by a tour guide in 1989 explaining it to a group of English-speaking tourists. The guide described the site, recited, more or less, a standard version of the Masada mythical narrative, and then arrived at the suicide. "You know," he told his eager listeners, "that the Jewish faith does not allow suicide. Those that commit suicide can not even be buried in a Jewish cemetery." Well, then, how to explain what the "Zealots" (never "Sicarii") did? Simple. There was no suicide on Masada. What really took place was murder. They murdered each other. A terrible thing to do, Judaism certainly does not allow it. One of the Ten Commandments specifically forbids it. However, murder is not suicide. If one commits murder, one can still be buried properly. Therefore, now that the suicide was turned into murder and was "undone" there is one problem left. What does the last person do? Well, the version that those attentive English-speaking tourists heard was that the last "Zealot" took his sword, ran out towards the Roman soldiers who were pouring into Masada through the breach in the wall, and yelled, "follow me." The Roman soldiers thought that he was the commander of the "Zealots" calling his warriors to follow him. So, they killed him. Again, no suicide. There are a few interesting things about this fairy tale. First, many Israelis will recognize the command of "follow me" as that given by Israeli officers to their soldiers. Israeli officers lead the way in battle. The connection to modern Israel is thus made. Second, how could the Roman soldiers understand what the last "Zealot" was yelling? Did he speak their language? Third, and this is the reason I call this "ending" a fairy tale, is what Josephus Flavius has to say about this, and here he is very explicit: "(H)e who was the last of all ... with the great force of his hand ran his sword entirely through himself, and fell down dead near to his own relations" (*Wars of the Jews*, book VII, chapter IX, p. 603).

Archaeology and Masada

Once the riddle of the Masada myth was solved, I knew what the nature of the myth was, how it developed, when its demise took place and why. That left open one very curious question. During 1963–65, Masada was almost fully excavated. Heading the excavations was a colorful and prestigious archaeologist—Professor Yigael Yadin of Hebrew University. There can hardly be a doubt that Yadin was the last powerful person to pour flammable liquids on the smoldering fire of the Masada myth. His 1966 book on Masada (in Hebrew and English), as well as his speeches, papers and media appearances, gave solid support to the myth. How did that take place and why? Clearly, the archaeologists read Josephus; they must have known that some major and significant differences between the historical and the mythical narratives existed. To solve this riddle, two methodologies were used. One, we interviewed each archaeologist who took part in the excavations. Two, the archaeologists convened every evening to discuss the findings of the day.

These meetings were recorded and later transcribed. I had full access to the daily transcripts. Combining these two methodologies gave me a powerful tool to decipher the excavations. The interviews revealed that indeed, there were some challenges to Yadin, but it was Yadin who took over the presentation and interpretation of the results. By the time I conducted the study, Yadin was no longer with us. However, it is not too difficult to realize, from his writings and public appearances, that he was captivated by the myth, embraced and believed in it. In short, he sacrificed his science in favor of his feelings and nationalistic identity. Let me use two illustrations. One is text-based, and refers to the finding in locus 8, on the northeast corner of the lower level on Masada northern palace.[2] The discovery was discussed on November 26, 1963, when the archaeologists and Dr. Haas (the pathologist) considered the findings there:

DR. [NICU] HAAS: Three skeletons were found in locus 8 ... One of a female ... aged 17–18, and one of a child aged 11–12 ... the third skeleton ... is that of a man and his age is between 20–22, also quite young.

YADIN: ... It is obvious that the child and woman cannot be mother and son because of the age difference, so if there really was a family here, the man might be the father of the child ... In those periods *Ya Habibi*! there is a plus-minus of a year ... here you make it 23 and there 10 and everything is OK ... The man and the woman can certainly be a couple! However, the son is not this woman's ... Maybe it is her brother or his.

No more physical evidence was found or added to this discovery. However, the interpretation given to this discovery evolved in a surprising way. Like others, Yadin was probably looking for empirical support for the Masada mythical narrative, some tangible "proof" that would end all doubts about the supposedly heroic acts that took place on Masada. Following Yadin's evolving interpretation of the find is fascinating. However, due to space considerations let me jump to the most intriguing interpretation of the discovery in locus 8, made on April 11, 1973. Then, Yadin addressed on the top of Masada members of the Society for the Study of Eretz Israel and its Antiquities, and of the Society for the Protection of Nature. This is what he said:

I shall mention the remains of the three fighters that we found in the northern palace: a very important commander, his wife and their child, just like in the description of Josephus Flavius ...

(Yadin 1973)

The gap between the April 11, 1973, statement and the November 26, 1963, factual discussion, as well as the departure from Josephus, are stunning. In the 1973 account, the three skeletons became those of a family (father, mother and child) of "warriors," headed by a very important commander. The 1973 text is much more congruent with, and can be easily interpreted within, the Masada mythical narrative. It was obviously a deliberate falsified interpretation, one that had nothing to do with the facts, and it was meant to make audiences believe in a mythical narrative, and hence it was deceptive. In 1991, the third volume of the Final Reports of the 1963–65 excavations was published, written by Professor Ehud Netzer. On page 167, Netzer describes locus 8:

> Near the bottom of the pool, in the southwestern corner, were found the remains of a boy aged about 10; beneath him was a large stone covering the skull of a woman aged about 18. Another concentration of human remains was revealed in the southeastern corner, also near the bottom.

To Netzer's scientific credibility, we must note how careful and factual he is. Moreover, Netzer did participate in the excavations. He does not mention an "important commander" or "family" or "last warrior" or even suggest that these skeletal remains had anything to do with the rebels on Masada.

The second illustration is from an interview (together with Iris Wolf) with Ze'ev Meshel (January 11, 1994). Meshel's version was:

> There is always a problem with historical sources ... In my view, even after the 70 A.D. conquest and the destruction of the Temple, Jews continued to uphold the independence of Judea in the Judean Desert and the Dead Sea basin ... This independence coalesced around three fortresses: Herodium, Macherus and Masada. That is why the Romans returned in 73 A.D., to suppress this independence. Thus, not only did those besieged on Masada believe in their power, but the Romans accepted it as well. They constituted independent Judea. There is no other explanation for the tremendous Roman effort in this God-forsaken outback. In addition, in my perception, Judean independence ended there in Masada.

When I pointed out to Meshel that, while his interpretation was interesting, it was most definitely not what Josephus wrote and there was not a shred of evidence for this speculation. Meshel responded by stating, "I ... am allowed to read in Josephus more than what is explicitly there ... "

Summary

My Masada project branched into two very different routes. The first focused on solving the riddle of the Masada myth. The solution of this riddle indicated that in order to help mold the new Jewish identity (mentioned earlier) in the twentieth century in Palestine and Israel, relevant heroic narratives were needed. Since not many were easily available, Masada's historical narrative was altered and reconstructed from a narrative of defeat and death to a narrative of heroism. The way this was done reflects how national collective memories are made—through an interactive process between the past and the present. Some elements from the past remain, others are made to disappear and new elements are invented and added. This process also means that it is very possible that at the heart of cultures one can find fabricated mythologies that form the central elements in the national and personal identities of members of that culture. While this may imply that the "past" may be viewed like clay—something that can be changed at the will and whim of artists, this process may also have limits that lie in personal memories, texts, and artifacts. Thus, and based on my Masada historical ethnography, the answer to whether the past is "there" for us to discover, or whether the "past" is a product of interests in the present, is that it is both. A related issue had to do with the angry, emotional response of people and interviewees when faced with the historical narrative. This anger is obvious because for many Israelis, mythical Masada has become a central ingredient in their identity as Jews and Israelis. Clearly, this effect is age-related and has a strong generational effect. Facing the possibility that a major ingredient in one's identity is based on a falsehood is not an easy revelation. The second riddle focused on the ways scientists, mostly so Yadin, supported a narrative that was inaccurate at best. While one can find a few challenges in the transcripts of the excavations, those did not change much. A reasonable hypothesis is that national motivation and beliefs probably took over scientific accuracy. More generally, this is another case when the primacy of ideology took over scientific methods and interpretations.

Overall, the Masada research project continued to solidify my conviction that studying cases and patterns of unconventionality and deviance per se is a barren direction. Contextualizing such studies in historical and contemporary cultures is the thing to do if we are to have better, more powerful and persuasive interpretations of social and cultural realities. In addition, this study showed me, once again, that social, cultural and historical realities are not to be revealed exclusively by deciphering the numbers and figures of such statistical methods as multiple regression analysis. These realities can be found easily and persuasively in people's accounts—written, given orally, and in the media, in texts, and in participant observations.

Notes

1 The "we" refers to my research assistants, and dozens of students who worked on this project.
2 Identified by Netzer (1991: 167) as "Frigidarium 8."

References

Aberbach, M. (1985) "Josephus and His Critics: a reassessment," *Midstream*, 31: 25–29.

Ben-Yehuda, N. (1995) *The Masada Myth: collective memory and mythmaking in Israel.* Madison, WI: University of Wisconsin Press.

——(1998) "Where Masada's Defenders Fell," *Biblical Archaeology Review*, 24: 32–39.

——(2002) *Sacrificing Truth: archaeology and the myth of Masada*, Amherst, NY: Prometheus Books.

——(2006) "Contextualizing Deviance within Social Change and Stability, Morality, and Power," *Sociological Spectrum*, 26: 559–80.

Best, J. (ed.) (1989) *Images of Issues: typifying contemporary social problems*, New York: Aldine de Gruyter.

Dayan, M. (1983) "The Victory of the Vanquished," in G. Israel (ed.) *Masada*, Paris: Armand and Georges Israel Publishers.

Flavius, J. (1981) *The Complete Works of Josephus*, trans. W. Whiston, Grand Rapids, MI: Kregel Publications.

Latour, B. and Woolgar, S. (1979) *Laboratory Life: the social construction of scientific fact*, Beverly Hills, CA: Sage.

Netzer, E. (1991) *Masada III: the Yigael Yadin excavations 1963–1965 Final Reports: the buildings, stratigraphy and architecture*, Jerusalem, Israel: Israel Exploration Society and the Hebrew University of Jerusalem.

Olick, J. K. (2005) *In the House of the Hangman: the agonies of German defeat, 1943–1949*, Chicago: University of Chicago Press.

Rapoport, D. (1984) "Fear and Trembling: terrorism in three religious traditions," *The American Political Science Review*, 78: 658–77.

Schwartz, B. (1991) "Social Change and Collective Memory: the democratization of George Washington," *American Sociological Review*, 56: 221–36.

Yadin, Y. (1965) *Masada: First Season of Excavations, 1963–1964: preliminary report*, Jerusalem, Israel: The Israel Exploration Society (Hebrew).

——(1966a) *Masada: Herod's fortress and the zealots' last stand*, London: Weidenfeld and Nicolson.

——(1966b) *Masada: in those days—at this time*, Haifa, Israel: Shikmona Ma'ariv Library (Hebrew).

——(1970) "Metzada," in *Encyclopaedia for Archeological Excavations in Eretz Israel*, vol. 2 (pp. 374–90), Jerusalem: The Society for the Investigation of Eretz Israel and its Antiquity and Masada Ltd. (Hebrew).

——(1973) "1900 Years to the Fall of Masada," *Ma'ariv*, April 16, pp. 15, 33 (Hebrew).

INDEX

INDEX

(fieldnotes 142, 149); *see also*
alternative data; fieldwork; grounded
theory; methodology
Denzin, Norman xii, 22, 152–68; AA
(Alcoholics Anonymous) 22, 152,
155, 157, 160, 162–63, 165–66; AA's
theory of alcoholism 22, 152, 161–65
(AA and the AA group as
interactional sites 162–63; AA and
science 162; AA's mode of
understanding 163–64; alcoholic
personality 161–62; self-help group
164–65); *The Alcoholic Self* xii, 22,
152, 160, 161; *The Alcoholic Society:
Addiction and Recovery of the Self*
152; anthropology of existential
experience 158–59, 161; Foucault,
Michel 22, 152, 154, 155; native 158,
160, 161; postmodern ethnography
22, 152, 153, 158–61, 166; *The
Recovering Alcoholic* 152, 158, 161;
scientific theories of alcoholism 22,
152, 153–58, 163, 166 (alcoholic
personality 154; reading treatment
155–56; scientific and clinical
treatment of alcoholism 155;
scientific, objective vs. subjective
stocks of knowledge 157–58);
symbolic interactionism 159;
theoretical frames 22, 153–61,
165–66; theory/research relationship
11; *Treating Alcoholism: An
Alcoholic's Anonymous Approach*
152; *see also* theoretical frames;
theory in ethnography
Dunn, Jennifer xii-xiii, 27, 277–88;
advocate 27, 278, 279, 280–81, 283,
284, 286; challenging established
wisdom 27, 277–88; conceptualization
27, 280, 286–87; *Courting Disaster:
Intimate Stalking, Culture, and
Criminal Justice* xiii, 27, 279–87; data
277, 278, 280 (interviews 279, 282;
notes 280–81); deviance 278, 279–80;
feminism 277, 278, 279, 284;
Holstein, J. and Miller, G. ('social
problems work' 281, 286; 'victim
accomplishment' 281, 286); Lofland,
Lyn 279, 280; media 277; methodology
277, 278, 279, 282, 286 (participant
observation 278, 280, 282); Mills, C.
Wright 277, 279, 280; reflexivity 277;

River City Survivors of Stalking 282,
285; social constructionism 27, 278,
281, 283, 286; stalking victim 27,
277–78, 280 (credibility 281, 282,
283, 284, 285; identity 278, 281, 283,
285, 286–87); symbolic interactionism
277, 279–80 ('aligning activities' 280,
282); theoretical framework 286–87;
see also challenging established
wisdom; theory in ethnography
Durkheim, Émile 162, 197, 209, 231,
254

empiricism 101–2; Blumer, Herbert 4,
19; empirical sociology 4; 'thick
empiricism' 79, 81, 89; *see also*
pragmatism
ethics 2, 8, 12, 15, 240, 313, 316
ethnography 73, 79, 147, 208, 210, 289,
296, 308; analytical ethnography 7,
15; 'auto-ethnography' 38, 74, 146,
208, 308; detective work 26, 263, 265,
267, 273, 274; *experimental
ethnography* 145–46; 'historical
ethnography' 29, 334, 336, 344;
postmodernism 15, 22, 38, 152, 153,
158–61, 166, 208; rethinking
ethnography 321–23; rhetorical styles
('four faces of ethnography') 15;
'thick empiricism' 79, 81; traditional
American ethnography 22; trends 65,
75, 79; *see also* alternative data;
research; social constructionism;
sociology; symbolic interactionism;
theory in ethnography; traditional
ethnography
Ethnomethodology 107, 113, 180, 300

Faulkner, Robert xiii, 19–20, 79–91;
Blumer, Herbert 80–81; data 79, 80,
81, 85 (interviews 82); grounded/
'theory-driven' approaches 15; *Music
on Demand* xiii, 19–20, 80; sensitizing
concepts 19–20, 79–89 (careers and
markets 82–89, 90, 91; desensitizing
89; knowledge, use, and shaping 89;
outcomes 80; shaping 81–89; sources
80; thick exploitation 82–84; thick
exploration 82, 85–87; thin exploitation
84–85; thin exploration 88–89); 'thick
empiricism' 79, 81, 89; thin/thick
theoretical exploration/exploitation

350

INDEX

native 145, 187; Collins, Harry 289, 300, 302; Denzin, Norman 158, 160, 161; Heilman, Samuel 201, 202–5; *see also* research

Pawluch, Dorothy xiv-xv, 29, 318–30; conceptualization 322; data 29, 321–22, 323–24 (interviews 29, 321; participant observation 29, 321); documentary 29, 318, 321–23; Glaser, Barney 29, 322–23; grounded theory 322–23; *The New Pediatrics: A Profession in Transition* 29, 318, 321–29; ontological gerrymandering 327–29; professions study 29, 318–19, 325–27, 328; research 320–21; rethinking ethnography 321–23; social constructionism 319–20, 327–29; Strauss, Anselm 29, 322–23; theorizing from alternative data 29, 318–29; traditional ethnography 29; *see also* alternative data; theory in ethnography

Pinch, Trevor xv, 12–13, 23, 180–94; *Analog Days: The Invention and Impact of the Moog Synthesizer* xv, 23, 181 (origin stories of the Moog project 182–83; sources of theoretical refinement 187–91; theoretical fictions 183–87; Trocco, Frank 23, 181, 184, 190, 191); ethnographic research 180–81, 182, 185, 189, 191; fieldwork 189; interpretative flexibility and closure 185–86, 187; memory 13, 23; methodology 183; narratives of 'theory-talk' 12–13, 180–81, 191–92; origin stories in science 181–82; Science and Technology Studies (S&TS) 188, 189, 191, 192; Social Construction of Technology (SCOT) 23, 185, 188; sociology of technology 184–85, 186, 187; theoretical frames 23, 183–87, 191–92; theorizing 23, 180–81, 191; *see also* theoretical frames; theory in ethnography

politics 235–36; battered women 265, 274, 275; ethnography 6, 10, 25–26; science 9

positivism 13, 51; criticism 152, 155; ethnography 13, 149, 161, 241, 245; positivistic sociology 4, 6, 13, 21

postmodernism 6, 13, 148; Denzin, Norman 22, 152, 153, 158–61, 166; ethnography 4, 5–7, 15, 22, 38, 152, 153, 158–61, 166, 208; reflexivity 146–47; social science 6–7; sociology 6–7, 13; *see also* Denzin, Norman

poststructuralism 309; reflexivity 146–47; Richardson, Laurel 309

pragmatism 79, 102; American sociology 4; *see also* empiricism

Prus, Robert xv, 7, 25, 238–50; community and social organization 25, 238–50; conceptualization 247–49; crime and deviance 239, 240, 241, 244, 245–46; data 241, 247, 248 (fieldnotes 239, 240; interviews 241, 247); 'generic social processes' 5; *Hookers, Rounders, and Desk Clerks* xv, 25, 238–46, 249 (Irini, Styllianos 25, 238–40, 247); methodology 241–42, 247 (participant observation 241, 247); *Road Hustler* 239, 240, 241, 246, 247; symbolic interactionism 5, 25, 241, 245, 247, 248; trans-situational properties of concepts 20, 105, 249; *see also* community and social organization; theory in ethnography

Puddephatt, Antony xv, 1–34, 59, 90, 249

qualitative research 3–4, 40, 106, 225, 307; data 40; ethnography 5, 8, 59; Glaser, Barney 60; Richardson, Laurel 307–10 (reconceptualization 308); theory 14, 60, 236; 'thick empiricism' 79; *see also* research

reflexivity 3, 6, 7, 56; anthropology 147; Dunn, Jennifer 277; ethnographic tradition 8–13; postmodernism 146–47; poststructuralism 146–47; science studies 8–9; Wacquant, Loïc 22, 137, 146–47 (epistemic reflexivity 137, 147–48)

research 1–15, 16, 37–38, 65, 79, 180–81; basic routes to 63; Becker, Howard 65; Collins, Harry 300–302; door-opening to 73; Gubrium, Jaber 127–28; Heilman, Samuel 197–98, 208, 210; key ethnographic question 70; Latour, Bruno 81, 189; Lofland,

Hassidic sect 24, 219–23, 224; overt/covert research 218–19; stigma 215–16; Tasher Hassidim 217–19, 224; *see also* community and social organization; theory in ethnography
social constructionism 72, 87, 125, 209; Ben-Yehuda, Nachman 333–34 (contextual constructionism 333–34, 335; strict constructionism 333); Dunn, Jennifer 27, 278, 281, 283, 286; Gubrium, Jaber 125, 132; Holstein, J. and Miller, G. ('social problems work' 275, 281, 286, 327; 'victim accomplishment' 281, 286); Loseke, Donileen 275; methodology 333–34; Pawluch, Dorothy 319–20, 327–29; Pinch, Trevor 13, 185, 187; scientific knowledge 333; *see also* sociology
social psychology 235, 254; Charmaz, Kathy 49; Karp, David 37, 38, 39; *see also* sociology
social science 6, 246; collective memory 335; ethnography as 4; methodology 10; reflexivity 9; research 37–38, 180–81; theory 6, 181; *see also* science; sociology
sociology 1; American tradition 4; American/European opposition 4; *carnal sociology* 146, 148, 149; Charmaz, Kathy 49; definition 308; deviance 68, 118, 239, 240, 241, 244, 245–46; European tradition 4, 6; Karp, David 37, 38, 43, 44, 45–46; knowledge 9; Mills, C. Wright 308; occupational 20, 82, 83, 89, 95–97, 102–3; positivistic sociology 4, 6, 13; postmodernism 6–7, 13; reflexivity 9–10; research 63; Richardson, Laurel 307, 308, 315, 317; Sanders, Clinton 67–68, 71, 72; sociology of art 71, 72; sociology of scientific knowledge 185, 294, 299, 300, 302, 333; sociology of technology 184–85, 186, 187; theory 13–14, 231; *see also* Becker, Howard; Bourdieu, Pierre; Chicago School; ethnography; Karp, David; Mills, C. Wright; qualitative research; research; social constructionism; social science; symbolic interactionism; theory in ethnography; Wacquant, Loïc

Stebbins, Robert xvi-xvii, 22–23, 169–79; *Challenging Mountain Nature: Risk, Motive, and Lifestyle in Three Hobbyist Sports* 22; Csikszentmihalyi, M. 171; data 173, 175; 'emergent theoretic codes' 169, 173, 174–78; 'established theoretic codes' 169–72, 173, 178; grounded theory 172–73; 'leisure theory' 22–23, 169–72 (casual leisure 170, 177–78; core activity 22, 169, 170–71, 177; epics 176, 178; hobby 170, 173; nature-challenge hobbies 22, 169, 174, 175; project-based leisure 170, 178; psychological flow 170–72, 174, 175, 177; risk 22, 172, 173, 174–75, 176, 178; self-fulfillment 22, 175–76; serious leisure perspective 169–78); sensitizing concepts 169–72, 173, 174–78; theoretical frames 22–23, 169–72, 177; *see also* theoretical frames; theory in ethnography
Strauss, Anselm 79, 325; *The Discovery of Grounded Theory* 5, 114, 322–23; grounded theory 16–17, 29, 50, 60, 79, 114, 228, 322–23; 'practical strategies' 108; 'social worlds' 131; *see also* grounded theory
symbolic interactionism 37; Albas, C. and Albas, D. 106, 109; 'aligning activities' 280, 282; Becker, Howard 241, 248; Ben-Yehuda, Nachman 333–34; Blumer, Herbert 4, 97, 103, 146, 241, 248; Chambliss, Daniel 254; Charmaz, Kathy 49, 55; Chicago School 4–5; Denzin, Norman 159; Dunn, Jennifer 277, 279–80; Goffman, Erving 241, 248; Karp, David 17, 37, 41; Lofland, John 109, 241, 248 ('mini-concepts' 20, 105, 108, 109, 114, 117); Prus, Robert 5, 25, 241, 245, 247, 248; Sanders, Clinton 65; sensitizing concepts 97, 103; theory 4–5; *see also* Blumer, Herbert; Goffman, Erving; sociology

theoretical frames 16, 21–23, 205; Collins, Harry 291, 301; Denzin, Norman xii, 22, 152–68; Dunn, Jennifer 286–87; Loseke, Donileen 264–66, 275; methodology 137, 144–45, 147, 183; Pinch, Trevor xv,

CPSIA information can be obtained at www.ICGtesting.com
Printed in the USA
LVOW10s2011031214

416794LV00005B/79/P